DATE DUE			

Lust for Fame

Portrait of John Wilkes Booth by Mathew Brady.
From the Brady-Handy Collection, Library of Congress.

Lust for Fame:
The Stage Career
of John Wilkes Booth

by Gordon Samples

 McFarland & Company, Inc., Publishers
Jefferson, North Carolina, and London
1982

792.028
Sa4L
130185
ort, 1984

Library of Congress Cataloging in Publication Data

Samples, Gordon.
  Lust for fame.

  Includes index.
  1. Booth, John Wilkes, 1838–1865.
2. Actors — United States — Biography. I. Title.
PN2287.B55S2   792'0924 [B]   81-20882

ISBN 0-89950-042-0   AACR2

Manufactured in the United States of America

To the memory of my parents and to my grandfather who served under General John B. Gordon, my father's namesake and mine.

Preface

This work is a chronicle of John Wilkes Booth's life on the stage and an evaluation of his performances through reviews from newspapers and opinions of his contemporaries. It is also an attempt to separate Booth the actor from Booth the assassin, limiting the present work to his theater and the theater of his time.

During the past century hundreds of books and articles have been written about the assassination of Lincoln, but relatively few have been devoted entirely to Booth. True, no biography of Lincoln can be written without the mention of the name of Booth, but in almost every case the biographer has limited his study to the retelling of the crime with little or no regard for Booth the actor. Aside from relating the narrative of the fatal night at Ford's Theater, Booth's notices in history books have been largely limited to stating that he was a second-rate actor, wild and exceedingly vain, a Southern sympathizer.

This work further attempts to disclose his multifaceted character and personality which heretofore have been obscured. To this end, a selected group of his letters, some previously unpublished, are included, thereby enabling Booth to speak for himself whenever possible.

Standardization in spelling in the quotations has been attempted wherever clarification was deemed necessary. Many words and names appeared spelled in various ways during this period: for example, Mark Antony was often Marc Anthony; Gloster often appeared as Glouster, or Gloucester; Monte Cristo became Monte Christo; Blount became Blont, etc. The reader is also reminded that certain forms of English usage, while called incorrect today, were in general use and considered correct during this period; for example, "He don't," and "I run." It is not to be misconstrued that writers of the period who used such forms were illiterate, but rather that this was then common usage.

Every effort has been made for accuracy in covering all known performances of Booth, giving a chronology of dates, theatres, and a summary of the stage during this time. Throughout the work there is attempted a running comparison of contemporary thought before and after 1865, giving the Lincoln-Civil War tie up, and a study of Booth's motivation in his drive for fame.

Acknowledgments

Of the many people who provided aid in research and encouragement toward this work, the author wishes to acknowledge a special indebetness to the following:

Miss Henriette Beal, Museum of the City of New York
Miss Rosa D. Burt, New York City
Mr. Patrick Carroll, the Players Club, New York City
Mrs. Ralph Catterall, Valentine Museum, Richmond, Va.
Mrs. Jack Crawford, Yale University Library, New Haven, Conn.
Mrs. Dorothy Thomas Cullen, the Filson Club, Louisville, Ky.
Mr. J.M. Edelstein, Library of Congress, Washington, D.C.
Miss Georgia Gambill, St. Louis Public Library, Mo.
Mr. Irving S. Greentree, Jr., Richmond, Va.
Prof. William F. Hanchett, Jr., History Dept., San Diego State University, Calif.
Miss Jeanne Hollis, Bradley Memorial Library, Columbus, Ga.
Mr. John D. Kilbourne, Maryland Historical Society, Baltimore.
Mr. Charles G. LaHood, Jr., Library of Congress, Washington, D.C.
Miss Elizabeth C. Litsinger, Enoch Pratt Free Library, Baltimore
Mrs. Marguerite McAneny, Princeton University Library, N.J.
Mr. Ridgway McNallie, Buffalo & Erie County Public Library, N.Y.
Miss Ester Merves, San Diego State University Library, Calif.
Mr. Lloyd Ostendorf, Dayton, Ohio
Mrs. Gertrude Morton Parsley, Tennessee State Library & Archives, Nashville.
Miss Jean Preston, Huntington Library & Art Gallery, San Mareno, Calif.
Miss Dorothy J. Smith, Reis Library, Allegheny College, Meadville, Pa.
Mrs. Daisy S. Tucker, Ledger-Enquirer, Columbus, Ga.
Mr. John J. Weisert, Louisville, Ky.
Miss Helen D. Willard, Harvard College Library, Cambridge, Mass.
Miss Clara Wright, Montgomery, Ala.

Contents

List of Illustrations

CHAPTER 1: Retrospection

What is fame but a generally diffused public opinion, resounding one day, diminishing the next. It is as with the rising crescendo of applause: fading, then rising, and falling again as the curtains rise and fall before the proscenium arch. To the true actor it is an inborn, all-consuming passion. John Wilkes Booth was no exception. As a child he dreamed of becoming such a famous actor that his name would last an eternity. This dream of fame obsessed him. At first he had little self-confidence and felt himself lost in a stormy sea of longing, not knowing how to remedy his dilemma. Then suddenly the theater was his; he was absolutely sure of himself; success was real. The absolute pitch of popularity was his, and it seemed that his overwhelming desire for fame was to be granted.

Was it compulsion for even greater fame that prompted Booth to assassinate Abraham Lincoln, the President of the United States, on April 14, 1865, at Ford's Theater? Who knew better than he how violence could move an audience? And what blood could stir the people more than that of a tyrant — or saint? Certainly the murder could hardly have been staged more theatrically.

Before 1865 he was called genius, brilliant raconteur, Victorian fashion plate, darling of the ladies, the Byron of the theater, a true scion of an illustrious father, Junius Brutus Booth, who was perhaps the greatest tragedian on the American stage.

Booth should have known that the assassination of Lincoln would bring him not fame, but infamy. His earlier reputation as an actor was lost in the storm of emotion that followed the murder. After 1865 he was called a wild bombastic poseur, dissipated beast, mad drunkard, the American Judas.

Since the time of the assassination, comment about Booth the actor has come predominantly from his actor colleagues. Francis Wilson, actor, biographer, and first president of Actors Equity, summed him up thus, for example:

> We scarcely know what Wilkes Booth would have been in maturity; he had but reached the formative period. But all evidence and indication point to the likelihood of a richly artistic development, provided that "strangeness" which was a part of his paternal inheritance did not overcome him.[1]*

Scant critical opinion of his talent survives past 1865, leaving the general public inclined to accept the verdict that Lincoln "snatched Booth from oblivion" — that he never *had* been a successful actor.[2] His repertoire covered a wide range of roles played to large audiences over the South as well

*See Chapter Notes, *beginning on page 181.*

Those eyes "blazing with hellish malignancy" John Wilkes Booth inherited from his father. From an engraving in Frank Leslie's Illustrated Weekly, *April 29, 1865.*

as the North and Midwest. His earnings as an actor during the latter years were over $20,000 per year, and ranged from $500 to $1,000 per week, a fabulous sum for the era, when his career had barely gotten underway.

His repertoire was an impressive one, especially when it is considered that he was only 17 when he played his first role. His last appearance was at the age of 26. It is no wonder that he was labeled "The Youngest Tragedian in the World," for what actor on our stage today could duplicate the strenuous roles he played in such short time, at that early age, and with equal acclaim? His contemporaries of the stage lauded him as a thorough artist, an actor's actor.

Did his lust for fame and acting fervor combine with his Southern sympathies to make him a madman unable to distinguish truth from melodrama? Was he playing Brutus when he murdered Lincoln, and Richard III in the Virginia woods at the close of the drama? The melodramatic oath scene with the conspirators before the murder and his letters and journal after the act provide some evidence for the hypothesis that he was playing a role. The complexity of motivation that made Booth a murderer remains a fascinating mystery.[3]

Even correspondence is filled with quotations from his plays. Even his letter to Dr. Stewart while hiding out in a black man's cabin in the Virginia woods after his escape contains lines from *Macbeth*, and the signature is a role he played. The actor, as always, comes through as the prime feature of Booth's character. It is illustrated in his letters and in all his actions. Neither pain nor fear of capture could diminish his vainglory. He was living his character roles.

The following is his letter to Dr. Richard H. Stewart, wealthy and prominent Confederate physician. His summer home on the bank of the Potomac River was where Booth went for aid and was refused:

> Dear Sir:
> Forgive me, but I have some little pride. I hate to blame you for your want of hospitality: you know your own affairs. I was sick and tired, with a broken leg, in need of medical advice. I would not have turned a dog from my door in such a condition. However, you were kind enough to give me something to eat, for which I not only thank you, but on account of the reluctant manner in which it was bestowed, I feel bound to pay for it. It is not the substance, but the manner in which kindness is extended, that makes one happy in the acceptance thereof. The sauce in meat is ceremony; meeting were bare without it. Be kind enough to accept the enclosed two dollars and a half (though hard to spare) for what we have received.
> Yours respectfully,
> Stranger.
> April 24, 1865.[4]

Booth wrote two versions of this letter, using pages from his diary. In the first he wrote five dollars, but after writing the note he reconsidered, feeling the gesture too extravagant, and changed it to two-fifty. The first version was folded and tucked inside the pocket of the diary. The second note was wrapped and pinned around the money and delivered by the black whose cabin he had taken over, all in the best melodramatic form of Booth's stage.

The diary he kept during the six days and five nights of the escape is dramatic in the same way. Whether he was in the dense thicket of the forest, on the rough board floor of the cabin, or on the plush gaslit stage "boards," Booth's responses exhibited the same melodramatic excesses. The following few lines from the diary allows Booth to speak for himself:

> After being hunted like a dog through swamps, woods, and last night being chased by gun-boats till I was forced to return wet, cold and starving, with every man's hand against me, I am here in despair. And why? For doing what Brutus was honored for. What made Tell a hero. And yet I, for striking down a greater tyrant than they ever knew am looked upon as a common cutthroat.... The little, the very little I left behind to clear my name, the government will no allow to be printed.... Tonight I will once more try the river with the intent to cross, though I have a greater desire to return to Washington and in a measure clear my name, which I feel I can do....

After being suppressed for two years, the diary with 18 missing pages came to light when it was referred to in testimony before the Judiciary Committee of the House of Representatives, February 1867.[5]

Much has been said about Booth's love for Shakespeare's characters, Julius Caesar and Brutus, and the analogy of his crime. Booth is supposed to have recited the play on the farm, in saloons, hotel lobbies, and interlarded bits into his stagey conversations, as he was likely to do with other classic quotations. Some of which were stated incorrectly or improvised as the notion struck him. The fact is, he appeared only briefly in this play. Once while recuperating from a shooting accident in Columbus, Georgia, he appeared on stage and recited Mark Antony's oration. He appeared only once in the complete play with his brothers in New York City. Once he carried a spear in it for an 1857 production at the Arch Street Theater in Philadelphia. As for quoting, he quoted and recited many things to his listeners. His pocketbook was crammed with little selections to be read, picked up at random. The fixation on *Julius Caesar* is one which has been built up by reporters for the effect and used by psychiatrists as a plaything. He probably recited "The Sermon on the Mount" and the poem "Beautiful Snow," spellbinding his listeners into mass weeping, more times by far than the lines from Shakespeare's play. He claimed the poem "Beautiful Snow" was his favorite piece. This poem played effectively upon emotions and conscience of the guilty, exposing their follies.

Actors of his day neglected Booth in their memoirs, except for a few stalwart friends like Clara Morris, Mrs. Gilbert, Sir Charles Wyndham, and John T. Ford. Other friends, John Ellsler, John Matthews, Edwin Varry, W.J. Ferguson, John McCullough, thought well of him but were reluctant to speak out because of fear. Because of this their articles and interviews were evasive and sketchy.

His brother Edwin, who loved him best of all the family, disowned him, burned his theatrical wardrobe and pretended he never existed, yet kept a framed picture of him in his bedroom as long as he lived. The very touching but senseless destruction of Wilkes Booth's personal effects in 1873 may be read in full detail in Otis Skinner's memoirs.[6] The contents of the ill-fated trunk which had been sent to Canada by Wilkes, included not only his large collection of costumes, wigs, daggers, swords, photographs, letters, prompt books, but also the priceless items of his father. The portrait of Wilkes hung in Edwin's bedroom "kept there doggedly as a symbol of pride or of futility of man's destiny to unhappiness..."[7] still hangs in Edwin Booth's room at the Players' Club in New York City just as he left it in 1893.

There is no doubt that John Wilkes Booth was well liked offstage as well as on, and the term "Darling of Misfortune" seems to fit him better than his brother Edwin, to whom it is applied.

The Civil War days were trying times for all actors, for war times and Lincoln's assassination threw everything out of focus. Even at best the actor was not generally accepted in good times. Clara Morris, an actress and close friend of Booth, had this to say about the days when she was first beginning her career:

> Theatrical people were little known and even less understood. Even the people who did not think all actors drunkards and all actresses immoral, did think they were a lot of flighty, silly buffoons, and not to be taken seriously for a moment.[8]

Whatever contribution the Booth family had given to bring dignity and status to the stage was broken down at this point. Hatred toward the theaters was exaggerated, and any small remark was magnified beyond reason. Laura Keene and her company were jailed after the climactic *Our American Cousin* performance. The cast was forced to give one extra performance of the play after the assassination, but to a select group of government investigators. John T. Ford was confined 39 days in Old Capitol Prison for nothing other than the fact that he was the owner of Ford's Theatre. Over 200 persons were imprisoned, many for the slightest implication or hearsay evidence. Anyone even remotely connected with the Booth family received the same treatment.

At first people were reluctant to believe that Booth was capable of such a crime. Joseph H. Simonds, Booth's business agent summed up the general feeling among his friends:

> Sudden, sharp and terrible was the blow upon all his *true* friends (and he had many) and it was one which at first could not be believed, cannot yet be realized and is a sorrow which time can never heal.[9]

The town of Franklin, Pennsylvania, where Booth was engaged in oil speculation, remembered him as "mild and retiring in his disposition and displayed none of the qualities of the desperado he has shown himself to be."[10] "He was not vicious," remarked one of his fellow players at the Arch Street Theatre, "nor was he, as has been represented, savage and morose. His address was remarkably winning, and insured the friendship of all with whom he came in contact. He was not a bad man and after all, was an innocent kind of fellow, who would not do a mean action for the love of meanness...."[11]

Rumors and stories spread rampantly and were often farfetched. Some even went so far as to question the legitimacy of his birth. *Harper's Weekly*, May 6, 1865, offered photographs in sensational advertisements: Lincoln at 10¢ each, Booth at 25¢ each. This was done in spite of General Lew Wallace's Order 95 issued on May 2, forbidding the sale of portraits "of any rebel officer or soldier, or of J. Wilkes Booth."[12]

Booth's photographs must have sold by the hundreds, for we are told that

> almost every family who kept a photograph album on the parlor table owned a likeness of John Wilkes Booth. After the assassination Northerners slid the Booth card out of their albums; some threw it away, some burned it, some crumpled it angrily but hung on to it as a momento of the nation's betrayal, and some wrote their hearts' prayers on the backs of the pictures.[13]

Any praise he had previously received for his talent was quickly forfeit. Even in places he had not performed, newspapers had spoken well of him by reputation, but following the assassination critics everywhere began to disclaim him as a very poor actor indeed.

Actors themselves propagated the rumor that J. Wilkes Booth was insane as a defensive attempt to save themselves from the raging mobs that threatened to destroy the theaters. On the morning after the tragedy, Booth's friend John McCullough was pacing the floor in Edwin Forrest's hotel room muttering "I don't believe it. I can't believe it." Where upon the great tragedian snarled, "Well, I do. All those goddamned Booths are crazy."[14] The cry was taken up and everybody began to remember oddities of the Booths; the insanity rumor persisted. So as time passed, the image of Lincoln, who was killed on Good Friday, became increasingly saintly, while conversely the image of John Wilkes Booth became increasingly insane. After all, who but a madman would kill a saint? John Hay, assistant private secretary and coauthor of a biography of Lincoln, called him "the greatest character since Christ."[15]

Of course every member of the cast of *Our American Cousin* and practically every member of the audience dashed home and wrote somebody about it, either to himself in a diary or to friends or relatives. These letters are still coming to light and continue to document holdings in museums. They reveal the excitement, inflamed passions, and the deeply-felt horror of the situation. But now there seems to be an indication that some historians are minimizing the crime, explaining it away with patriotic motives and behind-the-scenes intrigues. One may not get the full impact of the public reaction unless one reads letters written at that time.

Violent emotions reigned, so that anyone expounding heretical views was likely to get tarred and feathered, or even shot. And many who said they were glad about the assassination did receive such treatment.

Prompted by imagination, the audience at Ford's Theater gave accounts they could not possibly have witnessed from positions they occupied. With a little prodding by the police and the press, one got a variety of accounts of the evening of April 14, 1865. Even actors relaxing in the theater's greenroom gave accounts of having seen the event. Jennie Gourlay, a member of the cast that night said:

> Every now and then one friend or another sends me a clipping about what happened that night at Ford's Theater. As a rule, these clippings are so untrue to facts that they disgust me. Five of my family, counting myself, were in the theater that night, so I know just about what took place.[16]

Years later, a few people who had known and worked with Booth, began to reveal their true thoughts. In an interview with the press in 1914, 49 years after the tragedy, Jennie Gourlay, a "patrician beauty of sweetness and magnetism," was asked,

> "Wasn't J. Wilkes Booth sort of a barroom Thespis, a brawling tragedian?" Mrs. Struthers' [Jennie Gourlay] eyes flashed with a trace of annoyance at the question. "Indeed he was not. John Wilkes Booth was a gentleman, a high-minded, cultured man. They tried to make him out a barroom loafer, though.... I knew Booth well. I also knew his brother Edwin and supported him in several plays. I and the rest of our company like Wilkes Booth; everybody liked him ... [and] to us who knew him well it was hard to believe the worst of him."[17]

According to character reports, Wilkes was kind and thoughtful of his company, generous in his charity toward others and always ready to play a benefit performance for a fellow actor. Edwin Booth tells us: "His was a gentle, loving disposition, very boyish and full of fun—his mother's darling."

Clara Morris, "one of the very few American actresses to whom the gift of genius may be properly ascribed,"[18] offered this interpretation:

> He was so young, so bright, so gay — so kind. I could not have known him well.... There are two or three different people in every man's skin.... Who shall draw a line and say: here genius ends and madness begins? There was that touch of — strangeness. In Edwin it was profound melancholy; in John it was an exaggeration of spirit — almost a wildness.[19]

Physical descriptions of John Wilkes Booth by his contemporaries all seem to emphasize his classic features, his almost unreal, exotically theatrical character as he impressed it upon others. Clara Morris described him physically:

> He was rather lacking in height, but his head and throat, and the manner of their rising from his shoulders, were truly beautiful. His coloring was unusual — the ivory pallor of his skin, the inky blackness of his densely thick hair, the heavy lids of his glowing eyes were all oriental, and they gave a touch of mystery to his face when it fell into gravity — but there was generally a flash of white teeth behind his silky moustache, and a laugh in his eyes.... Now it is scarcely exaggeration to say the sex was in love with John Booth.... At the theater — good Heavens! as the sunflowers turn upon their stalks to follow the beloved sun, so, old or young — our faces smiling — turned to him.[20]

It was not just Clara Morris who was enchanted by Booth's physical qualities. Many others have set down their thoughts which coincide with hers. The *Detroit Free Press* in an article just after the assassination described him as follows:

> He had a vital head, vitally beautiful chest with broad shoulders gently sloping, arms white as alabaster and hard as marble....

But even though Clara Morris was one of the most talented, respected and beautiful actresses of the period, her praise of Booth was not well taken, even as late as 1901 when her memoirs appeared. Threatening letters and severe criticism were issued against her, as were any Booth articles written in a sympathetic vein. It was more popular to refer to Booth as "a dissipated star of the South who traded on his family name" — the one thing Booth did not want, a comparison with the other Booths, or an easy entrance by using the family name. That is why, for the first four years of his career he did not use the name Booth.

Only a few friends were willing to go on record as having anything good to say about Booth. John Matthews, a fellow actor and an intimate friend since boyhood, finally had the courage after many years to say:

> Poor John, he thought he was doing right, and had brooded so much over the terrors of war that he had reached a point where he looked upon his act as patriotic. He was a brave man. There was something exalted in his courage.[21]

In his testimony, now in the National Archives, Matthews describes Booth as a handsome and personable fellow, and if Booth had been a woman, Matthews could have loved him. Another close friend and fellow actor John Mc-Cullough always refused to discuss Booth. When his name was mentioned McCullough immediately left the room.

Clara Morris always referred to him as "that unhappy boy," and Edwin Booth, in one of his rare comments about his brother, said that Wilkes "possessed rare dramatic talent, and would have made a brilliant mark in the theatrical world."[22]

Francis Wilson, the first biographer of Wilkes romanticized about him by calling him "a man of refinement and ideals: a man to whom the rift of dawn, the reddening of a rose meant much." Wilson believed that his was "a self-sacrificing, albeit wholly fanatical devotion to a cause he thought supreme...."[23]

Just as every misfortune tended to raise Edwin Booth in the minds of the public, the crime of John Wilkes Booth killed every ounce of theatrical fame he had been accorded. Who can say where applause for Edwin's art ended and the applause of sympathy began? One might conjecture that it was largely emotion which caused the audience to stand en masse and cheer, the theater literally a sea of waving handkerchiefs, on Edwin's first return to the stage after the tragedy.

Understandably so, the uncomplimentary features of John Wilkes Booth were played up and any good features suppressed, just as there must have been some uncomplimentary aspects of Lincoln which were also suppressed. William Barringer, in *Lincoln's Rise to Power*, said:

> Not until Booth's bullet had let out life was there anything like unanimity in affirming that in the person of Abraham Lincoln a great man had done a great work.[24]

Partisans thought Booth a "Bonaparte in one great move." No one knew this feeling better than Lincoln himself. Prior to his second inauguration, he told John R. Briggs, husband of the authoress Susan Edson Briggs (Olivia):

> 'Don't let your wife come to my inauguration. It is best for our women to remain indoors on that day, as the bullets may be flying."[25]

Thus, Booth's merits as an actor have gone unnoticed; and, had he even been the world's greatest artist, there still might have been no recognition. The prevalent opinion handed down to us today is that he was merely a secondrate actor who killed the greatest man in history. All most people seem to recall about him is that he killed Lincoln and then shouted "Sic semper tyrannis!" after he did it. Even that famous remark was disclaimed by some who insisted he said nothing on the stage at Ford's Theater that evening.

There are a few historians who believe that Booth was quite different from the picture of him that has crept into history. Our only indication of this is to be found in the newspapers of the period prior to the tragedy, and the half-hidden comments about him by his contemporaries. In the interest of truth, however, or "giving the devil his due," so to speak, it would seem that theater historians can no longer ignore such talent as was his on the American stage during the decade from 1855 to 1865. Some are beginning to honestly ask what manner of man was this? The perspective of time does not produce a truer evaluation of historic events, but it does eliminate the personal and emotional elements: by burying the good, we get only evil; by burying the facts, we get folklore. Who can deny that the most attractive figures are those of legend: those half-mythical characters whose real selves must forever lie under a veil of the bizarre, involving sensational contrasts or striking incongruities.

A more realistic assessment may now be possible, since there is no longer anyone living to shudder or wince at the dreadful name. We may now endeavor to look at him objectively and dispassionately. But no matter how much looking one may do, one can never arrive at the complete truth, because the truth about any man, especially one of another era, is almost impossible to determine. If this man is in show business it becomes an even greater impossibility.

Unfortunately, those who knew him are all gone, and most of his effects have been destroyed. He has been almost obliterated from theatrical history. The mere mention of a play or two is the extent of it.

Consequently, any remaining playbills and personal items of John Wilkes Booth are scarce and command high prices when they appear on the collectors' market. Fortunately, a representative collection of his playbills, letters, broadsides, and photographs have found their way into the great theater libraries and are being preserved for study.[26]

Augustin Daly, master showman of the 19th century, gives a good picture of what the playbill of Booth's time was like:

> What bills of the play there were in those days! Such a night's entertainment is unknown in these degenerate times. A five-act tragedy, then a *pas seul* by a favorite danseuse, perhaps a comic song, and the whole to conclude with a rattling farce or a gorgeous extravaganza.... They were good generous bills of the play, a yard long, but known as the "small bills" — to which the public was referred by the advertisements, for "particulars" ... and how the inky blackness of the bills of the play is illuminated by strange meteors that flashed for their brief moment and were gone![27]

Perhaps the largest private sale of Booth items was from the Oliver R. Barrett Collection, which was sold at auction in 1952 at Parke-Bernet Galleries, New York City. Besides 13 playbills, there was a fine collection of photographs of Booth in a variety of roles, costumed as an actor and in poses and apparel he wore offstage. There was also a selection of handbills, broadsides and newspapers.[28]

But what was John Wilkes Booth the man really like? Where is the true Booth between "greatest tragedian on the American stage" and "posing, self-centered madman"? Writing in 1899, Joel Chandler Harris[29] has one of his characters describe Booth in the following way:

> He had all the elements of genius but seemed powerless to focus them.... To say that this young man was mad would be to dispose of the problem he presents in a very unsatisfactory way. He was as mad as Hamlet was; no more or less.... He was so infected and unbalanced by his profession that the world seemed to him to be a stage on which men and women were acting, living, their parts. There was nothing real to him but that which is most unreal, the theatrical and the romantic. He had a great variety of charming qualities, and his mind would have been brilliant but for the characteristics which warped it.[30]

Some contemporary writers have psychoanalyzed the tragedy by saying that Booth had a paranoid delusion motivated by fantasies set in motion by his mother.[31] Did his hatred of his successful father and brother Edwin prompt this deep paranoid delusion, causing the desire in Wilkes

Booth to kill a great man, any great man, in order to gain for himself a notorious place, even above that of the father and brother? This hypothesis, while highly interesting, is too speculative and farfetched to be accepted as truth. Because of the very nature of the legend, one which "stands unrivalled as raw material for the psychology of the unconscious, especially in the field of social illusion, of racial and national dreams,"[32] ever statement can be shuttled back and forth a thousand times, and each time given a different twist.

Advocates of the above theory forget the fact that John Wilkes Booth was an established actor of note in his own right. He was a success; although at the time of the tragedy he was still young. Even with his tremendous popularity he had not fully developed his artistic capacities. Many of his contemporaries believed that had he lived he would have come to rival or surpass his father and brother Edwin.

Humanitarian Horace Greeley, editor of the *New York Herald Tribune* at this period, advocated amnesty for all Southerners after the Civil War. This was his solution in 1866:

> Booth was simply one of the many badly educated, loose-living young men infesting the purlieus of our cities, who, regarding slavery as a chief bulwark of their own claim to birthright in a superior caste, and the Federal Constitution as established expressly and mainly to sustain and buttress slavery, could never comprehend that any political action adverse to whatever exactions and pretensions of the slave power could possibly be other than unjustly aggressive and treasonable.[33]

Before we bring to a close these examples of widely diverse views, two more should be heard. John T. Morse, biographer of Lincoln called John Wilkes Booth

> an unworthy member of the family of distinguished actors of that name ... of inordinate vanity and of small capacity in his profession; altogether a disreputable fellow, though fitted to seem a hero in the eyes of the ignorant and dissipated classes. Betwixt the fumes of the brandy he so freely drank and the folly of the melodramatic parts which he was wont to act, his brain became saturated with a passion for notoriety, which grew into the very mania of eogism.[34]

And finally Carl Sandburg's ranting epithets which emotionally describe Booth as

> a pitiless, dripping, carnivorous, slathered, subhuman and antihuman beast mingling snake and tiger; the unmentionable ... a madman or a snake — a lunatic, a diabolically cunning athlete, swordsman, dead shot, horseman ... a brain that was a haunted house of monsters of vanity, of vampires and bats of hallucination.[35]

Here we bring to a close the examples of widely diverse viewpoints spanning a period of a hundred years. The chief concern of this book is John Wilkes Booth the actor, based on his own writings and the criticisms and assessments of his contemporaries. He was a richly endowed, talented young actor who had everything to live for during the period that Winston Churchill has described as "the last of the romantic wars," but became misguided and sacrificed himself to a lost cause.

There is no one today to remember the handsome young actor who strutted the stage in stride and voice suited to Shakespeare, for his record as a performer was suppressed by the denouement which forever relegated him to the exile of murderers. Whatever Booth achieved as an actor has dissolved as a smoke or fog, for even so, as it is with all actors, their work is the most individual, the most fleeting.

Charlotte Cushman, whom Booth admired and imitated as a youth, and with whom he later appeared on stage, made this eloquent comment about the acting profession:

> [Actors] leave nothing behind them but the vaguest of memories. It is all gone; passed away. Now, other artists, sculptors, musicians—produce something which lives after them and enshrines their memories in positive evidences of their divine mission; but we,—we strut and fret our hour upon the stage and then the curtain falls and all is darkness and silence.[36]

Perhaps this is what Booth realized early in life and why he tried another route to make his name last, determined to have fame.

Was Booth the dissipated beast, the drunkard, the lover of pleasure houses he was painted to be? Perhaps he was this along with the polished gentleman, the actor and scholar, for liquor and such houses were an accepted part of the times. Actor Otis Skinner tells us that "these were days when liquor drenched the stage and few there were who escaped the flood."[37] There are many men in one frame; society and history create many more when called upon to do so. Historian Theodore Roscoe observes that "secrecy, propaganda and romanticism eventually combined to create a public portrait of Booth that bore about as much resemblance to the subject as do the profiles of public figures created by the modern artists of Madison Avenue for popular consumption."[38]

Deaf, dumb, and blind is the rule for Wilkes Booth's friends. Even his brother Edwin was said to have stuffed "cotton in both ears, wore a white felt hat, and had a piece of crape on his left arm, wore a Lincoln badge on the right breast in mourning."[39]

CHAPTER 2: Early Stages Juvenile Theater

John Wilkes Booth's interest in the theater started when he was quite young. In Baltimore he was a member of a group of boys who grew up to become prominent on the stage. These young hopefuls devised an amateur theater in a basement where they performed, before a select juvenile audience, classical and romantic dramas with the female roles left out. Admission was 3 cents for reserved seats and 1 cent for standing room. Edwin was the "star," with Stuart Robson (who grew up to become the prominent American comedian), but since Wilkes was only eight years old at the time, he seldom got to perform. The older boys thought him a nuisance because he often interrupted rehearsals by suddenly appearing and mimicking them. Finally he was allowed to take part in the plays. He beat on a triangle to announce the acts, and he had a specialty song to sing, "The Heart Bowed Down." The little theatrical group was well organized and so well attended that the shows were usually kept on for several weeks. The fact that each of the boys were clever at borrowing surreptitiously from their elders helped also.[1]

When the elder Booth learned that the children were secretly borrowing his costumes and altering them drastically to fit, he broke up the budding dramatic company. They were not to be outdone, however, for as soon as the elder Booth went away on tour, as he frequently did, the group of Baltimore boys opened up again in a stable loft on Smith Street. Written posters announced: "Boys, 3¢; little boys, 2¢ — Come early and bring your fathers and mothers."[2]

When the family moved to their new brick farmhouse called Tudor Hall, twenty-five miles from Baltimore, a new group was organized. This time a tent was set up in the Maryland woods. The Negroes called it the "lightning and thunder group." This too, was soon to see a bad end, for when the elder Booth returned from one of his theatrical tours, he immediately "closed their engagement."

Still another stage for the children was the immense cherry tree near Tudor Hall, where "the crotch of the tree, which spread like five great fingers from a hand" became a place for the Booth boys to declaim passages from Shakespeare.[3]

Wilkes' schooling was sporadic: elementary school in Baltimore and the Bel Air Academy; St. Timothy's Hall, a military school on Catonsville, Maryland, in 1852; Milton's, a Quaker school at Cockeysville, Maryland, in 1853; Bland's Boarding Academy in York, Pennsylvania; and St. Charles' College at Pikesville, Maryland.

James W. Shettel described his school days with Wilkes Booth as he remembered them. Richard Bland ran the Bland's Boarding Academy in York, where Wilkes attended for a short time; Bland always called him "Jack." He had been a transfer student from the Milton Boarding School, which was on the Baltimore and York turnpike, about seventeen miles from Baltimore, and three miles north of Cockeysville. Shettel had attended that school also, when Booth was there, and slept in the next bed to him in the dormitory. He recalled that "Jack was a bad boy and used to fag the smaller boys cruelly. He was a bully until another boy stood up to him and thrashed him terribly. He never crowed again. His scepter was broken; his thrown was destroyed; his dynasty was ended; he was thoroughly conquered, cowed and humiliated, and all the boys were glad of it."[4]

The one thing Wilkes Booth enjoyed most at school was appearing in the school plays. This held his interest where all other general school work was a bore to him. The discipline required of the students drove him away from the classroom. He would disappear for periods of time and when he returned he would refuse to tell where he had been or what he meant by his actions. But when he was cast in the school plays he showed quite a different side of his character. One of his schoolmates later recalled, "Johnnie was selected to take the leading role. When he stood on the stage speaking his lines his black eyes sparkled with intensity. Everyone could see that he would some day be a great actor like his father."[5]

One of his early appearances before an audience occurred at the Quaker school where at the end of the term a large gathering celebrated with a picnic and entertainment. Wilkes was on the program, and his mother and sister Asia had traveled by train to Cockeysville where 300 people gathered for the occasion. From Asia's memoirs we get a picture of the scene and how Wilkes performed:

> Wilkes stood there, watching his classmates with a nervous face.... The reason was obvious when, after a pause, Wilkes himself came upon the little stage with all the fury of old Shylock. A master, who stood screened by the boys nearest the platform, read out Salarino's, the servant's, and Tubal's lines, and Shylock had the stage to himself.... A swift torrent of applause recalled the young actor, who smiled, and blushed, and bowed repeatedly. A Quakereress beside me said, "What is his name? He is a comely youth...."[6]

That he was stage-struck from childhood there can be no doubt, for as a boy he dreamed of doing something so big that his name would be remembered a thousand years. "His was an inbred, lifelong ambition to be, not just an actor, but a star of the first magnitude."[7] This was a natural ambition for one in which all the members of the family lived and breathed theater. The family at home on the Maryland farm was ever eagerly awaiting news of the touring father and older brother.

To prove his ability at mimicry, Wilkes put on a girl's petticoat and bonnet, walked past a group of workmen, and succeeded in fooling the men with his "elegant deportment." Often he donned his sister's long-trained dresses and walked before the full-length mirror, declaring that he would succeed as Lady Macbeth. He proclaimed to the household that "all the perfumes of Arabia will not sweeten this little hand...." A little later he would appear in a toga with another role, and so continue from role to role in his one-man interpretations.

Another time he dressed himself as the leading actress Charlotte Cushman, playing an old hag (the first American actress to become a great star), and went into the fields where the Negroes were working. Suddenly he appeared before them in his hideous old hag dress and make-up. He jumped from out of a thicket loudly proclaiming Cushman's famous lines as Meg Merrilies in *Guy Mannering*. The surprised Negroes, thinking surely it must be some evil apparition, became so frightened that they threw down their hoes and took to the woods. And it was not until they were thoroughly convinced that the apparition was really Mars Johnnie that they returned shouting at Asia who was also taken in, "On-dress Mars Johnnie, on-dress Mars Johnnie, on-dress him!"[8]

Nothing fascinated him and Asia more than their mother's tales of their father's life on the stage, during which she showed them old playbills, prompt books and other mementos of the elder Booth. When Wilkes' father died the boy was only 13 years old. He felt the pang of what was said as the news was revealed over the country, "Booth dead? Now there are no more actors!"[9] When the news of his father's death reached them from New Orleans, Wilkes ran into the forest which surrounded their home and sat brooding all day. Later he persuaded one of the neighbor boys to run away with him and try to secure an engagement with a theatrical stock company in Baltimore. When this failed, the two boys went to the Chesapeake Shore and tried to join the oyster pirates. These adventurous episodes provided the start of his career several years later.

At best, Wilkes' training was gained from self-teaching, and reading the classics and the old plays with the family at home. He knew most of the parts from memory, for the family were all accustomed to recite, whether it be in the parlor or in the woods. Their audience was nature, the birds, the animals in this dense forest, a place where they had strict instruction from their father that no living thing was to be killed. Their audience also was composed of the Negroes who worked on the farm. The elder Booth owned no slaves, but rather employed them from the neighboring farms as workers when available. Many of the workers heard the recitations so frequently that they were able to join in and recite along too, being able to prompt each other.

Wilkes had had an opportunity to attend better schools than his brother Edwin, who began touring with his father while quite young, and was never afforded the same opportunity of formal schooling. Wilkes also had special training in music and dancing. He received flute lessons from one of the orchestra leaders at a Baltimore theater, while dancer J.R. Codet gave him instructions on dancing the "Highland Fling," "Sailor's Hornpipe," and a Polish dance. In those days, dancing fulfilled a useful requirement for actors, as it bestowed grace of movement and a suave deportment to the leading man, as well as to the beginner (known as the "first walking gentleman"[10]).

He studied elocution from all the books he could obtain on the farm; he devoured every scrap about his father that his mother would let him have. He and Asia visited old relatives and gleaned through the "hoards of precious

A young John Wilkes Booth, around 1855. From a daguerreotype owned by Robert G. Shaw, Harvard Dramatic Library; from a copy in the Library of Congress.

theatrical books." Being without the benefit of a speech tutor, which he longed for, one who could point out his errors and guide his study, he and Asia did the next best thing: they studied together and dreamed of the future.

CHAPTER 3: Baltimore
First Professional Appearance

Although memorization of lines heard over and over from the family may have made him "bedroom perfect," as actors put it, that does not guarantee a stage perfect performance. His father's costumes that his mother had given him, his handsome face, added to the confidence of the unschooled and the family name, ignited by his own passionate drive for fame, were to launch John Wilkes Booth into an acting career.

So it was on August 14, 1855, that Booth played his first part in a professional theater. He performed the role of Richmond in *Richard III*, at the St. Charles Theatre in Baltimore.[1]

This performance was for the benefit of John Sleeper Clarke, a rising young comedian, who was at the time courting Wilkes' sister Asia. Clarke, that night, played the lead in the afterpiece, *Toodles*, a part to become associated with him as one of his best characterizations. The announcement that the son of the great Junius Brutus Booth was to appear was enough to fill the house. Wilkes' mother thought the venture premature, and that Clarke was only after the family name to bring in a large crowd for his benefit performance.

According to most reports, Booth's first performance went very badly. It is said that he was petrified with stage fright, that when he did start to speak he stuttered and stammered, made every possible mistake in his playing, and was loudly hissed. Just how much of this is true and how much is prejudice against him, one cannot say. In all reports of his career, his failures have been unduly magnified. One thing is certain, however, that this first performance was premature. A 17-year-old boy jumping into an important Shakespearean role with little preparation and at the same time being expected to perform in the caliber of a famous family, would most certainly end in disaster. Wilkes had not had the opportunity of traveling with his father as Edwin had done, and thus lost the initial training and discipline for the stage he so needed. Edwin played his first part with his father at 16 after many months of touring and watching the father work.

Booth's first appearance was recorded by Alonzo May in his Baltimore theater records. Under the date, August 14, 1855, May states: "John Sleeper Clarke's benefit was the occasion of the first appearance of John Wilkes Booth, son of the lamented Junius Brutus Booth, on any stage."[2] In the leading role of Richard III was Mr. Ellis, and the cast also included John W. Albaugh, the Albany actor, whose name keeps occurring in connection with Booth during his career. May also states that "the press made no comment," although some other reports state that critics were kind to Wilkes, probably remembering his father, and said he had given a fair performance.

Asia describes Wilkes' return to the farm after the performance:

> "...Guess what I've done! I've made my first appearance on any stage, for this night only, and in big capitals." His face shone with enthusiasm, and by the exultant tone of his voice it was plain that he had passed the test night. He had made his venture in life, and would soon follow on the road he had broken.... Mother was not pleased as we to hear of this adventure; she thought it premature, and he had been influenced by others who wished to gain notoriety and money by use of his name.... We sat in the old swing-seat late that night, indulging romantic fancies. He could never hope to be as great as father, he never wanted to rival Edwin, but he wanted to be loved of the Southern people above all things. He would work to make himself essentially a Southern actor.[3]

This bad start, if indeed it was, did not seem to dim Wilkes' interest in the theater, although the next report of his professional appearance in the theater is not until the summer of 1857. This time he billed himself as J.B. Wilkes, saying he would take back the family name after he had made a name for himself on his own.

After the eventful first performance, Wilkes went to work to improve his elocution. The dense Bel Air woods rang with his voice reciting passages from Byron, Poe, Milton and as always, the family favorite, Shakespeare. He practiced charging on his beloved horse Cola, lance in hand, as he delivered the speeches from *Richard III*, trying to improve his delivery and projection, and at the same time expressing the prankish joy of youth: charging the trees, sleigh-riding in July. He and Cola were also preparing for the annual "Knights in Armour Tournament" held at Deer Creek Rocks.[4] Wilkes was known to exclaim of the joy of his youth on the farm:

> "Heaven and Earth! how glorious it is to live! How divine! to breathe this breath of life with a clear mind and healthy lungs! Don't let us be sad. Life is so short — and the world is so beautiful. Just to *breathe* is delicious."[5]

Ironically, it was acts of exuberance such as these that neighbors remembered after the tragedy and helped to establish the idea that John Wilkes Booth was insane. One of the neighbors recalled, "Sometimes he did things which seemed a little crazy, but so did his father. There were people around here who thought all the Booths were cracked."[6]

Wilkes was so greatly obsessed with his acting that he studied far into the night. There were times when he became despondent over the slowness of his career and exclaimed:

> "How shall I ever have a chance on the stage? Buried here, torturing the grain out of the ground for daily bread, what chance have I of every studying elocution or declamation?"[7]

Yet he kept doggedly at it, learning as much as he could from his father's old prompt books. The voice master he longed for was not to be. There was no one to help him. There on the Maryland farm he would recite the Shakespearean roles to the Negroes who would cue him on his lines, taking delight in joining him in the plays. As the group went through the scenes, one elderly black man named Old Joe, sitting in a corner, threw in "asides," thinking the Brutus of *Julius Caesar* was Wilkes' father Junius Brutus Booth. The scene went something like this (as Asia Booth later set it down in the dialect clichés common at the time):

> "....I come to bury Caesar, not to praise him."
> aside:
> "De Lawd hab mussy on 'im!"
> "...For Brutus was an honorable man."
> aside:
> "Dat's ah fac', Mars Johnnie, he was dat—jes dat, wuz Mars Brutus. Ax ole Missus, she'll tell you dat... ah hon'able man, if eber dar wuz one."[8]

These were joyful days. They romped through the woods, studied nature, planned for Johnnie's future. We are told that "at eighteen he was taller and bigger than Edwin, wonderfully good looking in an exotic, theatrical way. His dark eyes glowed, fascinating as a snake's eyes. His teeth flashed in an actor's smile. He was devouringly ambitious."[9] Asia describes him further at this time:

> He inherited some of the most prepossessing qualities of his father, and while that father's finely shaped head and beautiful face were reproduced in him, he had the black hair and large hazel eyes of his mother. These were fringed heavily with long up-curling lashes, a noticeable peculiarity as rare as beautiful. He had perfectly shaped hands, and across the back of one he had clumsily marked, when a little boy, his initials in India ink.[10]

The years 1855 to 1857 were spent in study with only amateur participation in the theater or in pageants such as was held at Deer Creek Rocks at annual festivals. Horses and skill in riding was his love at this point.

CHAPTER 4: Philadelphia First Stock Engagement

John Sleeper Clarke managed to secure a place for Wilkes in stock in William Wheatley's Arch Street Theatre in Philadelphia. There he was paid eight dollars per week to play any part assigned to him. At this time Wheatley and Clarke were joint proprietors of the theater, and it is said that Wheatley was one of the most careful and judicious stage managers in the country.

Philadelphia was then the theatrical showplace of the nation, just as New York City is today. As a cultural center, Philadelphia was ahead of the other cities in recognition of the actor, and at the same time more critical of his work. It was in direct opposition to Boston, where they would not allow Saturday evening performances; and where to be respectable, a theater had to call itself a "museum" or an "athenaeum." New York, although not yet the actor's Mecca, was striving hard to further the art of the theater. Editorials in the *New York Times* such as the following from October 7, 1857, attempted to impress the importance and potential of the theater:

> It is impossible that men should go through the wear and tear of business day after day and week after week, as many do in this city, without recreation and relaxation of some sort. It is, indeed, one of the first necessaries of life to thousands and tens of thousands of our working men. Those who work with the brain need it most, but those who labor with their hands need it also, and ought to have the means and opportunity for it much more abundantly than they have at present. It is for the lack of it that so many day-laborers resort to the rum shop, to find in the lights and hilarity, as well as in the drink of the place, some stimulus to the exhausted body and flagging spirits. The cause of morality would be greatly benefited by one who would devise a system of cheap, popular, attractive and innocent amusements for the poor....

So it was at this period that John Wilkes Booth started again, and this time in discerning Philadelphia, a city in which he never felt at ease, even as an established star in later years.

The regular season at the Arch Street Theatre opened on August 15, 1857, with a company of 29. Listed in a preliminary advertisement was "Mr. J.B. Wilks" (He had dropped the "e" as a still further disguise) "from the N. York Theatres, his first appearance in Philadelphia." This exemplifies that for even a period in theatrical history without press agents, the theater managers still managed to carry on the same routine as today.

At this time Philadelphia had several prosperous theaters, among which were the Walnut Street Theatre, the National Theatre, and the

Stanford Opera House, and several variety houses, or saloon theaters of song and dance, the parents of the latter day music hall. But it was the Arch Street Theatre that seemed to occupy a special place in the hearts of theater-goers down through the years. The papers referred to it affectionately as "the neat little temple" or simply as "The Arch."

Competition was strong among the rival theaters. At one point, simultaneously the Arch featured Charlotte Cushman, the National announced Edwin Booth, while the Walnut had Laura Keene. Operators thought nothing of stealing the very same play and making only the most minute alterations or title change. When the Arch played *The Poor of Philadelphia* to packed houses for over a week, the National retaliated with *The Poor of New York*. Both versions based on *Les Pauvres de Paris*, or *The Streets of London*, in a Boucicault rehash. Plays could be rewritten and altered in any way desired.

As a member of this company, Wilkes was under contract to play in any piece for which he might be cast, and to appear every day at rehearsal.

In the opening play his first part was that of the Second Mask in Hannah Cowley's *The Belle's Stratagem*. It is interesting to note that another young actor also had his first part, that of Thomas, in the same performance. This actor was John McCullough, who was to remain Wilkes' close friend the remainder of his life. It was McCullough for whom Booth played a benefit performance in Washington, March 18, 1865, his last performance. It is unfortunate that more about the friendship between these two actors is not known. It is felt by some that McCullough might have shed some more light on Booth, but he refused to discuss the tragedy or his friend.

During Wilkes' engagement at the Arch Street Theatre, he was nervous and blundered continuously, so some reports state. Even with abundant preparation, many times he was struck dumb, stood rigid upon entering the stage, his confidence seeming to leave him. His fellow actors had to play around him, cover up, improvise, cut, in order to get the performance through. This hurt him very much that he should have this deplorable stage fright. He claimed he studied faithfully, but his lack of confidence was ruining him.

William S. Fredericks, acting and stage manager, constantly complained of Booth's failure, and it was the general opinion of the company that he had no promise. It is said that he lacked enterprise, for while other young actors were studying and memorizing new parts in other plays in hopes of some day landing the parts, Booth was too indifferent to push ahead. He was compared to McCullough, who already had dozens of roles memorized, and could quote profusely from Shakespeare at any given point. The fact was pointed up that Booth was not applying himself in this way. Although he gave this impression to the rest of the company, he, it seems, was deeply disturbed by his failure. He realized he was jerky, stiff and awkward. Because of this his confidence was gone as soon as he entered stage. He lamented, "I shall never be a nimble skip-about like Romeo. I'm too square and solid. How shall I ever have a chance on the stage?" And his roommate at that time, another fellow actor, said that Wilkes would pace the floor in worry over his failure, crying, "I must have fame! fame!"[1] Yet his anxieties about his stage presence were finally overcome. It would be interesting to know just how and when this illusive stage confidence finally came about. His later portrayal of Romeo was hailed by many as just about perfect.

The following night after the opening play *The Belle's Stratagem*, Wilkes had four speeches as the Courier in *The Wife*. All he had to do was follow his cues and deliver such announcements as, "Here comes the Duke." Other small parts followed in a series of bills which changed almost nightly. There was always the main play with an afterpiece, and Wilkes sometimes had parts in both.

On February 19, 1858, John Sleeper Clarke was playing another benefit performance. According to the custom, the person being benefitted was allowed full choice of what was to be presented for the evening. Clarke arranged for Wilkes to again play the part that had launched his career, that of Richmond in *Richard III*. This time "Sleepy" Clarke was to do a comedy, or mock performance of Richard, burlesquing the old favorite. In this performance Wilkes was allowed to play his part straight in contrast to Clarke's comedy. For the first time Wilkes seemed to hold the audience and received token applause. And with it came better parts, but still embarrassing moments were in store for Wilkes.

George Alfred Townsend, or "Gath," as this special correspondent of the New York *World*, was called, tells of one performance at this time which illustrates Booth's confusion. The night was Tuesday, February 23, 1858. The play was Hugo's *Lucretia Borgia*. Wilkes Booth entered center stage, dressed perfectly in his brilliant court costume of the 1500's. He knew he looked good and he had his confidence and self-assurance about him. His opening line was to have been, "Madame, I am Petruchio Pandolfo." Instead he exclaimed:

> "Madame, I am Pondolfio Pet— Pedolfio Pat— Pantuchio Ped— Damnit! What am I?"

The audience roared, but Wilkes had enough stage presence to laugh along with them. Everybody both on stage and off was completely broken up with laughter.[2]

The next night he had a rather good part as Dawson in Moore's *The Gamester*, and for the occasion he had bought a fine new suit of clothes, and invited a lady friend to the performance. However, the moment he appeared on stage, the audience recognized him from the previous evening and started the hilarious laughter all over again, causing further embarrassment and turning the performance into shambles. Townsend reported that he saw similar occurrences on three other consecutive nights. But this may be an exaggeration, for Townsend has been accused of dramatizing much of his reporting.

The lady friend mentioned above was one of Wilkes' early amorous escapades similar to those of his father when the latter was a young actor in London. At the boarding house for budding artists and actors where Wilkes resided on Arch Street near the theater, lived the beautiful but unfortunate girl who had fallen desperately in love with him. We learn from historian Stanley Kimmel that

> the handsome Wilkes had the sort of appeal that no woman would resist. His fascinating dark eyes and melodious voice made them susceptible to his

advances.... Each night she entertained Wilkes with charms that finally got him into trouble and caused considerable expense. That he managed the entire affair with but few intimate friends knowing of it flattered his ego and gave him a false assurance. He considered himself especially adept at intrigue.[3]

But even with stage manager Fredericks declaring that there was little hope for him, Wilkes was nevertheless allowed to remain with the company.

All was not lost during this period of learning the theater, for Booth had the advantage of working with several prominent actors who appeared with the company that season. Dion Boucicault and his wife Agnes Robinson came for an engagement. Boucicault's *Jessie Brown* was first presented here. The play ran for 24 performances with only the afterpiece changing, an unusual run for the times, as most bills changed nightly. During the remainder of his brief career Wilkes was to appear in several of Boucicault's plays.

Visiting stars continued at the Arch Street Theatre, among them Susan Denin (later to become one of Wilkes' beautiful leading ladies), and in May, Charlotte Cushman, the lady whom Wilkes impersonated for the Negroes in the fields back on the farm, came for a week's engagement.

Miss Cushman was the most famous tragedienne of the period. Her voice has been described as one "saturated with anguish." When she appeared as Lady Macbeth, or as Nancy in *Oliver Twist*, she sounded as if she "spoke through blood" in her dying scene in begging Bill Sykes to kiss her. She arrived accompanied by flourishes of big, inky-black letterings on posters and playbills announcing "the great actress of the age" in her final professional engagement before retirement.

There are rare playbills of this period which show that Wilkes appeared nightly with her in small parts. For her Lady Macbeth, he was the First Apparition, for her Queen Katharine in *Henry VIII*, he was Capucius, ambassador from the Emperor Charles V, for her Rosalind in *As You Like It*, he was Silvius, the youth love-sick for Phoebe. This would indicate that the company stage manager was putting more confidence in Wilkes' work, as he would never have permitted anyone in the cast who might possibly disrupt the great Cushman's performances.

One of the longest runs at the Arch at this time was the spectacular *Last Days of Pompeii* and the afterpiece *The Scalp Hunters*. Advertisements called it "the most brilliant spectacle ever presented — over-flowing crowds and genuine success of the greatest combination in the world."

On November 13, 1858, each of the rival theaters cut prices in an effort to attract trade from the others. An advertisement ran in the *Philadelphia Public Ledger*:

Arch Street Theatre: Old prices restored to suit the times. 25 cts. to all parts of the house ... except orchestra 50 cts. and the private boxes 75 cts. Secured seats in the Dress Circle 27½ cts. Doors open at 6½; commences at 7...

And one share of stock for the Arch Street Theatre went on sale. The purchase of this share would entitle the buyer to a season ticket to the theater.

Wilkes remained "third walking gentleman" for the season through June. As is the case with all "third walking gentlemen," they are the first to walk. His failures in Philadelphia always worried him, and even after becoming well established he always hated to play there.

WHEATLEY'S
ARCH ST. THEATRE

SOLE LESSEE, ... W. WHEATLEY
ACTING AND STAGE MANAGER, . . . W. S. FREDERICKS

FAREWELL BENEFIT

AND POSITIVELY THE

LAST NIGHT

OF MISS

Charlotte Cushman

WHEN SHE WILL APPEAR IN

TWO FAVORITE CHARACTERS

FRIDAY EVENING, MAY 28th, 1858,

Will be acted SHAKSPER'ES Splendid Comedy of

AS YOU LIKE IT!

Banished Duke ....Mr GILE	Corin .... Mr McCULLOUGH
Duke Frederick ....Mr BRADLEY	Le Beau .... Mr WALLIS
Jaques ....Mr DOLMAN	Silvius .... Mr WILKS
Amiens ....Mr JAS. DUNN	William ....Mr TANNEHILL
Orlando.........................Mr WM. WHEATLEY	Charles, the Wrestler...................Mr F. JOHNSON
Oliver.............................Mr WM. H. MYERS	Celia ....Miss E. TAYLOR
Jaques Dubois ....Mr REILLY	Phœbe ....Mrs TANNEHILL
Adam ....Mr THAYER	Audrey........................Mrs THAYER
Touchstone........................Mr J. S. CLARKE	Courtiers, Shepherds, Hunters, &c., &c.

ROSALIND, - - - - MISS C. CUSHMAN

In the course of the Comedy, the following Music will be sung:

GLEE—" What shall he have who kills the Deer?" by Messrs. Jas. Dunn, Neel, Anderson and Poole.   SONGS—" Under the Green Wood Tree," Mr. Jas. Dunn, and " Blow, Blow, thou Wintry Wind."   SONG—" When Daisies wild and Violets blue," by MISS CHARLOTTE CUSHMAN.

The Orchestra, under the direction of Mr. CHAS. R. DODWORTH, will perform several Popular Musical Selections.

To conclude with the Admirable Comedietta of

SIMPSON & CO.

MRS. SIMPSON, - - - - MISS C. CUSHMAN

Mrs Bromley ....Mrs ELMORE	Mr Simpson ....Mr THAYER
Mrs Fitzallen ....Miss E. TAYLOR	Mr Bromley........................Mr DOLMAN
Mad. La Trappe ....Mrs THAYER	Foster ....Mr REILLY
	Servant..........................Mr BENN

SPECIAL NOTICE—The Lessee has great pleasure in announcing, that at the earnest request of numerous parties, MISS CUSHMAN has consented to give a

Day Performance To-Morrow, Saturday, May 29th

When she will appear, for the Last Time in Philadelphia, in her Great Unequaled Representation of

MEG MERRILIES.

The Performances will commence at HALF PAST 1 O'CLOCK, P. M.

Playbill of one of Booth's appearances with Charlotte Cushman, May 28, 1858. From the theater collection of Yale University Library. Previously unpublished.

Edwin Booth began a run at the Holliday Street Theatre in Baltimore, on August 28, 1858. This engagement lasted through September 4th. On the day before Edwin's regular run began, August 27th, Wilkes joined him for a performance of *Richard III*. In order to please his mother, Edwin had Wilkes billed under his own name, J. Wilkes Booth. Edwin played the title role, and Wilkes again tackled the part of Richmond. Evidently Wilkes got good direction and gained confidence under the tutelage of his brother, for reports of this performance were better than those he had previously received.

Some Quakers who had been in school with Wilkes in Cockeysville, Maryland, came to witness the two brothers on stage. Wilkes had played Shylock in the school play at Cockeysville, and was remembered by many in the Quaker settlement. One Quakeress who had never entered a theater before attended this performance. Her description of Wilkes was:

> He made me feel what a tyrant Richard had been. I seemed actually to be living at that time instead of in this quiet century. As for his appearance — Well, he looked like a new blown rose with the morning dew upon it.[4]

The Alonzo May Manuscript records: "27 August 1858 — Benefit, another Richmond in the field. *Richard III.* John Wilkes Booth as Richmond. This was incorrectly advertised as his first appearance in Baltimore. Actually his first performance was the same role which had launched him there in 1855.

Then Edwin Booth went on to other engagements, and Wilkes was engaged for another season of stock, this time in Richmond, Virginia.

CHAPTER 5: Richmond
The First Season

In the fall of 1858, John Wilkes Booth was engaged for a season of stock in Richmond, Virginia. At that time Richmond was the center of the entertainment world of the South. The Richmond Dramatic Star Company, known as Kunkel & Co., was a well-established part of Richmond, then in its third regular season at the old Marshall Theatre, or Richmond Theatre as it was later called. As was the custom in the theater of the day, many local dramatic companies prospered, each in turn readying the plays and settings for the "star" players who traveled from town to town. Such star players as Edwin Booth, Maggie Mitchell, Julia Dean, Barry Sullivan, J.W. Wallack, Dion Boucicault, and many others, announced ahead of time what plays they would be doing, and the company had the other parts cast and partially rehearsed as soon as the star arrived. Rehearsal up to a point, for on many occasions the star, upon arriving, did not like the casting or the stage blocking and had them changed to suit himself. This necessitated more rehearsals. Therefore the players were usually on call daily for rehearsals of new plays as well as appearing nightly (except Sundays) on a different bill. The bills always consisted of more than one play. This was before the days of one play for an evening, and no theater manager would dare risk losing the audience to another theater by not giving a patron his money's worth. A variety "bumper bill" (which consisted of several features and various acts) was usually presented in hopes of attracting more people. A ticket in the gallery could be purchased for as little as 12½ cents, or 15 cents in many theaters. There were usually two plays, sometimes three, the last on the bill being short ones, with added singing and dancing between the plays. There was a full orchestra to play the overture and to provide incidental music, while coy soubrettes took stage in the burletta, or musical burlesque. The program commenced at seven and lasted until midnight. Vaudeville, which was to come into its own about 1870, was still a thing unknown.

The old Marshall Theatre had been redecorated and painted for the new season, and according to the ads, George Kunkel, John T. Ford, and Thomas L. Moxley, lessees and managers, had left nothing undone so as to ensure the theater-going public with a most elegant season.

The company of "ladies and gentlemen of acknowledged ability selected with great care for the Richmond Theatre," also included J.B. Wilkes, now spelled with the "e" added, from the Arch Street Theatre, Philadelphia. Manager Kunkel paid Wilkes $20 per week, and he seemed to be getting better parts, better recognition, and was gradually developing into an actor of

Richmond Theatre, at a time when Richmond was the center of the entertainment world of the South. From the Irving S. Greentree Collection, Richmond, Virginia.

average ability. Wilkes' roommate was leading man H.A. Langdon, and both were swept into the whirl of Southern high society. So it was that the new season, "a company composed of artists from the theaters of the Union," opened on Saturday Evening, September 4, "at ¼ to 8 o'clock precisely."[1]

For a review of Saturday night's performance, a few lines follow from a lengthy article in the Richmond *Dispatch*, for the following Monday. There were no Sunday papers as well as no Sunday performances:

> *Opening Night at the Theatre.* – The Theatre Saturday night was un-comfortably crowded from the parquette to the highest gallery – the audience being the largest on the first night for four years.... The company is about fifty percent better than that of last season ... [and] took the audience by storm, and having youth and beauty on their sides, will play sad havoc, we fear, with the hearts this season....

Several days after the opening Wilkes wrote to Edwin telling him about his work with the Richmond Theatre company. As for addressing Edwin Booth as "Ted," one researcher observed, "It was the custom now even in a few journals to refer to him familiarly as 'Ted' Booth, a singular appropriation of the nickname 'Theodore' for which there seems to have existed neither reason nor precedent except perhaps the similar sound to Ed.[2]

Similarly, the following letter from Wilkes to his brother Edwin at this time reveals Wilkes' concern about his acting:

Richmond, Va.
Sept. 10, 1858

Dear Ted,
    I would have written to you before this, but I have been so busily engaged, and am such a slow writer that I could not find the time. I am rooming with

Three-quarter length carte de visite *of John Wilkes Booth at the time of his first Richmond engagement. From the collection of Lloyd Ostendorf, Dayton, Ohio.*

H. Langdon.³ He has stopped drinking and we get along very well together. This climate don't agree with me. I have felt ill since I have been here. I called on Dr. Beeal soon after I arrived here. He and his lady seem a very nice couple. I liked them very much. He has put me under a course of medicine, the same I have been subject to before. I understand it is that that makes me so languid and stupid. I have played several good parts since I have been here, Cool in *London Assurance* last night. I believe I am getting along very well. I like the people, place, and management, so I hope to be very comfortable. There is only one objection and that is I believe every one knows me already. I have heard my name—Booth—called for, one or two nights, and on account of my likeness the papers deigned to mention me. How are you getting along? I had hoped to hear from you before this. Give Mother my love. For I may not be able to write her this week, as they are casting Miss Mitchell's pieces, and I will have much to study. Excuse this dull letter. God bless you, and believe me I am as ever your affectionate Brother. John.⁴

This letter is a typical Booth letter in that Wilkes, too, complains of being ill. Many of the correspondences of the Booths allude to their tendency toward illness, depression, moodiness or reflect that they are being caught up in the essence of the tragedies they portrayed. Even at this age— Wilkes was 20 when he wrote the letter—one gets the feeling that he is indeed a Booth, a fact he was trying to hide from the public until he could make a name on his own. Probably because of criticism of his first performance, he decided not to use the name of Booth. He explained to his friends that he would take it back as soon as he made a success on his own.

The parts Wilkes spoke of in the above letter were in *School for Scandal, Extremes, The Wife,* and the one-act operettas *Swiss Swains* and *Jenny Lind.* He continued in such plays as *Old Heads and Young Hearts, La Tour de Nesle,* and *The Lottery Ticket.*

It was on Monday, September 13, 1858, that the top musical comedy actress of the day, Maggie Mitchell, came to Richmond for two weeks. This is referred to in Wilkes' letter when he speaks of having to learn many new pieces. Understandably, a good deal of preparation was required for Miss Mitchell's engagement, since she presented many short pieces, usually three per night, playing as many as seven parts in one piece herself. This meant that her supporting actors had to fill in with an equivalent number of straight parts to her many characterizations. Besides this, there were her specialty numbers of songs, dances, skits. She was the most popular star of her day. Possessing an effervescent and elfin-like personality, and a clever talent as a dramatic actress, she became the "peoples' favorite." Wherever she played she was referred to as "Our Maggie" and was received by ardently enthusiastic audiences. It is said that she was Longfellow's favorite actress. Her most famous role was as *Fanchon, the Cricket,* a part which showed off her subtle skill, and kept her a reigning favorite on the stage for forty years. Although born in New York City, she stopped many a show during the Civil War by doing her specialty dance numbers stomping upon the United States flag.

Being a strong Confederate supporter, it was natural for her and Wilkes to become good friends. They appeared together many times. It was she who gave him his first star benefit after he had gone out on his own in Montgomery, Alabama.

After Maggie Mitchell's engagement, Edwin Booth came to the Richmond Theatre for an engagement of three weeks. He opened on Monday, September 27, 1858, in his father's famous role of Pescara in *The Apostate,* a part to become more associated with Wilkes than with Edwin. Wilkes appeared every night with his brother, either in small parts or in the afterpieces.

An editorial in the Richmond *Examiner,* October 1, 1858, speaks of Edwin, then says, "There is in the company a young gentleman named Wilkes, a good deal like Edwin Booth in face and person. He is a man of promise, and might, with the approbation of the audience, be cast for a higher position then he usually occupies."

Then on Friday, October 1, 1858, the theater-going public was indeed informed in large capitals that Wilkes was a Booth:

RICHMOND THEATRE
To-night, Friday, Oct. 1, 1858
Unapproachable attraction for the
Benefit of
EDWIN BOOTH
when he will appear as
RICHARD III
on what occasion his brother

WILKES BOOTH
will appear as the
EARL OF RICHMOND

EDWIN BOOTH . . . . as . . . . DUKE OF GLOSTER
RICHMOND . . . . WILKES BOOTH

to Conclude with
THE SECRET; OR, THE HOLE IN THE WALL[5]

For this performance the press reported: "Theatre oppressively crowded; one of the most brilliant periods at the theatre for a long time."

This was to be the first appearance of Wilkes under his own name since the two brothers had appeared together in the same play in Baltimore on August 28th. Writing of this occasion to their older brother Junius, Jr., Edwin said of Wilkes, "I don't think he will startle the world ... but he is improving and looks beautiful on the platform."[6] And about this time his mother wrote to Junius, Jr., "John is doing well at Richmond. He is very anxious to get on faster. When he has a run of bad parts he writes home in despair."[7]

Edwin's run continued with an all Shakespeare bill. Wilkes supported him as Paris in *Romeo and Juliet*, Horatio in *Hamlet* and various other roles during the engagement.

On Saturday night, October 9, 1858, the brothers again performed *Richard III*. Wilkes was again billed as Booth. It was during this engagement that Edwin presented *Henry V*, his first time in the role, and the first time the play had been presented in the United States.

Edwin did all he could to further his brother's career, but some have said that Wilkes was hard to direct, resented the direction given by Edwin, became temperamental, wanted to do everything his own way. Naturally there was a clash between the two strong individuals as Wilkes continued to gain more confidence in himself.

Some felt that Edwin gave Wilkes every advantage before the footlights; he played so that Wilkes could be center stage, allowed him to "upstage" and to take every scene in which he appeared. Probably, Edwin was at times too patronizing. On October 5th, when they appeared together in *Hamlet*, at the final curtain, Edwin pulled his brother down to the footlights and said to the audience, "I think he's done well, don't you?"[8] The audience responded with cries of yes, yes! for even though his performance was not as polished as a tragedian's should have been, his handsome face and vibrant personality, coupled with the impact of the roles they had played: fond brothers playing fond parts, Hamlet and Horatio, had captivated the audience.

After Edwin's run, Wilkes went back to his billing as Mr. J.B. Wilkes. This seems strange, and one wonders why this shuffling back and forth in billing was necessary. One biographer has explained that the Booth name still needed protection, though by this time it was widely known that Wilkes was a Booth anyway. Whether or not his performances proved good or bad, the theater was still heavily attended.

It was in 1858 that the Booth brothers became acquainted with E.V. Valentine, the noted Richmond sculptor. Valentine was 20 years old at the time, the same age as Wilkes. A lover of the theater, he knew most of the players of the Richmond Dramatic Star Company, personally. On October 1, 1858, Thomas L. Moxley, Acting Manager, introduced Valentine to Edwin, and the next day Booth sat for his bust (now in the Valentine Museum). Booth sat on seven other successive occasions.

E.V. Valentine also wanted to sculpt John Wilkes Booth, but this was not to be. Valentine left Richmond late in 1859 for Europe where he studied sculpture, and did not return to that city until 1865. Valentine and Edwin remained good friends and kept up a correspondence over the years.

Extracts from Valentine's diary and his theater notes from Richmond newspapers include references to the Booths, e.g., Saturday, October 30, 1858:

> In the evening took a walk. Met John Booth. He told me he was going to Lynchburg with the company. At night went to the theatre. They played *La Tour de Nesle.* [9]

According to the papers, the plays given that night, Saturday, October 30, 1858, were *Dombey and Son* and *The Mysterious Panel. La Tour de Nesle* was given on Friday, the night before, according to the Richmond *Dispatch*. Performances could easily have been switched after the paper was printed, which seems most likely.

Be that as it may, the company did go to Lynchburg, Virginia, for a two-week run. There the company of 17 opened at Dudley Hall with *The Wife; or, My Father's Grave*. In this play Wilkes advanced from the smallest walk-on part to the leading role during his career.

The *Lynchburg Daily Virginian* was overflowing with praise for the company. It seems that "the house, crowded to suffocation, was filled with the beauty and fashion of the city." A lengthy editorial on Friday, November 5, 1858, said in part:

> In their ability to represent plays, and in a willingness to consult the moral health of the public while selecting them for the public, we believe the present management of our theatre has no superiors.... We bespeak for the Company, the kind remembrance of every true admirer of the drama.

Upon returning to Richmond, the company presented Avonia Jones as star for a two-week engagement. Wilkes appeared with the Richmond actress in several parts. Miss Jones was one of the most flamboyant and strikingly beautiful actresses among Wilkes' leading ladies. His leading ladies were selected for their beauty, temperament, and individuality. Mere prettiness would not suffice. It can be assumed that after becoming a star, Wilkes chose his leading ladies to suit himself. Certainly they all had that fire and personal magnetism he himself possessed, which, when coupled together, made for a dashing performance.

In a letter from Miss Jones to Augustin Daly, master theatrical producer, she described the type of role she most enjoyed playing:

> As you have never seen me act I must tell you that my style is passionate. When I love it must be madly; not the tender gentle love that shrinks from observation, but love that would sweep all before it and if thwarted would end in despair, madness and death. In fact in acting I am more fond of being bad than good. Hate, revenge, despair, scarcasm and resistless love I glory in; charity, gentleness and the meeker virtues I do not care for. [10]

Friday Evening, November 19th, 1858,

Will be presented the very successful Play, translated from the French, entitled

ADRIENNE

THE ACTRESS !

OR THE

YOUTHFUL DAYS OF MARSHAL SAXE.

Adrienne Lecouvrer,	- -	Miss Avonia Jones
Count Maurice de Saxe .... H A Langdon	Princess D'Bouillon, (her first appearance in 3 weeks,)	
L'Abbe .... D H Harkins		Mrs I B Phillips
Michoust .... W H Bailey	M'lle Angelique .... Miss Julia Irving	
Duke D'Aumont .... B T Ringgold	M'lle Jouvenot .... Miss Kate Fisher	
Quinault, (an Actor) .... S K Ch ster	M'lle Dangerville .... Miss Kate Pennoyer	
Paisson .... J B Wilkes	Marchioness .... Miss Taylor	
Valet .... W Mortimer	Actors, Actresses, Gents, &c.	

GRAND SPANISH DANCE,

Miss Kate Pennoyer

TO CONCLUDE WITH THE LAUGHABLE FARCE OF

JENNY LIND!

Or, The Swedish Nightingale.

Baron Swigitoof .... B Ringgold	Herr Kanaster .... W Mortimer
Mr Leatherlung .... W H Bailey	Her Spittoon .... C H French
Granby Gag .... T B Johnston	Her Koff .... R Meer
Her Cheroot .... J B Wilkes	Jenny Leatherlungs (with songs)... Miss Kate Fisher

In active preparation the new Tragic Play, written by Jonn Savage, Esq., of Washington, and received with marked success wherever it has been performed, entitled

SYBIL.

ADMISSION.—Dress Circle and Parquette 50 cts.; (no extra charge for Secured Seats.) Second Tier or Family Circle 45 cts. Eastern Gallery for colored persons 37½ cents. Western Gallery 25 cents — Gallery 50 cts. Doors open at 7 o'clock—Overture commence at ¼ before 8, precisely. Box Office open from 10 until 2, and from 3 until 5, daily

Hammersley & Co., Prs., Corner 13th and Main streets.

A rare playbill from the Richmond Theatre, November 19, 1858, showing Booth (as "J.B. Wilkes") in two roles. From the collection of Irving S. Greentree, Richmond, Virginia. Previously unpublished.

One can readily see why Booth would be attracted to Miss Jones as a leading lady, for her temperament would closely match his acting. Their last appearance together was for her benifit on January 20, 1865. The play was *Romeo and Juliet*, Booth's next to last appearance. He played Romeo in borrowed costumes, as his trunk was already on its way south to Richmond via Canada (a trip the ill-fated trunk never completed).

The 1858-1859 season continued with star players coming to join the stock company for a few weeks each engagement. Wilkes played small parts with such stalwart players as J.W. Wallack, Julia Dean, J.A.L. Neafie, William Wheatley, John Sleeper Clarke, James E. Murdock, and Barry Sullivan.

As they did in Lynchburg, the company traveled to Petersburg for a two-week engagement beginning Monday, December 20, 1858. Prior to their departure, Wilkes and several members of the company gave a special performance at the Powhatan Hotel on Saturday, December 18th. The Powhatan Hotel, located on the corner of Broad and 11th Streets, just four blocks from the theater, was where Wilkes and most of the company had rooms. On that Saturday, a special performance was given at the hotel presenting *Fazio* and *The Love Chase*.[11]

Petersburg was the scene of another meeting and series of performances with Maggie Mitchell. Wilkes is particularly remembered at this time by Leonard Grover, manager of Grover's Theatre, Washington, D.C.:

> At Petersburg, Virginia, in the latter part of 1858, I attended the theatre at which Maggie Mitchell was playing a star engagement. In the cast appeared the name of John Wilkes, playing the character of Uncas, an Indian. He seemed the most talented actor in the company, and I later learned that he was John Wilkes Booth.[12]

The play referred to was *Wept of Wish-Ton-Wish*, a dramatization of James Fenimore Cooper's novel.

Back in Richmond, January 3, 1859, the company continued their engagement through the winter and spring season. On Monday, January 24th, a "monster spectacle with nearly 100 persons" opened. This was based on Alexandre Dumas' *The Count of Monte Cristo*, and included a grand carnival, trained animals and trick horses. The advertisement for this show took up an entire column of the Richmond *Dispatch* for January 24th, and appeared daily during the run of the play. New scenery was designed especially for this production, and a "correct view" of the Port of Marseilles was staged. This was supposed to be the grand spectacle of all times, and it set a record for the company. It played for seven consecutive nights with no other piece on the bill. Then the carnival scene was used as an afterpiece with following bills. Wilkes played the part of Danglars, a supercargo, officer in charge of commercial concerns on a merchant ship's voyage. His roommate, leading man H.A. Langdon, played five parts, including the Count, Sinbad the Sailor, and Dante.

On Wednesday, February 23, 1859, there appeared in the amusement columns of the Richmond *Dispatch*, a correspondence. About a dozen citizens of Richmond presented a signed letter to Moxley asking that a benefit performance be given in his honor, and suggested a ticket price for all seats be

THE DISPATCH.

MONDAY MORNING.................................MAY 2. 1859.

AMUSEMENTS.

RICHMOND THEATRE.

GRAND RE-OPENING!
BENEFIT OF J. WILKES BOOTH,
Who will for the first time, sustain the arduous
character of OTHELLO; his brother
EDWIN BOOTH,
Who will remain for this night only, will appear in
his great character of IAGO.

MONDAY EVENING, May 2, 1859,
Will be presented Shakspeare's sublime tragedy of
OTHELLO, THE MOOR OF VENICE. Othello,
J. Wilkes Booth; Iago, Edwin Booth.

Popular Ballads, Mr J W Adams.

The evening's entertainment will conclude with La
Bayadere, Miss Kate Pennoyer.

BENEFIT OF J. WILKES BOOTH.—The benefit to this
young actor to night, affords an excellent opportunity of enjoying some very fine acting. He will ap
pear as Othello, and Edwin Booth, his brother, as
Iago. The bill also includes a variety of songs, and
a dance.

Announcement of John Wilkes and Edwin Booth in Othello, Richmond Theatre. *From
the Richmond* Dispatch, May 2, 1859.

fixed at $1 each. Moxley replied by way of the amusement columns with
thanks and suggested Friday, February 25th. Then members of the company
signed a letter offering their services for such a benefit. Among those signing
was J.W. Booth. One wonders if this was merely a polite, round-about way
of benefitting the acting manager; however this seems to have been
customary for theatricals in those days; and the company did enjoy great
popularity in Richmond.

The big performance for the benefit of Thomas L. Moxley, acting
manager, was *Romeo and Juliet*, with Maggie Mitchell cast as Romeo and
Mrs. I.B. Phillips as Juliet. Wilkes again played his part of Paris, while his
roommate, leading man H.A. Langdon, was relegated to the part of Friar

Lawrence, since Miss Mitchell had insisted upon "unsexing" herself and taking over the part of Romeo. Langdon probably felt as many others did concerning women playing men's parts. Many were violently opposed to such actresses as Charlotte Cushman and Maggie Mitchell in male roles, for no matter how good they were as actresses, the whole play was thrown off by the "unsexing." But those two ladies were top ranking stars and could demand any part they desired.

After the big benefit night, two celebrated comedians came to Richmond for a two-week run. They were William Wheatley and John Sleeper Clarke. They appeared in *Our American Cousin,* performing in Tom Taylor's dashing comedy, the original characters as performed by them at the Arch Street Theatre in Philadelphia for four consecutive months. Wheatley and Clarke had been managers of the Arch Street Theatre before Mrs. John Drew (grandmother of the Barrymores) took over in 1861. It will be remembered that Clarke, known to his friends as "Sleepy," had launched Wilkes' career in 1855, and later appeared with him at the Arch. It was only about two months after this 1859 engagement that Clarke married Asia Booth, Wilkes' sister.

On Monday, April 19, 1859, Edwin Booth again came to Richmond for two weeks. At the end of this run the theater closed for four days. On the following Monday, May 2nd, a grand reopening was announced. Edwin remained for one night only in order to give Wilkes a benefit. This was Wilkes' first benefit under the name of Booth, and his first time "to sustain the arduous character of Othello." Edwin stepped down a notch and played Iago. Again it is reported that the brothers played to standing room only and received a tremendous ovation. After this performance, Wilkes continued to play as before under the name of J.B. Wilkes, until the season closed on May 26th.

CHAPTER 6: Richmond
The Second Season

In the fall of 1859 Wilkes returned to Richmond for his second year. The company was basically the same as the previous season, except that Edwin Adams had replaced H.A. Langdon as leading man. This time instead of the theater boarding house, Wilkes stayed at the Powhatan Hotel. While he continued to use "Wilkes" on the programs, he was known as Booth off stage, and was listed in the Richmond city directory as Booth.

The *Dispatch* acclaimed the opening of the new theater season in a most lavish review, September 5, 1859:

> We attended the theatre on Tuesday night for the first time, so to speak, for, although we were there on Saturday, the crowd was so great that we could not get within seeing or hearing distance.... Most of the actors were new to us, though well known to fame.... The caste was inimitable, every actor and actress seemed to have been made for the particular personage he or she represented.... We do not recollect in some thirty years of theatrical experience, ever having seen a more unique or more decidedly good performance in every particular...

At the end of the first week, Saturday, September 10, 1859, *Richard III* was again presented, and it was brought to the attention of the public that it was Shakespeare's sublime tragedy in five acts, although one suspects that it was the same Colley Cibber version which had previously been given. The Cibber version of *Richard III* was the popular one for over 120 years. Known as "the blood and thunder version," or "the rapid action version," Cibber had taken parts of *Henry IV, Henry V, Henry VI,* and put them together in such a way as to get a *Richard III* which pleased the public far more than Shakespeare's original version. Such lines as "Off with his head; so much for Buckingham!" are not Shakespeare but Cibber, devised to catch the ear, and "to evoke the applause of the goundlings." Even though full of defects, Cibber's version was successful and made a reputation for all the tragedians of the day from Garrick to Edwin Booth. Booth and Forrest, however, regarded Cibber's version as a travesty. In correspondence to a friend in 1877, Edwin Booth tells of his intention of playing the original version:

> Did I tell you that I intended to restore Shakespeare's *Richard III* in lieu of Cibber's patchwork drama? If not, I'll tell you now that I have acted it several times to the satisfaction of even adverse critics, who, while abusing me declare the restoration a success. I shall endeavor to give it a good cast in New York, in order to make it run, and thus educate the ignorant, who suppose Cibber's bosh to be Shakespeare's tragedy.[1]

Others, too, attempted to restore portions of Shakespeare to Cibber's acting version. On Saturday, December 4, 1858, at the Richmond Theatre, J.W. Wallack, as star, announced his *Richard III* as "Cibber's adaptation of *Life and Death of Richard III*, with further restorations from the text of Shakespeare."

Whatever version, *Richard III* continued to be played by practically every leading star as he joined the Richmond company. The 1859-1860 season found still another Richard in the field, this time Edwin Adams, with Wilkes as Buckingham. Wilkes' old role of Richmond went to J.W. Collier. One wonders why, if Wilkes had been as good as reporters say, he played the part only when Edwin insisted, and why he used his own name only at such times.

This may be some indication of Wilkes' growing resentment toward stage manager I.B. Phillips, or "Old Phil" as he was called, and may account for his actions as reported by John M. Barron, a fellow actor:

> One day we had rehearsed *Much Ado About Nothing*. John [Wilkes Booth] was Don Pedro and I was Don Claudio, parts of equal importance, though dissimilar in character. After the rehearsal we wended our way homeward and fixed up our dresses for the evening's play. About four o'clock John suddenly turned to me.
>
> "You play Don Pedro tonight," he said.
>
> I looked at him in amazement. "I do not," I replied. "I play Claudio as I rehearsed it. What do you mean?"
>
> "No matter what I mean," he exclaimed. "You go and tell Old Phil that you play Don Pedro and he plays Claudio."
>
> I was dumbfounded, but I knew my man. To argue with him would have been as effective as trying to widen the Royal Gorge of the Colorado by whistling in it.
>
> "I am going to Petersburg," he said, and left me.
>
> Phillips was about as much like Claudio then as I am now; but I played Don Pedro and Phillips read Don Claudio. Of course the performance was marred. We did not see John for two or three days, when he walked through the stage door as if he had not absented himself.[2]

The performance Barron referred to was presented on November 10, 1859, during Barry Sullivan's engagement. This incident goes further to prove that all the company had to be "up" in a great many parts and able to substitute when the need arose. The stage manager was responsible for a full cast each evening. If someone were missing for any reason it was his job to find a substitute, much to the annoyance of all the company. Several who knew Booth during his school years further substantiate he then had that inherent air of mystery in that he would never tell anyone where he was going and what he meant by his actions. He could be stubborn and silent and no one could gain his confidence if he chose not to give it.

The 1859-1860 Richmond season continued with the star engagement of Mr. and Mrs. Waller, a traveling pair popular at the time, who filled the stages with the heaviest of theatrics. Mrs. Waller, not content to play Desdemona to her husband's Othello, undertook the role of Iago, "unsexing" herself amid the publicity of daily advertisements. Wilkes accompanied them in minor roles during the engagement.

Then came Jane Coombs, whom the *Dispatch* called "the accomplished and beautiful young American actress, her first appearance in this city ... whose recent artistic delineations of the principal roles in the higher walks of the legitimate drama in New Orleans created the greatest sensation! nightly attracting crowded and delightful audiences composed of the elite of the Crescent City." Miss Coombs opened in *Love's Sacrifice,* continued as Lady Teazle in *School for Scandal,* and *Romeo and Juliet.* This time leading man Edwin Adams got his role as Romeo, for Miss Coombs had no desire for men's parts. Wilkes again played Paris and the evening concluded with the "screaming farce," *A Kiss in the Dark.* Miss Coombs, "whose chaste and artistic delineations nightly continued to demand from crowded and delightful audiences the most flattering applause," continued in her celebrated renditions of unrequited love. Wilkes played the romantic lead opposite her in all her plays, including *The Love Chase,* which the press called this couple "everything the theater-going public could desire." Miss Coombs has been described by the press as a "well known but wandering star." This young debutante had traveled the states and played all the leading theaters. Later critics in evaluating her talent describe her as a refined and delicate actress.

As was the custom with Richmond society, this beautiful and gifted actress became the belle of the social season. The company members were frequently in the limelight of parties, balls, parades. Richmond at this time was a city of 35,000, and most of the players were known or recognized by the townspeople. It is said that the South accepted actors far more readily into their society than the North. The friendly hospitality afforded the Richmond company would indicate that this was so.

As for the theater itself, emphasis was still on the individual rather than the group as a whole. Advertisements usually carried announcements of the star players only, occasionally giving the entire casts, or partial casts. More often, one of two players and the roles they were to play were printed line after line for an entire column of the newspaper. This was a time when lead players took the stage and the supporting players served as supporting background. When a person in a small part was noticed by the newspapers, it was evidence that he had managed to accomplish something to make his part a standout.

A report from one who remembered Wilkes in a small part at this time was John S. Wise, who tells of attending the Richmond Theatre during this engagement. Wise tells of seeing a performance with his elder brother, who had just returned from Berlin as attaché of the American Legation:

> One night we attended the play *East Lynne* at the old Richmond Theatre. The performance was poor enough, to be sure, to a man fresh from Paris, but I thought it was great. On our way home, he remarked that the only performer of merit in the cast was the young fellow John Wilkes Booth. In him, he said, there was the making of a good actor. The criticism made an impression on me, who remembered the man and the name. Little did I imagine then that in seven years my beloved companion would be one of the victims of our great national tragedy, or that, at its close, the callow stripling who played before us that night would shock the civilized world with the awful assassination of the president.[3]

This is an interesting bit from Wise's most readable account of his times, but there are two things wrong with it. First, Wilkes never played in *East Lynne,* or at least it was not on any of the bills or advertisements during his two seasons in Richmond. Next, at that time Wilkes was not billed as Booth, except on special occasions when playing with Edwin, or in taking a benefit. There is a possibility that Wise had mistaken the one-act farce operetta, *Jenny Lind*, in which Wilkes did appear several times, and that he learned later that Wilkes was Booth. It should be noted that Wise, in writing his book in 1899, is telling of a performance he saw about forty years earlier.

For her farewell benefit, Jane Coombs and company surely must have given their audience full measure for their admission. Astonishingly enough, all in one night, Miss Coombs, "accompanied by the full strength of the company," consecutively performed Juliet in *Romeo and Juliet*, Julia in *The Hunchback*, Lady Teazle in *School for Scandal*, and finished with a light comedy, *His Last Legs.* Indeed, the actors as well as the audience must have been on last legs by that time. However, it might be assumed that these were cut versions of the plays mentioned. Let it not be said that Victorian actors did not work for the love of their art, catering to a devoted audience.

The season continued with a return of the perenially popular Maggie Mitchell, affectionately known as the "Pet of the Petticoats"; then a festival list of performances in conjunction with the Richmond Fair, when "great novelties, fun and amusements" were presented along with the plays by the "all star company.... After the fair go to the theatre," cried the bills, "where you will be amused, gratified, instructed."

But, in the middle of Maggie Mitchell's engagement, the Richmond Star Company split and went for a week's run to Dudley Hall in Lynchburg, Virginia. Apparently, Miss Mitchell, who was playing her "one woman show," could get along without the remainder of the company. On Monday, October 17, 1859, the *Lynchburg Daily Virginian* heartily welcomed the company. After the two leading players, Wilkes is listed first in the company which opened with Bulwer's *Lady of the Lyons.* The press advised "those lovers of the legitimate drama, in our midst, who are so quick to perceive merit in an actor, and to appreciate it always, will, we are sure, not allow the new candidates or the old favorites to act to a laggardly array of empty benches...." For the Lynchburg Fair celebration, the company presented practically the same bill as for the fair in Richmond. After a week they were back at their regular theater in that city.

Suddenly, Wilkes was to pull another disappearing act. After the close of *Heir at Law*, Tuesday, October 25th, he hopped the train for Boston. There he joined his brother Edwin for the last three nights of a two-week run at the Howard Athenaeum. Billed as "Mr. Wilkes," even thought he was with Edwin, he played the small part of Blount to Edwin's Richard, and not the usual Richmond. He followed with other walk-ons in *Richelieu, The Stranger*, and *Don Caesar De Bazan* with his brother as star.

Back again in Richmond the following Monday night he appeared as Horatio to the Hamlet of the celebrated Irish actor, Barry Sullivan. This was Sullivan's first tour of America. He was generally called superior to the general run of Hamlets, but "not superlative." He did not exaggerate like Forrest, nor did he mouth like Macready, but was a mild, sweet Hamlet, not given to ranting and roaring. He "does not astonish," continued the *Dispatch*, "He is not capable of electrifying by a sudden burst of inspiration, but is a

HOWARD ATHENÆUM

SOLE LESSEE & MANAGER.................Mr. E. L. DAVENPORT
Ass't Manager.......J. P. Price | Treasurer..........C. F. Davenport

NOTICE!—CHANGE OF TIME,

Doors pen at 6 1-2...........Commences at 7.

Second Week of THE GREAT AMERICAN TRAGEDIAN

MR. EDWIN BOOTH

This, WEDNESDAY EVENING, OCT. 26, '59.

Will be presented Shakespeare's Tragedy of

RICHARD III

Or,—The Battle of Bosworth Field.

DUKE OF GLOSTER, afterwards Richard III....Mr EDWIN BOOTH	
King Henry..........Mr Hanchett	Tyrell......................Mr Otis
Richmond..........Mr. Hardenburg	Blount....................Mr Wilkes
Duke of Buckingham......Mr Rand	Oxford....................Mr Snowden
Lord Stanley........Mr W. H. Curtis	Officer......................Mr Hills
Tressel................Mr Reynolds	Prince of Wales........Miss F. Price
Catesby................Mr Selwyn	Duke of York.............Miss Jones
Ratcliffe................Mr Browne	Queen Elizabeth......Miss Mestayer
Duke of Norfolk..........Mr. Price	Lady Anne..............Miss Sylvia
Lieut of Tower..........Mr. Verney	Duchess of York......Mrs Hanchett
Lord Mayor.............Mr Lennox	

Previous to the Play,—POLISH OVERTURE..........ORCHESTRA
☞The Orchestra is composed of First Class Performers, among them the Celebrated Cornet and Bugle Player, MR. EDWARD KENDALL,
Musical Director.... ....Mr. Thomas Comer

To conclude with the irresistibly funny farce entitled

ICI ON PARLE FRANCAIS !

Mr Spriggins...Mr Setchell
Major Rigalus Rattan..Mr Curtis
Victor Dubois..Mr Reynolds
Mrs Spriggins...Mrs Hanchett
Julia, wife of Major Rattan...................................Mrs Rand
Angelina..Miss LeClare
Ann Maria..Miss F. Price

NUMEROUS APPLICATIONS having been made at the Box Office, to ascertain if Richelieu will be repeated. the Manager begs to announce that Mr EDWIN BOOTH will appear in that character once more on Thursday Evening, Oct. 27th.

FRIDAY EVENING, Oct. 28th.

☞ Benefit of Mr. EDWIN BOOTH ☜
The STRANGER & DON CÆSAR DE BAZAN.

☞ During the Engagement of MR. BOOTH, he will appear in several New Characters.

Boston Mammoth Steam Job Printing Establishment, 2 Spring Lane

Wilkes Booth in a small role in Richard III, *a play his brother Edwin was the star of, Howard Athenaeum, Boston, October 26, 1859. From* Shakespeare Rare Print Collection, *ed. Seymour Eaton (Philadelphia: R.G. Kennedy, 1900).*

finished and elegant actor." Much of his business was new and "some of his novelties were effective."

Wilkes Booth's playing of Horatio on this occasion would have been most interesting to see, for how could it compare with his playing the same part opposite brother Edwin at the same theater the previous year. Very little time was left for rehearsal with the star, but the group had to be ready for him. This made it necessary to work long hours to be "up" in lines for a different play every night. Such was the rigorous routine of stock players.

On Wednesday, November 2, 1859, Wilkes again tackled the part of Dawson in *The Gamester*. It will be remembered that it was this part which had proven to be a traumatic experience for him with an audience laughing at his expense, only one year previously at Philadelphia's Arch Street Theatre. However, this time the celebrated tragedy got a more serious treatment under the hand of Barry Sullivan, as it was one of his most outstanding plays. Again, the star was always right — if the others did not fit in, they were replaced.

Apparently Wilkes had mastered the psychological effects of his stage fright which plagued him in Philadelphia, for when James E. Murdock came for his star engagement in January, 1860, the play was again presented with the same cast except for Murdock in the lead. Wilkes would have had to be letter perfect to pass the eagle eye of Sullivan or Murdock. It is said that "every scene bears marks of careful study, and is elaborated to the minutest details, nothing is slurred over, nothing is overdone." But the *Dispatch* critic continues, "Murdock was without that happy inspiration that gives life to the creation and awakens the enthusiasm of the audience," apparently the secret of Barry Sullivan's success in the role.

On Friday, November 24, 1859, Wilkes was to play in *Smike*, a dramatization from Dickens' *Nicholas Nickleby*, a role he had performed many times before. That afternoon, during rehearsal, he stepped outside the theater to see the company of Richmond Grays gathering and preparing to board a special military train which would take them to Charleston, South Carolina, to guard the captured abolitionist, John Brown, and his followers. The Richmond, Fredericksburg & Potomac Railroad had its track down Broad Street, and one had but to step outside the theater to board the train.

Wilkes immediately had a great desire to go with the Grays, and begged that he be permitted to do so. He was told that the train was strictly for military use, but he made such a convincing appeal that he was issued a uniform and allowed to join the company. Asked how the theater was going to get along without him, he replied that he didn't know and didn't care.[4] As he was familiar with military drill from his cadet training, he easily fitted into the ranks and was appointed Assistant Commissary, or Quartermaster.

The military aspect of Charleston was very gay and the troups explored the town and suburbs. "The Richmond Grays and Company F," said an edtorial, "which seems to vie with each other in the handsome appearance they present, remind one of uncaged birds, so wild and gleesome they appear.... Amongst them I notice Mr. J. Wilkes Booth, a son of Junius Brutus Booth, who, though not a member, as soon as he heard the tap of the drum, threw down the sock and buskin, and shouldered his musket with the Grays to the scene of deadly conflict."[5]

Richmond Dispatch.

THURSDAY MORNING, ... , FEB. 2, 1860.

RICHMOND THEATRE.—
Fourth Night of the Eminent Artiste,
MR. JAMES E. MURDOCH,
Who will appear in his celebrated character of
BEVERLY.
In Moore's great tragedy of
THE GAMESTER!
Which will be presented to our patrons in an un-
exceptionable manner, and with the following
powerful cast:
MR. JAS. E. MURDOCH as MR. BEVERLY.
Mrs. J. B. Phillips as Mrs. Beverly.
Miss Ella M. Wren as Charlotte.
Mr. Edwin Adams as Stukely.
Mr. W. H. Bailey as Jarvis.
Mr. J. W. Collier as Lewson.
Mr. S. K. Chester as Bates.
Mr. J. B. Wilkes as Dawson.
In addition to the above splendid tragedy, a new
and laughable Farce entitled the
BUZZARDS.
John Small .... Mr. B. G. Rogers.
Mr. Benjamin Buzzard... Mr. W. H. Bailey.
Mr. Glimmer .... Mr. J. B. Wilkes.
Miss Lucretia Buzzard . Mrs. C. Debar
Sally.................... Mrs. Edwin Adams.
TRULY A SPLENDID BILL.

Announcement of James E. Murdock in The Gamester, *showing Booth in two roles.*
Richmond Dispatch, *February 2, 1860.*

Wilkes stayed on with the Grays, also known as the "Dude Regiment,"
until after the hanging of John Brown on December 2nd. It is said that upon
viewing the execution he became ill at the sight of it.

During free evenings from guard duty he entertained his companions
with dramatic monologues, of which he had a great store in his fantastic
memory. His theater at this time was any shelter or lean-to; his audience of
soldiers sat around on mounds of straw, bales of cotton, or other warehouse
commodities available.

"Some little time after John Brown's raid at Harpers Ferry," writes
theater manager Leonard Grover, "I was in Richmond, where for the second
time I saw John Wilkes Booth. He had left his position at the theater and had

joined the Richmond Grays. Clad in Uniform of the battalion, and without any of his military companions, at least in uniform, he was visiting the bars of the hotels and earnestly asserting what manner of punishment should be meted out to John Brown.[6]

Wilkes later stated that he was proud of "my little share in the transaction," but in relating his impression of Brown to his sister Asia, said that "he was a brave old man; his heart must have been broken when he felt himself deserted."[7] A unique comparison has been expressed by G.S.P. Holland, Virginia historian, who said:

> John Brown was a worse assassin than John Wilkes Booth, for while the latter murdered one man, the former murdered more than a dozen and attempted to involve thousands in massacre. If the purpose of Brown was unselfish, the same could be said of the purpose of Booth. Brown wanted to rid the country of the tyranny of slavery and Booth of the tyranny of Abraham Lincoln, who had caused the slaughter of thousands.[8]

When Wilkes returned to the Richmond Theatre, he found that Kunkel had discharged him for his abrupt departure. But as soon as his military companions learned of this, a large number of the regiment marched to the theater and demanded that the manager take Wilkes Booth back with the company. Kunkel, aware of Booth's popularity and the added publicity generated, agreed. So, John Wilkes Booth again took up his "sock and buskin" and continued the season. A steady stream of plays continued with many visiting stars joining the company: James E. Murdock, Julia Dean Hayne, the Western Sisters, John Sleeper Clarke, and F.S. Chanfau, to name a few.

The theatre was closed the week of May 7-12 in preparation for the much publicized *Three Guardsmen; or, The Siege of Rochelle*, more popularly known as Dumas' *The Three Musketeers*. Wilkes played Aramis.

At the close of the season, in a benefit testimonial to George Kunkel, a drawing was held and three oil paintings were given away to those holding lucky numbers. Two of the paintings, by Rembrant Peale, were of Chief Justice Marshall and John Randolph, of Roanoke. There was another of a scene from *Rob Roy*, and a "painting taken from life" of Edwin Booth as Richard III. The paper on the following day made no mention of the winners. It would be interesting to speculate as to whether the paintings might still be in existence today, and how the present owners might have come by them. They had originally been won for a dollar theater ticket.

Three days after the close of the theater we learn of a special performance. Wilkes and his friend J.W. Collier decided to try for a joint benefit. The regular season having closed, these two players tried a performance at their own risk with only the offer of a few company players to support them. Said the press, "[B]oth of them have played well their parts and deserve a substantial token at parting.... [T]he first piece is the last act of *Richard III*, in which Mr. Booth appears as Richard and Mr. Collier appears as Richmond. There are recollections which crowd the name of Booth, when connected with *Richard III*, which will attract all to see in the character a promising son of the great master of the stage, struggling up by study and perseverance, into the path trodden by the father.... Let these young actors be encouraged tonight in a profession in which they have already made such rapid steps."[9]

Now, for the first time on his own Wilkes was announced as Booth, and for the first time as Richard. The advertisements carried the parts the two young players would perform:

RICHMOND THEATRE

EXTRA NIGHT!!
EXTRA NIGHT!!
EXTRA NIGHT!!

Benefit of Messrs
J.W. COLLIER and J. WILKES BOOTH

GREAT ATTRACTION!!!
GREAT ATTRACTION!!!
GREAT ATTRACTION!!!

J.W. COLLIER as The Son of Malta
J.W. COLLIER as The Fast Young Man
J.W. COLLIER as Heenan
J.W. COLLIER in a Sailor's Hornpipe
J.W. COLLIER as Richmond

J. WILKES BOOTH as Victim
J. WILKES BOOTH as Sayers
J. WILKES BOOTH as The Crook'd Back Tyrant
J. WILKES BOOTH as Richard[10] — first time

Fifth Act of *Richard III*
The Son of Malta
My Fellow Clerk
Also Songs . . . . Dances . . . . Recitations
POSITIVELY THE LAST NIGHT OF THE SEASON

Thursday, May 31, 1860

John Wilkes Booth had been a very popular favorite in Richmond. It is easy to understand this enthusiasm from an audience chiefly consisting of slaveholders, for Booth demonstrated his love for the Southern people and their cause. One can imagine the thunderous applause he is said to have received upon his return to the theater after his participation in the John Brown hanging. As Francis Wilson said, "He was in absolute sympathy and harmony with his surroundings. Indeed, it would have been strange had it been otherwise."

He had played two successful seasons in Richmond, made friends, and gained stage confidence. The following extracts of acquaintances' memoirs will give examples. From George Crutchfield, iron oxide merchant of Richmond:

> I knew Jno. Wilkes Booth quite well in 1858-1860 & frequently met him socially.... He was a man of high character & sociable disposition, & liked by every one with whom he associated. Was considered very handsome, having coal black hair & eyes, & frequently wore, when on the streets a fur trimmed overcoat, as shown in the photo I gave you of him.[11]

A member of the Richmond company, John M. Barron, tells that their life with the theater group was jovial and happy. They had adjoining rooms at the boarding house, and as brother actors, borrowed each other's wardrobe. Barron saw Booth every day and night and got to know just what manner of man he was. Booth was the absolute in determination as to his actions, but he was always so cool and calm that one did not detect that his determination was so unbending. He was quiet and unruffled, yet conveyed a certain power over others that allowed him to have his own way. Said Barron,

> He, like his brothers, was as generous as the balmy air on a glorious summer eve. Modest as a maiden, gentle, kind and considerate. While he was not much as a conversationalist, he was exceedingly companionable. John was quick in action and had eyes that were piercing and most expressive, with a perfect physical beauty and stately bearing.... The man was like Edwin — born with the divine spark. He was the mold of form, delicately organized physically, with beautiful hands and small feet, graceful by nature, and in all a most effective actor. His eyes, like all the Booths, were exceedingly brilliant and expressive of all the phases of his characters. Little did I dream while I was his companion that the time would come when those fingers, tapering like those of a 16-year-old maiden and with a touch as dainty, would pull the trigger which would put out the light of the greatest of mortals....[12]

There is no doubt that Booth made a deep impression upon everyone with whom he came in contact. He had that indefinable quality that actors today crave and press agents keep searching for; without this essence, good looks and talent are nothing.

People sought him out, eager to see him and to listen to anything he had to say. Eleanor Ruggles tells us that for every girl running after Edwin, there were two running after Wilkes. Ladies jammed the stage doors waiting for his exit, swarmed around him asking for his autographed "cartes de visite."

His carefully selected attire made of the finest material gained him the reputation of being the fashion plate of the times. He was invited to all the most elegant balls. No one passed him on the street without taking a second look, man or woman. Strangers lavished upon him ardent admiration and gifts. A dying Virginia belle willed him her beautiful light brown hair which had been cut during an illness of typhoid fever. Wilkes had it made into a wig and used it for many of his characterizations for the remainder of his career.

In Richmond he had been given the opportunity to play superior roles and had acquired a reputation for romantic gallantry and daredevil courage. Some, in comparison of the Booths, remarked that he had inherited his famous father's eccentricities of genius. In comparison, it would seem, Wilkes possessed far more charm, magnetism, and guts than any of his brothers, though like them, he had the peculiar reticence and aloofness of the Booths.

If he ranted and roared his lines, as some have stated, it was the custom of the day for all to rant and roar on stage. Edwin Forrest, for example, the most famous actor since Garrick, was known for his bombastic, robust style of acting, and called by some the worst ranter on the American stage. But it was the predominant style of the day to read "as if by flashes of lightning." It was to be many years later when Edwin Booth was to profoundly influence the acting profession by changing from the noisy, harsh style to the toned-down, more restrained, reflective, intellectual delivery.

Whatever Wilkes Booth's style, his delivery during his Richmond period seemed to please his audiences. His magnetic personality had made him a great social favorite, and "his physical perfections had reaped a harvest of hearts. His slender form, youthful but manly face, and the grace of his movements occasioned the remark that no photograph ever did him justice."[13]

This part of his career was over, but said Edward M. Alfriend, dramatist with the Richmond Theatre at that time, "his ability was unquestionable and his future assured."[14]

The days of the old Richmond Theatre were numbered. Only a season and a half later, on January 2, 1862, the theater where the elder Booth first applied for work after arriving in America, was burned, the company disbanded. The theater was rebuilt, however, on the very same spot the same year. The people of Richmond could not live without their theater and their pampered actors.

CHAPTER 7: Columbus–Montgomery
A Rising Star

In the fall of 1860, Matthew Canning, a Philadelphia lawyer turned theater manager, invited Wilkes Booth to star with his Southern theater company. Canning's group had previously appeared with success in Columbus, Georgia, and other Southern cities, but this season his plans were to expand the tour with a chain of engagements throughout the South.

So it was that the fall theatrical season opened in Columbus, Georgia, with the Canning Dramatic Company. The opening bill on that Monday night, October 1, 1860, was *Romeo and Juliet*. On his first star engagement, Booth was still billed as "Mr. Wilkes." Opening night he played the leading role to the Juliet of Mary Mitchell. Wilkes' repertoire for this engagement included roles that were to become his most successful for the remainder of his career: *The Stranger, The Wife, The Apostate, Marble Heart, Lady of Lyons* and *Richard III*.

The October 3 Columbus *Times* paid a very complimentary tribute to the new company, calling it "much superior to his corps of last year, and quite the equal of any which has appeared to the taste of a Columbus audience."

While the company was appearing in Columbus, announcements were being posted daily in the Montgomery, Alabama, newspapers that Canning's Company was to appear there following the Columbus run. The Montgomery *Daily Post* of October 5, 1860, said:

> Mr. Canning proposes to favor our city in a short time.... We may anticipate a treat for the lovers of the drama never before realized in Montgomery.

And on October 12th, the same paper stated:

> Columbus papers continue to speak in the most glowing terms of the theatrical performances of Mr. Canning's popular company in that city. Mr. Wilkes and Miss Mitchell are highly complimented.... The entire company are represented as giving universal satisfaction. Our city will be favored with the appearance of this splendid corps of performers in a few days.

This first starring engagement of "Mr. Wilkes" continued with great success in Columbus. A representative repertoire was planned which included tragedy, comedy, farce, and the usual songs and dances. Booth presented a "new comedy just received from England," Stitling Coyne's *Everybody's Friend* (which was not really very new, as Wilkes had appeared in it at the Richmond Theatre during the previous season). And now at last, he was able to play the leading roles in all the old favorites in which he had only been given bit parts before.

But sensational incidents were about to begin for J. Wilkes Booth. On Friday, October 12th, when he was to take a benefit for his first appearance as *Hamlet*, a shooting accident occurred at his hotel. The *Columbus Enquirer*, October 15, 1860, reported:

> Mr. John Wilkes Booth was accidentally shot in the thigh at Cook's Hotel. Mr. Booth and Mr. Canning were practicing with a pistol, when it went off in Mr. Canning's hand as he was letting down the hammer, inflicting a flesh wound in Mr. Booth's thigh.

Another report had the accident occurring in Booth's dressing room at the theater. Booth was with another actor when Canning came in on them and jokingly threatened to shoot both of them. The gun unexpectedly exploded and Wilkes "was shot in the rear."[1] By April 17, 1865, the New York *World* was saying:

> Wilkes became involved in a quarrel and was shot in the neck. The ball remained in the flesh for a period of perhaps two years, and came out unexpectedly during his first engagement at Grover's Washington Theatre, in the Spring of 1863.

It is at that time we hear about an operation on his neck to remove a tumor. The doctor is asked to call it a bullet.

From Matthew Canning's own biographical sketch of Booth we get what should have been the truth, since Canning himself fired the pistol, unless of course there was a desire to distort the story.

> In the season of 1859 he made his first appearance as a star in Columbus, Ga., the Theatre there being under the management of a gentleman from this city, who during the first week of his engagement, accidentally shot Booth in the side. After his recovery he made his appearance under the same management in Montgomery, Ala., where he played a highly successful engagement.[2]

Wherever the location of the scar, it postponed Booth's stage appearance for only eight days. J.W. Albaugh, stage and acting manager, and also a friend of Wilkes who had appeared with him in his first stage appearance, substituted for him in *Hamlet*, and then on successive nights for the remainder of the Columbus engagement.

On October 19th, the Columbus *Daily Sun* announced the "Benefit of Mr. John Wilkes, who has not yet recovered from the wound he accidentally received on Friday last." But because of "the inclement state of the weather on the 19th," stated the *Daily Sun* of October 20th, "the benefit of Mr. John Wilkes will take place this evening, when he will most positively appear as Mark Antony in the celebrated Forum Scene from Shakespeare's great tragedy *Julius Caesar*, assisted by the company."

The cast had tried to continue without him although business was growing slack. Everybody wanted to see the star personality as promised them. Already the wave of Booth's popularity was building up toward the gigantic proportions it was to become. The papers in Columbus and Montgomery told of his daily progress toward recovery, each day reaffirming that he would appear soon. In order to stall for time, Mr. Canning announced that "the success which has attended M.W. Canning's Dramatic Company has induced him to remain six nights longer."

It was a long build-up that preceded Booth's return to the company. The *Daily Sun's* news item of October 20th expressed pleasure that Booth was so recovered from his accident that he would be able to appear on stage that evening,

> although he is still too feeble to take an active part in the performance. At the earnest solicitation of numerous friends, he will attend the play and recite Antony's address over the dead body of Caesar. This piece is well adapted to the finely controlled voice of Mr. Booth, who has been especially praised in his readings and recitations....

The news item continued to stress the fact that the theater had been poorly attended since the accident, and that this night would be the last chance to see Booth in Columbus.

The company went to Montgomery, Alabama, and opened there on Monday, October 22, 1860 in *School for Scandal*. However, Booth did not appear. Advertisements that he would appear the following evening, called it the "first appearance of the young American tragedian, Mr. John Wilkes." But still Wilkes did not appear. Daily announcements told of his appearance for the following evenings; still no appearance. Obviously, the accident produced more than just a "flesh wound" as has generally been understood. Some five years later, Canning's wife said that her husband had informed her that the wound left a large scar on Booth's person and was "not to be mistaken once described."[3] Perhaps the report of the accident in *Spirit of the Times,* New York, October 28, 1860, was nearer the truth when the newspaper said the wound was quite serious and would "undoubtedly disable him for some time." The *Columbus Enquirer* of October 16th had said it was only a flesh wound and "not severe."

The following news item appeared in the Montgomery *Daily Mail,* October 26, 1860, giving some clue to his recovery and return to the stage:

> *J.W. Booth.* — We had the pleasure of an introduction to this young tragedian last night at the theatre. He is rapidly recovering from his unfortunate accident in Columbus, some time since, and informed us that he would make his first appearance on our boards Monday night.

It will be noted that although Booth was known as Booth, and referred to as Booth in articles in the paper, he was still billed as John Wilkes, or as J.B. Wilkes. Finally, on October 29, 1860, Wilkes returned to the stage, playing the leading role in one of his father's most successful plays, *The Apostate.* This was not his first starring role as some have stated, nor did he use the name of Booth. The advertisements and playbills announced him as John Wilkes, just as they had during his first star engagement in Columbus, Georgia.

One biographer has stated that while recovering from his accident, Booth read in the Montgomery *Daily Post* that his brother Edwin had just received $5,000 as his share of the profits for a month's engagement in Boston. This item was supposed to have resolved Wilkes to change from a stock player to a star performer. The fact is that Wilkes was hired as a star performer at the beginning of the season with Matthew Canning, and due to receive one-half the gross proceeds of every performance. He was scheduled to tour many Southern cities in Canning's chain of theaters. Stock players would be awaiting him in each city. Reading the article could have had little effect on one with already such a burning lust for fame. His plans had been in progress for many years. He was now far away from the $8 per week he received when he started as a stock player. Nor is it fair to say, as many have, that he traded on the family name. Determined to make his reputation before he took back his family name, he was reluctant to be billed as Booth, even though the newspapers and the audience all knew and referred to him as Booth. His billing was Wilkes during three years of stage appearances. Probably, however, the article in the *Daily Post* did convince him that the time had come for him to emerge completely as Booth. This he did with his next engagement.

In reviewing Wilkes' opening in Montgomery, Alabama, in *The Apostate*, the Montgomery *Daily Mail*, October 30, 1860, carried the following under city news:

> *Theatre:* — A fair audience greeted Mr. John Wilkes last night in his first appearance in the character of Pescara in *The Apostate* [he had previously played this role in Columbus]. While we do not think this character a good one to show to great advantage Mr. Wilkes' talents, and considering his late accident from which he was not entirely recovered, still the performance last night stamps him as a chip off the old block [indicating Junius Brutus Booth] which was received by the large audience with outbursts of applause.

Each following performance was covered by the Montgomery *Daily Mail*, both in advertisements and in city news sections. For *The Wife*, we learn that

> there was a rousing crowd at the theatre last night — decidedly the largest of the season. This great play ... was thoroughly presented and rendered quite effectively, to the entire satisfaction of all, judging from the demonstrations of approval with which they received. Mr. John Wilkes, Miss Mitchell, Mr. Albaugh and Mr. Chester won new laurels in the fine rendition of their respective parts....

For *Hamlet* we learn that the performance was a "refresher to Manager Canning's pockets, for his large theatre was full from pit to dome." The reviewer thought the performance seemed to give general satisfaction, but lack of space in his column forbade comment. As for *Richard III*, the reviewer said "there was another jam at the theater last night," and because of it he saw but little of the performance and could not speak knowingly about it. Incidentally, the *Daily Mail* carried notices of the Montgomery horse races, and among the horse entries was one named "Richard III" in honor of Wilkes Booth. "Sweepstakes opening day, $200 subscription, $50 forfeit. A horse, a horse! My kingdom for a...." Wilkes continued his engagement with *Romeo and Juliet*, which the reviewer said was

> very effectively and satisfactorily rendered. Mr. John Wilkes as Romeo, was all that could be desired, and his rendition was received with applause and approbation by the large number present. The same may be said of the beautiful Miss Mary Mitchell.... Tonight [will be] the last appearance on our boards of Mr. Wilkes, and we hope that his numerous friends will turn out and give him a "bumper at parting." He appears this evening in *The Robbers*.

Twelve days later Wilkes returned unexpectedly to appear in Kate Bateman's benefit night; Miss Bateman had almost completed a two-week run

MONTGOMERY THEATRE.

M. W. CANNING, Lessee and Manager. | J. W. ALBAUGH, Stage Manager.

THIRD APPEARANCE

OF THE POPULAR AND CHARMING COMEDIENNE,

MISS MAGGIE MITCHELL.

Grand Complimentary Benefit,

BY THE CITIZENS OF MONTGOMERY, TO

MR. J. WILKES BOOTH.

Miss Maggie Mitchell as Katy O'Sheal.

Mr. J. Wilkes Booth as Count Rafaelle, and in the Last Act of Richard III.

SATURDAY EVENING, DECEMBER 1,

The performance will commence with the elegant two act Drama entitled

R A F A E L L E.

COUNT RAFAELLE, MR. J. WILKES BOOTH.

To be followed by the Comic Drama in two acts, entitled

KATY O'SHEAL.

KATY O'SHEAL..MISS MAGGIE MITCHELL

To conclude with the fifth act of

R I C H A R D   I I I .

Box office open daily from 10 a. m. until 1, and from 3 until 5 p. m., when seats may be secured

---

MONTGOMERY THEATRE!

SOLE LESSEE & MANAGER..........M. W. CANNING.
STAGE MANAGER..................J. W. ALBAUGH.

SIXTH NIGHT OF THE SEASON.

Monday Evening, October 29, 1860.

It is with great pleasure the management announce an engagement of SIX NIGHTS ONLY with the talented young Tragedian,

MR. JOHN WILKES.

Monday Evening, will be presented

THE APOSTATE!

PESCARA...................Mr. JOHN WILKES.

SONG....................MISS EMMA MITCHELL.

To conclude with

COUSIN JOE'S VISIT TO THE FAIR.

☞ Box Office open daily from 10 until 1, and from 3 until 5 P. M., where seats may be secured without extra charge.

in Montgomery. The *Daily Mail* reminded the public that "Mr. Wilkes has in the kindest manner volunteered his valuable services, and will appear as Romeo. Friday evening, November 16." And on the same day, the city news column carried this suggestion, illustrating how the audience of the time played a more integral part of the production than is customary today:

> *Fashionable Night.* — ...We apprehend, that *the* fashionable night of the season will prove to be tomorrow, ... the complimentary benefit tendered to Miss Bateman by a large number of our families and leading young men. ...On that occasion, as full dress as possible will be desirable on the part of the audience, as we wish to make our Dress Circle as picturesque and brilliant as possible. Miss Bateman plays Geraldine this evening, and Juliet (Mr. Wilkes as Romeo) tomorrow evening.

In reviewing the play the following day, the Montgomery *Daily Mail* said that it "was given smoothly and effectively.... Mr. Wilkes showed that he can learn to play Romeo with great power, though as yet his conception is crude...." Evidently, there was some variance of opinion, for his previous performance of the role there had prompted the reviewer to state that Wilkes was "all that could be desired."

Two weeks later, during the engagement of Maggie Mitchell, the "little captivator," for whom, the press said, "praises are in everybody's mouth.... She has fused new life into our theatre-goers," Booth's name again suddenly appeared, only this time we are told that "a grand complimentary benefit by the citizens of Montgomery to Mr. J. Wilkes Booth" would be held on December 1st. Finally, Wilkes was billed as Booth, and all the advertisements cried, "Booth, Booth, Booth!!" The program presented Booth as Count Rafaelle in *Rafaelle*, followed by Miss Mitchell in the celebrated *Kathy O'Sheal*, and concluded with Booth in the fifth act of *Richard III*. City news column carried the following: "*Mr. J. Wilkes Booth.* — The many admirers of the young tragedian will be pleased to learn that a complimentary benefit, tendered by the citizens of Montgomery, will take place at the theatre this evening...." Concerning the performance the critic remarked the following day:

> A fine audience attended the complimentary benefit of Mr. J. Wilkes Booth on Saturday night. *Rafaelle* was well personated by Mr. Booth, and was well received by the audience, and at the close of the first piece, he was called before the curtain amidst loud cheering, then he returned his thanks in a very neat but short speech....

And so it was at the end of his Montgomery engagement, Wilkes was finally launched as Booth, both on and off the stage. He would now continue under his own name for the remainder of his career. Now full of confidence in himself, his eloquent speech and extravagant boasting were very much in evidence. Lloyd Lewis describes him thus: "Dressed to kill, and killing hearts right and left, he became a social lion among gay blades in barrrooms and ladies parlors. He had the voice, the eye, the vocabulary to gasconade with the fieriest of the fire-eaters...."[4]

Opposite page, left: *advertisement of John Wilkes Booth's first appearance in Montgomery, Alabama, from* The Daily Post, *ca. October 29, 1860;* right: *advertisement of the first time billed as "Booth," at the Montgomery Theatre, December 1, 1860, from* The Montgomery Daily Mail.

CHAPTER 8: Booth Emerges
An Actor at Mid-Century

The life of the actor in the 1850's and '60's was indeed a drudge. Travel, he must, for there were few long runs. And travel, even in peace time was hectic. One had to look to the road, particularly the rising young stars. The long, train rides, uncomfortable hotels, cold, makeshift dressing rooms in barn-like theaters required one to be in top physical condition and necessitated tremendous drive and love for the profession. Booth could no longer remain comfortably as a stock player for an entire season if he wanted to become a star, but had to endure the constant travel and endless waits between trains for the horse-cars or carriages from station to tavern, tavern to theater.

Added incentive was the money a star player was able to command, if he was able to acquire an active agent who would trumpet for him. Now Booth's popularity was beginning to be reflected in his salary as well as in his publicity. He was given regular benefits plus half the gross proceeds.

After becoming a star, a regular benefit performance was arranged, usually once per week, or the night before the final performance of the engagement. The custom of giving a starring player the receipts or "benefits" of one evening during his run, or during a season, originated in the English theater of the 17th century. If bad weather or other unpredictable obstacles kept away the crowds, another benefit was sometimes called. The authors got the proceeds of the third night of the run. Today a benefit performance for one player is rare, but sometimes benefits are given for organizations such as the Actor's Fund in New York. In the days of personal benefits, the actor relied on his benefit night for ready money, as his week's share in salary was hardly adequate to pay for current expenses. Usually the actor benefited could choose the play for that night, or even introduce one of his own. But in Booth's case, his popularity was such that he was one of the highest paid actors of the period. A benefit was the test of popularity.

Every theater of any importance had its permanent dramatic company which continued from season to season. Star performers traveled from city to city to join these companies. At this time there were established stock companies in residence, not traveling groups of performers as we have today. The stock players were generally good actors, and could be counted on to provide efficient support for the touring stars.

Actors worked hard to put over an evening's entertainment, which usually consisted of a five-act tragedy, a short comedy, and specialty acts with a full orchestra. All of this cost the patron from 15¢ to 75¢. The curtain usually rose at seven and fell well after midnight. During a season of rigid theater work, there would be a change of bill every night, plus occasional matinee performances on Wednesdays, Fridays and Saturdays. In addition there were rehearsals during the day for two or three new pieces. All this strenuous preparation would give any young actor with some talent and stamina a good theater background. Leading players were required to learn as many as 12 to 14 parts in two weeks. There was no type casting as we know it today, and the value of an actor resided in his ability to handle successfully the various parts for which he was cast. Necessarily, long hours of laborous study was needed, so that the actor had little time for leisure if he were to attain any statue at all. They all said it was a wretched life, yet powerless in its fascination.

One had to be a "quick study." There were no long runs; an entire week for one play was unusual. Except for the star and "second man" each player had no choice but to take whatever part was given him and to play it the best he could. If he already had the part memorized, he was so much ahead of the game. Actors had to be highly flexible — willing and able to try everything. Parts were distributed in "lengths" of 42 lines, a term which meant about the same as "sides" to a later-day actor. A typical schedule for the player might be as follows:

> Saturday: After the performance, Monday's part was given out.
> Sunday: All day devoted to study and rehearsal; his costumes for the next play (called dresses by all performers).
> Monday: Rehearsal; Tuesday's part given out; perhaps some time to study Tuesday's part Monday afternoon, and after Monday night performance.
> Tuesday: Rehearsal; Wednesday's part given out; after Tuesday's performance, begin work on Wednesday's play.
> Wednesday through Saturday, the same routine.

The coming night's play was studied piecemeal wherever a few minutes permitted. The actor had to have his "lengths" with him at all times, and study at every chance. Between acts or waits during a performance, actors sat in the wings studying for the following night's play: an eye on his new lines, an ear listening for his cue to go on stage. Thus, the term "winging the part" meant that the actor had learned one part in the wings while waiting to go on in another. While he took his cue on stage, his script was tucked in a crevice of the flats. These were units of stage scenery, stretched painted canvas on wooden frames, to make up three-dimensional sets. It was imperative for him to retrieve the script as soon as he left stage, for if the scene was changed and flats moved, pandemonium reigned in a tumult of searching.

The acting and stage manager did the casting, and parts for the following night's performance were posted on the call board in the greenroom, a place where the players gathered at free periods to study, chat, or wait for the callboy's summons. A player, upon checking the board, might find himself scheduled for parts in two comedies, three walk-ons in a tragedy, and a specialty act between plays, or only an appearance in the afterpiece.

John Ellsler, master theater manager of the period, tells us just how the situation was:

> Rehearsals were always called at nine, or half past nine, a.m. and rarely finished before five p.m. The performances ran until midnight, frequently

half an hour later, according to the bill. To witness these rehearsals would bewilder our present-day artists; indeed, I doubt very much whether they could endure the strain.... In the first place, the actor rarely knew what the succeeding plays were to be for the six nights, until possibly the three-sheet poster in front of the theatre furnished the information at the close of each performance. Out of the two or three pieces billed, it was quite possible that one or more were new to him. At the rehearsal the following day, notice would be given as to the part the actor would impersonate, and it was not unusual to wait until the part was copied, or be asked to perform the duty and pass the book to some other hapless wight.[1]

The elder Booth knew what a nerve-racking treadmill acting was and never encouraged his children to become actors. In fact he broke up their childhood stages at home so much that they had to build secret stages. But the theater was strong in their blood. Edwin Booth himself confessed the horrors of learning to become a star performer:

Before I was eighteen I was a drunkard, at twenty a libertine. I knew no better. I was born *good*, I do believe, for there are sparks of goodness constantly flashing out from among the cinders.... I was neglected in my childhood and thrown (really, it now seems almost purposely) into all sorts of temptations and evil society.... I was allowed to roam at large, and at an early age in a wild and almost barbarous country where boys become old men in vice.[2]

In spite of all the sordidness associated with the theater of the time, the Booth family lifted the acting profession to a new height. Since then the very name of Booth has taken on a scholarly connotation in the history of the theatre.

Wilkes Booth was greatly interested in all classes of people. He had the ability to learn insights from them into the various characterizations he was to portray on the stage. He listened raptly to them and learned what he could from their conversations. Stage hands, mechanics, and the riffraff of the saloons interested him as well as people of culture. They all gained his attention and respect. He had no pretensions whatever to literary ability. Said one reporter:

His father was a man of universal information. Wilkes had an idea that he was clever on this point, but his orthography was bad, and his syntax worse. He was exceedingly fond of poetry and his pocket book was filled with scraps cut from the papers.... His language was never ungrammatical nor vulgar, and he had great tact in avoiding matters of which he was ignorant. When impressed with a subject he was eloquent and always attracted a little crowd.[3]

Wilkes had the advantage of having worked with all the top actors and actresses of the day. He played many parts in all the current favorite plays, and was given the opportunity to try new pieces. He had a photographic memory and it was not difficult for him to jump into the leading roles. He also had the advantage of having played the same plays with different leading players, and could thus compare acting styles and formulate his own original interpretations.

His originality might have been what prompted remarks that he would not exert himself or apply himself to a word-for-word rendering of the part, but rather skim over the role, improvising, thus causing confusion on stage because the other actors would miss their cues. This new interpretation of roles brought him praise by some and censure by others. Such a problem occurred with an actor named Roberts, who refused to go on stage with him in Philadelphia. A fistfight ensued at the Girard House and Booth was fined in the police court.[4]

According to his sister Asia, Wilkes was most influenced by Edwin Forrest, another bombastic actor. However, Forrest did not hold so high an opinion of him. Once when John McCullough became too hoarse to play Iago to Forrest's Othello in Baltimore, manager John T. Ford suggested that Forrest engage Wilkes Booth, that Booth was in Washington, and he would telegraph him to come and play the part. Noted to be a tyrant of the stage and very profane, Forrest ripped out an oath and said scornfully that he would not "tread the boards with that goddamned spad!"[5] It has been suggested that Forrest, who was suffering with gout and feeling his rheumatic age, had become disillusioned with the loss of his youth, and perhaps resented Wilkes Booth. Forrest had seen Booth play in Philadelphia; his opinion of him as a "spad," is roughly equivalent to a later generation's "masher" or "dude."

Wilkes Booth also admired James E. Murdock for his grace and perfect elocution, and E.L. Davenport for his polish and correctness. He had a sincere affection for John McCullough, and unbounded admiration for him as an actor. He thought McCullough the only one fit to follow Forrest. He openly worshiped his brother Edwin as an artist. Wilkes was humble and had no illusions about his own acting. Reluctant to be billed under his own name, "he feared that people loved him for his father's sake," said Asia. "He yearned for criticism, no matter how severe, if just."

Before launching his famous characterization of the Crook'd Back Tyrant in *Richard III*, Booth had worked with the Richards of Edwin Booth, J.W. Wallack, Barry Sullivan, Edwin Adams, J.B. Roberts. And for *Hamlet*, he had had a chance to study and work with the performances of Edwin Booth, James E. Murdock, Barry Sullivan, J.A.J. Neafie. All of these were the very top ranking stars of the day. Each of them had his own unique approach to their impersonations, and each one probably contributed considerably toward Wilkes Booth's development as an actor. It is said, however, that he was like no other actor, with the exception of his father, whom he never saw on the stage. It is curious to note that while Edwin was trained by their father, and toured with him during the formative years, Edwin's acting turned out less like the father than Wilkes'.

Upon becoming a star, John Wilkes Booth did not appear in the after-pieces, except rarely when a part especially appealed to him, as in *Too Much for Good Nature*, a comedy he used frequently in contrast to his tragic roles. According to theater custom of the day, programs included one or two short pieces after the main play. These short plays were generally comedies or farces, supplementary entertainment for a public who liked some light diversion after sitting through a five-act tragedy. Often full-length plays were cut to required length for the afterpiece, but many short plays were written just for the purpose. The custom originated during the early part of the 18th century, and continued to be popular through the 19th century, when gradually, the afterpieces were reversed to "curtain-raisers," when one-act plays were given first on the program. These farces were written by theater managers, actors, or whoever happened to have a good idea for a skit. The author's name was seldom given, and most of the plays have passed into oblivion. Only titles remain among the newspaper announcements of the day. It could be said that these plays, however slight, were the first efforts of the American playwright. This American theater of American plays, was called "Yankee drama." Other than this, the American theater was practically nonexistent at this time, for most companies presented English plays, and only the tried and true classics. David Rankin Barbee said that John Wilkes Booth "was probably the sole actor of his day to try out new plays."⁵ Booth was also an innovator in the field of experimentation with classics.

The plays of Booth's day were farce, extravaganza, melodrama and comic opera, and of course Shakespeare was the great favorite. Most successful of all were plays of domestic situations, featuring broad comic characterizations. Broad comedy was a genre in which slapstick or farcical comedy was played with crude lines and all points labored. Comic bits were introduced for the sake of cheap laughs. This was a deliberate playing down to a less sophisticated audience on whom a subtler technique would be wasted. This does not mean that the entire evening's bill was played down, only relief from the heavy tragedies to give a more diversified program. These were the days when playwrights were not much concerned with distinct plot nor theme. In contrast, Booth's most successful plays were those that did try to offer more. Tom Taylor's and Dion Boucicault's plays were the most original and influential of the period. They represented conditions of real life, offering solutions for moral and social problems, though still retaining the broad humor, the romantic flavor, the spectacle and the patriotism that the public favored.

In such a time of conservative theater, when fresh ideas and style were lacking, Booth had the courage to try new tricks, endeavoring to break away from the staid traditions of the period. For these innovations he was criticized, called a gymnastic actor, accused of taking liberties with the classics. He introduced songs, tangential stage business and theatrical tricks where they had not previously occurred. However, most of the classics were butchered to start with (witness Colley Cibber's versions of Shakespeare). It was not until Edwin Booth began to restore the original text that the real Shakespeare was again played. This American restoration antedated the restoration even in England.

CHAPTER 9: Rochester–Albany–Portland–Buffalo Yankee Territory

John Wilkes Booth must have had misgivings about leaving the Southern theaters for a Northern tour, since he had become such a matinee idol in the South. His fiery, reckless, and debonair personality had captured the Southern theatergoers, but this was not the only reason for his Southern success. It is true that the South accepted actors more readily than the North, and the explanation is this. The Cavaliers, who had settled the South, had liked actors and perpetuated their legacy from old days in England, since the time when the Stuart kings made the London theater a thing of social prominence. In contrast, the Puritans, who settled the northern United States, had despised actors from the time that Cromwell shut up theaters as devil's dens and whipped players for performing. To Charles II's court, actors were lions to be wined and dined, while to their grim opponents, actors were godless vagabonds, painted tools of Satan. So it was natural that the first playhouses in America were in the South. Theaters spread rapidly northward, but the actor still received a hardier welcome in the South.

Nevertheless, Booth now tried his luck in Yankee territory. As he was now in the ranks of star performers, he had to travel from theater to theater as he had seen others do while he was a stock player. After his engagement in Montgomery, Alabama, Booth went to Philadelphia to spend Christmas holidays with his family. It was then that Matthew Canning persuaded Booth to tour the North for his theater work. War clouds were gathering in the South, making further touring very uncertain. Canning continued to be Booth's manager for the remainder of his career. From then on Booth was to receive half the gross proceeds of every performance plus his share in the benefit performances.

Canning's theater troupe did not expand into the larger theater chain as he had first envisioned. Theater troupes were becoming of less interest as war talk continued, and managers were hesitant about extending Southern tours. A few companies continued to play as long as possible, however. There was the "Mr. Fleming's Star Company from the Savannah Georgia Theater," for example, who presented many of the same plays Canning had presented, and held on for as long as a theater could be held together.

On February 18, 1861, Jefferson Davis was inaugurated president of the Confederate States of America, at Montgomery, Alabama. In reporting the event, the Columbus *Daily Enquirer* described Davis as one who "the ladies wreathed with flowers.... Ten thousand hearts beat high with joy, admiration and hope for the administration of the new president." Canning's stage and acting manager, J.W. Albaugh, one of the leading players of the period, was present. The coming war had changed many plans.

On January 21, 1861, John Wilkes Booth began a two-week engagement at the Metropolitan Theatre in Rochester, New York. *Romeo and Juliet* was the opening bill. The twin sisters Henrietta and Maria Irving joined him for this engagement.

Rochester's *Union and Advertiser* for January 21, 1861 announced:

> The Theatre. — Mr. Booth. — The lovers of the legitimate drama may congratulate themselves on a season of enjoyment in the theatre, now about to commence. This evening Mr. J. Wilkes Booth, a young American tragedian of great popularity, will make his first appearance in Rochester, and open a brief engagement. To add to the attraction of the theatre, and ensure Mr. Booth adequate support in the important parts he will sustain, the management has engaged the Irving Sisters. The play tonight will be the tragedy of *Romeo and Juliet*. Mr. Booth will take the part of Romeo and Miss Henriette Irving, Juliet. We expect to see this piece rendered tonight in a superior manner.

The same reporter the following day remarked that both leading players had "won warm applause for the manner in which they acquitted themselves ... [and] on the whole, the expectation of the play-goers in regard to these new candidates for favor at our theatres, were realized...." Similar announcements and reviews continued for the subsequent few nights of the engagement. Then on the fifth night a benefit for Booth was called, when *Richard III* and *Faint Heart Never Won Fair Lady* were presented. Prices for this benefit were: dress circle, lady and gentleman 50¢; single gentleman 35¢; family circle 25¢; private boxes $2, $3 and $5. In commenting, the critic gave Booth his best notice since the beginning of the engagement:

> The distinguished actor, Mr. Booth, has been honored with good houses since he commenced his engagement here, and has won golden opinions from those who have witnessed his acting. Tonight he takes his first benefit, on which occasion he will appear as *Richard III*, the great character in which his father won so much distinction. The son is said to play with greater success than did his father at his age.

The benefit was said to have been played to a "large and delightful audience" and that the engagement continued to draw crowds in spite of the competition of winter sports: sleighing and skating during moonlight evenings. A re-engagement followed with continued success. "He has played here for ten nights," said the reporter,

> to full and crowded houses, at a time when theatricals were languishing, and other amusements were diverting the attention of the people. This fact speaks more than anything else that can be said as a tribute to this genius. He has played a round of characters calculated to show the scope and versatility of his power, as well as to put his ability to the test of criticism. And all he has done well, making new friends and admirers in each new phase of character that he assumed. His Othello, Richard and Romeo, were as faultless as the same characters in the hands of his illustrious sire at the same age, and there is no reason to doubt that he is destined to fill his place upon the stage, and add new luster to the name he bears.

Booth's closing play, in which he played a dual role, *The Corsican Brothers*, was hailed for its skill and effectual use of modern stage machinery. His benefit night was so successful that he repeated the same play for his closing on February 2nd.

Booth's vigorous acting aroused considerable comment, and rumors long persisted concerning his productions. It seems that in almost every engagement of *Richard III*, either he or his combat partner was injured. During the Rochester engagement we find one of the first recorded accidents. The New York *Clipper* reported that "during the combat between Richard and Richmond, the latter was severely injured by the breaking of Richard's sword, the point of which struck Mr. Miles [Richmond] just above the eye, inflicting quite a wound." Booth's reputation as a violent, unpredictable actor was growing. Fellow actors noted that he seemed to be so completely involved in his characters that he lost his sense of reality. This was the same pattern development of his father, for many times the elder Booth did strange things in seemingly living his characters.

There was a continual comparison to his father, especially in the role of *Richard III*. Booth performed the play more and more during each engagement. He was becoming identified with the role just as his father was known for it. It is interesting to compare notices of Wilkes with that of his father at about the same age. When the elder Booth opened at the Park Theater, October 5, 1821, as Richard, among his notices was the prediction that with the aid of close study and practice, Junius Brutus Booth would become the first actor of the age. He was called astonishing, and of course he did become *the* actor of the age. Similar notices were being granted to his son John Wilkes forty years later.

After his Rochester engagement, Booth followed with what was to have been two weeks in Albany. Opening there on Monday, February 11, 1861, in *Romeo and Juliet* with Annie Waite costarring with him at the Green Street Gayety Theater, he received the usual praise to which he was becoming accustomed. Records of the Albany stage reveal that:

> Booth, at this time was only twenty-three years old, and as handsome a man as ever graced the stage ... for the romantic role of Romeo he seemed perfectly fitted. The fame of his dead father prepared the way for his reception, and the good reports of his brother Edwin, raised anticipation in relation to this younger aspirant, who was said to be equally, if not still more highly gifted. His success was immediate....[1]

On his second night he revived his father's role of Pescara in *The Apostate*, the first time it had been given in Albany since the elder Booth presented it. It was said that certain spiritualists in Albany declared that Booth so resembled his father in the role that the spirit of his father must have been hovering around to inspire him with his "energy, conception and soul." Booth had of course never seen his father on the stage.

Then while playing the last act in *The Apostate*, Booth's swashbuckling oratory turned the bloody villain Pescara into realistic staging. In simulating his fall in a combat scene, Booth's dagger fell first and he fell upon it. The point of the dagger entered his right arm-pit, inflicting a muscle wound, one or two inches deep, from which the blood flowed freely.

And so we find another sensational accident. Accidents, it seemed, continued to plague Booth from one engagement to another. According to *Atlas & Argus*, February 12th, his portrayals astounded other actors, who considered his performances marked more by vigor than artistic triumph. Although his wound was later reported as "not serious in character," the accident was serious enough to keep Booth off the stage for almost a week. When he returned the following Tuesday, he appeared in the same play with his right arm tied to his side, fenced with his left like a demon. Apparently he was determined to show super strength and continued passion in his acting style. Instead of returning in a less strenuous role, he chose the same one again. Thus he continued his two-week run. At the end of it he was promptly engaged for another two weeks.

On the night of Booth's return to the stage after this dramatic accident, Monday, February 18, 1861, Lincoln had reached Albany on his way to Washington to take office as president. The *Atlas & Argus*, in commenting on both Booth's and Lincoln's being in town at the same time, were much more complimentary to Booth. In reference to Lincoln the paper disdainfully expressed the following comment:

> But lo! the wine is out, the cord severed and the cork released, and instead of sparkling champagne that bubbled over, there is a frothy rush of root-beer — yeasty foam, inspired flatulence, slops and dregs.

In contrast, the review of Booth's performance read:

> The young gentleman has succeeded admirably in gaining many warm admirers in this city, all of whom he never fails to delight with his masterly impressions. Mr. Booth is full of genius, and this with his fine face and figure, and his artistic conceptions of the characters he performs, will always render him a favorite.

Following the Albany engagement, Booth opened in Portland, Maine, on Monday, March 18, 1861, again in his customary role of Richard. For this engagement he was supported by the Western Sisters, Helen and Lucille, and his old friend John McCullough. Booth and company gave Saturday matinee performances, as no Saturday night performances were allowed in the city. The stages in this area were still suffering from Puritan discipline. The admission for the afternoon performances was 15¢ for adults, and 10¢ for children. During the weeknights a variety of Shakespearean dramas were given, and many of Booth's choicest roles were presented. At the end of the first week, it was announced that a great desire had been expressed to see more of Mr. Booth, and that he had been engaged for another week.

On Friday night three plays were presented, *The Corsican Brothers*, *The Female Forty Thieves*, and *Raphael the Reprobate*. In this farewell benefit, Booth played two parts as the brothers, and also carried the lead as Count Raphael. The afterpieces were interspersed with songs and dances. The evening prices for the Portland Theater were 25¢ for the parquette, or pit, 50¢ for the gallery and cushioned seats, and 75¢ for a lady and gentleman. His concluding performance on Saturday, March 30th, was the popular *Corsican Brothers*, which was repeated. In describing the performance, a member of the audience recalled:

The afterpiece announced was *The Haunted Man,* but they played *The Flowers of the Forest* instead. I attended the afternoon. [This would have to have been Saturday, March 30, 1861.] I recall Booth's appearance in the tableau scene of the first play, *Corsican Brothers.* He was dressed in a loose white shirt and had on black pants and was bareheaded. He stood with a rapier in his right hand raised up and his left arm, about the same position and was looking backward. He was to be slid across the stage under an illumination of red fire. I suppose he stood on a plank which had not been properly greased, for it would stop, then start, with a jerk so pronounced, that he or his shirt could not stand without a sympathetic movement each time, which destroyed the impressiveness of the scene. I shall never forget it while I remember such things.[2]

Booth remained in Portland for about three weeks after his engagement and then returned for a third engagement to Albany. Signor Canito, the Man-Monkey, shared billing with him, and his leading lady was again Henrietta Irving, who had previously appeared with him in Rochester. During the week's engagement he presented the favorite *Richard III* and *The Robbers,* and in order to properly feature Miss Irving, her favorite play, *Evadne; or, The Statue,* was presented for the following three nights with Booth supporting her as Ludovico.

But again, sensational events were to color the engagement. For it was at this time that Henrietta Irving, the spectacular actress, aroused so much excitement by inflicting a severe wound upon Booth's face with a dagger. It seems that Miss Irving, madly in love with Booth, had decided it was unrequited love, as Booth had no intention of marrying her. During a drinking party in his rooms at the Stanwix Hotel, she accused him of having gained her favors under false pretenses, and in a jealous rage, slashed him across the face as he threw up his arms to prevent the blow that would have stabbed him in the heart. Here again, as in Columbus, Georgia, Booth barely missed death. His classic features were spared by a hair's breadth. Miss Irving related that she believed that she had killed Booth, rushed to her own room in the hotel and proceeded to stab herself, though not seriously. Since she tried to justify her actions by stating that "Booth had tampered with her affections," no legal action was taken. He packed his theatre trunk and went to Baltimore to mend his wound.

Later, at 1004 Chestnut Street in Philadelphia, Wilkes was resting and "closely occupied with so many business letters to answer." In a letter dated October 9, 1861, he told his friend Joseph Simonds in Boston, "I am at the best times, the worst letter writer in the world..."

Wilkes told his friend Joe about his concern over his standing as an actor and his efforts to increase his earning power. One gets the feeling here that Wilkes was smarting because he felt that he was still taking second place to his more popular brother Edwin. He related that theatrical manager E.L. Davenport wanted him for a run in November, but they were unable to come to terms at the Boston Museum. "Davenport wants me *bad,*" wrote Wilkes, "but the engagement is not satisfied yet, and it's doubtful whether it will be...." Wilkes wanted his friend to publicize the fact that he really preferred to play at Willard's Howard Athenaeum in Boston. "It will be a better move to bring our friend Davenport to terms," said Wilkes. "He thinks me a novice, crazy to play Boston and that he will get me for nothing (which to tell the truth is nearly as much as he has offered me.)"[3]

Edwin also played under the management of E.L. Davenport, who was renowned for his astonishing portrayals of Hamlet, Othello, Richard III, and other classic heroes in addition to his shrewd theatrical management.

As it turned out, Wilkes did not take the offer for the November engagement in Boston. It was not until May 1862, and again, in his most successful run in January-February 1863, that he played the Boston Museum. A later run at Willard's Howard Athenaeum finally occurred in September of that year.

CHAPTER 10: Detroit–Cincinnati–
Louisville–St. Louis–Chicago
"To Compel an Audience"

The Detroit *Daily Advertiser*, in announcing Booth's engagement there on November 11, 1861, gave him what was probably his heartiest welcome to date:

> *Mr. J.W. Booth.* — The brother of the great Edwin Booth is engaged by Mrs. Perry and will appear tonight. He is said to be both like and unlike his father Junius Brutus Booth, and his famous brother Edwin, and is by nature and education an actor. If all that we hear of him is true, he is the greatest tragedian on the American stage — the genius of the Booth family has been bequeathed to this third son — John Wilkes — without being diminished in fullness or dimmed in lustre.

Then the following day, rival newspaper the *Detroit Free Press* was in full agreement in its praise for the opening. This was Booth's first appearance in Detroit. For his opening he chose the biting romantic melodrama *The Wife,* a play in which Booth played practically every male part during his career from walk-on to lead role. The *Free Press* reporter felt that it was evident that the talent of the youngest Booth "bids fair to be almost equalled by that of his father.... The genius of Booth the senior has already descended in no small measure to the son." The reviewer believed that as St. Pierre, Booth's acting did not seem like acting, but was, "for the time being the reality." The reviewer continued by saying, "This we are aware is great praise of merit, but those who merit deserve great praise." Booth's long-time associate, J.W. Albaugh was praised for his work, as was Mrs. H.A. Perry, manager and leading player, but all the comments seemed to be centered around Booth. In announcing the following bill of *Macbeth,* the reader is advised: "If the words of Macbeth and Booth leave not force to compel an audience no words that we can write will attract one."

For his presentation of *Othello* on the 14th, although the weather was most unfavorable, there was a "goodly assemblage" at the theater. The same critic thought the play a decided success, and that "Mr. Booth sustained all that has previously been said of his qualities as an actor." Praise also was given to Mr. Albaugh as Iago, and to Mrs. Perry as Desdemona. Some of the cast, however, continued the critic, "were laboring under the disadvantage of having to assume their parts at short notice." This would indicate clearly the enormous strain, the drain on the nerves of the stock player who has to learn new parts at short notice.

64

The following evening was Booth's benefit, and "to judge his versatility" he appeared in both tragedy and comedy. Besides the favorite *Richard III*, Booth presented his frequent choice of afterpiece, *Too Much for Good Nature*, playing Romeo Jaffier Jenkins in "mock tragedy." The succeeding evening's *Hamlet* was greatly received, and because Kate Bateman was late arriving for her engagement, Booth filled in for her by again playing *Richard III* on Monday evening. One reviewer felt that "the sword combat in the last act between Richard and Richmond was decidedly the best and most thrilling scene that has ever been produced on the stage of the Metropolitan."

After Detroit Booth next played Cincinnati, fulfilling a two-week run. Adopting the custom of his father, he was now habitually opening with his most successful role of Richard at each of his engagements. During this run at Wood's Theater, the tragedian J.A.J. Neafie was appearing at Pike's Opera House. Booth had appeared with Neafie in minor roles when the latter was starring in Richmond. Now that Booth was of star magnitude,

Playbill showing Booth in a double-bill, Metropolitan Theatre, Detroit, November 15, 1861. From the Yale University Library Theatre Collection. Previously unpublished.

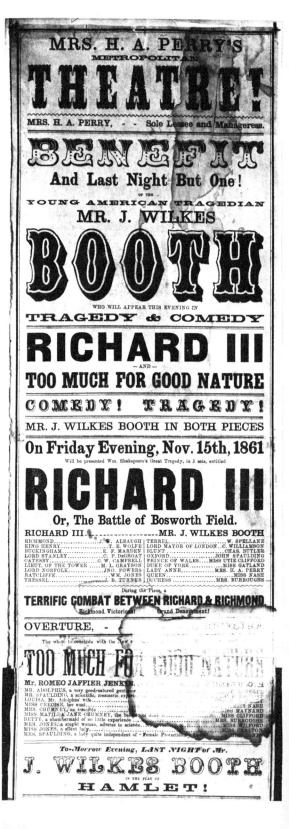

he and Neafie were in fierce competition. The young Booth attempted to out-do his rival by presenting the same play the following evening. When Neafie presented *Hamlet,* Booth presented *Hamlet* the following night. When Neafie presented *The Corsican Brothers,* Booth came forth the following night with an even greater spectacle of the dual role "embracing all the latest machinery never before equaled upon the stage." Apparently the Cincinnati *Enquirer* review editor preferred Neafie, as Booth was hardly mentioned in the theater columns, whereas about a paragraph per day was devoted to Neafie. But Neafie was an old established favorite, twice the age of Booth, welcomed back from his tour abroad, where "he had mellowed by travel," and had been a great success in England that same year, 1861. The Cincinnati audiences for Neafie were slim, however, a fact bemoaned by the reviewer. Booth's good looks and youth were bringing in the crowds. In spite of the build-up given to Neafie, he closed in nine days. His benefit was slight, the excuse was the horribly cold weather. He was shown up by his young rival who stayed on for two weeks.

Immediately after the Cincinnati engagement, Booth went to Louisville, Kentucky, opening as usual in *Richard III* on December 9th. This engagement was exceedingly successful, running for four weeks, and was Booth's longest engagement to that date. He presented all the old favorites of his repertoire, and many not previously presented. One new play, *The Fairy and the Demon,* ran for 11 consecutive performances, an unusual event since most bills were changed nightly.

Speaking of his opening night, the Louisville *Daily Democrat,* December 10, 1861, reported:

> Severe as was the test for so young a man, Mr. Booth proved himself fully equal to the appointed task. He has fire, energy, fine personal appearance and good talent. Some eccentricities of style and some apparent imitations of other actors alone marred the beauty of his personation.... He is evidently a young man of very great promise, and will doubtless add to the already great distinction attached to his family name.

On the same date, another Louisville newspaper, the *Daily Journal,* was full of praise. There was still the comparison of father and son:

> He reminds us more of his father than his brother Edwin does.... Mr. Wilkes Booth is a young man of extraordinary genius, and when his voice is matured by practice and he has succeeded in shaking off some mannerisms, he will become a great actor.... We have never seen the last act of *Richard III* played with more power, spirit and originality than he did it on Monday.

Five days later, the most laudatory comments were by the *Daily Democrat:*

> Mr. Booth played to another excellent house last night. His rendering of Charles de Moor in Schiller's play of *The Robbers* was marked by evidence of originality and boldness of conception characteristic of his *Richard III* and *Macbeth.* Mr. Booth is the most original actor we have seen in a great many years....

It would seem now that Booth's only criticism centered around his mannerism and his voice. At 23 one might imagine that his voice for heavy drama might not yet have the depth and fullness required for the roles. One gets the feeling he might have shouted his lines in a strained delivery, rather

John Wilkes Booth and the so-called "Idle Group." St. Louis, January 1862. Posed with three other men in classical motif by Mathew B. Brady. This portrait was made soon after the Southern theater engagement began. The seated man in civilian clothes is probably J.W. Albaugh, stage manager, and the one who substituted for Booth on several occasions. From the Brady and U.S. Collection, Library of Congress. Previously unpublished.

than projecting in a quieter yet powerful way. It is interesting that the reviewer, in speaking of his opening performance, said there were "some apparent imitations," yet in five days the same reviewer is saying that Booth is the "most original actor."

Booth's successful engagement at Louisville continued through January 4, 1862. Immediately following, he opened on January 6th at Ben De Bar's St. Louis Theatre, again with the customary Richard. This was to be the first of five engagements in St. Louis. For his first St. Louis run he had Charlotte Wyette as leading lady.

The *Daily Missouri Democrat* gave the following report of Booth's opening in St. Louis:

> Mr. Booth had a most rapturous reception last night as *Richard III*. He is an
> actor of the highest order, with all the fire and enthusiasm of his father or

brother Edwin, being taller and better formed; also a fine expressive face. As a declaimer, he is unexceptionable; careful and correct, never evincing a disposition to rant.

The above comments would indicate that to some critics, Booth did not "rant" his lines, but was a "careful and correct declaimer." Later critics gave the opposite impression of his delivery. It is hard to explain this variance in opinion.

It was Booth's intention to give a series of Shakespearean plays during this engagement. Each of these seems to have attracted "full and fashionable houses." His *Hamlet* was thought to be a "well studied and highly finished performance," *Macbeth* was "brilliant," but of course the favorite was *Richard III,* in which "the fight between Richard and Richmond in the last scene is most terrific; indeed, we have never seen it equaled on the stage...."

The followng hurriedly written note was addressed to Joseph Simonds, his business agent [see illustration]. Booth had been giving Simonds money all along to invest for him in various ventures. The letter indicates the money problem during Civil War times.

St. Louis, Dec. 10th [i.e., January 10, 1862]

Dear Joe

Both your letters Rec'd. You must not flatter yourself that your letters are too long, or that you write too often, for although I hate writing myself, I can read your letters, if you send three or four a-day. My bus [business] here so far has been fair As you may see by the papers. I play here all next week and then may go to Chicago, but not sure of it. I think I have one of those pictures you alluded to, Nevertheless you can take <u>two</u> for me. I can get nothing but St. Louis money here, and they won't take that East, or I would enclose the funds. The first Eastern note I get I will send it then you can send the pictures. Let me hear from you often, Joe. Always delighted. Excuse this as I write it in a hurry, as I always do it seems. Remember me to all my friends. I will write again soon God bless you. Your True Friend.

J. Wilkes Booth.

I wrote this in the dark. Excuse mistakes, & et.[1]

It is evident that Booth did write this quite hurriedly, and probably backstage in the dark. His postscript was written in a slanting way across the back of the page, and a blob of ink is with it. The letter is dated Dec. 10th, but obviously it should have been Jan. 10th, judging by its contents and Booth's known engagements. He was always in a hurry and always apologizing for errors.

At the close of his St. Louis engagement, the *Daily Democrat* had not changed his mind about Booth. In part he said, "Mr. Booth has made a highly favorable impression each night, increasing in the number and the fashion of the audience.... Mr. Booth is in every sense a great actor, well read, and of commanding appearance...."

Immediately following the close of his St. Louis run on Saturday, January 18, 1862, Booth opened in Chicago, as he had written to Simonds, on January 20th. McVicker's Theatre was the most costly and impressive theater in the "West." It presented only "distinguished drama" and it is here that J. Wilkes Booth achieved a personal triumph.

He was keeping close and continuous engagements now, with only

I wrote this in the dark
excuse mistakes &ct

St Louis, Dec 14th

Dear Joe

Both your
letters reach'd me (and must
now plead guilty) to neglect
of your letters are
too long, or that you
write too often, for
although I have neither
myself. If you read them
as I do read these
or Louis A. Clark (my friend
here so far has been far)
do you may see by the reason
I play there off upon I
accept and then heartily
go to Chicago, and
I have one of these without
you already ho! nevertheless
You can take care for me

I can get nothing but
to lend money there, and
they won't take that
check, or I would enclose
the friends, the first
Earthen cuse I get I
will send it. When you
can send the picture—
Let me hear from you
often you always follow
"excuse this" as I never
it in a hurry as I always
do it in a hurry. Remember
me to all my friends
I will write again soon
God bless you. Your
True Friend

J. Wilkes Booth

Sundays allowed for travel, and with at least two weeks in each city. It would seem that he was making every effort to perfect his art, attempting in a most serious way to present his plays, yet bring to the roles a new freshness which sometimes astounded the conventional theater patrons. Increasingly, reviewers, in discussing his performances, could find fault only in the fierceness of the "inherited fire in his blood," feeling that if he conquered this, he would achieve greatness. But Booth, knowing full well the importance of that fire, was not about to give the audiences a tame performance. They came to see a show, not a recitation. The following is the reaction from the *Chicago Tribune*, January 21, 1862, regarding his first appearance there in *Richard III*:

> Under whatever circumstances Mr. Booth may take his farewell of the Chicago public, he can find no fault with his reception, which was as hearty and generous as those accorded to older and, perhaps, better actors. We regard the selection of *Richard III* as being unfortunate for Mr. Booth's opening night. The hunchbacked, crooked and deformed Richard was certainly not pleasing to the eye. Those essential points of a good actor: a fine commanding figure, easy carriage, etc., were concealed, if they exist at all, in the humpbacked Richard. Even the voice, —full, rich and distinct, which is, of course, requisite to a good actor, can be poorly judged in the husky soliloquies, the dissemblings, or the frantic ravings of Richard. If originality is a virtue, Booth is virtuous to an intense degree. No actor ever displayed more independence of, or disregard for, the old beaten path than he does. Mr. Booth's delivery of the text in one less studied and scholarly, would be pronounced careless.

It is obvious from this review, that Booth was striving for realism and characterization first. He was not trying to make pleasing-to-the-eye scenes or to present Richard as a drawing room character with perfect diction. Booth might have been called vain because of his handsome features, but certainly in his role of Richard they were hidden. He did not care to stand center stage with proper posture and eloquently voice the lines of a character who possessed anything but these qualities. If the character of Richard was ugly in the extreme, then his impersonation of him must be the same, posture and voice included.

But Booth shattered the *Chicago Tribune's* opinions and showed his audiences that he could enact a part of more attractive countenance. He followed the ugly Richard with the romantic play of *Lady of Lyons*. This Bulwer-Lytton drama was enlivened by Booth's touch of color and romance; its settings created pretty pictures that everyone delighted in. Reviewers often referred to the play as one which would be "especially pleasing to the ladies."

For yet further contrast, Booth followed this with the arduous character of Pescara, another role of blood and thunder. He followed this with Romeo, to fully display his poetic artistry. Critics lauded him as the most brilliant actor ever to play Chicago. This was quite a superlative for that rough and critical city.

During the Chicago engagement Booth attended a charity party where he was asked if he would sell his autographs and donate the money to

Opposite page: *facsimile of Booth's letter to Joseph Simonds (see text). From the Andre deCoppet Collection, Princeton University Library. Used with permission.*

charity. We are told that "he demurred on the grounds that his signature was worthless," but a young girl convinced him she could sell all he would provide at 25¢ each. When Booth's murder of Lincoln assured the actor of a prominent if villainous role in American history, many Chicago families spent hours trying to salvage these autographs from attic trunks and cluttered bureau drawers.[2]

There is no doubt that Booth made a deep impression with the people of Chicago. In 1862 he played two engagements there, one of two weeks, another of three weeks. The impact of his "Force to Compel an Audience" is graphically set down three years later in the Chicago *Post*:

> Younger by far than any actor who had gained like prominence upon the American stage, whose lustre saw little prospect of being dimmed. That he is possessed with histrionic ability far beyond his years, none can deny, and for him has been predicted a future, which a lifetime of assiduous and unremitting labor often fails to achieve. That future is ended. The star of his destiny is set in blood...."[3]

CHAPTER 11: Baltimore
A Native Son Is Welcomed

At the end of his Chicago engagement Booth traveled homeward to Baltimore. He opened for a three-week engagement at the Holliday Street Theatre there on Monday, February 17, 1862, with the usual opener, *Richard III*. The newspapers announced this as his first Baltimore appearance, but this was in error, as Booth had appeared there twice previously: his first stage appearance in 1855, and again with Edwin Booth in 1858. Perhaps this was a deliberate oversight, as his earlier appearances had not been very praiseworthy nor was he yet a star. On opening day, the Baltimore *Sun*, carried the following:

> *Holliday Street Theatre.* — Engagement of Mr. J. Wilkes Booth. Public interest and curiosity are enlisted in the announcement that a second son of the great tragic artist, J.B. Booth, is a candidate for professional distinction in the same range of dramas as that occupied by his renowned father. We know nothing whatever of his talents or skill, but his reception is represented to have been of the most favorable character, and marked by a steadily growing approval wherever he has appeared....

Richard Cary, a friend of Edwin's, after having seen Wilkes in *Macbeth* on February 27th, of this engagement wrote Edwin of his impressions. He thought Wilkes too melodramatic, woodenfaced, although in part his rendition was remarkably like Edwin's. He said it reminded him of "a blood-and-thunder melodrama full of sheet iron and burnt rosin and ghosts and other horrors...."[1]

The opening bill in Baltimore carried the words "I am myself alone," an indication that Booth wished to be judged for himself instead of the usual comparisons with the other Booths. Yet, the reviewer persisted in making comparisons along with daily praise. "A recognition of home genius," the critic said; "... A bright and glorious success, Booth received last evening by an ovation of genuine and continuous applause from an audience tremendous in numbers and brilliant in fashion. The storm no impediment...." The second night the audience members were "all uniting with vehement pleasure in the fact that Richard's himself again" in a repeat performance "...ending with that scene of preternatural and terrific grandeur, the Battle of Bosworth Field.... [S]ecure your seats during the day ... 25, 38, and 15 cents."

Two large columns daily were devoted to the company. Many of Booth's old friends and former fellow actors were in the casts. His leading costars were Mrs. Farren and Annie Graham. In a review of the *Richard III* production, the Baltimore *Sun* said:

"None of the printed pictures I have ever seen do justice to Booth. Some of the cartes de visite get him very nearly..." — Townsend. *A rare such card, date unknown. From the Lloyd Ostendorf Collection, Dayton, Ohio. Previously unpublished.*

This young artist was favored with another large and distinguished audience last night, and the repetition of Richard was received with the warmest demonstrations of cordial esteem. That he is in the career to eminent popularity is quite evident, and that he possesses the elements of true greatness in his profession we cannot doubt. Indeed, with allowance for the exuberance of youth, the energy of an apparently healthy and substantial physique, and the consequent overworking of some lineaments of character in Richard, the exhibition of great genius, originality and reserved power — that reserve which will chasten and endure with classic grace his maturer performances — is manifest and incontestable. The peculiarity of voice and tone constantly reminds us of his father, and there are frequent graces of expression which carry with them the assurances that the American stage has the acquisition of a good hope in this young man.

For his Romeo he was hailed thus:

> unexcelled in the originality and delightful freshness of his style, rare evidence of genius, a passionate earnestness and intense fervor which invests his personations with the charm of reality, and have already excited in the minds of the intellectual and discriminating a profound sensation of admiration and delight. The voice of the people uttered in thunders of heart-cheering applause, has declared his engagement a most brilliant and successful hit! Mr. Booth's personation of this character is the very embodiment of youthful ardor, and has been recorded as one of his best performances...

Although it was reported that Booth was laboring under a severe cold, "he looked and acted the devoted and jealous young lover of Shakespeare's creation with the happiest effect. Miss Graham's Juliet made a very favorable impression...."

Booth followed Romeo with the dual role of *The Corsican Brothers*: "sparkling with fire of original genius and rendered fervid by the passionate earnestness of youth...." The special effects of this psychological drama were widely applauded. Booth employed the use of such devices as trick mirrors, sliding panels, revolving platforms, and special lighting to give the effect of consuming flames. Some theatergoers consider special effects used today as entirely modern, not realizing that many basic stage mechanisms known today were in use in Booth's time, producing as exciting and as startling results then as now. By 1849 gas lighting in theaters had progressed to such a degree that dimming was possible, resulting in more effective shading. Previous to this, the whole theater had remained in an even glare of light regardless of the type of scene played.

Booth employed the use of the "limelight," or calcium light, that had come into general use in 1860. This instrument produced an extremely white and concentrated beam of light by directing an oxyhydrogen flame on a cylinder of lime. This could be used with varying colors of lenses, and probably helped to produce the startling effects in *The Corsican Brothers.*

Some other plays also produced novel effects far ahead of their time. Dion Boucicault, leader in new theater staging, contributed much toward the advancement of new ideas. Revolving stages, cutaway sets showing various rooms in the same house, sound effects and shades of lighting were used to develop a broader scope of realism through the use of special effects. Booth appeared in many of Boucicault's plays and gained ideas from his genius.

Booth's contrasting bill of tragedy and comedy, *The Apostate* and *Too Much for Good Nature*, brought forth these flowery words of praise from the Baltimore *Sun*, February 21, 1862:

> 'Mid the galaxy of stars that have illuminated our theatrical firmament, reflecting upon the genius of America, the lights of a fame unsurpassed in brightness, none have shown with greater brilliancy than our young artist; admiring audiences throughout the country, comprising the learned, the discriminating, and the better judgment still, the people at large, whose honest hearts respond with generous sympathy to the fervid expression of genius, have conferred upon him their warmest admiration; and here in his native city, crowded audiences have nightly listened to and marked his personations with that riveted attention, which is the greatest compliment that art can command, or appreciation bestow.

Baltimore had claimed him as a native son, and although the advertisements and reviews were putting it on pretty thick, one can still surmise that Booth was a popular success. The audience reveled in the horror of Booth's blood-stained sword as he spoke such lines from Shiel's play as, "Ha! ha! a Moor ... one of that race we have trodden down...."

The following description was given the performance of *The Apostate*, which was highlighted by Booth's impersonation of the evil Duke Pescara, a character full of ghosts and bloody horrors. After calling the performance one of thrilling effect and a discussion of good audience reaction, the critic singled out those scenes he thought best. Said he,

> The passionate interview between Pescara and Florinda, with which the fourth act closes, was sustained with such power and such influence upon the audience that the house called for a complimentary appearance of Mr. Booth and Mrs. Farren before the curtain, and the demand was reiterated at the close of the piece."

It should be remembered that in Booth's day, the play was stopped quite frequently by applause. If this was strong enough, the play was completely stopped and the actors of the particular scene were brought forth for a curtain call in the middle of the play. Today, a complete "show-stopper" is rare unless it is in a vaudeville type performance. Rarely today is a scene broken by the actors stepping to the footlights for an appreciation speech in the middle of the play. Possibly, only in opera in this done. But in Booth's day, this was quite common to stop the show if a player gained such audience approval.

The Baltimore *Sun*, February 24, 1862, continued coverage of Booth's engagement:

> The audience thronging all parts of the house, and the satisfaction enjoyed was manifest in the performance. That this young tragedian is destined to achieve great distinction, and possibly peculiar eminence in his profession, there can not be a doubt. There is a freshness, energy, physical vigor, earnestness and dash in his personations which challenging and defying the austerity of criticism delight the audience and command the artist to popular favor.

His *Hamlet* was called a "rare treat," especially since this demanding role was played well by one so young. "His bright, glowing, impulsive acting wins every heart.... [T]he presentation of Mr. Booth is really worthy of, nay, it commands admiration...." The reviewer felt that many of the scenes in the play were like "select gems from a great painting.... It confirms the opinion we have heretofore expressed, that this young tragedian is to occupy a most distinguished rank on the American stage."

As for Booth's *Macbeth*, the critic thought he sustained the character with great vigor and effect, but it was Mrs. Farren who, being the "best Lady Macbeth upon the stage," commanded a dignified personation, and took most honors. The combat scenes between Macbeth and Macduff were comparable to those in *Richard III*. The entire music of Locke was played by the orchestra, and a powerful chorus was most effective.

Charles Selby's *Marble Heart* was one of Booth's most popular plays. He altered, adapted and partly rewrote this play to suit his own designs, and thought of it as a sequel to the famous French play *Camille*, with "illustrations of life" in Paris about 1856. *Marble Heart* is an allegorical experiment of the times, and not just another melodrama, but genuine tragic material. The story concerns the sculptor, Raphael Duchatlet, rejected by the "marble hearts" of the time, who goes mad and dies, and of the counterpart with Phidias, of the ancient world. In this play, Booth played both parts. The fact that John Hay, one of Lincoln's secretaries, said in his journal, "rather tame than otherwise,"[2] might indicate that he had expected the run-of-the mill melodrama rather than the experimental allegory, in which a beautiful girl chooses a rich old man to a poor handsome one. Certainly it was tame in comparison to *Richard III.*

Booth, essentially a tragic actor, excelled in parts of this nature and after reaching stardom seldom wasted his time on plays having only conventional characters with series of sentimental intrigues. Shakespeare occupied most of his repertoire, as was the custom of all the Booths.

On Friday, March 7, 1862, the young men of the city of Baltimore gave Booth a testimonial benefit, called a "Boothenian Festival," in which the young men "graced the house with the fair" in a "memorial in the chaplet of fame." For this high occasion Booth presented *The Robbers* by the "German Shakespeare," Schiller, and the "Jew that Shakespeare drew," Shylock in the *Merchant of Venice.* After this, "Baltimore's favorite son" closed his engagement with the customary *Richard III,* and took a week's rest and preparation before opening in New York City.

CHAPTER 12: New York City
The Broadway Engagement

Mary Provost, popular New York actress, had just returned from five years of touring in California, Australia, England and Ireland when she reopened Wallack's old theater, then located at 485 Broadway near Broome Street, and proceeded to be its new manager. The New York *World*, in reporting the transaction, said:

> Miss Provost, we take pleasure in announcing, has had it washed. She has, moreover, signalized her opening attempt at New York management by engaging a star of real magnitude, and singular though fitful brilliancy....

J. Wilkes Booth was the star engaged, and he brought with him several members from the Baltimore company, among them Mrs. Farren and E.L. Tilton. The opening bill on Monday evening, March 17, 1862, was the usual opener, *Richard III*. But let us hear firsthand reaction from one member of that company:

> Monday morning came the rehearsal with the star, and the company had all assembled awaiting him. Many were the stories of his wonderful gifts and eccentricities. One old member of the company, who had played with him through Georgia, prophesied he would make a terrific hit. Said he: "I am an old man at the business and have seen and played with some of the greatest tragedians the world has ever known. I've played second to Macready. I've divided the applause with Charles Kean. I've acted with Forrest, but in all my long years of professional experience, this young man Wilkes Booth (I might call him a boy), this boy is the first actor that ever (to use a professional term), knocked me off my pins, upset and completely left without a word to say! Yes, sir, an old actor like me that you suppose an earthquake could not move, was tongue-tied — unable to speak his lines.... I tell you gentlemen, there is more magnetism in Wilkes Booth's eye than in any human being's I ever saw."[1]

The company listened with pleasure to the old actor. Some of them disbelieving, and thinking him overly enthusiastic, others agreeing that Wilkes was surely to be all he said since genius ran in the blood of the Booth family. Old stories of the elder Booth were then retold, and comparisons between the Booths were discussed. Another actor related a similar time of "being knocked off his pins" while acting with the elder Booth. He too agreed that the company was in for a surprise.

Soon a commotion was heard at the back of the stage, and striding down the center of the stage came J. Wilkes Booth in a dramatic entrance of half darkness. The footlights and borders were suddenly turned up and "revealed a face and form not easily described or forgotten. You have seen a high-mettled racer with his sleek skin and eye of unusual brilliancy chafing under a restless impatience to be doing something. It is the only living thing I could liken him to...."

The stage manager then introduced Booth to all the company, and Booth, "with a sharp, jerky manner" started the rehearsal. The actor recording the scene for history continued:

> I watched him closely and perceived the encomiums passed upon him by the old actor were not in the least exaggerated. Reading entirely new to us, he gave; business never thought of by the oldest stager, he introduced; and, when the rehearsal was over, one and all admitted a great actor was amongst us.

Booth then proceeded to go to each individual in the cast and chat with them, setting them at ease, that they should not "be affrighted that night" because, he said with a smile, he might "throw a little more fire into the part than at rehearsal." Each member of the cast was given a few words of criticism: "Lady Anne was gently admonished; Richmond was bluntly told to look out in the combat scene, and in a sotto voice, said to Jim Ward [who played Ratcliffe], "Keep your eye on me tonight."

When the evening of the opening arrived, the house was only fair, but word of mouth hastened to make Booth's Richard a success, "a positive and unqualified success, so much so that it was kept on the balance of the week." A new interpretation seemed to attract the audience, because there was a

> breaking loose from all the old orthodox, tie-wig business of the Richards since the days of Garrick down to Joannes; he gave such a rendition of the crookback tyrant as was never seen before, and perhaps never will be again.... [O]riginality was stamped all over and through the performance. It was a terrible picture...."[2]

And from other critics we hear the same type of description for Wilkes' performances; they mention frequently the fire, the abandon, the unpredictable staging. For Wilkes Booth, like his father, relied almost entirely on impulse of the moment. Neither of them cared for set rules. To feel the part was the thing; to make the audience feel it, the ideal. In order to better achieve this, the elder Booth often spent the entire day before an evening performance actually *being* the character he was to perform. Thus there were the extremes on and off the stage.

Wilkes, too, often became so absorbed in his characterizations that he carried his intensity to extremes. There are many tales of his dueling scenes in *Richard III*, most of which make him out to be a complete madman on stage, slashing savagely with little regard for his fellow players. The truth is that Wilkes was an expert fencer and an outstanding athlete. He gained a reputation for his realistic combat scenes and his acrobatics. The Baltimore *Sun* called him "a gymnastic actor; his heels in the air nearly as often as his head...." And because of Booth's fire and enthusiasm, reporter Townsend commented that he was "too energetic to be correct." Another reporter giving his views a year after the assassination stated:

> Booth as an actor did not, except in some parts, deserve the exalted eulogiums bestowed on him.... In all acting that demanded delicate characteriza-

tion, or carefulness, Booth was at sea,* but in strong physical parts, requiring much declamation, the due need of praise was not bestowed. His conception of Richard was vivid and original, and resembled very closely his father's great personation, which no one who had ever seen it, could forget. His Romeo was greatly admired by competent judges a faultless piece of acting. Though the tubes of his throat were somewhat affected, his voice had not failed, and his charge to the cavalrymen [those involved in Booth's death] was as sharp and clear as in his palmiest days.[3]

Wilkes probably remembered the accounts of his father's characterization of Richard and was determined to equal the famous father, if not surpass him. All the Booths discarded the old fixed form of theater, and portrayed their characters with their own excessive passion. The results were startling and different and these portrayals left their mark upon the memory and imagination of the audiences.

Believing that it was more wonderful to stun audiences with a brilliant personality than to capture them with art, he was forever rearranging Shakespeare and Schiller so that his entrances could be more electrifying and startling. He made staggering leaps off precipices and battlements. For example, when he appeared before the witches in *Macbeth*, he was not content to enter in a normal fashion, but had to jump from a high mound of rocks down into the scene, where limelights produced effective boiling cauldrons for the witches, illuminated his flying entrances and pinpointed faces in the dark muslin trees of the stage forest. An analogy to this in modern times is quite evident in the swashbuckling of Douglas Fairbanks and Errol Flynn. We cannot however call Wilkes the first swashbuckler, for his father would seem to have gained that title.

It was said of the elder Booth that he presented his Richard in such variety that the audience never knew what to expect next, yet his impersonation was such that judges call him the great actor of the age. In the elder Booth's dueling scene in *Richard III*, at times he fought out his scene over the footlights, down the aisle, out the door, down the street, up the alley, and back to the stage again while the audience sat gasping for breath. This may be why Wilkes kept telling his Richmonds to "Come on! harder!!" He expected his opponent to deliver an equally vigorous fight. The fact that Wilkes had to sleep padded with oysters in order to relieve his cuts and bruises might have seemed in order to him, if not to his Richmonds.[4] Naturally, this was the scene everybody talked about, the climax of the play.

Actor James H. Stoddart remembered the time that he appeared with both Edwin and Wilkes Booth in the play at the Holliday Street Theatre, Baltimore, in 1858:

> During this season I participated in an exceedingly interesting performance of *Richard III*, with Edwin Booth as Richard, and his younger brother, John Wilkes Booth as Richmond. Both performances were superb. I shall never forget the fight between Richard and Richmond in the last act, an encounter which was terrible in its savage realism.[5]

An audience is either moved by effective staging, or they remain unconvinced by what they see. That is why our great names of the theater have

*Other critics felt that his sensitive playing of Romeo was "just about perfect."

MARY PROVOST'S THEATRE

LATE WALLACK'S THEATRE.

485 Broadway, near Broome Street.

Doors open at Seven.   Commence at a quarter before Eight o'clock.

BENEFIT

And last appearance but one of the

YOUNG AMERICAN TRAGEDIAN

J. WILKES

BOOTH

Who, in consequence of previous pressing engagements, is compelled,(notwithstanding the strong importunities of the management, and unanimous call of the public, to

Decline any Present Re-engagement.

ORCHESTRA, under the direction of Mr. KOPPITZ

Friday Evening, March 28th, 1862

Will be presented, Shakspeare's great Tragedy, of

MACBETH

WITH ALL THE ORIGINAL MUSIC.

MUSICAL CONDUCTOR..MR. KOPPITZ

Macbeth, King of Scotland - - - - -
J. Wilkes Booth

Lady Macbeth...Mrs. Farren
Macduff...Mr. E. L. Tilton
King Duncan..Mr. George Ryer
Banquo...Mr. Carter
Rosse...Mr. J. W. Collier
Malcolm...Mr. Rand
Donalbain..Miss Smith
Fleance..Miss Mary Bullock
Hecate..Mr. Spackman
1st Witch...Mr. Lewis Baker
2nd Witch..Mr. McCloskey
3d Witch...Mrs. Rand
Bleeding Captain..Mr. Pemberton
Chamberlain..Mr. Thompson
Singing Witch..Mrs. Chasteau
Gentlewoman..Mrs. Floyd
Physician...Mr. Crosta
                                                                          Mrs. Floyd
Apparitions {   Mrs. Rand
                                                                        Miss Bullock
1st Officer...Mr. Ward
2nd Officer...Mr. Walsh
Singing Witches...........................Messrs. Rea, Oliver, Waldron, and Mortimer
Witches, Soldiers, Nobles, Retainers, &c..............by...............Auxiliary Corps

TO-MORROW SATURDAY,

LAST APPEARANCE
OF

J. WILKES BOOTH

MARY PROVOST,

Who has achieved a marvellous success, during the last five years, throughout California, Australia and Europe, having partially recovered from her late severe indisposition, will soon have the honor of appearing before an audience of her own Country in her native City.

PRICES OF ADMISSION :

Orchestra Chairs - - - Seventy-five Cents | Family Circle - - - - Twenty-five Cents
Dress Circle and Parquette - - Fifty Cents | Private Boxes - $4 to $7, according to location

Seats may be secured, without extra charge, at the Box Office, from 9 A. M. to 4 P. M.

MARY PROVOST'S THEATRE

LATE WALLACK'S THEATRE.

485 Broadway, near Broome Street.

Doors open at Seven.   Commence at a quarter before Eight o'clock.

LAST NIGHT OF THE

Triumphantly Successful Engagement

OF THE

YOUNG AMERICAN TRAGEDIAN

J. WILKES

BOOTH

Who, in consequence of previous pressing engagements, is compelled,(notwithstanding the strong importunities of the management, and unanimous call of the public, to

Decline any Present Re-engagement.

ORCHESTRA, under the direction of Mr. KOPPITZ

Saturday Evening, March 29th, 1862

Will be presented, Shakspeare's great Tragedy, in five acts, entitled

RICHARD III

BY

PARTICULAR AND SPECIAL
REQUEST,

SUPPORTED BY

J. Wilkes Booth - as - - - Richard

Queen Elizabeth...Mrs. Farren
Lady Anne...Mrs. Chasteau
Duchess of York..Mrs. Rand
Prince of Wales..Little Mary Bullock
Duke of York..Mr. E. L. Tilton
Earl of Richmond..Mr. Lewis Baker
Tressell...Mr. George Ryer
King Henry VI...Mr. Carter
Duke of Buckingham...Mr. Spackman
Lord Stanly...Mr. Collier
Catesby...Mr. Walsh
Duke of Norfolk...Mr. T. J. Ward
Ratcliffe..Mr. Crosta
Lord Mayor..Mr. McCloskey
Lieutenant of Tower..Mr. Davenport
Blunt..Mr. Walter Birch
Tirrell..Mr. Rand
Officers, Soldiers, Lords, Ladies, Pages, &c...........by..........Auxiliary Corps

Mary Provost

Who has achieved a marvellous success, during the last five years, throughout California, Australia and Europe, having partially recovered from her late severe indisposition, will soon have the honor of appearing before an audience of her own Country in her native City.

PRICES OF ADMISSION :

Orchestra Chairs - - - Seventy-five Cents | Family Circle - - - - Twenty-five Cents
Dress Circle and Parquette - - Fifty Cents | Private Boxes - $4 to $7, according to location

Seats may be secured, without extra charge, at the Box Office, from 9 A. M. to 4 P. M.

Two playbills from Mary Provost's Theatre, New York, March 28 and 29, 1862. From the collection of the Museum of the City of New York. Both previously unpublished.

succeeded in characterizations by the sheer force of dynamic personality to make the stage come to life.

Just as Wilkes Booth was a crack shot with the rifle and an expert horseman, so he was an expert fencer. He was reputed to have taken on two men concurrently, disarming them both in a matter of seconds. Several accidents occurred during the fierce dueling scene in *Richard III*, and publicity distorted his dashing technique all out of proportion. Yet, how much of it was actually true? In a sketch of E.L. Tilton, the actor who played Richmond to Booth's Richard in New York City, we are told:

> During the engagement of John Wilkes Booth at Mary Provost's Theatre, New York, Mr. Tilton one night, while playing Richmond, accidentally stepped off the stage, dislocating his shoulder, which was the ground-work of the story about Booth's getting so excited that he knocked him off.[6]

This story was magnified to gigantic proportions, relating how Tilton was frequently wounded in the swordplay with Booth, and that he, for one, had no respect for Booth, since Booth would go wild without consideration for his fellow players.

Another incident during rehearsal of the same scene in Cleveland resulted in Booth's being accidentally cut on the forehead and his eyebrow slashed by J.C. McCollom who played Richmond. Wilkes made nothing of it, begging McCollom not to apologize, and seemed more concerned that he had wounded his opponent. In describing the combat scene for a Detroit engagement the *Detroit Free Press*, April 30, 1865, remembered that "he fought like a demon, but never viciously." And Clara Morris, who was a member of his cast, said, "There are not many men who can receive a gash over the eye in a scene at night, without at least momentary outburst of temper."[7]

Yet, when he wounded his opponent, Booth would be quite upset by the accident, more so than had he himself received a cut or bruise. When his Richmond in the Rochester engagement had been wounded, Booth bent over him and cried under his breath, "Oh, God! Oh, God! I've hurt you!" The version of the play then acted required Richard to die on stage, as opposed to later versions where "Enter King Richard and Richmond; exeunt fighting." It is said that on this occasion Booth continued to moan as Richmond finished his speech with a bloody face, and the curtain fell. Thus John Wilkes Booth was not totally insensitive toward his fellow actors, as some have implied.

Although many compared Wilkes most favorably with his father, others observed that he did not have his father's ability, only his father's traits. Walt Whitman, who had seen and admired the performances in the Bowery of Junius Brutus Booth, had this to say about Wilkes, after having seen him in his New York City debut on March 17, 1862:

> I went to see the old man's son, Wilkes, play his Richard during his engagement a month or so ago at Mary Provost's Theatre, having heard the said Wilkes' acting praised. It is about as much like his father's as the wax bust of Henry Clay, in the window down near Howard Street, a few blocks below the theatre, is like the genuine orator in the Capitol, when his best electricity was flashing alive in him and out of him.[8]

Years later, August 16, 1885, Whitman wrote of the elder Booth in the *Boston Herald*. Fifty years had not dimmed his memory of the great Booth's acting. Whitman wrote what is probably the best description of him on record. It is interesting to compare criticisms of both father and son in their favorite role of Richmond. Whitman called the elder Booth's performance of Richard "one of the most marvellous pieces of acting ever known." Whitman continues with his poetic description:

> I never saw an actor who could make more of the said hush or wait, and hold the audience in an indescribable, half-delicious, half-irritating suspense.... He vitalized and gave an unnameable race to those traditions with his own electric idiosyncrasy. The words, fire, energy, abandon found in him unprecedented meanings. I never heard a speaker or actor who could give such a sting to hauteur or the taunt. I never heard from any other the charm of unswervingly perfect vocalization without trenching at all on mere melody, the providence of music.

This further substantiated in the memoirs of actor Walter M. Leman, who carefully studied the elder Booth's performances:

> Mr. Booth's absolute identification with the character he represented, I think, can never have been exceeded by any actor of any era or clime ... the lightning glance of eyes that flashed defiance — pity — despair — revenge or love, with equal power, they impressed upon the listener the actuality and presence — not of Booth — but of Richard, King of England.[9]

And critic H.D. Stone particularly remembered the elder Booth's death scene in *Richard III*:

> His eyes, naturally large and piercing appeared greatly to increase in size and fairly to gleam with fire, while large drops of perspiration oozed from his forehead and coursed down his cheeks.[10]

Those electric eyes "blazing with hellish malignity" Wilkes inherited from his father. Those who saw both of them perform declared the look was the same in both: the father image, which could have been inherited and not imitated. When the elder Booth died, Wilkes was 14 years of age and had had no opportunity to see his father perform. During the last ten years of his life, the elder Booth spent considerable time with his family on the farm 25 miles outside Baltimore, making only occasional professional tours. It was Edwin who toured with their father and provided a strong backbone during Booth's last years, which were dominated by physical and mental illness.

In comparison, John A. Ellsler remembered that fiery, untamed method of Wilkes Booth, and remarked:

> Indeed, to my mind, he was the only Richard, after his father. His fifth act was terribly real, while his fight with Richmond was a task that many a good swordsman dreaded. John Wilkes, as Richard, never knew when he was conquered, consequently he was never ready to die, until it was evident to him that his death was necessary to preserve Richmond's life according to the story and the text of the tragedy. In many instances he wore poor Richmond out, and on one occasion Richmond was compelled to whisper, "For God's sake, John, die! Die! If you don't I shall."[11]

Wilkes underwent several narrow escapes due to his overplaying the part. Frequently he missed his cues which resulted in knifing himself or his opponent. Dueling scenes on stage have to be carefully planned and exacting routines worked out. Booth did have a plan for the fight scene. He and his opponent were supposed to count and time each thrust, which placed the actors at a certain place on the stage. Stage business such as this is risky; even at best, accidents do occur. Stage lighting affects the actor's perspective. Emotional tensions and the excitement add to the hazard.

At the time Wilkes was playing in New York City, his brother Edwin was appearing abroad. Wilkes sent his brother clippings of his reviews, among which was this review from the *New York Herald*, March 18, 1862:

> Mr. Booth undertook no small task when he attempted at act a character in which his father was famous, and which his brother Edwin plays so well; but the result justifies the undertaking. As Edwin in face, form, voice and style resembles the elder Booth, so the debutant last evening is almost a facsimile of Edwin, and in the first three acts of the play these brothers could no more be distinguished than the two Dromios. But in the fourth and fifth acts, J. Wilkes Booth is more like his father than his brother. He reads the play capitally, and makes all the well known points with ample effect. But in the last act he created a veritable sensation. His face blackened and smeared with blood, he seemed Richard himself; and his combat with Richmond (Mr. Tilton) was a masterpiece. An audience packed and crammed beyond the usual limits of the theatre applauded him to the echo. Mr. Booth has had much experience in the provinces, and his conception and rendition are most mature, his self-possession extraordinary.

Richard III was so successful that Booth presented it 11 times during his New York engagement. Contrary to procedure in "the provinces," where the bill was changed nightly, with added attractions each evening, Booth presented one play each evening with only the orchestra as accompaniment. Booth successfully packed the old Wallack Theatre (Mary Provost's) for three weeks, in spite of competition from the numerous other theaters of New York City.

Because of the success of Richard, Booth did not have much opportunity to present many other plays. *Hamlet* was presented once, March 24th. The *Herald*, the following day, thought his Richard superior to his Hamlet:

> Mr. Booth's Hamlet is not so excellent and consistent a performance as his Richard Third or Charles de Moor [in *The Robbers*], but it is very well read throughout, and has evidently been carefully studied. The melancholic, philosophical scenes were only good; but when the action was hurried and the passion intense, Mr. Booth was more like himself, and marvellously like his father. Decidedly, his forte is in melodramatic, rather than in quiet, classical, intellectual characters.

The *New York Times* liked him in other characters. Pescara in *The Apostate*, "immensely effective"; in *The Robbers*, "admirable" and the New York *World* felt his faults could be overcome to produce a truly great actor.

Perhaps the most lengthy and detailed reviews of Booth's New York engagement appeared in New York's *Spirit of the Times*, March 29 through April 12, 1862. To begin his series of articles, the critic outlined the work of the great actor families, comparing the styles and prominence of the Booths, and declared that "dramatic talent often perpetuates itself in a remarkable degree." Wilkes had not yet passed his 24th birthday but, the critic remarked, he had had "a protracted and successful career in the country, marked with every general approbation." Edwin was already an established star, and the memory of the elder Booth's 25 years of unrivalled mastery on the stage presented no small challenge for the younger Booth.

In describing Wilkes Booth and his performances, the critic of the *Spirit of the Times* continued his articles:

> In person he is very like his brother Edwin, though considerably stouter. This surplus strength is of great advantage, however, in such work as he has to do in the last act of Richard. He has a fine presence, but lacks in grace and dignity of carriage — a slight fault, a country habit, that will soon wear away under the influence of city experience. He has a quick, expressive eye; and his other features are mobile and under good control. His voice is so much like Edwin's that it is only in its greater power a casual hearer can detect the difference. With such advantages in the way of solid capital, advantages of hereditary talent, person, features and voice, it is safe to predict that study and practice alone are required to raise the young artist to the first rank of historic merit.
>
> My memory is not very distinct of his father's Richard, but I think in the main he has pretty closely followed that excellent pattern.... Young Booth makes Richard a stirring, active villain, busy with his grand ambition; soliloquizing, scheming, making love, dissembling.... With a firm step he hastens on from point to point, his eye constantly seeing in the near future the crown, the "bright reward of ever-daring minds." His soliloquies are full of restless gesture, and declamation of doubtful propriety in artistic view, but then it is Gloster all over; no one would suspect that uneasy villain of wasting time in smoothly-spoken sentences, said to himself only; he had no minutes for oratory, nor desire to spout if he had, since the Demosthenean "action! action!" was his rule of life. This uneasiness from "Now is the winter of our discontent..." Mr. Booth gradually increases, until, in the last act, it culminates in a whirlwind, a tornado of rapid execution, hurrying the spectator along, with resistless power, to a climax unequalled in thrilling effect by any Richard that I have seen, not excepting the father himself.

The critic felt that Wilkes Booth's Richard was just about what most thinking people would judge the character to be, and under his interpretation Booth gave "an embodiment at once vigorous and truthful, full of excellent acting, and with fewer defects, to my mind, than any actor that I have seen in the part for many years." He called the combat scene a wonder of art, and played with thrilling effect. He gives a detailed analysis of Booth's power, when Richard makes his final effort, grasping his two-edged sword with both hands and chopping at Richmond "with the ferocity of hate and desperation, foot to foot, breast to breast, hewing over his shoulders...."

For Booth's characterization of Charles de Moor in Schiller's *The Robbers*, "a play bloody enough to satisfy the appetite of a cannibal," the same critic thought Booth "admirable, and in scenes with the father was great.... Booth's playing rose gradually in power and intensity, and wrought his audience to the wildest enthusiasm."

However, this critic, continuing in the *Spirit of the Times*, April 5, 1862, did not appreciate Booth's rendition of *Hamlet*:

> Not that he conceived wrongly, or played badly.... Mr. Booth seems to me, too energetic, too positive, too earthy, real and tangible for Hamlet.... He failed to convey and enforce that sympathy to and from the audience.... I found coming upon myself, a sensation of dullness...

The critic liked Booth best in melodramatic parts. There he felt he was perfectly at home. In *The Apostate*, Booth played "that condensed epitome of villainy, Count Pescara.... There is a terrible earnestness in his eye, a waking of every nerve and fibre in his frame, that gives immense effect...." Comparing the role to that of Richard, the critic noted:

> He seems to revel in rascality, to enjoy the devilish tricks he puts upon his victims, to glory like another Lucifer in the misery he has caused. His Mephistophelean sneer, his demonic glare, and pity-murdering laugh, fairly curdle the blood, and haunt one like the spectres of a dream.

After seeing Booth as Macbeth, the critic carefully outlined his impressions of that performance. He thought his Macbeth not as good as his Richard, but better than his Hamlet. He felt that Mrs. Farren, famous for her role as Lady Macbeth, "was everywhere equal, and in some points superior to her Macbeth." On the whole, however, he felt:

> Mr. Booth finely portrays the irresolution of Macbeth, from the first interview with his wife, giving by his restless eye and troubled visage, the cue which makes her say: "Your face, my Thane, is as a book, where men may read strange matters." The whole scene with Lady Macbeth was well done. The dagger scene was not great; Mr. B. lacks the delicacy of execution necessary to embody the emotions of supernatural fear. Further on he was better, and went through the murder scene exceedingly well. His reading of "Duncan is in his grave," was a fine touch of pathos, made solemn by remorse. In the banquet scene, he was forcible without ranting, a fact greatly in his favor, since so many Macbeths tear themselves in these celebrated speeches. The sudden transition from quivering fear to courteous and even careless ease, on the final exit of the ghost, was a good point. Thenceforward he was good throughout, working up to the requirements of the text with fine effect, and keeping well in view the remorse and fear which struggle in Macbeth's troubled heart. The semi-soliloquies about his age, the flight of time, were very well done. Of course the combat was good, though less terrific than in Richard.

In summation of Booth's New York engagement, the critic concluded that Booth had proved himself to be an actor of genius and talent, with the capacity of becoming very great in "the more tempestuous sort of tragedy and melodrama, but all his rude strength wants toning, refining, and educating into tractable harmony...."

A rival critic, reporting in the April 7 New York *Herald*, concluded that

> in the round of characters that he performed he displayed unmistakable evidences of original talent, often crude in its conceptions, it is true, and unequal in its power of expression, but still developing great future promise.... He has had an opportunity of testing before a metropolitan audience the abilities that have won him such a reputation in the provinces. That he has passed through the ordeal with so fair a success is a proof that there is the stuff in him to make a first class tragedian, if he chooses to correct by study the extravagances that disfigure his impersonations, and which, we fear, have been more or less confirmed by the undiscriminating applause of country audiences. Mr. Booth leaves town today to fulfill a long list of engagements in the Eastern and Western cities. We wish him every success, and trust that when he again returns to New York he will show that he has benefitted by the criticism to which he has been subjected to here.

During his New York engagement, Booth was having to make decisions as to his next move. Theater schedules had to be arranged, managers and agents had to work out the runs in concurrence with him. The following abrupt letter written from the St. Nicholas Hotel to his friend and business manager, Joseph Simonds, gives an idea of the necessary theatrical planning.

St. Nicholas
March 23d [1862]

Dear Joe

Telegraphed you yesterday that De Bar [manager, St. Louis theater] won't let me off, so if I come to Boston, it must be for the two weeks commencing May 12th. So tell Keach [acting and stage manager, Boston Museum] to write at once, that I may answer Milwaukee and Cincinnati.

Just rec'd yours of 22d. No news of Joe. Have hunted every place I can think of. I can't tell what to do. Poor Mother will take it so hard. I will write you again in a few days. Excuse this hasty scrawl. Remember me with best wishes to the Rugebur [?].

Your true friend.

J. Wilkes Booth.[12]

The "Joe" referred to was Booth's youngest brother, Joseph Booth, who had disappeared. A failure on the stage, he had become a doctor. It was rumored that he was doing undercover work for the Confederacy, which might account for his disappearance. Astonishingly enough, he was finally reported to be in Australia. But the disappearance of Wilkes' brother coming at the time of the New York City engagement, probably was added anxiety just when he was most anxious to make a good metropolitan showing.

And so the New York engagement came to an end. Wilkes was not destined to play again in New York City except for one special performance of *Julius Caesar* with his brothers.

CHAPTER 13: St. Louis–Boston "I Am Myself Alone!"

Booth's next engagement brought him back to St. Louis and Ben De Bar's Theatre. For this new offering, the *Daily Missouri Democrat* (which was a "Republican" paper) offered this superlative report on April 21, 1862:

> The greatest tragedian in the country, Mr. J. Wilkes Booth, will commence an engagement at the St. Louis Theatre this evening, appearing as Charles De Moor in Schiller's great play *The Robbers*. This young tragedian has just concluded a successful engagement in New York City, and was acknowledged by the press and public of that city, as being equal to his father, the great Booth, as we were fond of calling him. Mr. Booth is only engaged for a very few nights, and we would impress upon all those who love to witness good, legitimate acting, the necessity of availing themselves of the present opportunity, as Mr. Booth will shortly leave for Europe to fulfill an engagement. Our citizens have now an opportunity of showing their willingness to support the legitimate drama by filling the house during the engagement of Mr. Booth.

After the opening, the following day's paper stated:

> The greatest tragedian now in America, Mr. J. Wilkes Booth, made his appearance last evening and was greeted with a crowded house.

And for the following performance of *Hamlet*:

> A full and fashionable house last night witnessed his superb performance of *Hamlet*. He is, undoubtedly the best and most original tragedian now on the American stage; his style is entirely his own, never showing the least symptoms of imitation...

For the *Richard III* performances, we again find overwhelming praise. Continuing their series of reviews, the *Daily Missouri Democrat* unequivocally stated:

> His *Richard III* is unsurpassed by any other living actor, his performance of the part being entirely original, introducing many new and startling effects. The fight with Richmond (played by J.E. Carden) in the last scene has never been equalled by any of his predecessors.

and for the romantic *Marble Heart*; the critic called it

> the most decided success of the season; Mr. Booth's acting of the double part, Phidias and Raphael, was inimitable. It is by general desire to be repeated tonight, after which, although so great a success, it must be withdrawn, this being the last night but four of the engagement of Mr. Booth, and he promised to perform a different character each evening.

The engagement closed on May 3rd, and Booth left his quarters at Scollay's Planters' House in St. Louis for Boston. In Boston — no easy place to

Portrait of John Wilkes Booth by Mathew Brady. Half-length seated with hand on hip. From the Brady-Handy Collection, Library of Congress.

please—Booth was again hailed for his originality in *Richard III.* Leading ladies in his support were Kate Reignolds and Emily Mestayer. Following the opening night, May 13, 1862, the *Boston Daily Evening Transcript* gave this articulate report:

> Last evening J. Wilkes Booth made his first appearance in Boston in the difficult character, Richard the Third. The house was crowded to its utmost capacity by the intelligent, brilliant and sympathetic audience, and he was called twice before the curtain to receive the reward of his exertions in hearty plaudits. His personations was in many respects original, and showed a close study and vivid conception of the individuality of the character.... Richard's jests are more terrible than other men's imprecations, and the essential wickedness which penetrates his whole character and speech was never lost of by Booth for the purpose of making points.

88

The critics felt that Wilkes reminded one of his father in many respects, but that he did not imitate him. He felt that there was strong indication of genius in his acting, and that he was "perhaps the most promising young actor on the American stage." The standard was high, for here the elder Booth was greatly admired, and Edwin Booth was also popular.

After the first week of Wilkes' engagement, which had been played to "prolonged and enthusiastic plaudits from the largest audience even assembled within the walls of the Museum," a different kind of review was published in the Boston *Daily Advertiser*, May 19, 1862. In this we get the first of a series of criticisms regarding the clinical aspects of Booth's elocution:

With a view to observing if Mr. Wilkes Booth were winning for himself his father's triumphs, or if he were likely to do so, we have taken pains to see him in each of the characters which he assumed during the last week: Richard III, Romeo, Charles de Moor, and Hamlet. We have been greatly pleased and greatly disappointed. In what does he fail? Principally, in knowledge of himself – of his resources, how to husband and how to use them. He is, apparently, entirely ignorant of

Playbill of Booth in The Stranger, *Boston Museum, May 20, 1862. From the Harvard College Library Theatre Collection.*

BOSTON MUSEUM

ACTING AND STAGE MANAGER... ....Mr E. F. KEACH

THE LAST WEEK

POSITIVELY, OF THE YOUNG AMERICAN TRAGEDIAN,

MR. J. WILKES BOOTH

☞The Management would urge an early application for seats on the remaining nights of Mr BOOTH's engagement, as the

EXTRAORDINARY FURORE

Excited by this Young Artist's histrionic efforts has never been equalled by any star at the Museum. He will have the honor of appearing this evening as

THE STRANGER!

Mrs HALLER...................... ....Miss KATE REIGNOLDS

THE GLORIOUS FARCE,

LEND ME FIVE SHILLINGS

GOLIGHTLY.....................................Mr W. WARREN

ON TUESDAY EVENING, MAY 20th, 1862,

The Performance will commence with the Overture...... . ...,,..LE SERMENT.

Leader and Musical Director..............................Julius Eichberg.

After which, the Ever Popular and Pathetic Play, in 5 acts, entitled the

STRANGER!

Or—MISANTHROPY AND REPENTANCE·

THE STRANGER...........Mr J. WILKES BOOTH

Baron Steinfort.......Mr F. Hardenburgh	Wilhelm.....................Mr Bartlett
Count Wintersen.......... ...J. Whiting	George... ....Bennet
Francis....... ....J. Wilson	Countess Wintersen......Miss L. Anderson
Solomon.... ....R F. McClaunin	Charlotte....... ..Miss Josephine Orton
Peter ....W. Warren	Annette, with Ballad, 'I have a silent sorrow
Tobias...............Sol. Smitn, Jr	here'.............Miss Oriana Marshall
Karl.. ....Delano	Claudine.................Miss L. Baker
Mrs Haller.... .... Miss Kate Reignolds	

LA MANOLA.....................................Miss ROSE WOOD

BRILLIANT SELECTIONS BY THE.............................ORCHESTRA

To conclude with the Favorite Farce, entitled

LEND ME FIVE SHILLINGS!

Mr Golightly......... ...Mr W. Warren	First Waiter......... .....Mr Bartlett
Major Phobbs........ ...J. F. Ketchum	Second Waiter ....Delano
Capt. Spruce..................Whiting	Mrs Major Phobbs......Miss L. Anderson
Moreland.... ....Wheelock	Mrs Capt. Phobbs. ..Miss Oriana Marshall
Sam................. . ...Blake	

☞Mr BOOTH'S impersonation of CHARLES DE MOOR having been received with immense enthusiasm, the Play of the " ROBBERS !" will be repeated on WEDNESDAY EVENING.

WEDNESDAY AFTERNOON—the New Comedy, "SHORT AND SWEET!" and the "INVISIBLE PRINCE!"

Admission 25Cents. Orchestra and Reserved Seats 50 Cents Children under 12 years of age 15 Cents.

Exhibition Hall open at 6 1-2 ......Evening Performance commence at 7 1-2 o'clock. Afternoon Performance at 3 o'clock.

TREASURER.. ....Mr GEO. W. BLATCHFORD

F. A. Searle, Steam Job Printer—Journal Building—118 Washington Street the main principles of elocution. We do not mean by this word merely enunciation, but the nature and proper treatment of the voice, as well. He ignores the fundamental principle of all vocal study and exercise — that the chest, and not the throat or mouth, should supply the sound necessary for singing or speaking.... When Mr. Booth wishes to be forcible or impressive, he produces a mongrel sound in the back of the mouth or top of the throat, which by itself would be unintelligible and without effect; by a proper use of his vocal organs he might draw from that fine trunk of his a resonant, deep tone whose mere sound in the ear of one who knew not the language should give a hint of the emotion to be thereby conveyed. In this connection we need simply say that his proclivity to a nasal quality is more apparent, and bodes great harm to his delivery if not checked at once...

Whether or not Booth took any of the criticisms seriously is not known. It is doubtful, at this late date, if he could have changed his delivery from throat to chest, for the habit had already been established. There are many contradictory statements as to the quality and tone of his voice. Some have insisted that his voice was nasal, harsh and ill-trained, while others have recounted (as late as the summer of 1864) that "he possessed a voice so smooth and yet so strong and forceful."[1]

At this time, the Boston *Post* offered this comparison of the Booth brothers:

Edwin has more poetry, John Wilkes more passion; Edwin has more melody of movement and utterance, John Wilkes more energy and animation; Edwin is more correct, John Wilkes more spontaneous; Edwin is more Shakespearean, John Wilkes more melo-dramatic; and in a word, Edwin is a better Hamlet, John Wilkes a better Richard III.

This is probably the best comparison on record of the two brothers. It would also seem to fit in with Walt Whitman's impressions. He loved the fire and genius of the elder Booth, and he thought Edwin "had everything but guts.... Edwin was never supreme, perhaps his one defeat was that he did not let himself go.... He is a man of bright parts, interesting: you can enjoy him: but he is not a genius of the first class — not anywhere near first class...."[3]

In comparing their own roles, Wilkes admitted that Edwin's Hamlet was the better. Edwin admitted that he was a failure as Claude Melnotte and as Romeo, two of Wilkes' outstanding roles. At rehearsal one day, some of the players were praising Wilkes' Hamlet, when he declared with truth and modesty, "No, no, no! There is but one Hamlet to my mind; that's my brother, Edwin. You see between ourselves he *is* Hamlet, melancholy and all!"[4] And at a later date, Edwin was reported to have said, "John Wilkes had the genius of my father, and was far more gifted than I."[5]

To the satisfaction of many, however, Wilkes also played a pleasing version of Hamlet. Wilkes knew the value of interpreting the character differently, because all the star tragedians tried their luck with this complex character. He was never one to copy, but to strike out on his own as he felt it. His staging was different; actors appearing with him learned to expect the unusual, the daring, the bold departure from the set ways of presenting well known plays. According to fellow actor E.A. Emerson, Booth's directing was not only outstanding but ideal in relationship to his cast. Emerson had these comments:

He was the gentlest man I ever knew. He was not feminine, yet gentle as a
woman. In rehearsal he was always considerate of the other actors, and if he
had a suggestion to make, made it with the utmost courtesy, prefacing it
with; "Now Mr. _____, don't you think that perhaps this might be a
better way to interpret that?" In this he differed from his older brother,
Edwin, who was always harsh and commanding, showing little feeling for
the young actor.[6]

It might have been Wilkes' desperate motivation for fame that pushed
him on and made him try to outdistance his father and brother, but then
again it might have been just a genuine love of the theater, an all-consuming
desire to achieve greatness in the field of his inheritance. Others have said
that he was exceedingly jealous of the successful father image. Booth himself
told Emerson that "his father told him that he would never make an actor,
and if he turned out a failure, he did not want the family name engaged in
it."[7] As indicated already, Wilkes kept this request and did not use the family
name during his first few years on the stage.

It is true that Wilkes had never seen his father on the stage, but he had
heard many tales about the eccentricities of the elder Booth. Wilkes Booth
once said:

I know these good old tales are only lies ... I cannot see why sensible people
will trouble themselves to concoct ridiculous stories of their great actors.
We know that two-thirds of the funny anecdotes about our father are dis-
graceful falsehoods.... I often wonder where the fun is, where the merit lies.[8]

The many comparisons with his father and his brother were beginning
to provoke him. Once while sitting in the saloon-billiard parlor of John
Deery, next door to Ford's Theatre in Washington, D.C., one of his drinking
companions told him, "You'll never be the actor your father was!" To which
Booth ironically replied with a frown on his heavy brows, "When I leave the
stage I'll be the most famous man in America."[9]

Here again, we have the possibility of the significance of the father
image, an image which at the beginning of his career he hoped for, but later
on we find him hoping the public would accept him for himself and stop the
comparison. His playbills and newspaper advertisements had begun to carry
the phrase: "I am myself alone!"

John Wilkes Booth got carried away with the fierce realism of his portrayals. When he fought, it was no ordinary fight. Kate Reignolds, his leading
lady, related her harrowing experiences during her performances with him:

It is my earnest belief that if ever there was an irresponsible person, it was
this sad-faced, handsome boy. He was as undisciplined on the stage as off....
He told me that he generally slept smothered in steak and oysters to cure his
own bruises after *Richard III*, because he necessarily got as good as he
gave—in fact more, for though an excellent swordsman, in his blind passion
he constantly cut himself. How he threw me about! Once even knocked me
down, picking me up again with a regret as quick as his dramatic impulse
had been vehement. In *Othello*, when with fiery remorse, he rushed to the
bed of Desdemona after the murder, I used to gather myself together and
hold my breath, lest the bang of his scimitar gave when he threw himself at
me should force me back to life with a shriek.... In the last scene of *Romeo
and Juliet*, one night, I vividly recall how the buttons on his cuff caught my

hair, and in trying to tear them out he trod on my dress and rent it so as to make it utterly useless afterward; and in his last struggle literally shook me out of my shoes! The curtain fell on Romeo with a sprained thumb, a good deal of hair on his sleeve, Juliet in rags and two white satin shoes lying in the corner of the stage! He was ever spoiled and petted, and left to his unrestrained will. The stage door was always blocked with silly women waiting to catch a glimpse as he passed, of his superb face and figure.... He succeeded in gaining position by flashes of genius, and the necessity of ordinary study had not been borne in upon him. No life could have been worse for such a character than that of an actor....[10]

Kate Reignolds' impressions of John Wilkes Booth are further confirmed by Walt Whitman, who saw him perform several times. Whitman recalled that "he was a queer fellow: had strange ways: it would take some effort to get used, adjusted, to him: but now and then he would have flashes, passages, I thought, of real genius."[11]

CHAPTER 14: Chicago–Louisville–Lexington–
St. Louis–Cincinnati–Boston
"Youngest Star in the World"

On June 2, 1862, Wilkes Booth returned to McVicker's Theater in Chicago for three weeks, where he set up his private quarters at the Tremont House. Opening in *Richard III*, he again made a very favorable impression. His *Hamlet* was compared to the *Hamlet* of Murdock with divided opinions. He was most lauded for his romantic roles in which his youthful appearance made him ideal for such parts as Claude Melnotte, Charles de Moor, and Romeo.

His popularity was now at its height, and his income accordingly soared to figures only dreamed of by others in the acting profession. He was giving stiff competition to the older players, for this was a time when youth and beauty dominated the stage. No longer could aging actresses and actors get away as coy sobrettes and rakish first walking gentlemen. Forrest, the king of players, was feeling his rheumatic age, and quarreling with the critics when they panned his performances.

With only a three-day break, Booth went from Chicago to fulfill a three-week engagement in Louisville, Kentucky — back again to the Louisville Theater where the previous December and January he had played to "large and fashionable audiences" for four weeks. His popularity was undiminished. Crowds packed the entrance to the stage door following each performance. Shops sold his photographs by the hundreds. His fan mail reached epic proportions. Even so, this Louisville engagement lasted only six days, or one "split week," "other commitments" not being explained. On his closing performance, Tuesday, July 1st, Booth presented a new play, the first presentation of George L. Aiken's *The Gun-Maker of Moscow*.[1]

Booth was receiving offers from theater managers from all over the country. By this time he could pick and choose to fill his schedule as he pleased. He dictated terms as to salary, benefits, and plays.

Back in Philadelphia for the remainder of the summer, we find him answering a request:

> No. 923 Chestnut St.
> Philada.
> Aug. 3d /62
> T.V. Butsch, Esq.
>
> Dear Butsch
> In answer to yours of July 31st, which has just come to hand. You must know that my time till after March, is all filled up with the exception of the

two weeks mentioned in my last, Nov. 24th /62 and Jan 5th /63. If Miss Thompson will not let you off, why then I will come for the one week beginning Jan. 5th. Share after eighty dollars. And half clear benefit. I would like to come for two weeks, but you see its impossible on a/c of other engagements. If this suits you, and she lets you off from Nov. 24th, why you can book me for <u>both dates</u>, if not, I will come Jan. 5th. Let me know as soon as she writes. Excuse this hasty scrawl.

Yours truly
J. Wilkes Booth.[2]

Reporting the opening of the fall season, the Lexington *Observer and Reporter*, October 25, 1862, tells us that "the elite of Lexington theatergoers were thrilled by the first appearance of the greatest tragedian of the age, Mr. John Wilkes Booth," who appeared at the Opera House in two of his favorite roles, *Richard III* and as Charles de Moor, in *The Robbers*.

The following Monday, Booth made a return engagement to Louisville for two weeks. There we are told that he was welcomed with the usual crowds and flattery. Indeed, "the theatre opened last night under the happiest auspices, that is to say, with a suffocating, crowded auditorium...." Then with only one day to travel, he went directly to Cincinnati for another two-week engagement.

The first of December he again played McVicker's Theater in Chicago. For three weeks he presented a wide variety of plays to "much praise and criticism from the drama critics." So great was his variety that the popular *Richard III* was now being kept to one performance per week.

Booth's Chicago success is mirrored in his correspondence to friend and business manager Joe Simonds. Also typical in the following letter is Booth's usual compassion toward the distress of another. It would be interesting to know more about Frank Hardinburgh and why Booth felt that he could appreciate his sad unexplained bereavement more than anyone else:

Chicago
Dec. 6th [1862]

Dear Joe

Yours of the 1st rec'd. Am much obliged to you, my dear boy, for attending to my bus. with so much punctuality. Have rec'd dresses [costumes]. Am much pleased with them.

Poor Frank Hardinburgh. I have been wanting to write to him every day, but know not how to do it. The more quiet we can keep in such sad afflictions, I deem is better for the mourner. I do not like to write him for fear of opening his wounds afresh. Yet would not have him think me indifferent to his misery. For I am sure there is no one <u>except himself</u>, who can appreciate his sad bereavement <u>more</u> than I.

I must now run to the theatre, Joe. It seems always the case when I am about to write to you. My bus. here has been great, near $900 on my first week. Remember me with best wishes to Monty Field, Keach, Warren and all my friends.

Excuse this.

Yours as ever
J. Wilkes Booth.[3]

Chicago papers announced that "John W. Booth is to make his first appearance in the Brooklyn Academy of Music on Dec. 30th, playing the role

archers extending in line of battle. Carrying
out that line I draw down right of stage.
And the Lord, Mayors scene too (but of 9 act)
could be made something of. Think of it.

I am glad Ned is doing so well
Give my love to him. Arrange but: as you
think best,   Excuse this hurried scrawl.

Wishing you all that's good, I am to you
now and ever the same————

                              J. Wilkes. Booth.)

P.S.
Best wishes to Monty. Warren. Wolff & Simonds.
                                                    yours
                                                    JWB.

Chicago Dec 8th /62

"Friend" Keach

I will endeavour to write
a few lines in answer to yours
of the 1st so here goes. The
Scenes I rec'd all right and am
highly delighted with the
thought's I wrote you of the
other day etc. Now I
would either send them
the scenery scene, on stage of
either the "Cathn. As I other
most fame: scenes". Among the
Bailiff (which all the Baltimore
in the world) ran over two
weeks. to him of $800. I sent
to my mother.

(Dry goods does indeed hang high
(dear Mary she meant) I have picked up

1/2 on an average this year;
over $650 per week. By first
week here I rec'd one $900.
And this week has earned
better.

I am glad
the Numerous holds her own.
Pray I fear Tony will be
in the most unless I get there.
If you will go I would then
be for Richmond. I think
we can make up a front.
Card for three or four nights
in the first and last will
be the engagement, Viz — No 3
of all. (plenty of information
(with out rehearsal) and the
Coronation scene and
the scene "who saw the sun to
could be made find
Richmond the latter to bring
the left flat haunted through
turning off in Richmond Richard
tent (turned at in his previous one)
by this picture J.W.B. find on right flat

of Richelieu in response to an invitation from New York's mayor and prominent citizens." However, this did not come through at this time; Booth had other plans. His Brooklyn debut had to wait. New Yorkers were told that "the younger brother is represented to be equally, if not more gifted, than Edwin."

So, with only a Sunday break, Booth opened again at Ben De Bar's St. Louis Theater on December 22nd, and continued through January 3, 1863. We learn of his income at this time and also of his plans for the next Boston engagement, from a letter to Boston Museum manager, E.F. Keach:

Chicago
Dec. 8th /62

Friend Keach

I will endeavour to write a few lines in answer to yours of the 1st — so here goes. The dresses I rec'd all right and am highly delighted with the Romeo's. I wrote Joyce the other day, telling him I would either send him the money, or pay him when in Boston. I prefer the latter, as I do not fancy sending money by express. I have now been waiting (with all the patience in the world) for over two weeks to hear of $800 I sent to my mother.

My goose does indeed hang high. (Long may she wave.) I have picked up on an average this season over $650 per week. My first week here paid me over near $900. And this week has opened better.

I am glad the Museum holds her own. But I fear *Trag* will be in the mud when I get there. If you will go to some trouble for Richard, I think we can make it a strong card for three or four nights in the first and last week of the engagement, Viz — First of all, plenty of supernumeraries (with one rehearsal,) and then the Coronation scene. And the scene "Who saw the sun today." Could be made fine pictures. The latter by having the left flat painted camp running off in distance. Richard's tent (furnished as in his previous scene) set L.U.E. [left upstage exit]. And on right flat archers exiting in line of battle. Carrying out that line I draw down right of stage. And the Lord Mayor's scene too (but of 3d act) could be made something of. Think of it.

I am glad Ned [Edwin] is doing so well Give my love to him. Arrange bus. as you think best. Excuse this hurried scrawl. Wishing you all that's good, I am to you now and ever the same

J. Wilkes Booth

P.S. Best wishes to Monty [R.M. Field, assistant to Keach], [William] Warren [Boston actor], Wally & Simonds.

Yours
JWB.[4]

When most actors were creating the illusion by voice and body along, Booth was using many tricks of lighting, mechanics and special scenery to gain added effects, or "fine pictures" as he says in the letter above. One rehearsal with plenty of "supers" would indicate the close concentration and skill he expected from his company.

The engagement alluded to in his letter at the Boston Museum proved to be one of his most successful and longest runs. To be enthusiastically welcomed and praised in Boston spoke well for Booth, for the Boston

Opposite: facsimile of Booth's letter to Keach, Chicago, December 8, 1862. From the Gratz Collection, Historical Society of Pennsylvania.

BOSTON MUSEUM

ACTING AND STAGE MANAGER.................. ....Mr E. F. KEACH

ENGAGEMENT OF

J. WILKES

BOOTH

THE BRILLIANT RECEPTION OF THIS YOUNG AMERICAN TRAGEDIAN
IN THE CHARACTER OF

ALFRED EVELYN!

And the Unqualified Eulogiums bestowed upon the efforts of the general Dramatic
Persons, in Bulwer's Great Comedy of "Money," induces the Management
to announce it for repetition this Evening.

First time this season of the Excellent Farce,

CHRISTMAS BOXES!

JACKLEY...Mr W. WARREN

On Tuesday Evening, Jan. 27th, 1863,

The Performance will commence with the Overture....... "William Tell," Rossini.

Leader and Musical Director, JULIUS EICHBERG.

After which, the Celebrated Play, in 5 acts, entitled

MONEY!

BY SIR EDWARD LYTTON BULWER.

ALFRED EVELYN...................J. WILKES BOOTH			
Graves ....Mr W Warren	Flat............ ...W J. Hill
Sir John Vesey ....R F. McClannin	Greene........ ...H. Peakes
Sir Frederick Blount.......J. A. Smith	Sir John's Servant.... Hunter
Lord Glossmore...........J Wheelock	Toke.......... .....Delano
Stout.... .....F. Hardenbargh	Waiter at the Club........ Pitman
Captain Dudley Smooth. ...J. Wilson	Clara Douglas.... Kate Reignolds
Old Member........J. H. Ring	Lady Franklin ...Miss Emily Mestayer
Sharp ....G. F. Ketcham	Georgina... ....Miss Annie Clarke

PAS DE DEUX........ NAPOLITAINE!

MISS ROSE WOOD AND THERESE WOOD.

BRILLIANT SELECTIONS.............................ORCHESTRA

To conclude with the New and Successful Farce, entitled

CHRISTMAS BOXES!

Mr Jackley.... ....Mr W Warren	Mrs Jackley............ ...Miss Annie Clarke
Mr Holly ....Mr L. Mestayer	Mary ....Miss L. Baker
Mr. Holly .... Miss Josephine Orton	

WEDNESDAY EVENING,

J. WILKES BOOTH as OTHELLO!

(FIRST TIME IN BOSTON.)

☞ MR. W. WARREN will appear on WEDNESDAY AFTERNOON in his inimitable impersonation of **PAUL PRY.**

**Admission 25 Cents. Orchestra and Reserved Seats 50 Cents
Children under 12 years of age, 15 cents.**

Exhibition Hall open at 6 .... Evening Performances commence at 7 o'clock.
Afternoon Performances at 2 1-2 o'clock.

TREASURER.................... ......Mr GEORGE W. BLATCHFORD

F. A. Searle Printer—Journal Building—118 Washington Street Boston

---

BOSTON MUSEUM

ACTING AND STAGE MANAGER.............. ....Mr E. F. KEACH

POSITIVELY THE LAST WEEK OF

J. WILKES BOOTH

Who will assume, for the first time in Boston, the Characters of the Twin Brothers,
FABIAN and LOUIS DEI FRANCHI, in the Great Legendary Drama of the

CORSICAN BROTHERS!

☞ This remarkable piece will be presented for the first time at this establishment with New Scenery, Costumes and Mechanical Effects, and no pains will be spared to render the representation thoroughly complete in every particular. WONDERFUL ILLUSIONS WILL BE WROUGHT BY ELABORATE SCENIC AND MECHANICAL APPLIANCES.

"LOOK UPON THIS PICTURE AND ON THIS,
THE COUNTERFEIT OF TWO BROTHERS."

Mr WARREN as.........................SMASHINGTON GOIT

Monday, Tuesday and Wednesday Evenings.

FEBRUARY 9, 10 AND 11, 1863.

The Performance will commence with the Overture. "Angel of Midnight," EICHBERG,
Leader and Musical Director, JULIUS EICHBERG.

After which, the Legendary Drama, entitled the

CORSICAN BROTHERS!

FABIAN DEI FRANCHI........ { Twin		
LOUIS DEI FRANCHI............ { Brothers, }.......Mr BOOTH		
Chateau Renaud........Mr Wm. Whalley	Boise........	
Alfred Maynard............L. Mestayer	Tomaso...... ....J. H. Ring
Baron Martelli...........J. Wilson	Francoise.... .....Delano
Baron de Montgiron......J. A. Smith	Chicago Metamorandors, &c. Bartholo
M. Beauchamp...........J. Peakes	Emilie de Lesparre...... Kate Reignolds
M. Verner ....Delano	Madame de Franchi.... Emily Mestayer
Judge....................Mr Dunn	Marie......... Mrs J. Wheelock
Orlando ....G. F. Ketcham	Coralie...... ...Miss L. Baker
Coloma....................Sol. Smith, Jr	Estella...... Miss Annie Clarke
......................Hunter	Celestine..... Miss M. Andrews

Synopsis of Scenery, Incidents and Tableaux.

ACT FIRST. Room in the Chateau of the Franchi Family, at Corsica. THE VENDETTA. The Reconciliation. The Warning—"Ten Minutes past Nine."

FIRST TABLEAU..THE SPECTRE OF LOUIS

SECOND TABLEAU......THE DUEL IN THE FOREST OF FONTAINBLEAU

ACT SECOND. Interior of the Opera House, Paris during a Masqued Ball and Carnival

PAS DE TROIS..SABOTIERE

Miss ROSE WOOD, THERESE WOOD and Mr G. F. KETCHUM

DANS..DU VAISSEAU AMIRAL

Miss ROSE WOOD, THERESE WOOD, Mr G. F. KETCHUM and all the Characters

Scene 3, Montgiron's House. The Rendezvous. The Insult. The Challenge. Scene 4, The Forest at Fontainbleau. DOUBLE TABLEAU.

RE-PRODUCTION OF THE DUEL! DEATH OF LOUIS!

FABIEN AT CORSICA.

ACT THIRD. Forest of Fontainbleau. The Escape of Chateau Renaud. His Meeting with Fabian. STAY! The Challenge. The Defiance. "Guard dir!!" The Fatal hour of Nine.

The Terrific Encounter.

THE DEATH. THE APPARITION. FINAL TABLEAU.

BRILLIANT SELECTIONS............................ORCHESTRA

To conclude with the Admired Farce, entitled

SMASHINGTON GOIT

Smashington Goit....... Mr W. Warren	Mrs Fluttersome..... .Mrs J. R. Vincent	
Mr Twittely Fluttersome.R. F. McClannin	Clara....... ...Miss L. Baker	
Mr Jonas Closefist....... Sol. Smith, Jr	Nelly....... Miss Josephine Orton	
Carpenter................Delano		

☞ WEDNESDAY AFTERNOON—Mr W. WARREN will appear in his Great and Original Character of JEFFERSON S. BATKINS, Member from Cranberry Centre.

☞ THURSDAY—The Last Representation of Richard III.

☞ FRIDAY—Farewell Benefit of J. W. Booth.

☞ MONDAY, FEB. 16th—BENEFIT OF MR. W. WARREN.

**Admission 25 Cents. Orchestra and Reserved Seats 50 Cents.
Children under 12 years of age, 15 Cents.**

Exhibition Hall open at 6.............Evening Performances commence at 7 o'clock.
Afternoon Performances at 2 1-2 o'clock.

TREASURER...........................Mr GEORGE W. BLATCHFORD

F. A. Searle Printer—Journal Building—118 Washington Street, Boston.

Playbills: left, Booth in Money, Boston Museum, January 27, 1863; from the collection of the author. Right: Booth in The Corsican Brothers, Boston Museum, February 9-11, 1863; from the William Seymour Theatre Collection, Princeton University Library. Both previously unpublished.

Museum then possessed the most critical audiences in America, according to E.S. Bates, author of a series of biographical articles on the Booths.

After opening on January 19th, he continued through February 13th, playing all his popular pieces with repeats of as many as four consecutive performances of some plays. His rendition of the two Corsican Brothers, "for the first time presented with new scenery, costumes, and wonderful illusions wrought by mechanical effects," made it one of the most popular plays. Booth's leading lady was Kate Reignolds, who had previously appeared with him in Boston.

On Wednesday, January 21, 1863, Edwin Booth took his wife Mary Delvin to see Wilkes perform Pescara in *The Apostate*. Edwin related his delighted reaction in this letter to his friend Richard Henry Stoddard:

> I saw last night — for the first time — my brother act; he played Pescara — a bloody villain of the deepest red, you know, an admiral of the red, as 'twas, and he presented him — not underdone, but rare enough for the most fastidious "beef-eater"; Jno. Bull himself Esquire never looked more savagely at us poor "mudsills" than J. Wilkes, himself, Esquire, settle the accounts of last evening. Yet I am happy to state that he is full of the true grit — he has stuff enough in him to make suits for a dozen such player-folk as we are cursed with; and when time and study round his rough edges he'll bid them all "stand apart" like a "bully boy, with a glass eye"; I am delighted with him and feel the name of Booth to be more of a hydra than snakes and things ever was.[5]

Wilkes' Boston engagement was called "truly extraordinary" by the *Transcript*, and judging by the backed houses, Booth could have played on for two months instead of one. However, because of another engagement on February 23rd in Philadelphia, he had to close his Boston run with Bostonians crying for more.

CHAPTER 15: Philadelphia
Booth vs. Forrest

John Wilkes Booth had been itching to try his luck in Philadelphia, the city where his first season of stock proved to be so unflattering at the beginning of his career. Now, a complete master of himself, he would not stammer and forget his lines as he had done six years earlier. Besides, he wanted to challenge the great Edwin Forrest on his home ground. It is interesting that the elder Booth thought so highly of Forrest that he named a son after him. Yet the sons were never to appreciate Forrest. There was always this jealousy, or an invasion of territory between them. The work of both Edwin and Wilkes was enviously watched by the aging Forrest, who felt that both of them were a threat to his supreme popularity. Wilkes was also keeping a close watch on criticism of both Forrest and his brother, so that he would know when it was safe to spring. Said biographer Kimmel, "Encouraged by notices, and attendance at his performances, Wilkes decided to pursue Forrest to Philadelphia. The opportunity to compete with this great American tragedian submerged his painful memories of his earlier disagreeable reception there and he made arrangements for an engagement at the Arch Street Theatre, the scene of his former failures."[1]

As it turned out, Booth did not open in Philadelphia until March 2nd, since Edwin's wife Mary Delvin died that February 21st. This small actress had been frail and in poor health so that she could not throw off an attack of pneumonia. Wilkes had taken time out from his engagements to attend their wedding only three years previously. It was said that after the ceremony Wilkes instead of kissing the bride, threw his arms around his brother Edwin and kissed him warmly. Sister Asia did not attend or approve the match. But at Mary Delvin's death, Wilkes cancelled his performances. A "card to the public" headed the Arch Street Theatre playbill for February 23rd, stating that Wilkes had "felt the necessity imperative upon him to join his afflicted brother."

Opening a week later at the Arch Street Theatre in Philadelphia — the same theater that had heckled his performances in 1857 and 1858, brought a different reaction from the critical Philadelphia audiences. At this time Philadelphia was the center of the theatrical showmanship as opposed to New York City today. The "Arch," which was now under the direction of Mrs. John Drew, glorified Booth as a star performer. The *Press* saw "no reason why he shouldn't become a great actor," stating that his genius needed only cultivation and development.

Mrs. Drew, the grandmother of the latterday Barrymores, John, Ethel and Lionel, was Booth's leading lady. Also in the cast was his old friend J.W.

Albaugh, who had substituted for him during the recovery from the shooting accident in Georgia. William Fredericks, the acting and stage manager who had given Wilkes such a bad time several years previously, was still at his post. This was possibly another reason why Booth was anxious to prove himself in Philadelphia: to show up those who had belittled him. He was now in the position of giving orders to managers.

Booth was now beginning to speculate with investments. His future seemed assured. He was making at least $20,000 per year at this time. "For one single season his cash book showed earnings deposited in the bank of twenty-two odd thousand dollars."[2]

Booth's manager friend, Joseph Simonds, received the following letter about this time:

> Philadelphia
> Feb. 28th [1863]
>
> J.H. Simonds, Esq.
> Dear Joe
> Yours of 26th rec'd. I think with you that the water power stock is a good investment and am only sorry I did not buy long ago. When you get this we can not tell what it will be selling for. However, I would invest at once. I send you by this draft for fifteen hundred dollars ($1500.) Invest it for me at once, dear Joe. I think I will have to make you my banker and give you an interest in my speculations, so that if we are lucky you may be able in a few years to throw aside those musty ledgers. I am anxious to hear from you about the Ogdensbergh mail road. I can find the town but no road on the map. To where does it run. Find out all about it and let us invest at once if it is all you have heard it is. I would like to risk about $2000 in it. Telegraph or write on the receipt of this, to 1021 Race St. Am anxious to hear from you.
> Your true friend
>
> J. Wilkes Booth.[3]

On the very next day, Booth wrote again to Joseph Simonds, his broker, at the Boston Mechanics' Bank. This time Booth was a little worried after noticing the theater situation in Philadelphia for shows running prior to his own opening. Could his engagement in Philadelphia be a failure also? His old anxiety of Philadelphia seemed to return as he cautions Joe:

> Philada.
> March 1st [1863]
>
> Dear Joe
> I open here tomorrow. I don't expect to do much, The theatres here seem filled nightly with empty benches.
> I sent you a draft yesterday for $1500. I want you to be careful of my money as if it was your own (but there's no good in saying that, for I know you will, and in fact more so) but what I mean is to "look before you leap." If we make any good speculations you can count on a good percentage of profits when I sell. For you should have something for the great trouble I put you to. And I am sure you will need something to get you in time from that old desk of yours. How about the Ogdensbergh stock. Let me know too, all about the water power. Do they divide their dividends in land or money, and when and how is it paid. The draft I sent is on Spencer & Bilo [?] Co., Boston, from Drexel of Philad.
> What did Henry say about his money. Was it enough. He wrote me about it (but I guess it was before I gave it you) telling me to send it. It's raining here

Portrait of Booth by Mathew Brady. Half-length seated, looking right. From the William Wyles Collection, Princeton University Library. Previously unpublished.

very hard. I have not struck your *game* yet, but I may, and be sure I will not let them slip. I am in great haste. God bless you.

Your true friend

J. Wilkes Booth.[4]

Some scholars have attempted to find hidden meanings and coded messages in Booth's letters. It is interesting to note that someone has penciled in on the original of the above letter an asterisk after the word *"game,"* and at the bottom the asterisk indicates "Lincoln, Seward, Stanton," the three men the later conspiracy had in mind to eliminate. It is true that the last few lines of the letter do not make much sense. One would hardly think however that Booth could be giving so much time to conspiracy plans at this time, since he was so intent upon making a good showing for himself in Philadelphia, and proving himself equal if not superior to Forrest.

It cannot be assumed, as many have done, that since there were few drama critics in Booth's day, that the papers praised any theatre troupe who advertised with them. Quite the contrary, many spoke out their displeasure for some under "Local Matters" while flowery praise filled the advertisements under "Amusements." Booth came under fire of several critics, especially for his off-beat and unusual impersonations of familiar characters. The reviews from his Philadelphia engagement might have prompted this comment to his brother Junius, who was playing there: "I don't know how the Philadelphia papers will use you," wrote Wilkes from Washington, January 17, 1865, "but if they are as kind to you as to me, *why God help you say I*."[5]

The Philadelphia *Press*, March 5, 1863, devoted almost an entire column to Booth:

> The Arch Street Theatre.— Mr. John Wilkes Booth is playing what we believe is his

Playbill for The Merchant of Venice *and* Catharine and Petruchio *(i.e.,* The Taming of the Shrew*),* Arch Street Theatre, Philadelphia, March 6, 1863. From the Theatre Collection of the Yale University Library. Previously unpublished.

first star engagement in Philadelphia. He is a young man of promise, and he belongs to a great family. His father is remembered as one of the most renowned of our modern actors; his brother stands high in his profession. Mr. Booth, therefore, comes among us with many claims upon our affection and esteem. We have not seen enough of him to give a mature opinion, but we have seen enough to justify us in saying that he is a good actor, and may become a great one. His figure is slender, but compact and well made. He has a small, finely-formed head, with cold, classic features, a bright eye, and a face capable of great expression. He very much resembles his brother Edwin in tone and action. Like Edwin, he occasionally minces his words, and uses quaint pronunciation. Indeed, the resemblance is very marked.

Without having Edwin's culture and grace, and without that glittering eye that gives so much life to his Iago and Pescara, Mr. Booth has far more action, more life, and, we are inclined to think, more natural genius. He does not play *Richard III* as well as Edwin, but he plays some parts of it in a manner that we do not think Edwin can equal.

His last act, and particularly his dying scene, is a piece of acting that few actors can rival, and is far above the capacity of Edwin Booth. It is, of course, a different style from that in which we are accustomed to see the elder brother, who is great in quiet scenes, but it was wonderfully done, and shows the possession of a genius that is now rough and rugged, but may become great by constant cultivation.

And having said this much of John Wilkes Booth, our commendation must cease. We think he has a wrong conception of the character of the Duke of Gloster. He makes him a slinking, malignant cripple, so deformed as to be almost unpleasant to the eye; one who loved murder for murder's sake alone. Shakespeare has done enough to make us hate him, and some think unjustly hate, Richard III, and it seems cruel to the memory of one, who with all his vices and many noble qualities, to add intensity to the black colors of the dramatist, and the blacker daubs of Mr. Colley Cibber. We know it is the custom of actors to make Richard do nothing but murder while he smiles, but Mr. Booth even disdains to smile. His look, from the beginning to the end, is almost demoniac, and it was our constant wonder that he succeeded in making love to Lady Anne, in deceiving the mayor and Buckingham, and making all men his victims or his tools.

The Richard of Mr. Booth is, in these respects, an impossible personage. He dabbles in blood; sprinkles it on the stage after the murder of Henry; wipes his sword on his mantle (a very vulgar and disgusting thing to do), and revels in it from the beginning to the end. This all combines to make a very original and effective conception, but so much truth and poetry is sacrificed that we advise Mr. Booth to abandon it. He can be a great Richard, but he must return to his studies and endeavor to give the part a new life....

We make these suggestions to Mr. Booth in the best of feeling. We welcome him to our stage as a rising man and as the possessor of a name which we cannot regard without interest. He has our best wishes for his success. It is, perhaps, unfortunate that he has become so soon a star; but it shows ambition if not judgment, and he will find the buffs and tumbles of the young tragedian's life a fine field for experience and instruction....

But apparently, Booth knew what was good box-office. He also knew that he was striving toward an original characterization of realism. Butchered though the Cibber version of *Richard III* was, it is a fact that the restored Shakespearean version was never as popular as the Cibber version. As for the realism of the character, it was not until 1876 that Edwin Booth presented Richard without distortion, without limp, without hump, and without distorted speech, and made him more of an inwardly wicked man of genius and a human being. The Cibber version did not give opportunity for this type of approach to the character.

During the Philadelphia engagement the *North American* also commented on Wilkes' Richard:

> Every nerve quivers with the passion which his words give vent to; crime healed on crime only seems to afford fresh scope for his determined will — whilst the climax of the play, the fight between Richard and Richmond, was never given with such energy.

At the same time, the great Edwin Forrest was playing at the Chestnut Street Theatre in William Wheatley's company which included Booth's old friend John McCullough. The two theaters competed in heated rivalry with two such outstanding companies. It is said that audiences preferred the handsome and fiery Booth to the aging, vapid Forrest. It is sad to realize that when Forrest was Wilkes Booth's age, he too was extremely handsome and in great demand of his audience. The fire of Booth and the talents of Mrs. John Drew seemed to draw the crowds, and it is said that Forrest would go into a swearing tantrum whenever the name of Booth was mentioned. Says George S. Bryan:

> It is obvious that this young player, not only sought by managers as good box-office but greeted in such fashion by the press of the leading theatrical centers of the East and acclaimed by seasoned patrons of the drama in an era of gifted actors — was not, as had been misrepresented, either a foolish tyro or an empty swashbuckler. Indeed, the New York *Herald* specified that he was "most mature, his self-possession extraordinary"; and the *Times,* that he was "intellectually impressive"; and in Philadelphia the *North American* added a good word for the "poetic spirit of his Raphael" [in the play *Marble Heart*]. In Boston he made the greatest hit of any actor of his time. At twenty-five, after but a half-dozen years on the stage, he had a repertoire of at least a score of leading parts, nine of them Shakespearean — evidence that he could not have been exactly lazy.[6]

E.S. Bates' biographical sketch further reveals that:

> his acting was marked by inspiration rather than finish, and he was given to daring innovations, rendering the death of Richard III, for example, in a realistic manner that astounded his contemporaries. Although careless in his enunciation and prone to slur passages in his haste to reach the big scenes, his fire and passion more than atoned for these defects. Had his temperament permitted whole-souled attention to his art, he would probably have become one of the leading figures in American theatrical history.[7]

Comedian Roland Reed, who was a call boy at Mrs. Drew's Arch Street Theatre during this time, remembered the celebrities of that historic theater. He related that he had to sit at the stage door, but when the fight scene came in *Richard III* he would get somebody to watch for him so that he could see the scene. He would steal up to the gallery of the flies "to witness the blood-curdling combat." Reed remembered that of all the celebrities who played the Arch, Booth impressed him the most "by the elegance of his dress and manner, and his handsome face, which was so striking that no one could

fail to be impressed by it." Reed had a fond remembrance of Booth which
shows his thoughtfulness of others:

> Once, in passing out, Booth looked closely at me, and, seeing what a small
> boy I was for such a position, turned back, shook hands with me, leaving in
> my palm a substantial present, which I made all haste to spend, not fore-
> seeing what a momento of the man it would be now.[8]

John Wilkes Booth's fondness for children is alluded to in various
other stories. Such incidents recur as when he would pick up dirty street ur-
chins and affectionately say a few words, soothe a crying child who was lost
and forlorn, or pass out candies to the little children as he rode through the
streets on his horse. "Remember me, babies, in your prayers," he was wont to
tell his sister's children. The black children on the farm knew that his saddle
bags were stocked with sweets for them each time he returned to the farm.

Joseph Hazelton, program boy at Ford's Theater remembered kind
words he had received from Wilkes. He was asked, "Joseph, is that your best
cap?" "Yes, Mr. Booth," he answered. "Well, Joseph, it pleases me not at all. I
like not your cap. Come with me and we will find another." And Booth
marched Joseph off to a shop where he told the proprietor, "Kindly fit my
young friend here with a cap befitting his professional duties. One who
makes known the players of great parts should be surmounted with a proper
crown."[9] Joseph proudly wore his new cap while calling to the patrons to
direct their steps to the theater and to the stars of the evening.

Amid all the glitter of the theater and the strenuous routine, Booth
kept up a regular correspondence with Joseph Simonds regarding their investments. Again comes the following letter from Philadelphia:

> April 3d [1863]
> Dear Joe
> Did you or Orlando send me that catalog of Back Bay lands to be sold
> April 9th. However, find out about them. For lots No. 5. 6. 7. or 9. (any one
> of them) on the north side of Commonwealth Avenue. I will bid as high as
> $2.70 per foot, (their minimum value is $2.25) If you fail to get any one of
> the above, I will bid on corner lot (Commonwealth Avenue) No. 20. as high
> as $3.25 per foot. If you are not out big and fail to get any of them, I will bid
> on any one (single lot) on south side of Marlborough Street as high as 20 per
> cent above its minimum valuation, (a corner lot preferred.) Attend to this,
> dear Joe. See Keach who said something about the auctioneer being sorry he
> did not know I wanted to buy last time. Let Orlando see this. Advise with
> him about it. He promised to buy from me, or to let me know about it.
> I don't care about the lots on Marlborough St. If I buy one of them, it will
> be on spec. So if you miss the Commonwealth Ave., strike light on the first.
> When did you see Ned [Edwin]. Love to him and Mother and remember me
> to Orlando, Keach and Monty [Field].
> I have written to my old Rector in behalf of Steffin. Will send it today. I
> hope you have pretty well got over your trouble. Bless you my dear boy.
> Keep your eye open a little wider.
> Yours truly
> J. Wilkes Booth.[10]

Evidently Booth was planning to build a home for himself as well as
make investments. The piece of real estate he referred to was to become a
fashionable and aristocratic area in Boston.

CHAPTER 16: Washington, D.C. "Star of the First Magnitude"

Following his Philadelphia engagement, Booth went to Washington, D.C., then known as Washington City, for seven performances. Upon opening in *Richard III* at Grover's Theater, the Washington *Intelligencer* reported: "He played not from the stage rule, but from the soul, and his soul is inspired with genius." It was said of his *Hamlet* that the scene with his father's ghost was so realistic that one would have sworn that Booth had actually seen a ghost. People called him the "Darling of the Gods" and commented that they had never seen such fire in anyone's eyes. It was, they said, "the fire of passion whipped high."

On April 11, 1863, his opening announced him as "The Youngest Star in the World; the Pride of the American People." He had all Washington City at his feet. It was a cultural city, and beautiful in the spring, but a mudhole in winter. Pennsylvania Avenue and about a mile of Seventh Street were practically the only paved streets, and these were paved with cobblestones, which were described as having slime oozing from the stones when wet and clouds of dust arising when dry.

It was on Pennsylvania Avenue between 13th and 14th streets where Grover's National Theatre stood, and still stands as a professional theater today. It had been in operation almost thirty years before Wilkes Booth made his appearance.

In Hunter's record of the Washington theater, we are told that Wilkes Booth made his first appearance before a large and fashionable audience, and that President Lincoln and Senator Oliver P. Morton occupied a private box. "As the great Lincoln sat there, heartily applauding the young actor, how little he imagined that he beheld his fate...."[1]

But, according to the press, Lincoln saw Mrs. Drew in the farce *Pocahontas*, at a rival theater that evening. Perhaps Lincoln changed his mind as to play selection at the last minute, although he believed "a farce, or comedy is best played; a tragedy is best read at home."[2]

Yet we find William Seymour's notes, left on the Booth playbills themselves, now in Princeton University Library, which tell us that Lincoln's box was the lower one at stage level; for on the night mentioned above, Booth in the final scene, boldly knocked his Richmond, player J.M. Ward, into the presidential box. The *Intelligencer* remarked that "the effect produced upon the audience was absolutely startling and bordered upon the terrible," and that "a brilliant and fashionable audience gave unbounded applause."

106

The *Daily Morning Chronicle* believed that he had inherited much of his father's ability and talent;

indeed, when we have seen him in some of those old Shakespearean plays in which his father was so renowned, we have almost thought that the elder Booth was before us, and have been carried back to the days of our early play-going, when J.B. Booth was to our mind the real Richard, and the illusion was so complete that we involuntarily paid to him the homage belonging to a king. None of the younger Booths so often remind us of the great tragedian, their father, as John Wilkes. Edwin will doubtless be claimed by the critics the better actor, but in our judgement John exhibits more of those peculiar qualities which distinguished his great father, who had no superior and rarely an equal, upon the American or English stage.

John Wilkes is a very young man, but he has sprung at once to fame solely upon his own merits, and not upon any facetious fame which belonged to his great father.

Following the opening night, the critic continued his comparisons of the Booths, concluding that "it is difficult to determine which of the brothers excels in their representation of the bloodthirsty monarch."

Playbill of Booth in Richard III, *Grover's Theatre, Washington, D.C., April 11, 1863; from the William Seymour Theatre Collection, Princeton University Library.*

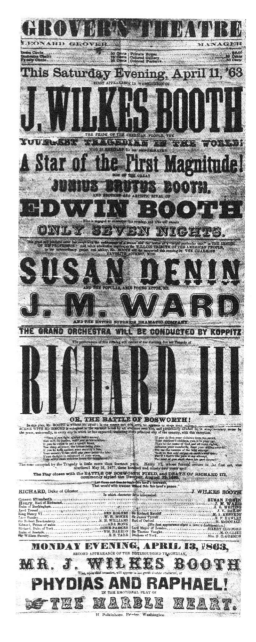

Daily praise continued as Booth played out his engagement. The Washington *Evening Star*, April 16, 1863, thought that "Young Booth has made a fine impression here, and veteran play-goers see in him a worthy son of a worthy sire." The *Daily National Republican* cited Booth's benefit performance in the following day's news:

> Mr. Booth is a young man of rare abilities, and considering his experience, really wonderful in his impersonations. His representations, notwithstanding the severe surgical operation of Monday last, entitle him to the admiration of the public.

This was the time Booth had a fibroid tumor removed from his neck. Booth's doctor, John Frederick May, in recalling the operation 24 years later, told of "a fashionably dressed, and remarkably handsome young man" who came to his office and complained of being "much annoyed by a large lump on the back of his neck, which for some time had been gradually increasing in size, and had begun to show above the collar line of the ordinary theatrical costume." The imaginative young Booth succeeded in persuading the doctor to say, if questioned, that he removed a bullet from his neck. May agreed to remove the tumor on the condition that Booth suspend his theatrical engagements and observe complete rest. This, Booth said, he could not possibly do, as he was playing an engagement with Charlotte Cushman, and must continue, but he would be very careful in his acting, and moderate his movements, so as to make no strain on the wound. But before the wound had completely healed, Booth was back in the doctor's office with the wound torn open and gaping wide. He said that "in some part of the piece he was playing with Miss Cushman, she had to embrace him, and that she did so with much force, and so roughly, that the wound opened under her grasp."[3]

Either Dr. May had confused names of actors and actresses after a 24 year period when he recalled this incident in 1887, or a deliberate contradiction concerning details of the event was instigated by Booth for some unknown reason. For Charlotte Cushman was not performing in Washington at that time, nor had she appeared with Wilkes Booth since he had appeared in minor parts with her company way back in 1858.

It would be difficult indeed to separate truth from fiction regarding the many strange and fantastic tales that have surrounded John Wilkes Booth. Most of these rumors were probably initiated by Booth himself. He gloried in dramatic effect and knew its value in building a character, both on and off the stage; and it would be in keeping with his character for him to invent the story, for example, of a jealous Montgomery, Alabama, actress shooting him in the neck. The legend of Booth was being established long before the assassination.

Among the many tales is the one about Booth throwing a wooden stool at an actor during his Washington engagement. Actually Booth had thrown a wooden wedge, about six inches long and three or four inches thick, that was being used under the stage flats and in the wings — not a stool at all. This incident occurred during a performance of *Richard III*. At a certain cue, as Richard was about to exit center stage with an escort of soldiers, the trumpets were supposed to sound off vigorously. Booth gave cue after cue but there was only silence. The prompter had failed to give the signal to the musicians. At that moment Booth, screened by the soldiers, stooped over, picked up one of the wedges, and with a quick jerk, sent it flying against the wall just a fraction of an inch above the prompter's head. W.J. Ferguson, callboy at the time, told of this instance. He related that the prompter collapsed in fright and waved the late signal frantically from the floor. Booth strode from the stage quite as if nothing unusual had happened—the delayed trumpets blaring out in full force.

Booth's erratic behavior probably resulted from fits of temper caused by persons in the company who did not perform their jobs as Booth thought they should. He was such a perfectionist and a thorough artist that he could not tolerate an inadequate or sloppy performance in his company. To say that Booth intended to kill the prompter as some have claimed would be a gross misunderstanding indeed.

Edwin Forrest often pulled similar stunts. It is said that in a certain scene he had to throw a player off stage. If the player happened to be a good player, Forrest would *carefully* throw him. But if he were a bad player, Forrest would give the poor devil such a jolt as to almost break every bone in his body: every bad actor of all time was embodied in that one thrust! Possibly in the rivalry of the two players, Booth was copying Forrest's eccentricities.

Even the mild and melancholy Edwin Booth was wont to discharge a temper on occasion. It is reported that he said, "It annoys me to see some gaping super stand where the audience can see him and I once threw a book at one."[4]

Another instance which has often been quoted is the time Booth blackened the faces of each member of his cast with pork fat dipped in lampblack during a performance. This would seem to be an insane thing to do if one does not know the ways of the stage, and as Edwin said, the comic relief of the nerve-wracking business of acting, so needed to "open the safety valve of levity." This was during a Washington performance of *The Taming of the Shrew* (then usually called *Catharine* [or *Katharine*] *and Petruchio* in Garrick's version) and Wilkes was playing the devilish Petruchio. In the banquet scene, the stage business calls for Booth to practically wreck the dining table, spank his leading lady and generally rough her up. What he did was more in line with his custom for satirical jokes and fitted the role perfectly. Beforehand, he had secretly arranged with the property man to prepare imitation slices of ham with the underside coated with lampback—the ham being merely cut out pieces of canvas painted to resemble ham on one side. At the height of his presumed fury with the player guests, Booth seized the ham and smeared each actor's face. One by one they magically turned into stage Negroes while the audience shrieked with laughter and applause. This abuse of fellow actors, his manipulation of them to their surprise and expense to achieve his own desired effects, would indicate that he treated colleaguges like props rather than people. Yet in contradiction to that the reader will recall the statement of a fellow player, E.A. Emerson, who claimed Booth was always kind and considerate and a joy to work with.

To the purist, the instance above was possibly thought of as being out of place in Shakespeare, but Booth was constantly trying out new pieces of

Three-quarter length portrait of Booth with cane, hat and gloves. From the collection of the Museum of the City of New York.

business, new ways of doing old plays, striking out in a most individual way to practice his craft. One would say that he was far ahead of his time in this respect. At a time when most actors were standing center stage and declaiming, Booth was utilizing the whole stage with acrobatics as well as voice. He habitually took his business of acting very seriously and expected his company to do the same. His productions were noted for their bits of surprise staging and unusual interpretations. He could not content himself to present any part in a conventional way. Satirical twists to old romantic parts seemed to come to him naturally. He loved joking and fun along with the work. One observer remembered him as having "a twinkle in his eye that seemed to say, if I could only think of a good joke to play on you I should be supremely happy."[5]

However, where the business of constructing a character was concerned, Wilkes, like his father before him, always completely lost himself in his characters. This absolute identification often caused strange quirks to emerge. Edwin remembered the strange temperament of the father, and he realized the strangeness that was in Wilkes. In a like mixture of tragic acting and ribaldry, the elder Booth would do unpredictable things. Edwin explained:

> Great minds to madness closely are allied.... At the very instant of intense emotion, my father while turned from the audience, would whisper some silliness or make a face.... My close acquaintance with so fantastic a temperament as my father's so accustomed me to that in him which appeared strange to others that much of Hamlet's mystery seems to me no more than idiosyncracy. It likewise taught me charity for those whose evil or imperfect genius sways them to the mood of what it likes or loathes.[6]

On April 18, 1863, Wilkes closed his Washington engagement, The Washington *Evening Star* summed it up thus: "It has been a most successful one, though short, and our play-goers feel that the name of Booth is yet to hold its own on the stage." The *Chronicle* declared his Romeo the best ever rendered in that city.

The next day after closing Booth wrote to his friend Joe Simonds about the success and also about the operation which Dr. May had performed on his neck. Booth still stuck to the story of the bullet wound rather than the removal of a tumor.

> Washington
> April 19th [1863]
> Dear Joe
>   I have just finished a fine engagement here. I am idle this week but stay on here in hopes to open the other theatre next Monday for a week or two before going to Chicago. I am glad to hear of your investment in our different specs. Try it again in anything you think will pay.
>   I enclose a letter from my old Rector which you can show our friend Stephen. In my letter to Van I said I had met Mr. Stephen very often. Also that he was a fine linguist. He wishes him to write. Excuse this, dear Joe, have a very bad pen. And am far from well. <u>Have a hole in my neck you could run your fist in. The doctor had a hunt for my bullet.</u> Once more, excuse this.
> Yours truly
> John Wilkes Booth.
> Rose sent Orlands a draft from Phila. and I sent one from here. Has he enough.[7]

So another near fatal accident failed to stop the run of performances, the tours and the strenuous routines of the actor. The scar from the above

Opposite, playbills of two of Booth's Washington D.C., appearances: left, in Hamlet, *Grover's Theatre, April 14, 1863; right: in* The Robbers, *Washington Theatre, May 9, 1863. Both from the Harvard College Library Theatre Collection. Both previously unpublished.*

ROVER'S THEATRE

NARD GROVER............................MANAGER

is Tuesday Evening, April 14, '63

THIRD APPEARANCE
OF THE DISTINGUISHED AMERICAN TRAGEDIAN,

WILKES BOOTH

APPEARANCE OF THE CHARMING FAVORITE ACTRESS,

MISS SUSAN DENIN

SPECIAL APPEARANCE OF THE YOUNG, BEAUTIFUL AND VERSATILE ACTRESS,

MISS EFFIE GERMON!

APPEARANCE OF THE POPULAR, TALENTED YOUNG ACTOR,

R. J. M. WARD!

FIRST APPEARANCE OF A GIFTED YOUNG ACTOR,

MR. CHARLES WYNDHAM!

WILL BE PRESENTED THIS EVENING THE

SUBLIME SHAKSPERIAN MASTERPIECE
DEEMED BY THE MAJORITY OF THE

PRESS, PUBLIC AND PROFESSION OF AMERICA!

To be the most thrilling effort of man's genius known in the English language. A play the beauties of which are ever so evident to foreigners that various and repeated efforts have been made to present it on the

French, German and Italian Stages

The charms of Shakspear's poetry and eloquence, displayed in this play, belongs solely to his native tongue and cannot be diverted from it.

ppitz will conduct the Grand Orchestra

WILL BE ACTED THIS EVENING

HAMLET!
PRINCE OF DENMARK.

HAMLET, Nephew to King Claudius......................J. WILKES BOOTH
In which he is unequaled by any living Actor.
Gertrude, Mother of Hamlet, (first time)..................SUSAN DENIN
Ophelia, Daughter of Polonius.........................EFFIE GERMON
Hamlet's Father..W. H. BOKEE
Lord Chamberlain.......................................BEN G. ROGERS
son to Polonius...J. M. WARD
friend to Hamlet.......................................J. B. WHITING
....J. V. DAILEY
anta,   Courtiers,..................................WM. BARROW
stern,..E. S. TARR
o,   Officers.....................................N. A. KENNEDY
lo,...M. COLLIER
o, a Soldier...HARRY CLIFFORD
ator..F. A. MONTAGUE
aradigger...EDEN ATLMER
Gravedigger..CHAS. WYNDHAM
....J. B. EVANS
Queen..FANNY RYAN

IN GREAT PREPARATION,

MACBETH.

Will soon be produced, for the first time this season, Schiller's great Tragedy,

THE ROBBERS.

H. Polkinhora, Printer, Washington

WASHINGTON THEATRE!
COR. 11th AND C STREETS, NEAR PA. AVENUE.

LESSEE AND MANAGER......................J. WILKES BOOTH

PRICES OF ADMISSION:

Parquette and Dress Circle............50 cents | Balcony Seats......................75 cents
Orchestra Chairs............................75 cents | Parterre............................25 cents
Private Boxes, $5. No Extra Charge for Secured Seats.
Doors open at 7 ; Curtain will rise at 8 o'clock.

LAST NIGHT POSITIVELY!
OF THE ENGAGEMENT OF THE EMINENT YOUNG TRAGEDIAN,

J. WILKES

BOOTH!

At the request of many citizens who were unable to witness Mr. BOOTH'S rendition of the character of CHARLES DE MOOR, on its first representation, the great Tragedy of

THE ROBBERS!

WILL BE REPEATED THIS EVENING.

J. WILKES BOOTH - as - CHARLES DE MOOR

This being positively the last appearance of Mr. Booth, in Washington, those persons desirous of witnessing him, in this great character, should not miss this opportunity.

The character of Charles De Moor is claimed by the Philadelphia Press to be Mr. Booth's best effort, excepting Richard III, and one which surpasses in true power, and brilliancy of genius, even Murdoch's noted performance of the part.

From the Daily (Baltimore) Gazette.

The young favorite acted Charles De Moor, in Schiller's sombre tragedy of "The Robbers," with great intensity and a bold originality of conception. The malediction which Charles hurls against his unnatural brother, the parricide was terrible in its deep earnestness of passion, and reached, in effect, to the thrilling. We do not hesitate to say that it is the most effective and exciting representation of the character ever presented from the stage of a Baltimore Theatre.

| Miss Alice Gray | as | Amelia |
| Mr. E. H. Brink | as | Francis De Moor |

SATURDAY EVENING, MAY 8, '63

Will be presented Schiller's great Five Act Tragedy of

THE ROBBERS

Charles De Moor,	- - -	Mr. J. WILKES BOOTH
Count de Moor		Mr. W. H. BAILEY
Francis de Moor		Mr. E.H. BRINK
Roller		Mr. N FORRESTER
Switzer		Mr. J. EDWARDS
Speigelberg		Mr. J. PARKER
Grimm		Mr. J. P. KILBOURN
Commissary		Mr. R. STEPHENS
Herman		Mr. W. BARRON
Schufterle		Mr. E. W. ACKER
Raseman		Mr. C. HILLYARD
First Robber		Mr. C WYBROW
Daniel		Mr. D WALTERS
Amelia		Miss ALICE GRAY

H. Polkinhorn, Printer, Washington

mentioned wound was to be a prime factor in the controversial identification
of his body a few years later. Whether it was a saber wound which caused
him to fight with one hand tied to his side, or a painfully sore neck, Booth the
trouper would carry on, nevertheless, endeavoring to please the public.

In 1866, an unidentified reporter was writing his impressions of Wilkes
Booth in the Capitol City as he remembered them three years previously, and
after the national tragedy. His graphic description follows:

> A sculptor would not have asked a better model for the head of Apollo....
> His eyes were dark but full of expression — those orbs that can meet in love or
> flame with passion; his glances were keen and he read character intuitively.
> In fact, he exercised a kind of magnetism over the person with whom he con-
> versed, and no one could resist his fascination. This was the secret of his
> influence over Herold, Atzerodt and Paine [three of the Lincoln assassination
> conspirators]. A mass of curling, jetty hair crowned his square forehead and
> brow.... When he spoke his eyes kindled with enthusiasm, and his voice
> which was always sweet in conversation, thrilled on the ears of his auditors,
> and they tacitly acknowledged the force of his genius. He was then in the
> very morning of life.... A blush mantled in his cheek, and his eyes shown
> with an unwonted fire....[8]

It is quite evident after a study of the individual conspirators that each
of them looked upon Booth as a kind of God, ready to do his bidding. Some
of them were stagestruck, the others thoroughly enamored of Booth as a
celebrity. Each of them was cleverly chosen by Booth to serve a special purpose in his plans. Gradually, these conspirators were included in Booth's
theater life, where he found it easy to make them ingratiate themselves.

The high society and fashion of Washington as well as the rowdies in
the balconies cheered Booth's performances. Although Washington's theaters
were high-class places of entertainment, and sections were reserved for ladies
(this was not segregation of the sexes, but a provision for safety) raucous
crowds still tended to take over the back of the house with ribald jesting, to
the annoyance of the rest of the audience.

The *Washington Sunday Chronicle* made this descriptive comment
regarding the state of the theaters: "If a gentleman were forced to sit in the
back of the house, he needed an umbrella and a life preserver to protect him
from the sluices of tobacco juice, which ran under his feet in a yellow sea,
laden with peanut and chestnut shells."

Nevertheless, there were seldom empty seats, and Washington
audiences eagerly awaited Booth's return about a week later. Booth was quite
a businessman and leased and managed the Washington Theater for a run of
two additional weeks. An old establishment, the Washington Theater stood
at the corner of Eleventh and C streets, near Pennsylvania Avenue. It was not
as elegant as its rivals, Ford's and Grover's, but still used as a legitimate
theater. Booth had a devoted following, a demonstrative audience, full of
good will. His benefit performances were played with people standing in the
aisles. For the Washington Theater engagement, April 27th through May 9th,
1863, Booth introduced new staging with his new company. His leading lady
was Alice Gray, and this time his Richmond was E.H. Brink. The *Intelligencer*
reported that "J.W. Booth has that which is the grand constituent of all truly
great acting, intensity."

Then for some unexplained reason, Booth relinquished Wednesday and Thursday, May 6th and 7th, to J. Grau's Italian Opera Troup. Booth returned the following night for a benefit, then closed on Saturday. Theater box-office receipts for the city of Washington were down considerably at this time, probably because the Union had beed defeated at Chancellorsville, casting a gloom over the city.

But news correspondent "Gath" Townsend had another idea why Booth relinquished some of his engagements at the Washington Theater:

> The [Washington] Theater was not one of the fashionable pair in the city [Ford's and Grover's], but an audience of notables gathered there. Booth was inflamed with brandy; he ranted and leaped for three acts.... In the fourth act John Wilkes Booth found he could not articulate at all. As sometimes had happened to his father, after a fellow had broken his nose in a drunken bout, the wanton son was dumb as a pantomimist. The most he could do was to speak in a whisper.[9]

It was during the Washington run that Sir Charles Wyndham first acted with Booth. Besides his theatrical interests, Wyndham had a medical degree from Dublin University, and later was appointed military surgeon in the Union Army. He was reputed to be a very fine comedian. In speaking of his introduction to Booth, he recalled:

> My first part was Osric in *Hamlet* [April 14, 1863]. During my introductory rehearsal I wandered about the stage and finally chose an advantageous position at a little table where I could command a good view of all the proceedings. John Wilkes noticed me there and smiled. A few minutes later the stage manager caught sight of me and rushed up in a great state of mind. It seemed that I had been sitting at the star's table, whereas my proper place was far back in the wings. I apologized, of course, but Booth didn't seem to mind. He spoke pleasantly to me and we spent some minutes in conversation.... The courtesy and kindness shown to me by John Wilkes made way for friendship between us, and we frequently were together after the play. He was a most charming fellow, off the stage as well as on, a man of flashing wit and magnetic manner. He was one of the best raconteurs to whom I have ever listened. As he talked he threw himself into his words, brilliant, ready, enthusiastic. He could hold a group spellbound by the hour at the force and fire and beauty of him. He was unusually fluent, and yet throughout the spell he wove upon his listeners there were startling breaks, abrupt contrasts, when his eccentricity and peculiarity cropped to the surface.... At all times his eyes were his most striking features, but when his emotions were aroused they were like jewels. Flames shot from them. His physical defect was his height (for certain heroic characters), but he made up for the lack of his extraordinary presence and magnetism.... I was strongly attracted to him in the first place by his effective, thrilling presentation of *Hamlet*. Edwin's was a reflective *Hamlet*. As John Wilkes Booth played it, the Danish Prince was unmistakably mad throughout. Edwin's conception of the part was that of uneven and unbalanced genius, and wonderfully he portrayed it. But John Wilkes leaned toward the other view of the character, as was in keeping with his own bent of mind. His *Hamlet* was insane, and his interpretation was fiery, convincing and artistic.... As an actor, the natural endownment of John Wilkes Booth was of the highest. His original gift was greater than that of his wonderful brother, Edwin.... He was the idol of women. They would rave of him, his voice, his hair, his eyes. Small wonder, for he was fascinating.... Poor, sad, mad, bad, John Wilkes Booth...[10]

But at this time Booth was not sad or mad. With at least $700 a week guaranteed him, and more offers from theater managers than he could fulfill, he had all audiences at his feet.

Opposite: full-length portrait of Booth standing by column and leaning on post. From the Brady and U.S. collections, Library of Congress.

CHAPTER 17: Tour-Hopping at a Frantic Pace and an Unheralded Trip to Paris

A June engagement at Ben De Bar's St. Louis Theatre followed the May closing in Washington. Booth had the same supporting players as in his previous St. Louis engagements, Charlotte Wyette and J.E. Carden, and brought forth the same comments of success as before.

After two weeks in St. Louis, Booth followed with a four-day engagement at the Academy of Music in Cleveland, June 30–July 3, 1863. John Ellsler, actor-manager of this theatre, thought highly of Booth, and left these words about him:

> John has more of the old man's power in one performance than Edwin can show in a year. He has the fire, the dash, the touch of strangeness. He often produces unstudied effects at night. I question him: "Did you rehearse that business today, John?" He answers: "No; I didn't rehearse it. It just came to me in the scene and I couldn't help doing it, but it went all right, didn't it?" ... Full of impulse just now, like a colt, his heels are in the air nearly as often as his head, but wait a year or two till he gets used to the harness and quiets down a bit, and you will see as great an actor as America can produce.[1]

Ellsler himself played Sir John Vesey to Booth's Alfred Evelyn in *Money*, with Rachel Noah playing the leading lady. In a small part was the rising young actress Clara Morris. *Money*, originally written in the 1840s, was Lytton's comedy of poverty versus riches. It was one of Booth's most successful plays. He gave the piece a thorough revision and cutting. It became streamlined, more satirical, and the character of the handsome prig became a work of delicate characterization in the hands of Booth. In its original version it was exceedingly long, and would have run a good six hours. His was a bold departure from the old style, and it proved to be popular. Earlier in his career, Booth had played in it as "third walking gentleman"; now as a star with the authority to revise and restage, he played the lead as his own creation.

There has been a lot of controversy and speculation among historians as to John Wilkes Booth's alleged trip to Paris. Was it the summer or winter of 1863, or the spring or summer of 1864? Checking the chronology of Booth's theatrical engagements and dates of his letters, one finds that between July 4 and September 22 in 1863, is the longest unaccounted-for period of time that year in which he could have made the trip. It should be noted that the crossing alone from New York to Liverpool and back would have taken at least 22 days. It is true that he did not play during the summer of 1864, but his time and travel for that period is fairly well accounted for.

The first indication that Booth had ever been abroad came from the journal of the French actor, Edmond Got, of the Comédie-Française (who was said to be "one of the finest and most dependable actors of his day, and played innumerable new parts, as well as most of the classic repertory"[2]). Got's *Journal* was published in Paris in 1910, and covers the years 1840 through 1892. One entry in the journal states that Booth had been a houseguest in Got's home, bringing with him an introductory letter written in London by the noted Hamlet interpreter Charles Albert Fechter. Fechter was a popular actor who played in French and English, in Europe and America, with equal success. It is easy to see why Booth would be attracted to Fechter, as both gained prominence for their revolutionary Hamlets. "Fechter's reading brought out the subtlety and depth of the part, and even those who clung to the other view of Hamlet were impressed by his interpretation, while his admirers were fervent in his praise."[3] Fechter played in London during all the Civil War years, and did not come to America until 1869, when he became a rival Hamlet to that of Edwin Booth.

We find the following revelations recorded in Got's *Journal* for April 30, 1865. Unfortunately, Got did not give the exact date that Booth came to him, for he was writing retrospectively about Lincoln's assassination. The *Journal* is not in a sense a diary, but more in keeping with a memoir. The following is a translation from the French:

> Fechter sent me an urgent letter of introduction to a celebrated tragedian of New York, Booth, who was desirous of passing some time in Paris.
>
> He was a tall, handsome bachelor of energetic appearance, of distinguished manners, well educated, but scarcely speaking French. I courteously received him and aided him in renting an apartment and a carriage by the month, for he acted like a gentleman.
>
> He lived for three days at my house, seeking through me to place himself au courant with the art and the fashions here. I remember that, while smoking, he several times spoke to me of Julius Caesar, of Shakespeare and of Brutus, particularly of Brutus. Once he asked me: "What do you think of Brutus, in France?"
>
> "We admire him at college, in the Greek version as imparted by Plutarch. Still what was Brutus, at the bottom, but an ungrateful and sinister dreamer, a sophist even in his blood. Does he not so decree himself in his role, in his last cry, 'Virtue, thou are but a name.'"
>
> And Booth, thus questioned, nervously changed the conversation. I remember that now. After he left my house I saw him quite often. He ran about the theatres, the town, and made rapid progress in Parisian civilization. On one occasion, at his request, I presented him to the beautiful daughter of one of my women friends, whom he had noticed at the Porte-Saint-Martin, in *Les Filibustiers de la Sonora*. But what was my surprise one morning to hear the girl, who was, nevertheless, hardly timid, telling me, all "époustouflée" [astounded], that he was a madman; that he arose at night in his sleep in order to converse with spirits, and that she was so afraid that she was fleeing to Nice without saying goodbye ... Bon voyage.
>
> Soon after this Booth came to take leave of me, the sanest man in the world at least in appearance, and started back for America. "I must return!" he exclaimed.[4]

Portrait of Booth by Mathew B. Brady: three-quarter length, seated in Gothic chair. Brady-Handy Collection, Library of Congress.

Another report undoubtedly with the same girl is to be found in an article by Jules Claretie in *L'Illustration* for March 28, 1868. The young lady, only further identified as an actress, Mlle T. related how Booth had been unusually attentive to her at each of her performances. She became acquainted with him intimately. He spoke of violent love and passion, then suddenly, as if seized by rage, or hallucination, he would be striding about the boudoir with great steps, treading on the carpet with rage and waving his right arm as if he were brandishing a dagger. She became alarmed and asked him to leave. Later in trying to locate him at the Grand Hotel (indeed!), she found that he had completely disappeared. After the assassination of Lincoln, she recognized Booth's photograph as being that of the handsome acquaintance.[5]

Whatever the exact date, it seems fairly certain that Booth did make a clandestine trip to Paris. The trip is further verified by a letter from actress Charlotte Cushman to her niece in St. Louis, who claims to have seen both Edwin and John Wilkes Booth in Paris during the Summer of 1863.[6]

The purpose of the trip we can only surmise. Some researchers believe it might have been in an effort to gain financial support for the Confederacy. It is most certain he had no intention of a professional engagement, although he had had several offers to play in London and abroad. This was most likely a secretive visit, since there would otherwise have been considerable publicity of his going. Actors usually go on trips to act, and any publicity gained along the way is usually welcome.

The fall of 1863 found Booth again in Boston, planning ahead for engagements to come. The following typical note to Ben De Bar in St. Louis, indicates the rising salary he was able to command.

Sept. 22' /63

B. De Bar, Esq.
  Dear Ben
    Yours of 20th rec'd.
All right, Book me for the two weeks to begin Jan. 4th/64. Share after $140 per night, and benefit each week.
    With regards to all,

I am Truly Yours,
J. Wilkes Booth.[7]

One year earlier he had quoted his fee as "share after $80, and half clear benefit."

On September 28, 1863, Booth opened in Boston, this time at Willard's Howard Athenaeum in *Lady of Lyons*. Playing Claude Melnotte, he again found himself highly praised for his individualism, his beauty, his fire by the critical Boston audience. Booth shared top billing with the popular Mrs. Julia Bennett Barrow. There was such a tremendous turn-out of women rushing to fill the theatre that Booth complained because they far outnumbered the male audience. Perhaps it was not just the overabundance of women comprising the audience, but their undignified behavior of which he complained. Probably Booth felt that the women were not coming to enjoy a drama and his art of acting, but to stare and gawk.

Booth's engagements continued with little respite. Now, he would more frequently be hopping from town to town with only a few performances in each theatre rather than the usual week or two week engagements. The notices continued favorably as he toured from company to company. On a short tour of October 1863, Booth gave one performance in Providence, three in Hartford, two in Brooklyn, and two in New Haven. Several critics spoke of his hoarseness which ruined an otherwise fine performance, indicative of his relentless drive to continue at a frantic pace. It was obvious that Booth was driving himself too hard. He seemed to think little of his physical condition, only of his insatiable lust for fame. It was at this time that he found a new leading lady, Fanny Brown, billed as "Pretty Fay Brown." She was one of the six whose photographs were found on Booth's body after his death.

FORD'S NEW THEATRE.

Tenth Street, near E.

JOHN T. FORD - - - - Proprietor and Manager.
(Also of Holliday street Theatre, Baltimore.)

MONDAY EVENING, NOVEMBER 9, 1863.

Last Week of

MR. J. WILKES BOOTH,

And Messrs. CHAS. WHEATLEIGH,

HARRY PEARSON,

G. F. DE VERE,

AND THE GRAND COMBINATION COMPANY.

THE MARBLE HEART.

Phidias-- }
Duchalet } ....Mr. J. Wilkes Booth.
Diogenes }
Volage   } ....Mr. Chas. Wheatleigh.
Georgias }
Chateau Margeau } ....Mr. Harry Pearson.

ON TUESDAY—HAMLET.

ADMISSION:

Dress Circle.......50 cents | Orchestra Chairs....75 cents
Family Circle......25 cents | Private Boxes....$10 and $6

☞ Box Sheet now open, where seats can be secured
without extra charge.

nov 4 —

WILLARD'S

HOWARD ATHENÆUM

ALBERT D. BRADLEY..............STAGE MANAGER
ISAAC B. RICH.....................TREASURER

THIS AFTERNOON,

SATURDAY, OCT. 10,

AT 3 O'CLOCK,

MR. J. WILKES

BOOTH

MARBLE HEART!

OR, THE SCULPTOR'S DREAM.

PROLOGUE. THE DREAM.

PHIDIAS, THE SCULPTOR, MR. J. WILKES BOOTH

Diogenes, the Cynic Philosopher........................Mr. Jas. Duff
Georgias, a Rich Athenian..............................N. D. Jones
Alcibiades, the General................................J. G. Boyd
Strabon, a Slave.......................................J. H. Conner

ASPASIA. }   MRS. JULIA BENNETT BARROW
Lais,   } Statues,   { Mrs. L. Anderson
Phyrne, }   { Miss Mollie Newton
Thea, a Slave.   { Miss Lizzie Anderson

Soldiers, Citizens, Slaves, &c.

SCENE—Studio in Athens. Study and Poverty have turned his brain. Georgias claims
the Statues. Bark, masters, you must not see them. Who will dare prevent us? The man whose
genius formed them, and the offspring of his Genius, the philosopher, in rags.

THE SWORD OF JUSTICE AND CHAMPION OF FREEDOM.
The Statues—LAIS, ASPASIA, PHYRNE. The Slave's Devotion. The Appeal. The Power of
Gold. Phidias Forsaken. Marble Hearts. False one of the past, false one of the future, woe to the
man who loves you!

THE DRAMA.

RAPHAEL DUCHALET. - - MR. J. WILKES BOOTH

Many of his *Richard III* playbills during this time carried the quotation from the play which apparently represented Booth's political views on the war: "Let them not live to taste this land's increase, / That would with treason wound this fair land's peace." The troubled times were being reflected in his work more and more, although it would seem that success as an actor was still his greatest ambition. He had developed rapidly through an aptitude for the theatre and through his stubborn persistence to show those who were skeptical, that he, as a Booth, could make it on his own.

One researcher offered this dramatic and curious allusion:

> As John grew older he acquired a likeness to Edgar Allan Poe although, with curly black hair, black eyes, the classic Booth head, he was far more handsome than Poe. He was also small of stature and bowlegged, a defect which later in life he always carefully concealed by wearing an ankle-length cloak. Yet in spite of these handicaps his determination to succeed with whatever he professed made him an athlete, a skilled marksman, an able fencer and horseback rider.[8]

It is questionable just how bowlegged Booth was. Pictures of him do not show it, and critical descriptions of his physique do not mention it. It is possible this arose from the boyhood nickname "Billy Bowleggs" his playmates bestowed upon him in their makebelieve world of pirate characters. He did wear an elaborate cape, but, one suspects, for reasons of fashion.

Booth seemed to be a success wherever he went. He could choose his engagements, decline all if he so chose, demand rearrangements which suited him, select his company, and be assured a large percentage of the box-office. When he spoke the opening lines of *Richard III*, "Now is the winter of our discontent...," the audience felt the pang of the war times and were moved by his presence.

At a time when many actors were oblivious to costuming, Wilkes Booth invested substantially to make an impressive showing. Oldtimers in the theatre were very indifferent to costume. Even Edwin Booth is said to have played *Macbeth* "in a cheap property crown and very queer robes" as recalled by character actress Mrs. Gilbert. "Most anything an actor had he could make do, or borrow from wardrobe actors."

Wilkes' wardrobe was different. It was the talk of the theatre. Valued at $25,000, it contained in addition to many of his father's costumes, the intricate changes needed for his repertoire on stage. His trunk was filled with a fascinating motley of theatrical finery: velvets, ermines, fake jewels, wigs, swords, daggers, sandals, silk and cotton tights, opera shirts, plays and manuscripts and properties of every description. And of course, every star tragedian carried a skull in his trunk to be used in *Hamlet*.

Opposite, left: short bill announcing Booth in Marble Heart, *Willard's Howard Athenaeum, Boston, October 10, 1863. From the Harvard College Theatre Library Collection. These "short bills" were passed out on the street by program boys. Boston would not permit Saturday evening performances, much less any on Sundays, so the closing performance of the week was the Saturday matinee. Right: Advertisement for same play at Ford's Theatre, Washington, D.C., November 9, 1863. From the Rare Book Division, Library of Congress. The short bill (left) is previously unpublished.*

Among his many costume changes for his favorite role of Richard, he wore a long, belted, purply velvet shirt, ornamented with jewels. Over this he wore an arm-hole cloak trimmed in fur. For the dual role in *The Marble Heart*, Booth costumed his Raphael Duchalet in a regal velvet coat and gray trousers for the contemporary scenes, and for the sculptor Phidias, a slate-colored mantel with white Grecian border and a Phrygian cap. A small beard was added to the familiar mustache. For Hamlet he wore a black-beaded hauberk, black silk stockings, and black velvet slippers with silver buckles. For Iago in *Othello*, black tights in silk with white velvet trim; for Othello, a robe made from two East Indian shawls of the finest gossamer materials. Slippers were royal purple Genoa velvet, richly embroidered in gold and lined with white silk. The entire Othello costume was of Turkish origin, and highlighted by touches of glitter in jewels, amulets, sabers, dirks, rapiers, heavy necklaces, medallions. For the evil Duke Pescara in *The Apostate*, he wore a vividly contrasting costume of blood red and black. So carefully worked out in every detail were these costumes that one may well imagine the effective and spectacular staging of his productions under the amber glow of gas light or the bright spot of the calcium lights (which prompted critics to exclaim about Booth's appealing ethereal quality as well as his fiery emotional scenes).

Off stage as well as on, his was the last word in fashion. Quite a dapper dandy, his street clothes were in good taste without being gaudy or flashy as was the custom with other members of the theatrical profession. His street attire might be a contrast in colors: a claret coat with velvet lapels, a pale buff waistcoat, dove colored trousers lightly strapped under boots of the finest workmanship, a broad Guayaquil straw hat with a broad black ribbon. His after theater evening attire was often a full suit of black to match his raven hair and mustache, with a small diamond glittering in his cravat, another on his finger. His evidently was a striking appearance not easily forgotten, since so many of his contemporaries took the time to write down their descriptions of him.

CHAPTER 18: President Abe Lincoln Theater Enthusiast

John Wilkes Booth's next engagement was at the now historic landmark, Ford's Theatre, located on 10th Street between E and F Streets, or "2½ squares north of Pennsylvania Avenue." In 1967, Ford's Theatre underwent a complete restoration to become again a useful legitimate theater, the same as it was when it opened in August 1863, after a former theater on the site had burned. This "magnificent new Thespian temple" was said to be the finest in America. It boasted superior ventilation, acoustics, and hydrants with hose attachments. There were seats for 2,400 persons, and the admission was 25¢, 50¢, and 75¢. "Painted Jezebels were barred from the audience by police officers stationed at the door."[1] Only the cream of society was encouraged to patronize the theatre.

On Sunday, November 1, 1863, before the Monday opening, we find the following anticlimactic remarks in the Washington *Sunday Chronicle* regarding John Wilkes Booth's acting ability by a bold critic, who signed himself "Bizarre" and was known for his witty sarcasm:

> We do not regard Mr. Booth as an eminent tragedian. We can scarcely call him a tragedian. Unless he has improved very much since we last saw him, he is little more than a second-rate actor, who, as the possessor of a great name, and with a fine presence, sweet voice, and much natural and uncultivated ability, has seen proper to come upon the stage as a representative of tragedy. It is possible that Mr. Booth will in time become a great actor...

Following his opening in *Richard III*, on November 2nd, the *Washington Daily Chronicle* gave a full column review of the performance. The reviewer expressed the opinion that Booth made the character too sanguinary. It was too murderous and too unlovely for refined audiences, although the critic admitted that "from the day of Garrick to this present time, Richard III has been the most improbable monster upon the stage." He also thought that "most tragedians are convinced that "Richard the brute is more popular in the galleries than Richard the genial and courtly Prince," and that Booth conveyed this message with all the brute force of which he was capable. Continued the *Chronicle*:

> He certainly deserves the merit of giving us the very worst Richard now upon the stage. In plainer words his Richard is as bad as it is possible for an actor to make him. It is possible that there might have been such a Richard as Shakespeare drew ... but such a creation as that of Mr. Booth never existed. He does not seem to be satisfied with the text before him. That is bad enough.... He evidently thinks that his audiences desire gross food.

Here are a further glimpses into Booth's techniques of portraying Richard according to the same critic:

> When Mr. Booth comes upon the stage, he looks like a rascal ... he scowls in certain parts ... he rubs his hands in a coarse, fiendish manner, as though there was as much brutality in his nature as in one of his own murderers.... He must be a tragedian, an inheritor of his father's genius. He insists upon being mentioned in the same sentence as Forrest, Macready, Davenport, Wallack and Edwin Booth. This is an attempt to obtain fame under false pretenses. We do not express it in any spirit of unkindness to this young man. He has many natural gifts — a fine figure, expressive face, and a rich eye that seems capable of intense expression. His voice is very much like that of his brother Edwin, without, perhaps, its sweetness of melody.

Furthermore, Booth's efforts to portray a realistic but different version of the character brought forth this adverse criticism. The *Chronicle* reviewer felt that Booth was a

> representative of a vicious and depraved school of tragedy ... who make it their business to gain applause and notoriety by departing as far as possible from the duty that lies before them. *Richard III* as Shakespeare wrote it was unjust in a political sense, but still it was a tragedy.... *Richard III* however, as Mr. Booth plays it is neither tragedy nor a drama, but something noisy, unpleasant, and improbable, which should not again be played before an audience of judgment and taste.

Here is evidence that Booth was first in his field to try new versions of the old familiar roles. It seemed to be more than critics could take, as they felt that the established tradition of presenting certain roles should not be tampered with. Dramatists of today would laugh at this, for a new and different twist to any old "war horse" is what makes for successful theater.

After the first week of the Washington engagement, "Bizarre" again came forth on Sunday, November 8th, with another piece of criticism. He had not changed his mind about Booth, and continued his thoughts in the same vein. He did, however, like Booth's impersonation of Shylock in *Merchant of Venice*, and particularly the trial scene, but still he did not approve of Booth's violent and noisy delivery. Moreover, "Bizarre" was appalled by the audacity of Booth in his incorporation of sentimental Civil War songs in the production, which he thought resulted in a most incongruous travesty of Shakespeare. He sarcastically said that "Mr. Booth might make a greater success in *Richard III*, if he permitted his Richmond to sing 'When the Cruel War is Over' on the morning of the battle."

But nobody seemed to pay any heed to "Bizarre," for Booth continued his run of two weeks playing to packed houses. Every seat was sold with additional seating provided in every available space, and Standing Room Only was at a premium. The money was rolling in and his name was described in box-office terms as "brilliant and lucrative." The ads stated that he was "assisted and supported by the strongest dramatic combination ever in Washington." It may be of some significance that the *Chronicle*, a strong supporter of Lincoln, may have known of Booth's political opposition, while the *Intelligencer*, who praised Booth so highly on his previous engagement in Washington, carried the opposite view.

There are many contradictory tales as to just how many Booth performances Lincoln attended. There is no question but that Lincoln loved the theater and gave his wholehearted support to it, often writing letters of praise to certain players he particularly enjoyed. Also there is the touching tale of the time in November 1864 when 53 players sent Lincoln a petition asking that he show clemency toward one of their fellow actors who was under sentence of death as a deserter from the U.S. Army. Upon receipt of the petition, Lincoln telegraphed General Thomas at Nashville, Tennessee: "Let execution ... be suspended until further order, and forward record for examination."[2]

The picture comes to mind of the familiar face of Lincoln seated in his rocking chair in the presidential box enjoying a play. He consults his "yard-long program" frequently under the gas light of the chandelier which hangs just outside of the box. "This is act two eyes," says he to his young son Tad, or 'This is act vee one eye coming up." (This was Lincoln's manner of interpreting Roman numerals.) He is very conscious of the "supers," and says, "I wonder if those red-legged, pigeon-toed chaps don't think they are playing this play. They are dreadfully numerous...."[3]

According to Leonard Grover, manager of Grover's Theater, Lincoln attended his theater over 100 times during his four-year administration,[4] and possibly he attended the two rival theaters of Washington as frequently. After Ford's New Theater was opened on August 27, 1863, Lincoln is known to have attended it on eight occasions. When his favorite player J.H. Hackett presented an engagement as Ford's, December 14–19, 1863, Lincoln attended three times, two of which were consecutive performances of *Henry IV*. Hackett seemed to hold a special place in the heart of Lincoln, although he did not have the genius of Forrest or of the Booths; yet he was a major star. Forrest, Lincoln saw three or four times, and "in February 1865, he came twice to watch the engaging comedian, John Sleeper Clarke, who had married Asia, sister of Edwin and John Wilkes Booth."[5]

Some say that Lincoln saw John Wilkes Booth play on many occasions and particularly admired him. It is possible that Lincoln did see him many more times than are recorded, for according to Noah Brooks — Lincoln's friend in the newspaper business who accompanied him on such jaunts — they were able to slip into any performance at any time and no one would know. The audience never knew that their president was among them. Sometimes at the last minute the Presidential Box was not readily available, so Lincoln and his companion had to slip into whatever the manager could find and still be unobserved by the audience. This would account for many of Lincoln's theater visits going unrecorded. The press of the following day usually gave the details of his previous night's entertainment unless he had made secret visits.

Brooks describes such a time when they occupied a lower box at Ford's to see Edwin Booth in *Merchant of Venice*. On this occasion Brooks has confused the two rival theaters, as it was Grover's, not Ford's where Edwin played at that time.

"Gath" Townsend reported that "on one occasion Lincoln applauded the actor [John Wilkes Booth] and his performance rapturously, and with all that genial heartiness for which Lincoln was distinguished." It is also said that Lincoln wished to meet Booth and had said so, but Booth had evaded the interview. Booth is credited with saying that he would rather have the applause of a Negro to that of the President![6]

But in direct contradiction to the above statement, we have quite an extreme view on the subject. John A. Ellsler, Cleveland theater manager, business partner and lifelong friend of Booth, remembered:

> The frequent engagements he had played in Washington, brought him in contact with most of our notable men, in civil and military service. Their names were all familiar to him, and he would descant on their deeds of valor and service to our cause with knowledge and eloquence; nor was it a rare thing to hear him mention "Uncle Abe" with the greatest reverence and respect. He spoke of his performances being honored by the President, and members of his family and cabinet; how "Uncle Abe" enjoyed his efforts, and how proud he felt of such encouragement. To quote from his own words, "It is most gratifying to see the President, the head of our country, personally recognizing, and by his presence, endorsing the theatre and the profession. I tell you, we owe him all honor and respect; God bless him.[7]

Lincoln did attend the theater at least once during the November 1863 engagement of Wilkes Booth.[8] In his diary for November 9th, John Hay, one of Lincoln's secretaries, wrote that he "spent the evening at the theatre with the President, Mrs. Lincoln, Mrs. Hunter, Cameron and Nicolay. J. Wilkes Booth was doing *Marble Heart*. Rather tame than otherwise."[9] The two secretaries, Nicolay and Hay, later wrote their monumental ten-volume biography of Lincoln. They describe Wilkes Booth "like a young god in beauty ... handsome as Endymion upon Latmos, the pet of his little world...." However they belittled John Wilkes Booth's acting talents thusly: "His value as an actor lay rather in his romantic beauty of person than in any talent or industry he possessed."[10]

Carl Sandburg wrote that Lincoln was "a practiced actor and an individual artist in the use of his face." And Lincoln biographer James G. Randall surmised, "Doubtless he would have made a powerful tragic actor as well as a discerning drama critic."[11] It was said of Lincoln that he astounded people in reciting scenes from *Richard III*.

Although interested in attending the theater, Lincoln had no desire to go back stage, saying to do so would spoil the illusion of the play. It was said, however, that when actors appeared in whom he was specially interested, he would invite them into his private box for a chat. Lincoln's clandestine theater attendances were not limited to the two rival houses, Ford's and Glover's, but said Noah Brooks, close friend and reporter who later replaced Nicolay as secretary to Lincoln, "He would sally forth in the darkness, on foot, accompanied only by a friend"[12] to the old Washington Theater and also to the variety [later called vaudeville] house, Canterbury Hall.

The theater caught the fancy of Lincoln's young son Tad, who frequently attended with his father or his tutor. (He was with his tutor seeing *Aladdin, or the Wonderful Lamp* at Grover's Theater the night his father was assassinated at Ford's Theater.) A mere ten years of age at the time, "Tad" became so infatuated with the theater that he frequently came alone to rehearsals where he made the acquaintance of the stage hands. He was so well liked that he was given considerable freedom backstage where he aided the property men in setting the scenes and frequently appeared on stage in walk-on parts. Theater manager Leonard Grover said that nobody in the audience had the remotest idea that the President's son was taking part in the plays. Little "Tad" was so stage-struck that he had one of the rooms at the White House converted into a theater, complete with stage, curtains, orchestra pit, parquet and other paraphernalia.[13] It was the custom for theater people to be always welcome at the Executive Mansion where theatrical readings were given as entertainments at gatherings. It was at such a gathering about three weeks before the assassination that John Wilkes Booth was "at the White House and specially introduced. The President greeted him very cordially, and taking him by the hand said: 'Mr. Booth, I am proud to meet you as a son of the elder Booth.'[14]

After Lincoln's death, various biographers attempted to conceal Lincoln's love of the theater. They were perhaps still under the influence of the puritanical belief that theaters were the devil's workshop, and felt that the man in the office of President should not frequent such places. One biographer even tried condescendingly to whitewash this chief diversion of Lincoln by saying "Rulers of men must occasionally appear among the people; and it was more for this reason than for personal entertainment that Mr. Lincoln with his wife and a few attendants visited Ford's Theater." Grover expressed the truth of the matter when he said, "There was not the slightest atom of hypocrisy about Mr. Lincoln. He visited the theater to be entertained and for relaxation ... to have his mind taken from the sea of troubles which awaited him everywhere."[15]

The Washington *Evening Star*, in telling of this performance of *Marble Heart*, which the Presidential party attended, described it thus:

> One of the most popular, as it is one of the most sensational dramas.... In his personation of the romantic young sculptor, Mr. Booth concentrates many of his best qualities as an artist. The part is exceedingly picturesque and engaging, but Mr. Booth, by his earnestness, his vigorous grasp of genius, and his fervor of style, invests it with an interest beyond the author's ideal, and claims in the result the most brilliant honors of his art. The role is peculiarly well fitted to Booth, and it is not to be wondered at that he has achieved in its embodiment his richest distinction.

And for his Romeo during this engagement, the *Daily National Intelligencer* proclaimed it "the most satisfactory of all renderings of that fine character." H.L. Bateman, later the manager of the London Lyceum, was so impressed that he wanted to present Booth to English audiences as Romeo. W.J. Ferguson, callboy at Ford's Theater, remembered the Washington performance, and adds another stage accident to a long list of Booth mishaps:

> Particularly was I impressed by the sincerity of his acting. Playing Romeo, he so gave himself up to emotion in the cell of Friar Lawrence, that when he threw himself down on the line, "taking the measure of an unmade grave," he wounded himself on the point of the dagger he wore suspended from his girdle. It was on the very spot on the stage where he was to fall again, in the course of a tragedy of tragedies....[16]

John T. Ford, proprietor and manager of several theaters, and personal manager of many of Booth's engagements, held a very high opinion of the actor. In a Washington interview on December 3, 1881, Ford was asked if he thought Booth was a great actor. Ford replied:

Yes, sir. Doubtless he would have been the greatest actor of his time if he had lived. Besides being the handsomest man I ever saw, he was an athlete. He put into all his impersonations the vitality of perfect manhood. He added a fine physical organization to his marvelous mental powers. His Macbeth and Richard were different from any other I ever witnessed. In the scene in *Macbeth* where he enters the den of the witches, Booth would not content himself with the usual steps to reach the stage, but had a ledge of rocks some 10 to 12 feet high erected in their stead, down which he sprang upon the stage. His Richard was full of marvelous possibilities, and his fighting scene was simply terrific.... He was very fine in *The Apostate*, and his Raphael in the *Marble Heart* was simply matchless. He was an ideal Raphael. When he was playing in Boston he doubtless made the greatest success of any actor of his day. People waited in crowds after the performance to catch a glimpse of him as he left the theatre.... I have paid him $700 a week, and he could easily earn $20,000 a year, and he was only 26 years old when he died.[17]

Washington journalist Ben Perley Poore, whose *Reminiscences* are still a standard reference work, set down his thoughts about John Wilkes Booth's Washington engagement:

He had given unmistakable evidence of genuine talent. ... [A]dded to his native genius, the advantage of a voice musically full and rich; a face almost classic in outline; features highly intellectual; a piercing, black eye, capable of expressing the fiercest and the tenderest passion and emotion, and a commanding figure and impressive stage address. In his transitions from the quiet and reflective passages of a part to fierce and violent outbreaks of passion, his sudden and impetuous manner had in it something of that electrical force and power which made the elder Booth so celebrated, and called up afresh to the memory of men of the preceding generation the presence, voice, and manner of his father. Convivial in his habits sprightly and genial in conversation, John Wilkes Booth made many friends among the young men of his own age, and he was a favorite among the ladies of the National Hotel, where he boarded.[18]

CHAPTER 19: John Wilkes and the Ladies

Fashionable women continued to pursue Booth blocking the stage doors. Reporter "Gath" Townsend said that women of all ages and social classes pursued Booth more than he them, and that his path was waylaid by married women in every provincial town or city where he played. Said Townsend:

> His face was so youthful, yet so manly, and his movements so graceful and excellent, that other than the coarse and errant placed themseves in his way. After the celebrated Boston engagement, women pressed in crowds before the Tremont House to see him depart. Their motives were various, but whether curiosity or worse, exhibiting plainly the deep influence which Booth had upon the sex. He could be anywhere easy and gentlemanly, and it is a matter of wonder that with the entry he had to many well-stocked homes, he did not make hospitality mourn and friendship find in his visit shame and ruin. I have not space to go into the millionth catalogue of Booth's intrigues, even if this journal permitted further elucidation of so banned a subject....[1]

He received thousands of love letters in the mails. In an era which preceded films, radio, and television, this was especially significant. Clara Morris tells of watching him open and stack such letters before beginning a rehearsal. She said that he would carefully open, cut off and destroy every signature. "They," he told Miss Morris, pointing to the letters like a hero in a Congreve play, "are all harmless, little one – Their sting lies in the tail!" And when one of the actors picked up one of the letters saying, "I can read it, can't I, now the signature is gone?" Booth chivalrously replied: "The woman's folly is no excuse for our knavery – lay the letter down, please!"[2]

Waitresses, laundresses, and hotel maids vied with each other as to which of them would be so fortunate as to serve his food, deliver his laundry, make his bed, etc. It was said that hotel maids tore up his bed for the sheer joy of making it again. It was Townsend's opinion that Booth was licentious as men go, and particularly as actors go, but not a seducer. "The beauty of this man and his easy confidentiality, not familiarity, but marked by a mild and even dignity, made many women impassioned of him."

There was the instance of the young girl in Philadelphia who became particularly enamoured of him. She sent him flowers, notes, photographs. Booth, to whom such things were common, ignored her, but finally as the love tokens kept coming, granted her an interview. He was surprised to find that so bold a correspondent was so young, so refreshing, and so beautiful. Booth told her, sympathetically, the consequence of pursuing him; that he

Seated portrait of Booth, hand under chin, by Charles D. Fredericks, New York, 1864.
From the William Wyles Collection, University of California, Santa Barbara Library.

Booth told her, sympathetically, the consequence of pursuing him; that he
entertained no affection for her, though a sufficient desire, and that he was a
"man of the world to whom all women grow fulsome in their turn. Go home,"
he told her, "and beware of actors. They are to be seen, not to be known."
The girl was more infatuated than ever and still persisted. So, Booth, "who
had no real virtue except by scintillations," said Townsend, became what he
had promised, and "one more soul went to the isles of Cypress."[3]

       After Wilkes died, Edwin received a number of letters from self-styled
"widows" of his brother who wrote from various cities demanding that the
Booth family acknowledge their claims.[4] There was also a flood of anxious
requests from young women, who "feared they might be compromised, for
the return of letters they had written and gifts they had given. He loved
lightly and well, did Wilkes. It was argued for him however, that he never
knowingly deflowered virgins."[5]

John E. Owens, a fellow actor and comedian who knew Booth from childhood, cryptically remarked: "He was all man from the child, and the feet up."[6]

Stories of Booth's philandering escapades seem endless. He had several narrow escapes from getting into real trouble, among them: his reported rape of a girl with the Philadelphia stock players when he was 19; his legendary marriage in Connecticut on January 9, 1859; his fleeing from adultery charges in Syracuse; his "nestings" with landladies in Manhattan, Niagara Falls, Montreal, and other citites, to his seemingly favorite sporting house, that of Ella Turner Starr in Washington, D.C. Legend would have one believe that Booth had affairs with most of the young starlets and leading ladies in one theatrical troupe after another.[7]

Of the five photographs found on Booth's body, four were well-known actresses: Alice Grey, Effie Germon, Helen Western, and Fanny Brown. The fifth, supposedly his fiancée, whose name was withheld until 1929, was Bessie Hale, daughter of U.S. Senator John P. Hale. Yet the amorous tales of Booth did not cease even after his death. The legend, probably encouraged by Booth's own vanity, refused to die.

With all his easy accessibility to women of every standing, Booth seemed to have had an unnatural attitude toward women, which resulted in his being incapable of relating to them as people. The above-cited examples of his coldness to them and the impersonality of his sexual relations with them lead one to believe that perhaps he was revealing an inadequacy in his character.

An examination of the formative years of his childhood might provide further illumination. When John Wilkes Booth was growing up he was virtually a fatherless boy on the farm, since his father and brothers were so often away on tour. He was overly pampered and protected by his mother and sisters, who had visions of grandeur concerning his future. "The favorite was always Wilkes ... so fiery, so reckless, so debonair. He was his mother's particular love.... She gloried in him and feared for him."[8] Therefore, the adoration from women which he received in his manhood was simply a continuation of the pampering and adoration which he had received during his childhood. He came to expect it, and take it for granted; although excessive adoration made him tire quickly and look toward to variety. In his psychoanalysis of Booth, Philip Weissman believed Booth's artistic and personal failure to have been caused by "the early parental attitudes toward the future artist.... Such attitudes can be crucial determinants for the final outcome of success or failure."[9]

John Wilkes Booth was one of the great romantic figures of the stage, despite his omission from the annals of theatrical history and despite the reluctance of historians to mention it. He *was* the matinee idol of his time, not his brother Edwin, who never evoked passion as did Wilkes. "Twenty years before anyone had heard of a matinee idol, Booth was the recipient of a hundred love letters a week, was followed home by women, was carried off the stage by them, and was the first actor on record to have his clothes shredded by a gang of zealous fans."[10]

CHAPTER 20: Cleveland and
Cleveland Again
The Third Identifying Scar

Booth's next engagement after Ford's Theatre was a return to the Academy of Music in Cleveland.[1] Arriving a few days before the opening, we find the following news item in the *Cleveland Leader*, November 23, 1863: "J. Wilkes Booth, the celebrated actor, Col. Humphreys, of the U.S. Army, Capt. Sypher, of the 1st artillery, and J. Visselier of New York City, are at the American House, which is now doing a deservedly big business." One can assume that Booth did not particularly relish his name being linked with these Unionists, and certainly they were not there as a group. But it is interesting that even in war time, the top brass took second billing to that of the popular actor, regardless of his political views.

As with his two previous Cleveland engagements, Booth's manager was John A. Ellsler. Booth's first introduction to Ellsler was through the well known actor Joseph Jefferson, of Rip Van Winkle fame, a long-time friend of the Booth family. Jefferson once declared that John Wilkes Booth was one of the most promising actors of the day.[2] According to Ellsler's reports, Booth made a hit with his company and was welcome back at any time. So typical of the Victorian style of expression, one of his leading ladies, Clara Morris, stated: "At the theatre, as the sunflowers turn upon their stalks to follow the beloved sun, so old and young our faces smilingly turned to him."

On Saturday evening, November 28th, during a performance of *Richard III*, another of the many publicized accidents in the fight scene occurred. This time Booth got the worst end of it, and as Clara Morris told, because fencing partner McCollom was a cold actor, Booth kept after him to "Come on hard! Come on hot! hot, old fellow! harder—faster! I'll take the chance of a blow—if only we can make a hot fight of it!"

So McCollom, in his efforts to become a fiery man, became nervous, forgetting to count his number of blows in the action. Striking once more, McCollom, wielding his sword with both hands, brought it down with awful force across Booth's forehead. A cry of horror rose, said Miss Morris (who was standing in the wings holding McCollom's watch),

> for in one moment his face was masked in blood, one eyebrow was cleanly cut through—there came simultaneously one deep groan from Richard and the exclamation: "Oh, good God! good God!" from Richmond [McCollom], who stood shaking like a leaf and staring at his work. Then Booth, flinging the blood from his eyes with his left hand, said genially as man could speak: "That's all right, old man! Never mind me—only come on hard, for God's

sake, and save the fight!" Which was resumed at once, and though he was perceptibly weakened, it required the sharp order of Mr. Ellsler, to ring the first curtain bell, to force him to bring the fight to a close, a single blow shorter than usual.... There was a running to and fro, with ice and vinegar-paper and raw steak and raw oysters. When the doctor had placed a few stitches where they were most required, he laughingly declared there was provisions enough in the room to start a restaurant. Mr. McCollom came to try to apologize — to explain, but Booth would have none of it; he held out his hand, crying: "Why, old fellow, you look as if *you* had lost the blood. Don't worry — now if my eye had gone, that would have been bad!" And so with light words he tried to set the unfortunate man at ease, and though he must have suffered much mortification as well as pain from the eye — that in spite of all endeavors would blacken — he never made a sign.[3]

Let us view this scene through the eyes of still another player, who according to reporter Townsend, was an almost literal transcript from the observer's reminiscence:

The wings were thronged to see the broadsword encounter, by carpenters and supers, hot for a real fight. The two began with single-hand exercise, and the Earl scratched Booth's cheek. He whispered to Booth to pause and end it there. Booth objected, and, in the stage phrase, "led up with two hands." The manager and ladies now hurried to the entrances to see a combat of real blood. Booth rushed forward with both hands grasping his weapon, and there was a short series of clashings and sparks, when down came Richmond's temperate and accurate sword, severing Booth's eyebrown and clipping the cheek. "My God! I've killed you!" said the Earl, in an undertone. Booth staggered, bleeding and stunned, and sought the support of the tree-bough that, in the tradition of his father, he always nailed to the wing in *Richard*, and there with sparkling eyes and white glistening teeth, and blood-stained countenance, he sought to renew the fight. The manager ordered the curtain to be rung down. Booth was led, faint and blind to his dressing-kennel. "That's all right, old fellow," he said to Richmond's apologies, "that was splendid!"[4]

As seen from the front, the accident took on a different view to the reporter from the *Cleveland Leader*. Reporting the accident the next day, the paper said that Booth had broken his sword, thus had to fight out the scene holding it by the blade. But since his grasp was loose, the next blow from his opponent caused the broken sword to fly back and cut his forehead above the eye. "He nevertheless fought the scene out, its effect being greatly heightened by the accident." Fortunately the next day was Sunday, and rest. Booth made two more appearances in Cleveland: Monday, November 30th, and the following Saturday, December 5th. The accident in Cleveland gave Booth one of his three identifying scars. One in helping to shift scenery during Edwin's run in Baltimore, Wilkes twisted his thumb out of place. And in Washington he had had the celebrated bullet (tumor) removed from his neck.

We know that Booth remained in Cleveland a few days after the close of his engagement, for as late as December 11, 1863, a news item in the *Cleveland Leader* related that he and James Ward, "the young and talented comedian" were stopping at the American House."[5] This is important in establishing a date for Booth's alleged trip abroad. We know from his letters that he was in Leavenworth, Kansas, late December and early January 1864. The time element would rule out a trip during this period.

CHAPTER 21: The Snows of Leavenworth St. Louis–Louisville–Nashville–Cincinnati

The next engagement we find for John Wilkes Booth is at the St. Louis Theatre, again under the direction of Ben De Bar.[1] For two weeks in St. Louis he was offered $150 per night, with a weekly benefit performance. He was announced to open in *Richard III* on January 4, 1864, but did not appear. Then on the 6th, then for the remainder of the week, but still he did not appear. Substitutions were made. Ben De Bar himself appeared in several plays to fill in. From Booth's letter to his friend Kimbal, we learn the reason for his delay in getting to St. Louis:

St. Joseph
Jan. 2d, 1864
10. P.M.

Dear Kim

Here I am snowed in again, and God knows when I shall be able to get away. I have telegraphed St. Louis for them not to expect me. It seems to me that some of my old luck has returned to hunt me down. I hope you passed a delightful New Years, you and your kind lady, but I fear not. I will give you a slight glimpse of mine. I arrived at the Fort [Leavenworth] with one ear frostbitten. I saw our friends there, had a _____ well, I won't say what, and then after giving my boy my flask to keep for me, I started for a-run and made the river (four miles) on foot. I run without a stop all the way. I then found my boy had lost that treasured flask. I had to pay five dollars for a bare-backed horse to hunt for it. I returned within sight of the Fort, and judge of my dismay upon arriving to see a waggon just crushing my best friend. But I kissed him in his last moments by pressing the snow, to my lips, over which he had spilled his noble blood. I got back to the river in time to help and cut the ice that the boat might come to the shore. And after "a sea of troubles," reached this hotel, a dead man. Got to bed as soon as I could where I have been ever since. Am better now though and will I expect get up tomorrow. You must excuse this scrawl. I am the worst letter writer alive. And I am trying to get through this on a cold bed. Give my best wishes to Mrs. Kimbal and ask her to forgive me for keeping her husband out so late at night. I guess she is glad I am gone. We may get away from here Monday or tomorrow, we can-not tell. Hoping you will remember me to all my friends, and that you will look over this poorly written letter.

I remain
Yours truly,
J. Wilkes Booth.[2]

We noted here Booth's fondness for his flask, and comparing its spilled "noble blood" and his hyperbolic analogy to the loss of a best friend. It is interesting to note that each time this letter was sold at auction, it was taken literally. Description of it always read that it was a letter about Booth's loss of his best friend. The line borrowed from *Hamlet* concerning his decision to cross the frozen river is interesting in that Booth used such quotations constantly in his letters. This highly descriptive letter whets one's appetite for more information and background for the events he relates. It is typical of the style of his correspondences in their lack of explication and his now archaic English. One wonders why he was there and who his friends were at Fort Leavenworth, Kansas, then reported to be a town of proslavery Missourians. One could even speculate that Booth was there on some secret mission for the Confederacy.

There is also an interesting letter in the National Archives from a fellow actor, Edwin Adams, which substantiates this strange tale. Adams said that Booth was boasting of a long and tedious journey over the frozen prairies from Leavenworth to St. Louis, trying to get to his engagement on time. Adams said that Booth told them that the train was stalled because of the snow, but he placed a pistol at the conductor's head and made him continue his journey to St. Louis.

Another Booth letter gives further details about the perilous trip. This one to theater manager John A. Ellsler, in Cleveland, a longtime friend and associate. The business referred to is the purchase of property and the start of an oil well.

> Woods Theatre
> Louisville,
> Jan. 23d/64
>
> Dear John:
> I know you will not believe me when I say that this is the only moment I have had in which I could sit down and write at my ease. Every day I have thought of writing you, for I am as anxious for our bus[iness] to go on, as you can be. I have written to Mears several times. The last time I wrote him I requested him to have the agreement drawn up and to send it to me and I would sign it. He said he wanted about $500 to begin with. I told him if you could not spare it that I would send it to him.
> I have had a rough time John, since I saw you. It was hard enough to get to Leavenworth, but coming back was a hundred times worse. Lost all but <u>four nights</u> of my St. Louis engagement. In St. Joe I was down to my last <u>cent</u> and had to give a reading to pay my way. It gave me $150 with which I hired a sleigh and came 160 miles over the plains. Four days and nights in the largest snow drifts I ever saw. It's a long story which I want to tell you when I see you, but I will say this, that I never knew what hardship was till then. Write to Tom, John, and let us push this thing through. Give my love to all. How's my little girl? [Ellsler's little daughter]
> Your friend
> J. Wilkes Booth.[3]

The above letter reveals another of his little known performances, the solo reading in St. Joseph, Missouri.

Federal law was always a thorn in Booth's side, for his outspoken utterances for the South often got him into hot arguments. St. Louis seemed to be a place where strong feeling on both sides were held. It was here two years earlier, during his engagement, April and May 1862, that he became en-

Jan 2d 1864
10. PM

Dear Kim

Page above and this page: Facsimile of Booth's letter to "Kim" Kimbal, St. Joseph, Mo., January 2, 1864. From the Charles C. Hart Manuscript Collection, Library of Congress.

tangled with federal law enforcement. He and another member of the theater, T.L. Conner, were arrested for utterances against Lincoln's administration. Booth said he "wished the whole damn government would go to hell." It is not recorded what his friend said, but Booth was released after paying a fine and taking an oath of allegiance to the Union. His friend was not so lucky and was committed to a military prison. It was said that Ben De Bar's theater was a hotbed of rebels.[4]

From St. Louis, Booth went to Louisville, Kentucky. In the light of history, this was his most interesting engagement, since this period of his stage work has been overlooked. The engagement was not played in the larger Louisville Theater, where he had previously appeared, but in a smaller house known as Wood's Theater. The building was originally Mozart Hall, intended for nondramatic performances, but remodeled several times.[5] Mrs. McKee Rankin, wife of the prominent actor-manager, and herself an actress under her own name, Kitty Blanchard, a member of the Louisville company, remembered that engagement, and set down these particulars about it:

> I had never seen John Wilkes Booth when I began my engagement with the stock company in Louisville, and this is the reputation which had preceded him: "Good actor. A little inexperienced for a star. Extremely handsome. Good-natured. Very dissipated. A great lover of horses."

Under the old stock system one star came to a theatre each week, depending entirely upon the stock company to be "up" in all the standard and legitimate plays. John Wilkes Booth was one of those stars. "It meant very hard work for the beginners, as there were six parts a week to study, and frequently the farces as well, but it was great practice for them. It was before the day of understudies, but the actors and actresses seemed equal to any emergency." There was always some ambitious actor who was ready to jump in a needed place. True he had to learn many parts he never had a chance to perform. Mrs. Rankin remembered the instance which threw the company into a frenzy. Booth had missed a railroad connection out west, between Leavenworth, Kansas, and St. Louis, which "compelled him to lose his first night with us. This might have given Mr. John Albaugh (our leading man) and the company no end of bother if we had not been prepared to substitute something at a moment's notice."[6]

Again, as in Columbus, Georgia, John Albaugh substituted for Booth, his friend since boyhood, who, according to Mrs. Rankin, said: "I would stake my life on his integrity." Mrs. Rankin gives a detailed account of the perilous trip mentioned earlier in Booth's letters. Through Booth's "wonderfully sweet tones" she learned of the help of his trusted young black servant Leav, the trials to try to run 18 miles by sled through the snow drifts to catch the train in Kansas City, the difficulty in getting their whiskey jug filled so late at night, and the fight with wild animals on the snowbound prairie. This was all quite adventuresome as reported by Mrs. Rankin as she heard it spoken directly through the "small transom for ventilating purposes, which made it possible to hear every word that was spoken." She and Alice Grey, one of Booth's favorite leading ladies, shared a dressing room just off the greenroom.

During this two-week engagement in Louisville, January 18–30, 1864,

Mrs. Rankin recorded another amusing incident, a "serio-comic incident" as she called it, which occurred during a performance of *Richelieu*. On Monday evening, January 25th, there was a scene being played with Kittie Miles, "a charming young lady, but one who was suffering terribly from stage fright." Miss Miles was playing Marian de Lorme, and of course there was Wilkes Booth in his Richelieu robes for the character. Said Mrs. Rankin:

> Mr. Booth had been dining out and arrived at the theatre late, barely in time to get on the stage for the first scene. There must have been a good many courses at that dinner, and wine with every course, for his colored valet [Leav] found it necessary to lift him, place him on his feet, and lead him to the entrance for every scene he played. Once there he got through fairly well, when closely watched by the prompter. But the prompter slipped into the greenroom for a moment, thinking it safe to do so, and left poor Miss Miles to the mercy of Mr. Booth, who, seated in a large, high-backed arm-chair, commenced very well. During the scene "Mariane de Lorme" is supposed to kneel at the feet of the "Cardinal." The "Cardinal" should give her the cue to rise, when — awful experience — he went fast asleep, breathing so heavily that Miss Miles in alarm, believing him to be in an apoplectic state, tried in vain to signal the prompter. A scene shifter, with great presence of mind, stooped down and tried to reach Mr. Booth's foot by lying down flat on the stage and poking a brace out as far as possible. It was too short, and he tried another, which just touched the "Cardinal's" foot and made it wobble, but it didn't wake up John. At this the prompter turned and shouted at him, finding it impossible to touch him because of the high-backed chair. Finally Miss Miles, ignoring stage directions, rose from her knees, touched him on the shoulder, and, forgetting her dignity, gave him a good shake, which partially roused him. Then unluckily she started to repeat her last line, stuttering and stammering painfully, at which Mr. Booth looked at her and said, "Wha's s'matter, don' you know your lines yet?" and settled himself more comfortably in his chair to resume his nap. The prompter rang down the curtain and rang in the orchestra. The audience gave a round of questionable applause, accompanied by one or two shrill whistles from the gallery, when Mr. Booth suddenly arose from the chair, ordered the curtain rang up again, resumed the scene, and played it beautifully to the end.[7]

Nashville, Tennessee, was Booth's next stop where on February 1, 1864, he began a two-week engagement. Booth's plans for continuing his career, one engagement closely following another, is verified by a letter from him to Boston theater manager and impressario, E.F. Keach, in which Booth asks Keach to inqure about an offer he has had from Blatchford, a rival theater manager. He mentions that he will open in Nashville on Monday and will be in Cincinnati in two weeks.[8]

In Nashville crowds greeted him with the same familiar enthusiasm to which he was accustomed, but one critic there thought Edwin Booth and the elder Booth far superior to Wilkes. The critic thought his performance twice as violent as it should have been. Another critic in Nashville remarked that while Wilkes insisted that Edwin as the better Hamlet, Nashvillians thought Shakespeare could scarcely have wished for a better Hamlet than Wilkes Booth.

Immediately following his two weeks in Nashville, Booth went again to Wood's Theater in Cincinnati, where as usual the papers stated that he "was welcomed by a large and enthusiastic audience." Scheduled to open in the usual *Richard III*, he played Iago in *Othello*, instead, on February 15th. The reason stated for the change was "Booth's indisposition." Supposedly his hoarseness which had been bothering him lately, was the reason for the switch to a less strenuous role. The Cincinnati *Enquirer* for February 16th stated: "His interpretation of the great 'Boothonian' character of Richard III was a masterly histrionic effort." That the last part of this sentence was an unlucky guess is shown by the review in the *Commercial*, which stated that *Othello*, with Booth as Iago, was presented, Booth being indisposed.

Because of freezing weather which kept the theaters half empty, Wood's was not filled as it would have been, noted a critic. Still, Booth suffering with a severe cold continued for two weeks. On the third night of his engagement, Booth was to have presented *The Robbers*, but was too ill to appear. The play was presented anyway with a substitute in the leading role. In telling of Booth's illness, the paper stated that he had "labored (the past two nights) under the disadvantage of performing when he should have been in the care of a physician."

On the 18th, he had recovered enough to return in *Richelieu*, followed by *Money*, and then the strenuous *Richard III*. For Washington's birthday, he presented *Hamlet*, when the paper remarked that "a bird's eye view from behind the curtain revealed a packed house" in spite of the competition from P.T. Barnum's famous midgets, Tom Thumb and Commodore Mutt, at another theater.

After a series of plays for a Bulwerian revival, and several Shakespeare favorites, Booth closed on Friday, February 26th, at Wood's "popular and neat establishment." His engagement was followed by a benefit for the one and only Mrs. G.H. Gilbert, noted to be the finest character actress of the period.

Mrs. Gilbert, who appeared with all the Booths, remembered Wilkes Booth most favorably in her memoirs. She said that he was "the most perfect Romeo, the finest I ever saw. He was very handsome, most lovable and lovely." She continued to say that the character of Romeo is perhaps Shakespeare's most difficult role. Few had excelled in it. The elder Booth never tried it "because it was beyond his powers.... Edwin Booth failed in it so often that he had to withdraw it from his repertory." She knew only two other actors, the giants in the theater David Garrick and Spranger Barry, who had succeeded in the role. Yet she called John Wilkes Booth "perfect" in the role. "I assume," said she, "that when an actor is perfect in the role that few have succeeded in, he is pretty near the top of his profession...."

In describing Booth, Mrs. Gilbert thought him "eccentric in some ways, and he had the family failings, but he also had a simple, direct, and charming nature. She substantiates the theory put forward in a previous chapter concerning Booth's relations with his mother. "The love and sympathy between him and his mother were very close, very strong. No matter how far apart they were, she seemed to know, in some mysterious way, when anything was wrong with him. If he were ill, or unfit to play, he would often receive a letter of sympathy, counsel, and warning, written when she could not possibly have received any news of him. He has told me this, himself."[9]

Booth next planned a five-week engagement in New Orleans, arranged for him by Ben De Bar. We learn of his plans from one of his letters to a friend, just after he had recovered from a severe cold in Cincinnati. Even so, his illness had kept him off the stage only one evening. He had forced himself through the strenuous routine, and after presenting Hamlet wrote the following:

> Wood's Theatre
> Cincinnati
> Feb. 22d/64

Dear Monty

It's all right. Yours I have just read and hasten to answer it. Depend on me for April 25th. I start from here (God willing) on Saturday for New Orleans, where I play a five weeks engagement, have two weeks to get from there to Boston. If you wish to write me direct, care St. Charles Theatre. I have been very sick here, but am all right again, thank God.

Joe [Simonds] told me I would be astonished when I found out my new manager's name. And I am so. I wish you more success than you have ever hoped for. Excuse this.

I wish to be remembered to all

I am your true Friend

J. Wilkes Booth.[10]

"Monty," as R.M. Field was called by his friends, had been made acting manager of the Boston Museum, taking over Keach's job—thus the explanation of the last part of the above letter.

CHAPTER 22: New Orleans: Crescent City Under the Yankee Yoke

Since the city of New Orleans had fallen early in the war to Union forces on April 25, 1862, Booth had to get a military pass in order to travel through to fulfill his engagement. General Grant issued him this pass at Vicksburg which allowed Booth freedom to travel through the Union lines.

Traveling on the train to New Orleans, Booth was appalled and greatly distressed to see the countryside, once so beautiful, now devastated by the war. When he arrived in New Orleans, he was even more heartsick to see the city overrun with 15,000 Federal troops. The whole social structure had crumbled in a vast upheaval. Booth had seen the horrors of war as he traveled. Tension ran high everywhere, and quick tempered fights, looting, and corruption were commonplace. In order to carry on at all, theaters had to adjust themselves to such circumstances. Sudden changes of theater programming became more frequent as performers and stage hands suddenly found themselves marching or caught into a swirl of mobs, so that one seldom knew what, if any, performance would be given that night.

A prominent actress of the time, Mrs. Gilbert, in a graphic description, told how everyone became calloused and accustomed to violence. There was bitter feeling everywhere, separating friends and families. Union and Confederate flags were rung up on private homes. There was a great deal of quarrelling and free shooting. "It got so that no one minded; they simply said: 'Another man shot,' and went about their business. In those times of hot words and quick firing there was no time to draw pistols, and they shot through their pockets.... There were alarms and wild ringing of bells ... martial law would be declared, and every one would have to be indoors by nine at night. At such times there was no performance, of course; but at other times our theatre would be full, for in such a whirl of excitement, people liked to be constantly amused...."[1]

Booth's own cry at the horror he had witnessed seems to echo the remembrances of Mrs. Gilbert:

> I have never been upon a battle-field; but oh! my countrymen, could you all but see the *reality* or effects of this horrid war as I have seen them, I know you would think like me, and would pray the Almighty to create in the Northern mind a sense of *right* and *justice* (even should it possess no seasoning of mercy), and that he would dry up this sea of blood between us, which is daily growing wider...[2]

During such times of strife the theaters carried on as best they could, providing the necessary relaxation from tension, if one were able to relieve his mind of worry for an evening of farce.

At the time of Booth's New Orleans engagement, the city was under the yoke of oppression, and was being dragged to the depths of every depravity. In this situation, the theater, the saloons, the pleasure houses flourished as long as one said the right things, didn't sing certain songs, pretended to support a certain cause. Many of the concert-saloons were vividly described as "coarse and without female patrons. Men smoked cigars, and waiters peddled liquors up and down the aisles. After minstrelsy, dancing, and other variety entertainment, a loud howl arose from the motley audience for the fresh favorite that is ever requested and devoured, like fresh babes by the sacred crocodile...."[3]

The company at the St. Charles Theater was busily rehearsing and preparing for the arrival of the star. Among the players was Lizzie Maddern, mother of the famous star of the following generation, Mrs. Fiske. The theater, also known as "The Old Drury," had been closed from 1861 through January 1864, when Ben De Bar sent down a stock company for the reopening, and a long line of distinguished star players came for engagements.

A new play was presented each evening including Sundays. Rehearsals were called every day in preparation for the coming play. Before Booth arrived, the company had been rehearsing his repertoire for weeks, and there was wild anticipation as to how the new star would react to the company, what changes he would make in the staging, since many stories concerning Booth's staging had preceded him there. The resident players found Booth congenial to work with. Though a big star, he was not exceedingly egotistical nor difficult with his supporting actors, but merely suggested changes here and there so as to heighten the effectiveness of certain scenes.

The richly ornate St. Charles Theatre with its four horseshoe balconies and gaslit chandeliers had been the scene of the elder Booth's last performance in 1852. It also proved to be one of the supreme achievements of J. Wilkes Booth.

His opening of *Richard III* on Monday evening, March 14, 1864, brought a heterogeneous audience filled to capacity which included Union soldiers, freed slaves, townspeople and carpetbaggers: the new poor (Creoles stripped of their wealth, former slaves on their own) and the new rich (Northern profiteers).

The *Daily True Delta* gave the following reportage:

> On the American stage the name of Booth is truly a tower of strength.... The Old Drury welcomed the youngest of that gifted family to those boards which had been the scene of the many and oft-repeated triumphs of his distinguished father and scarcely less distinguished brother. The fame of Mr. Booth, as a young tragedian of extraordinary promise, had preceded him, and if his powerful delineation of the bloody-minded Gloster is to be taken as a sample of his ability, then we cheerfully add our mite of admiration to the general praise and commendation his efforts have met with wherever he has appeared.

The critic pointed out certain scenes in which he felt Booth was outstanding: "with Lady Anne, with the queen mother and princes in the council chamber, and with the Lord Mayor and aldermen, were all masterpieces of satanic

ST. CHARLES THEATRE.

FRIDAY, MARCH 25, 1864.

PROGRAMME FOR THIS EVENING.

The performance will commence with the

MERCHANT OF VENICE.

Shylock,..........J. Wilkes Booth

DUKE,...J. WELKINS
ANTONIO,...E. L. MORTIMER
BASSANIO,...G. D. CHAPLIN
GRATIANO,...E. MARBLE
LORENZO—With Song,........MISS L. MADDERN
SALANIO,..C. L. FREEMAN
SALARINO,..E. MACKWAY
OLD GOBBO,................................A. H. CAMPBELL
LAUNCELOT,.......................................J. A. GRAVER
TUBAL,..H. MELMER
BALTHAZAR,..H. MELLEN
PORTIA,.......................................MRS. C. P. WALTERS
JESSICA,...MISS E. CASSEL
NERISSA...MRS. CHIPPENDALE

To conclude with

KATHARINE AND PETRUCHIO !

OR,

TAMING THE SHREW.

Petruchio,........J. Wilkes Booth

BAPTISTA,..G. G. TURNER
HORTENSIO,..C. L. FREEMAN
BIONDELLO,...MR. LEONARD
GRUMIO,...J. A. GRAVER
MUSIC MASTER,..........................A. H. CAMPBELL
PEDRO,..E. MACKWAY
TAILOR,..T. DAVEY
COOK,...H. MELMER
SERVANT...H. MELLEN
KATHARINE,........................MRS. C. F. WALTERS
CURTIS,..MRS. J. W. THORPE
HORTENSIA,..MISS E. CASSEL

☞NOTICE—During the engagement of Mr. BOOTH seats may be secured three days in advance by applying at the Box Office from 9 A. M. to 4 P. M.

FREE LIST WILL BE ENTIRELY SUSPENDED EXCEPT THE PRESS.

☞Doors open at 7 o'clock, Curtain rises at 7½

The yard-long playbills had diminished to under eight inches in war-torn New Orleans. This one is of Booth in Merchant of Venice *and* Katharine and Petruchio, *St. Charles Theatre, March 25, 1864. From the collection of the Folger Shakespeare Library, Washington, D.C.*

dissimulation, and scarcely inferior to his lamented father. In the tent scene and on the ensanguined field of Bosworth, he was absolutely horrifying...."

Booth's fighting partner this time was G.D. Chaplin, and appearing as Duke of York was the boy prodigy, Willie Seymour, for whom the Seymour Theatre Collection at Princeton University is named.

The *Picayune* found that Booth exhibited "that subtlety which was so prominent in Gloster.... In the tent scene, on waking from his horrible dream, his acting was remarkably fine. We cannot imagine a more terrible picture of phrenzied guilt."

During his stay in New Orleans Booth made many friends. He had a boyish charm which captured the hearts of the people who regarded him with respect and admiration. He was a great social favorite as well as a stage favorite, and townspeople who never saw him on the stage enjoyed his wit and dash in the saloons and entertainment establishments throughout the city.

John Wilkes Booth's leisure activities included horseback riding, billiards, and tenpins. He was a perfectionist even in his games; and was not content unless he excelled. Frequently, he would play for the remainder of the evening, even after a performance, in order to beat his friends at the games. One of the members of the family where Booth boarded while in New Orleans later wrote that "the New Orleans people loved him for his gentleness, for his extraordinary histrionic ability, for his power to make them laugh or cry, for jest and quip, and for the many things an actor can do to lighten the burden and make easier the way of life."[4]

After the evening performances, Booth, who was never too tired, would accompany his friends to the various places of amusement which abounded in the city. One of these friends tells an interesting story of Booth and his companions at this time:

> Booth and some friends were out one night playing billiards and after the games were over, concluded to walk down the street. Booth was challenged by one of his companions to sing "Bonnie Blue Flag," a popular Confederate ditty then forbidden by the military authorities in control of the city. Without a moment's hesitation he broke into the words of the song. The rest of the party was too scared to think. It was treason to sing that song, and so they ran away. Booth calmly continued to the end of the first verse and then, surrounded by excited Union soldiers, who thronged into the streets on hearing the prohibited lyric, managed to escape from their hands, by the excuse of his marvelous power of fascination. He even made the soldiers believe he did not know anything about the law against a song of that kind, and that he sang it just because he had heard it on the streets of this city, and liked the words and the tune. If any of the other members of the party had uttered the words, they would probably have been in jail at this moment or, anyway, till the war was over. Butler[5] had forbidden anyone to sing the Confederate songs under pain of imprisonment over an indefinite period of time. But Booth could do pretty much what he pleased. He had a way about him which could not be resisted, the way which permits a man to overstep the boundaries of the law, and do things for which other people would be punished.[6]

Here again, as in St. Louis, Booth had been able to talk his way out of a tight situation. His daredeviltry in exercising freedom of expression showed his contempt for the military authority in power.

John Wilkes Booth's version of Hamlet, mustachioed and wild, seemed to be not completely appreciated by the New Orleans critics as had some of his other roles. Said the critic of the *True Delta*: "The large audience seemed pleased with Booth's idea of the Prince of Elsinore. This is perhaps as much as can be said of the efforts of any actor to portray that incomprehensible character.... Booth's reading was very pure and chaste.... There was more in the performance to admire than to censure."

In his next performance Booth played Shiel's *The Apostate*, which seemed to be more to the liking of the *True Delta*. The critic believed that "Booth realized to the full all of our anticipations. The subtle hate and malignity of Pescara were depicted with a fidelity and an intensity that stamp Mr. Booth as a son worthy of the sire, who excelled in that line of characters. The scene in which Pescara relates his dream to Florinda was a piece of acting which evinced great power and excellent judgment. It was one of those test scenes which distinguish the actor from the mimic, and well did Mr. Booth acquit himself therein."

After the first two weeks of nightly appearances, Booth again fell ill. The combination of damp winter weather, his run-down condition due to his constant drive to fulfill nightly performances, his hectic social life which kept him up most of the remaining hours of the night after a performance, the drive to establish and hold an image of fame, all contributed toward the eventual time when he would have to give in. The paper stated that it was a cold and laryngitis which kept him off the stage for three nights. The absences were growing longer. His previous illnesses he had been able to shake off in one night. His recurring hoarseness made his speech labored and indistinct, and since this was an age before blurred and husky speech was thought of as a virtue on the American stage, critics began to be concerned and to apologize for him. The New Orleans *Times*, March 19, 1864, stated that "it is a matter of regret that he is at present laboring under a severe hoarseness, in consequence of which his efforts have been much less satisfactory to himself than to his friends, but we trust his speedy recovery may enable him to consent to the merit of his endeavors. He has certainly created a furor here, which will continue through his engagement."

But Booth's illness was more serious than anyone would like to admit. Finally he had to give in completely to the ailment. A notice appeared in the Sunday New Orleans *Times*, March 27, 1864:

> Notice. — The management of the St. Charles Theatre regret to inform the public that in consequence of the severe and continued cold under which Mr. Booth has been laboring for several days, and at the suggestion of his medical adviser, he is compelled to take a short respite from his engagement. Due notice will be given of his next appearance.

Booth's successful five-week New Orleans engagement, so right for him in every other respect, seemed to be shortening in spite of all other good fortune. He did not allow himself full recovery from his illness before returning to work. He lacked the patience needed for recuperation. His restless nature and energy of youth did not provide for the luxury of relaxation. Booth's old luck had returned to haunt him. The voice for the actor is the prime factor, and if that is not functioning adequately, the rest is silence indeed.

But after three nights' rest, Booth returned for a benefit on Tuesday, March 29th, in *Marble Heart*. Still, critics mentioned that his hoarseness and marred articulation kept his performance from being at his top. Still Booth managed to continue through Sunday, April 3rd, when he closed in the favorite and most taxing *Richard III*. Summing up, the *Daily True Delta* said:

> Critics have carped at his personalities and found fault with his readings. True in some instances he has departed from the traditional renderings of certain personages, and so must every man do who is an actor and not a mere mimic. We well remember the elder Booth, than whom we have never had a more scholarly, chaste and correct actor, who not only departed from the example of his predecessors, but from his own, and so absorbed did he become in his performances, that it is probable that he never enacted the same play twice in the same fashion.... We do not pretend that Mr. Booth is the greatest actor on the stage, but we do say that we have yet to find any young gentleman who gives promise of such excellence.

Rival newspaper the *Daily Picayune*, April 3, 1864, remarked:

> Actors are not over prone to praise each other, but we have heard a good actor say that J. Wilkes Booth had quite as decided theatrical talent as any member of his talented family. It is a matter of regret that a physical disability (we trust temporary) prevented his engagement from being so gratifying to himself or to his friends as was desirable, and we look for his return here next season under more favorable auspices.

It is at this period in Booth's career that we find much later criticism and speculation as to whether or not he was only suffering from laryngitis, or indeed losing his voice from improper training and lack of voice control. Several historians have insisted that the severe cold and laryngitis which kept recurring with every engagement, was not merely a cold, but the beginning of the end of his career.

Working conditions for the actor during the war years were deplorable, and it is no wonder that so many suffered from laryngitis and colds. Drafty theaters, cold dressing rooms, long working hours, traveling in all kinds of weather, all actors had laryngitis from time to time, but no actor ever quit the stage because he had a sore throat or had temporarily lost his voice. The voice would almost always be restored. He might have been forced to lay off a few days, but an actor had to be hardy and capable of enduring such conditions.

As Augustin Daly put it so graphically in his description of the times, October 1864, "I poison each tumblerful of water with half a dozen drops of whiskey...." This would indicate that the water in so many places was contaminated. "Railroad accommodations are horrid," continued Daly, "dirty floors, no ventilation ... filthy stations and long waits ... in the cold night air ... crowded with noisy, blasphemous and filthy soldiers and conscripts."[7]

Wilkes was not the only Booth to be plagued by laryngitis. In a letter to his friend Adam Badeau,[8] Edwin said: "I am sick — took physic last night to make me sleep and laid awake all night; my cough is worse and my hoarseness damnable! I am tired and in bad humor!"[9] And years later we still find the same complaint: "I've been so sick — from gargling and dosing myself for this infernal hoarseness — that I've been negligent of all notes and callers...."[10]

Upon reading letters of the Booth family, the predominant impression one perceives is of their predisposition toward gloominess, illness, hoarseness, and general depression. They were a moody lot, reminiscent of a family out of the pages of a Gothic novel. Still, they marvelously managed to dominate the American stage for over 70 years!

Wilkes in his boyhood, had been warned of his ill-fated destiny by a gypsy fortune-teller. He wrote this oracle down and gave it to his sister, Asia, though he said it was no use to write it down as he was not likely to forget it, and he never did. Often he was to remember the words and to refer to their message as "my old luck":

> Ah, you've a bad hand; the lines all cris-cras. It's full enough of sorrow – full of trouble – trouble in plenty, everywhere I look. You'll break hearts, they'll be nothing to you. You'll die young, and many to mourn you, many to love you too, but you'll be rich, generous, and free with your money. You're born under an unlucky star. You've got in your hand a thundering crowd of enemies – not one friend – you'll make a bad end, and have plenty to love you afterwards. You'll have a fast life – short, but a grand one. Now, young sir, I've never seen a worse hand, and I wish I hadn't seen it, but every word I've told is true by the signs. You'd best turn a missionary or a priest and try to escape it. [11]

CHAPTER 23: Boston: The Favorite City
Montreal: Pleasure vs.
Business

Booth's illness in New Orleans did not keep him from other long engagements. After about three weeks' rest, he fulfilled five successful weeks in Boston, where he gave the greatest number of parts in his career: 34 performances in 29 days, consisting of 18 different leading roles, a rigorous schedule which would no doubt strain the talents of any young actor of today.

After the summer of 1864, Booth made definite plans for continuing his career. He had leased a theater in Washington, engaged a cast, staged a heavy repertoire, and billed himself pompously as "The People's Choice." His voice was reportedly as clear as a bell when he played Mark Antony in New York on November 25, 1864. No actor with a poor voice could have performed the demanding role of Antony and still have received the tremendous ovation which reviewers tell us he received.

Booth was also planning a Canadian theatrical engagement. Early in October 1864, he arrived in Montreal and rented a room on fashionable Coté Street near the Theatre Royal. The Montreal *Telegraph* conducted an interview with Booth where it was learned that he had plans to appear with the Theatre Royal under the management of J.W. Buckland. He announced that he was in Montreal on oil speculation, although he intended to do some readings at Corby's Hall and a performance or two at the Theatre Royal.

On October 18, he checked in at the elite hotel, St. Lawrence Hall, which was packed with well-bred Southern gentlemen plotting to involve Canada in their war with the North. His actor friend, John McCullough, had brought Booth's entire wardrobe up from the States, and plans were in progress to present *Julius Caesar*. Booth checked on the Theatre Royal, small by American standards, and wondered if it were large enough for his productions.

The engagement with the Theatre Royal never materialized. Instead Booth spent his time in pleasure, drinking wine, reading books, lounging and playing billiards with rebel agents and Secessionists. Friends remembered him as a striking figure sleighing in his yellow foxskin cap.

However, Booth did present an evening of solo dramatic readings at Corby's Hall to quite a receptive audience. In scenes from *Merchant of Venice*, *Julius Caesar*, and *Hamlet*, Booth gave "an electric performance" playing all roles in each scene with "marvellous effect" and "thunderous applause." His readings of "The Charge of the Light Brigade," and "Remorse of the Fallen One" brought tears to the audience as they associated the poems with the terrible slaughter on the battlefield going on that very time.

Booth did not pursue any other theatrical engagements in Montreal. It was likely that more serious political plotting was occupying his mind. His remark to a billiards playing companion gained full significance some six months later, "I have got the sharpest play laid out ever done in America...."[1]

Still other plans indicated that Booth intended to continue his acting career. In the Montreal *Telegraph* interview he disclosed that he was anxious to get back to Richmond, Virginia, and play for the Confederate hospitals.

As late as April 5, 1865, we have another report of his plans. At that time Edwin was appearing at the Boston Museum in *Hamlet*. Wilkes was back stage chatting with Rachel Noah, Ophelia to both the Booth brothers on several occasions. When she asked Wilkes if he planned any engagements during the current season, he replied, "Oh, perhaps, a few in New York and Philadelphia."[2] He was in excellent voice and joked with her about her recent marriage. Wilkes also had several benefit performances promised to friends. Then too, he was expected to do another New York benefit performance with Edwin on April 22, 1865, for the Shakespeare Statue Fund which was gathering donations for a memorial in Central Park. The reader will remember the date of the assassination was April 14, 1865.

There were only occasional comments about Wilkes' voice during his five-week engagement at the Boston Museum. On this third engagement there, his opening bill of *Richard III* was welcomed by the usual large audience with much praise. The *Transcript* described it as "very successful," giving "much satisfaction to the admirers of this young actor."

Booth was in excellent spirits during this long Boston run. We have a description of him as this time from the memoirs of A.F. Norcross, a relative of the Mestayer family of players. When she was a little girl, Miss Norcross remembered her father's house as being continually filled with the players of the Boston theaters. It was a jolly household, and the rafters of the old residence often rang with the peals of merry laughter accompanied by favorite scenes from the plays. She reminisced of John Wilkes Booth as being "extremely popular with everybody.... He loved a jest and in his quiet, quizzical way made friends everywhere...."[3]

The Boston *Transcript* reported the following comment on Booth's April 27th performance in *Money*:

> Mr. Booth played the part of Evelyn at the Museum last evening with a tact, grace and appreciation of the character such as few but himself can exhibit upon the stage, the only drawback being the cold which restrains his voice. The company, too, put their best feet foremost, and the large audience was kept in excellent humor throughout the evening.

And the Boston *Post* the following day commented:

> Crowded houses have thus far attended the performances of J. Wilkes Booth and this notwithstanding the prevalence of a severe storm from the very

Opposite, left: Playbill of Booth in Othello. *Boston Museum, May 2, 1864. From the Theatre Collection of Yale University Library. Right: In* Romeo and Juliet *the next night. From the Harvard College Library Theatre Collection. Both previously unpublished.*

BOSTON MUSEUM

ACTING MANAGER . . . . Mr. R. M. FIELD

SECOND WEEK OF THE

☞BRILLIANTLY INAUGURATED

ENGAGEMENT OF

J. WILKES BOOTH

WHO WILL APPEAR

This Monday Evening, May 2, 1864,

IN SHAKSPERE'S TRAGEDY OF

OTHELLO!

WITH THE FOLLOWING POWERFUL CAST:

OTHELLO	J. WILKES BOOTH
Iago	Mr L. R. Shewell
Cassio	Mr J. Wilson
Duke of Venice	Mr J. Wheelock
Roderigo	Mr J. A. Smith
Brabantio	Mr F. Hardenburgh
Ludovico	Mr G. F. Ketchum
Gratiano	Mr T. M. Hunter
Montano	Mr Walter Benn
Julio	Mr J. E. Adams
Marco	Mr J. Peakes
Messenger	Mr J. Delano
Senators, Gentlemen, etc.	
Desdemona	Miss Kate Reignolds
Emelia	Miss Emily Mestayer

DANCE . . . . ARIEL!

Miss ROSE and THERESE WOOD.

DURING THE EVENING,

Mr. EICHBERG'S ORCHESTRA

WILL PRESENT THE FOLLOWING:

OVERTURE--Midnight Angel	EICHBERG
SELECTIONS FROM RIGOLETTO	VERDI
ST. PATRICK'S QUADRILLE	D'ALBERT
COL. CHICKERING'S BATTLE MARCH	EICHBERG

To conclude with the Laughable Farce, entitled

"JOHN WOPPS!"

Or--FROM INFORMATION I RECEIVED.

Sam Snug (Independent)	Mr J. Wilson
Chopps (a Journeyman Butcher)	G. F. Ketchum
John Wopps (Policeman (A. 1.)	W. Warren
Tom Chaffer (Ditto, A. 2.)	Hunter
Mrs Wopps	Mrs J. R. Vincent
Mrs Chopps	Mrs J. Wheelock

☞ Tuesday--"ROMEO AND JULIET!"

☞ Wednesday--"DAMON AND PYTHIAS!"

☞ Due notice will be given of Mr BOOTH'S appearance as "IAGO!" and also of a repetition of "RICHARD III" and "THE APOSTATE!"

☞ Wednesday Afternoon--A glorious bill! "CHARLES II" and "BLACK EYED SUSAN."

Seats Secured One Week in Advance.

Admission 30 Cents. . . . . . .Orchestra and Reserved Seats 50 Cents

Children under 10 years of Age, 15 Cents.   Children in Arms not Admitted.

Exhibition Hall open at 6 1-2 o'clock . . . Evening Performance commence at 7 1-2 o'clock Afternoon Performance at 2 1-2 o'clock.

TREASURER . . . . Mr. GEO. W. BLATCHFORD

F. A. Searle, Printer, Journal Building, 118 Washington Street, Boston.

BOSTON MUSEUM

ACTING MANAGER . . . . Mr. R. M. FIELD

SECOND WEEK OF

J. WILKES BOOTH

THE EMINENT YOUNG TRAGEDIAN,

Who has been honored by the attendance of

☞LARGE AND ENTHUSIASTIC AUDIENCES,

AND WILL APPEAR

This Tuesday Evening, May 3, 1864,

IN SHAKSPERE'S PLAY OF

ROMEO AND JULIET!

ROMEO	J. WILKES BOOTH
Mercutio	Mr L. R. Shewell
Benvolio	Mr J. Wilson
Tybalt	Mr J. Wheelock
Capulet	Mr R. F. McClannin
Friar Lawrence	Mr F. Hardenburgh
Paris	Mr Walter Benn
Peter	Mr J. H. Ring
Apothecary	Mr Sol. Smith, Jr
Balthazar	Mr T. M. Hunter
Gregory	Mr J. Delano
Page	Mrs T. M. Hunter
Juliet	Miss Kate Reignolds
Nurse	Mrs J. R. Vincent
Lady Capulet	Miss M. Parker

DANCE . . . . ARIEL!

Miss ROSE and THERESE WOOD.

DURING THE EVENING,

Mr. EICHBERG'S ORCHESTRA

WILL PRESENT THE FOLLOWING:

OVERTURE--Midnight Angel	EICHBERG
SELECTIONS FROM RIGOLETTO	VERDI
ST. PATRICK'S QUADRILLE	D'ALBERT
COL. CHICKERING'S BATTLE MARCH	EICHBERG

To conclude with the Laughable Farce, entitled

BROTHER BILL AND ME

Archibald Noodle . . . Mr R. F. McClannin	Policemen . . . . . Messrs. Delano and Hunter
William Wiggles . . . . J. Wilson	Seraphina Noodle . . . Miss Emily Mestayer
Benjamin Wiggles . . . . W. Warren	Wilhemina Noodle . . . . Mrs Hunter
Simon Squib . . . . Sol. Smith, Jr	Martha Wiggles . . . . . Miss Josephine Orton

WEDNESDAY EVENING,

DAMON AND PYTHIS!

DAMON	Mr BOOTH
Pythias . . . . Mr L. R. Shewell	Calanthe . . Miss Kate Reignolds

☞ Due notice will be given of Mr BOOTH'S appearance as "IAGO!" and also of a repetition of "RICHARD III" and "THE APOSTATE!"

☞ Wednesday Afternoon-- A glorious bill! "HUNTER OF THE ALPS!" DANCING and "BLACK EYED SUSAN."

Seats Secured One Week in Advance.

Admission 30 Cents. . . . . . .Orchestra and Reserved Seats 50 Cents

Children under 10 years of Age, 15 Cents.   Children in Arms not Admitted.

Exhibition Hall open at 6 1-2 o'clock . . . Evening Performance commence at 7 1-2 o'clock Afternoon Performance at 2 1-2 o'clock.

TREASURER . . . . Mr. GEO. W. BLATCHFORD

F. A. Searle, Printer, Journal Building, 118 Washington Street, Boston.

BOSTON MUSEUM

ACTING MANAGER .... Mr. R. M. FIELD

~MR.~
J. WILKES BOOTH

~THIS~

Wednesday Evening, May 4, 1864,

IN THE FINE PLAY OF

DAMON AND PYTHIAS

DAMON	Mr J. WILKES BOOTH
Pythias	Mr L. R. Shewell
Dionysius	Mr F. Hardenburgh
Philistius	Mr J. Wilson
Damocles	Mr J. Wheelock
Procles	Mr T. M. Hunter
Lucullus	Mr Walter Benn
Naxilus	Mr J. Delano
Petrus	Mr M. Woolf
Senators	J. Peakes, Adams, Knowlton Launders, etc.
Calanthe	Miss Kate Reignolds
Hermion	Miss Annie Clarke
Damon's Child	Miss Susie Swindlehurst

Senators, Soldiers, etc.

The Piece will be admirably mounted as regards

☞ Scenery, Costumes and Appointments. ☜

DANCE .... ARIEL !

Miss ROSE and THERESE WOOD.

DURING THE EVENING.

Mr. EICHBERG'S ORCHESTRA

WILL PRESENT THE FOLLOWING :

1. OVERTURE--Jeannette	EICHBERG
2. IL BACIO VALSE	ARDITI
3. PAISLEY SCHOTTISCHE	LABITZKY
4. SELECTIONS FROM LA TRAVIATA	VERDI

To conclude with the Glorious WARREN FARCE, entitled

FITZSMYTHE, OF FITZSMYTHE HALL !

Fitzsmythe of Fitzsmythe Hall, W. Warren	Bey .... Miss Kate Harrison
Frank Tottenham .... J. Wilson	Mrs Fitzsmythe of Fitzsmythe Hall,
Gregory .... Sol. Smith, Jr	Mrs J. R. Vincent
Cricketers .... Delano and Pitman	Penelope .... Mrs J. Wheelock

THURSDAY EVENING,

THE APOSTATE.

Received with universal applause by a Crowded Audience on Wednesday last.]

SATURDAY AFTERNOON,

ROMEO AND JULIET !

ROMEO ... . Mr BOOTH
Mercutio .... Mr L. R. Shewell | Juliet .... Miss Kate Reignolds

Seats Secured One Week in Advance.

Admission 30 Cents........Orchestra and Reserved Seats 50 Cents

Children under 10 years of Age, 15 Cents. Children in Arms not Admitted.

Exhibition Hall open at 6 1-2 o'clock...Evening Performance commence at 7 1-2 o'clock
Afternoon Performance at 2 1-2 o'clock.

TREASURER .... Mr. GEO. W. BLATCHFORD

F. A. Searle, Printer, Journal Building, 118 Washington Street, Boston.

BOSTON MUSEUM

ACTING MANAGER .... Mr. R. M. FIEL

FOURTH WEEK OF

J. WILKES BOOTH

WHO WILL APPEAR, THIS EVENING, AS

ST. PIERRE

For the first time in Boston, supported by a

☞ SPLENDID CAST. ☜

Mr WARREN in the .... TWO BONNYCASTLE

THIS THURSDAY EVENING, MAY 19, 1864

The Performance will commence with a .... FAVORITE OVERTURE

Leader and Musical Director .... JULIUS EICHBERG.

After which, will be presented the much admired Play of

THE WIFE!

CAST AS FOLLOWS :

JULIAN ST. PIERRE	J. WILKES BOOTH
Leonardo Gonzago	Mr L. R. Shewell
Ferrardo Gonzago	Mr F. Hardenburgh
Antonio	Mr W. H. Smith
Bartolo	Mr R. F. McClannin
Lorenzo	Mr J. Wilson
Count Florio	Mr J. Wheelock
Hugo	Mr G. F. Ketchum
Bernardo	Mr M. Woolf
Carlo	Mr Sol. Smith, Jr
Cosmo	Mr Delano
Courier	Mr T. M. Hunter
Officer	Mr J. Peakes
Pietro	Mr J. E. Adams
Mariana	Miss Kate Reignolds
Floribel	Miss H. Orton

DANCE .... LA VIVANDIERE !

Miss ROSE and THERESE WOOD.

BRILLIANT SELECTIONS .... ORCHESTRA

To conclude with, 2d time this season, and by request, the capital Farce of

TWO BONNYCASTLES !

Mr Smuggins .... Mr R. F. McClannin	Mrs Bonnycastle ... ... Miss Annie Clarke
Mr J. Johnson .... J. Wilson	Helen .... Mrs T. M. Hunter
Jeremiah Jorum .... W. Warren	Patty .... Mrs J. Wheelock

☞ Friday--BENEFIT OF Mr BOOTH and production of MACBETH.
☞ Saturday Afternoon--Mr BOOTH in the MARBLE HEART !
☞ In Preparation for Monday next--THE CORSICAN BROTHERS !

Seats Secured One Week in Advance.

Admission 30 Cents........Orchestra and Reserved Seats 50 Cents

Children under 10 years of Age, 15 Cents. Children in Arms not Admitted.

Exhibition Hall open at 6 1-2 o'clock...Evening Performance commence at 7 1-2 o'clock
Afternoon Performance at 3 o'clock.

TREASURER .... Mr. GEO. W. BLATCHFORD

F. A. Searle, Printer, Journal Building, 118 Washington Street, Boston.

commencement of his engagement. Seats are in demand for a week ahead, and there is every indication that his present visit to Boston will be crowned with greater success than any heretofore made.

The stage door was always crowded, and the Tremont House became another waiting place to catch a glimpse of Booth before and after a performance. He smiled at the long lines of fans and joked with the cabmen as he hurried through the crowds. Miss Norcross remembered that after a performance and a hearty meal late at night as all good actors did, Booth liked nothing better than to curl up in a chair and become engrossed in reading some book from her father's library. Booth was indeed a lover of books, for from various sources we get a verification of this. His library on the Maryland farm was impressive considering the time and the isolation he faced in growing up. His mother gave him autographed books on his birthday; and his trunk in traveling was always heavily stocked with the classics. Books or title pages from his books turn up occasionally and bring handsome prices on the collector's market.

Since Saturday evening performances were not allowed in Boston because of the so-called Blue Laws, the company gave Saturday and Wednesday matinee performances. Boston had not yet progressed to the point of nightly shows as had New Orleans, which not only presented performances on Saturday evenings, but Sunday evenings as well.

Besides his usual Richard, Romeo, Hamlet, and other Shakespearean roles, Booth's five-week engagement included a variety of romantic roles of the day. Several of his seldom played parts were presented, such as *The Wife, Ugolino*, and the Greek legend *Damon and Pythias*, the story of two men whose names are a symbol of ideal friendship. Booth played Damon to the Pythias of L.R. Shewell, and to the Calanthe of Kate Reignolds, the actress who graphically wrote her on-stage memories of Booth.

One other play was planned. On Wednesday, May 4th, the play *Charles II*, which he rarely performed, was announced on the handbills for a matinee performance, but the production did not come off as planned and substitutions were made for the afternoon without Booth. Speculation might be that rehearsals did not come up to expectations, and Booth walked out.

Perenially popular afterpieces included such comic satires as: *Hit Him, He Has No Friends; Truth in the Rough; Loan of a Lover;* and *Why Don't She Marry?* Of the wide variety of plays offered by Booth at this time, one wonders which one Julia Ward Howe had in mind when she remarked: "Ah! Have you heard young Booth yet? He's a man of fine talents and noble hopes in his profession."[4] It was at this time that Mrs. Howe (who wrote the familiar "Battle Hymn of the Republic") was on a lecture tour espousing reforms: abolition, women's suffrage and world peace.[5]

For a picture of the Boston Theater at the time Booth played there, we turn again to Miss Norcross' memoirs:

Opposite, left and right: playbills of Booth in Damon and Pythias, *May 4, and in* The Wife, *May 19, 1864, both at the Boston Museum. From the Harvard College Theatre Library Collection. Both previously unpublished.*

People paid more attention to dress in those days, and there was more visible enjoyment of life. Theatre going was an important social function. We always went in our carriage, and every box was filled with ladies in full evening dress, feathers and flowers in their hair, wearing beautiful jewels and carrying magnificent fans, many of them jeweled and costing hundreds of dollars. The Boston Theatre, with its brilliantly magnificent chandelier lighted, was a gorgeous sight. Between the acts the audience visited and paraded up and down in the lobby. The aisles of the orchestra were filled with marvelously gowned women and handsome men.[6]

Booth brought his longest star engagement to a close on Friday, May 27, 1864, in a farewell benefit of *Ugolino; or, The Innocent Condemned*, a tragedy written by his father who possessed a talent for writing in addition to his great acting ability. This play was first presented by him in New York 30 years previously. Wilkes revived this blank verse tragedy in honor of his father's birthday.

The Boston Museum was not really a museum at all, but a living, active theater hiding behind the pretentious label of "museum."[7]

CHAPTER 24: Parlor Performances Among the Oil Fields of Pennsylvania

At the end of his Boston run we find Booth traveling widely from Washington to Canada, but there are no recorded theatrical engagements during the summer and fall of 1864 unless one considers the scattered hotels where he gave readings and special dialogues in parlor appearances. He could always pick up a few hundred dollars at any hotel where he might be staying for an evening's readings. This he did on many occasions, most of which are unrecorded as they were spontaneous and not advertised.

Several trips during the latter part of 1864 were made to Franklin, in the Pennsylvania oil region, on speculative leases and prospecting in the area. In Ernest C. Miller's studies on this period of Booth's life, we find an interesting collection of interviews with various people of Franklin, who 29 years after the tragedy, set down their thoughts about Booth's visits there. According to Miller, this was a trying time for Booth. His throat was bothering him, and he had to take a rest from the stage for a while. As Booth had expensive tastes, he wanted to maintain his income at a high level, and had no intention of lowering his standard of living. Although whenever he appeared he would average from $500 to $1,000 per week, he was refusing engagements which could have gained him ever greater returns. Whether his throat was bothering him or his time was taken up in undercover activities for the Confederacy, he was still expending large sums of money for his pleasure as well as contributing to the Confederate cause; and the boom-town of Franklin seemed to be another way of supplementing his income.

It was at this time that Booth, along with Cleveland theater manager John A. Ellsler and Thomas Y. Mears, a gambler and former prizefighter, formed the Dramatic Oil Company, and Booth's well was being drilled. It seems that the idea for the company was first created in January 1864, and the most of the summer of that year Booth spent in Franklin watching the progress of the well.

Ellsler describes those days of oil speculation when excitement over the new discovery even took precedence over Booth's theater work: Through a mutual friend, Ellsler and Booth had been persuaded to invest in a piece of oil land during the mania for oil territory in Pennsylvania. The understanding was that at the conclusion of the dramatic season, the new property owners would go to their exciting adventure. As arranged, Booth preceded Ellsler to the area and began to purchase the necessary machinery and get things in operation. Ellsler detailed the situation as he found it:

155

"He had all the elements of genius but seemed powerless to focus them..."—Joel Chandler Harris. Booth in Napoleonic pose. From the National Archives, Washington, D.C.

When I reached him, I found him hard at work, dressed in a slouched hat, flannel shirt, overalls, and boots. He was a sight to behold. Who that had ever seen him as Hamlet, Claude Melnotte, Richard, Raphael, Romeo, Petruchio, etc., would suppose that such a transformation would be possible!... But there he was, a handsome picture of manhood, even in his working garb. The little town of Franklin being at the time crowded, Wilkes had provided himself with a "sky parlor" in a frame skeleton, called by courtesy a house. This he had furnished with a bachelor's paraphrenalia. There was quite a library of interesting reading matter and a few engravings, together with photographs of his family that decorated the wall. In one corner stood the bedstead and a double barreled shot gun, with its accompanying powder flask. In another corner was his fishing tackle, etc., and last, but not least, on a shelf reposed four well-colored meerschaum pipes, a five pound box of killikinick,[1] and a variety of clay pipes. To this cozy establishment Wilkes invited me as his guest, and it was here we learned to know each other, as only men can know each other who live together, week in and week out....[2]

There are many interesting incidents of Booth's stay in Franklin, as recorded by people who knew him. The same observations keep recurring wherever we find him: that he was a polished gentleman, "courtesy incarnate — with the manners of a Virginian of the old school," kind, considerate, a lover of fun, though subject to moody spells. He loved children; was free with his money. Everywhere people seemed to notice the piercing magnetic gaze, the Booth look, the poetic face, the expensive wardrobe, the aristocratic stature, the shrewd and keen intellect, and the fiery temperament when provoked.

During this interim summer away from the theater he did not completely give up acting. After a day's surveying the oil fields on horseback, his evenings were usually spent in performing for his friends and select groups of other oil prospectors and townsmen. His ability to converse and sway his listeners was renowned. He was described as one who could "dim his beauty as you turn down a lamp in men's company, so that their natural suspicions were lulled and they took him in."[3]

The nightly gatherings among the oil fields was described thus:

> Booth and several cronies had a room over an old barroom where they congregated in the evenings to enjoy themselves. All were jolly whole-souled men, each well-to-do, who had come to Franklin to have a tussle with this new way of making fortunes. The genial spirits who met in this room with Booth were men of education and much means. Besides Booth, there were many other Shakespearean scholars ... and two or three first rate comedians.... Between Shakespeare readings, recitations by Booth ... comedy work ... some very interesting evenings were spent in the old room. This crowd repaired to this room in the evenings only, after having covered a good deal of territory during the day looking for promising leases or merely standing around town or loitering in the numerous real estate offices, where the avaricious farmer was constantly repairing to lease his farm. ...The fun grew fast and furious at these meetings of the club and the entertainment was sometimes as interesting as the most fastidious taste could wish. Booth always took an active part in whatever was going on. Comedy or tragedy, it was all the same to him... One peculiarity of Booth's was the fact that he never indulged in a hearty laugh. Nothing more than a smile could be brought to his face by the most amusing of actions or utterances on the part of his fellow members of the impromptu club. Booth never laughed; he merely smiled.[4]

Here we get what might be an implication of Booth's abnormal inadequacy, a change of his personality, or perhaps in his mental health. Previously, he had been recorded just the opposite.

Another interview recorded how Booth, after having spent an evening drinking the strongest brandy available, decided that he would like to perform his favorite role of Richard III. A member of his audience that evening recollected that "Booth was as drunk as he could possibly get and was covering the whole sidewalk in a rendition of the play. He carried a broomstick in his hand which he wielded as the rendering of the part demanded, and the exhibition was very strong and made more than one bystander overlook Booth's condition in their admiration for his acting of the part."[5]

This instance will again remind the reader of the similarity between Booth and his father, who acted in much the same manner, playing his role even into the street and forgetting his audience entirely until the spirit moved him to fight his way back into the theater again.

Others noted an example of Booth's arrogance, a new development in his personality, when they observed that he was a cynic of the most pronounced type, inclined to sneer at "a great many things an average man would do. He sneered at religion and at the religious professions of his friends. His cynicism was an all prominent feature, but it was never offensive...."[6]

His conversations were filled with sarcasm and sharp wit, and he could hold forth on any subject. "He had the shrewdest and keenest intellect of any man I ever met," said one acquaintance. Six weeks before the Ford's Theatre tragedy Booth was again in Franklin. Upon his departure some of his friends asked him where he was going, to which he nastily retorted, "I am going to Hell" — another contradiction of his joking spirit, and one which emphasized how morose and brooding he could be.

Yet others of those interviewed mentioned his great popularity with the ladies, the same in the oil town as in the plush drawing rooms of the cities. They speak with awe of his manners, and tell "stories of the magnetisim and the fascination in the man's face are strictly true no matter how strongly drawn...." It was said of his readings, that "the most hardened drunkard would weep copiously on hearing John Booth's rendering of 'The Sermon on the Mount'."[7]

A compulsive actor, Booth would draw his own audience wherever he found it that summer. He was always ready with a poem or a characterization, whether he was walking with the workmen in the hills or lounging in the barrooms, harness shop, barbershop, or hotel parlor. He loved to chat, and would discuss any topic be it politics, literature, theatre, or nature.

There are several references to a performance given in Meadville, Pennsylvania, although search has failed to uncover any definite evidence that he gave a professional performance there. We are told that he was an "overnight guest at the McHenry House on August 13, 1864, after a theatrical performance at the Opera House on Water and Chestnut Streets."[8]

The only reason one learns of this performance is in connection with the diamond-scratched windowpane in his hotel room. Apparently Booth amused himself by removing his diamond stickpin or his diamond ring, both familiar objects to his friends, and etching the following on his bedroom windowpane: "Abe Lincoln, departed this life August 13, 1864, by the effects of Poison."

Although the chambermaid reported the etched windowpane the following morning, nothing was done about it until after Lincoln's assassination eight months later. The manager of the hotel removed the glass, mounted it on black velvet, and framed it together with Booth's signature cut from the hotel register. It remained in the possession of Mary McHenry, daughter of the hotel owner, until 1879. At that time she sent it to Judge-Advocate-General Dunn in Washington, D.C., where it was added to other Booth relics in his office.

Probably Booth did give unadvertised performances, or solo readings in Meadville as he had done for his friends in Franklin. There are many more

"Doubtless he would have been the greatest actor of his time if he had lived..."—John T. Ford. Booth in three-quarter length portrait with cape. From the William Wyles Collection, University of California, Santa Barbara.

such unrecorded performances wherever Booth happened to be, such as those in St. Joseph, Mo., or Niagara Falls, and Troy, N.Y. Those improvisational performances were briefly alluded to only in letters to friends, or found entered in diaries of those in attendance.[9]

Here is one interesting report of a performance Booth gave one

afternoon for four people. The story goes that one day two ladies and a gentleman escort in Franklin went to have their photographs taken. In the gallery
upon their arrival was a stranger. While the camera, subjects, and back-
grounds were being prepared, a heavy rain storm began to rage, which kept
the four people stranded in the studio for some time. The stranger, as it was
learned later, happened to be John Wilkes Booth. He suggested that as they
were all stormbound together, that they might as well have a group photograph taken. The ladies were reluctant as they did not know the stranger, but
finally agreed to a group posing and a photograph was taken. As the storm
persisted outside, it seemed the group would be inconvenienced for a long
time. Making the most of an awkward situation, Booth undertook to amuse
the two ladies, their gentleman escort, and the photographer by an impromptu divertissement. Jumping upon the gallery platform, Booth quickly
improvised a tiny stage and began impersonations from parts he was familiar
with as an actor. He presented part after part in rapid succession, jumping
from one role to another, with abrupt and vivid transitions from comedy to
tragedy. His private audience sat spellbound as the storm continued to rage
outside. Later, one of the ladies present recalled how especially entertaining
was one of these scenes in which Booth portrayed a comic Irish cook preparing an evening meal, which he had quickly improvised with props and
deft pantomime. As soon as the storm was over, Booth made his exit from
the tiny stage, and in true actor fashion, bowed graciously and departed. It
was then that the ladies learned that their gallant entertainer had indeed been
none other than John Wilkes Booth. A few days later, each of them received a
copy of the photograph sent by him from Baltimore.[10]

Back in Franklin, his old theater friends were avidly playing the role of
oil men. They were Jo Simonds, John Ellsler, and Tom Mears, the "all around
good sport" and tough fighter who enjoyed music and poetry. There were
also several others in this bachelor group who had left the oppressive summer
heat of the city in exchange for a refreshing summer of roughing it with
nature.

Although Booth threw up his own "sky parlor" as mentioned, he at
first shared quarters with some of the group. Since Franklin was a boom-
town, there was little choice in sleeping accommodations.

Probably Booth's closest friend during this summer was the oil and
pipeline operator A.W. Smiley. Booth usually preferred nonactors for his
personal friends; he would choose mechanics and other down-to-earth,
rough and ready men, for his off-stage associates. Such a man was Smiley,
who gave the following interview which he set down in the third person,
giving us some interesting details of these times:

> The town was full of people at that time so Booth and Jo Simonds, who
> came with him, occupied Smiley's room in the old U.S. Hotel. Smiley, Phil-
> lips, and Stevens had the same room. Booth and Simonds had the same
> room. After a week, Booth slept with Smiley and put Simonds in with Phil-
> lips who was an immensely large man.[11] This was a result of a scheme of
> Booth's and Smiley's with that object.... Booth took quite a fancy to Smiley
> who was only 21 years old at the time. Smiley worked at the Atlantic &
> Great Western R.R. Depot. Booth had plenty of money and was very free in

spending it. Would not let Smiley pay for anything, saying, "I have plenty of money and you are only working for a salary. I enjoy your company and I am going to pay for all our fun together." ... Smiley accompanied Booth on all the little sprees around town. Went to dances together and drank together ... thrown out of a dance hall ... after a hard fight. Booth and his partner had bloody noses but there were many bloody noses inside the hall. Booth was a hard drinker of the strongest brandy. Sometimes he drank rum.... Smiley always knew that Booth was a perfect gentleman. In the presence of ladies his manners were the most refined.

Most of the summer of 1864 Booth spent in Franklin, but he made many trips back and forth from Baltimore to Washington during this time. In mid-June he was at home in New York, Edwin's home, where he and his brothers made plans for benefit performances for the Shakespeare Statue Fund. While the plans were still in progress, Wilkes took off for Cleveland, went back to the oil region, and up to Niagara Falls and then to Montreal again.

CHAPTER 25: New York–Washington Rationales: "To Whom It May Concern"

During his absence from the stage, it has been surmised that Booth had given up the stage because of his voice, or as some have said, a fall in popularity. It was probably more likely that this absence may be attributed to his undercover work for the Confederacy, smuggling drugs and medical supplies across the lines. The South needed medicine badly. Quinine was a costly drug and urgently needed. Booth's contacts supplied him with this scarce and vital drug and he had money to buy it. Many are the tales of how the smuggling was accomplished; one way was to hide the drug in horse collars. Medicine was thus supplied for places as distant as Kansas and Texas.

Booth's name provided him with easy access and virtually assured his freedom of travel. He told his sister, Asia:

> I have only an arm to give. My brains are worth twenty men; my money worth an hundred. I have free pass everywhere, my profession, my name, is my passport; my knowledge of drugs is valuable, my beloved precious money — oh, never beloved till now! — is the means, one of the means, by which I serve the South.... Grant has given me freedom of range without knowing what a good turn he has done the South. Not that the South cares a bad cent about *me*, mind — a mere peregrinating play-actor.[1]

The Shakespeare statue benefit performance which the Booth brothers had been planning all summer finally took place on Friday night, November 25, 1864, at the Winter Garden Theater, on New York City's Broadway. Edwin played Brutus, Junius Brutus played Cassius, and John Wilkes played Mark Antony. Their brother-in-law John Sleeper Clarke, who was managing the Winter Garden, ceded the evening for the occasion. Announcements stated that "The evening will be made memorable by the appearance of the sons of the great Booth ... who have come forward with cheerful alacrity to do honor to the immortal bard from whose work the genius of their father caught inspiration and of many of whose greatest creations he was the best and noblest illustrator the stage has ever known."

Prices skyrocketed for this special performance to $5 for the orchestra, $1.50 for the parquet and orchestra circle, and $1 for the family circle: unusual for those days when prices ordinarily ranged from 15¢ to 75¢ to see a play. But the people were reminded that they were "contributing to a great national work and not to the personal advantage of any individual" (from the playbill). The New York *World* reported on the 28th that nearly $4,000 dollars had been gained toward the statue by this performance.

An eloquent description of the performance before a packed audience of 3,000, was offered by the sister of the Booth brothers:

> The theatre was crowded to suffocation, people standing in every available place. The greatest excitement prevailed, the aged mother of the Booth's sat in a private box to witness the performance. The three brothers received and merited the applause of that immense audience, for they acted well, and presented a picture too strikingly historic to be soon forgotten. The eldest [Junius Brutus], powerfully built and handsome as an antique Roman; Edwin, with his magnetic fire and graceful dignity, and John Wilkes in the perfection of youthful beauty, stood side by side, again and again, before the curtain to receive the lavish applause of the audience mingled with waving handkerchiefs and every mark of enthusiasm.[2]

At the end of the first act amid outbursts of applause and cries of "Bravo! Bravo!" the three brothers stood before the private box their mother occupied and bowed to her. This spectacular event must have been the proudest of her life.

Wilkes had shaved off his familiar moustache for his portrayal of Marc Antony. Attired in Roman toga and

Playbill of the three Booth brothers in Julius Caesar. *Winter Garden, New York, November 25, 1864. From the collection of the Museum of the City of New York.*

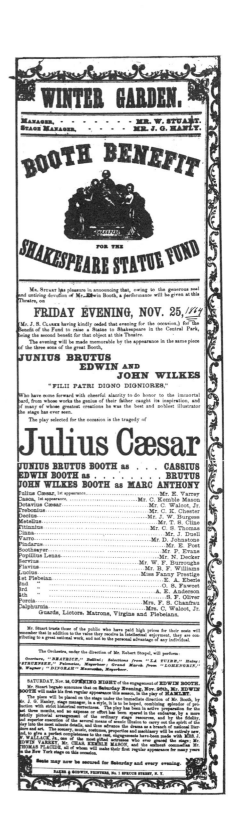

"The audience was fairly carried by storm from the first entrance of the three brothers side-by-side..."—New York Herald. *From left to right: John Wilkes Booth as Marc Antony, Edwin Booth as Brutus, and Junius Brutus Booth as Cassius, at the Winter Garden, New York, November 25, 1864, in a benefit for the Shakespeare Statue Fund. From the Brady and U.S. Collection, Library of Congress.*

sandals laced high on the legs, his striking appearance elicited reports over the audience. Asia overheard a Southern voice exclaim while staring as if transfixed: "Our Wilkes is like a young god!"

The *New York Herald*, the following day, gave ample coverage. The reviewer liked best the scene of Brutus and the conspirators; also the death of

Caesar, and the quarrel scene "were perfect pieces of dramatic art...." He said that the vast audience was "fairly carried by storm from the first entrance of the three brothers side by side.... Brutus was individualized with great force and distinctness—Cassius was brought out equally well—and if there was less of real personality given Marc Antony, the fault was rather in the part than in the actor.... He played with a phosphorescent passion and fire, which recalled to old theatregoers the characteristics of the elder Booth."

At breakfast the following morning the family all gathered at Edwin's home on 19th Street. What had been a happy occasion was then marred by a heated political quarrel among the brothers.

That evening, Saturday, November 26th, Edwin began what was to be his famous 100 consecutive nights of *Hamlet*. He never forgot the spectacular night when the three brothers played for the only time together. Two years before his death, we have a record of his thoughts on Wilkes in that performance. From the diary of E.V. Valentine, set down after a visit to Edwin at The Players, October 6, 1891:

> Edwin spoke of his early success and of fame—that illusive, undefinable, mysterious status that sometimes comes easily and quickly, or not at all. He gave as an example, the time his father was to play but got quite intoxicated so that he could not. Yet the papers next morning told what a fine performance it was, though the elder Booth had not played at all! Edwin Booth said that his brother Wilkes had fine talent, but he did not like correction.... Spoke of how strong he was physically.... Spoke of how finely Wilkes Booth had played Mark Antony....[3]

About this time Wilkes began his famous "statements" or "To whom it may concern" letters detailing his political views. He wrote at least four versions of these rationales; however, only two have been thoroughly treated by the historians. The first version, left for safekeeping with his brother-in-law, J.S. Clarke in November 1864, has been the one most often published. Then there was the version Booth gave to his friend, John Matthews to be delivered to John F. Coyle, editor of the *National Intelligencer*, which Matthews committed to memory and then destroyed. Then there is the version that Booth himself gave to his editor friend, Coyle. On the night of the April 15, 1865, assassination, Coyle and several other gentlemen were having a private dinner party in a back room at Wormley's Restaurant in Washington. During dinner, the waiter came in and told them that Lincoln had been shot at Ford's Theatre, and that the suspect was Booth. It was then that Coyle remembered an incident earlier, and with blanched features and trembling lips, said: "My God, gentlemen, this very day I met John Wilkes Booth in the market space. He was on a bay mare, and rode up to me and handed me a sealed envelope, saying, as he did so: *If you hear of me in twenty-four hours publish this. If you do not hear of me in that time destroy this,* and he rode away. Here is the package.... What must I do with it?" All the gentlemen were horrified and agreed that the document should be burned at once without its being opened for anyone would surely hang who knew anything about the assassination no matter how innocent.

> The doors were carefully locked, and the mysterious envelope and its contents were carefully burned. Even the ashes were carefully collected and

placed in a dish, mixed with water, and made into a paste, which was afterward put into the fire and burned again.[4]

Even with two versions addressed to the *National Intelligencer* supposedly destroyed, there was a third such statement addressed to that newspaper. Apparently, none of these ever reached the newspaper office, yet one addressed "To the proprietors of the *National Intelligencer*" was published in full in 1866.[5]

Finally, there is still a fourth known version of the statement which survived and is still in perfect condition; its purple ink is as clear today as when Booth penned it in 1865. This 16-page proclamation addressed "To the People of the United States," is in the collection of the library of the Players' Club, New York City. The library calls it "the original draft" and it has never been published. Its context is similar to the published and "memory" version of Matthews,[6] except that it is quite different in wording.

During the latter part of 1864 and the beginning of 1865, Booth spent a large part of his time in Washington where he was flattered by the attentions of people in many walks of life. He lived at the National Hotel and apparently was a man of leisure. Obviously, he was preoccupied with subversive plans more important to him than the theater. He had plenty of offers for engagements from many theater managers, but he seemed uninterested. His mother sensed something was wrong, wondering why he did not accept other engagements since he had been such a success at the Winter Garden. His connections with two senator's daughters, Eva and Bessie Hale, enabled him to get tickets to most presidential functions. He was welcomed at high society functions in Washington as well as by the low-lifes of John Derry's Billiard Parlor Saloon next door to Grover's Theater.

He frequently lounged in the parlor house of his favorite mistress, Ella Turner Starr, whose sister Nellie ran the most expensive and also the coziest establishment in Washington. Yet it was rumored that he was engaged to Bessie Hale, while still keeping company with another senator's daughter. It would be hard to say which of these women was more enamored of him. Ella, upon hearing of the tragedy, took chloroform, placed Booth's picture underneath her pillow and prepared to die. When officers found her she told them she did not thank them for saving her life. Bessie Hale wrote to Edwin declaring she was ready to marry Wilkes "even at the foot of the scaffold." Miss Hale was exiled abroad by her family, but she kept Booth's letters until the end. Her will requested they be burned. It would be revealing if one could read them today. Could they compare with the one to Ella Turner Starr:

> My Dearest Love —
> Although I have not been long away from you, still it seems an age. I divide the world into two parts, where you are, and where you are not. I am indeed separated from you in body, but joined to you in soul.
> I was detained longer in Baltimore than I anticipated, but I hope it will all be right in the end. There will be a change before long, which will greatly influence my fortune, but of one thing rest assured, that whatever may occur, whether in time or eternity,
> I am ever yours,
> J. Wilkes Booth.[7]

Rumors of his girl friends, his illegitimate children, his secret marriage, his perversions, seem to mount with the years. It is obvious that he dabbled in all forms of the above, but any proof so far has been only speculation.

As to girl friends, we get an idea of one girl whom Booth indicated as the "serious one." This might mean one would could do him the most good politically, since he had had numerous advantages to choose from all areas of society. He had two senator's daughters on the string who helped him to gain admittance to governmental functions. Booth's close friend John Matthews recalled an incident which might throw some light on the "serious one":

> He had some words at the National Hotel upon the subject of the exchange of prisoners with a United States Senator, and, coming up to my room, he spoke of the subject with great feeling. Finally, he threw himself upon my bed and seemed to be a good deal distressed. He lay for a moment in deep thought, and then, quickly turning to me, said: "John, were you ever in love?" "No, I never could afford it," I replied. "I wish I could say as much. I am a captive. You cannot understand how I feel. What are those lines in *Romeo and Juliet* describing love? I have played them a hundred times, but they have flown from me." "Will you stand a bottle if I'll give them to you?" I asked. "I will—two of them," replied Booth. "Here are the lines," I answered:
>
> *O! anything, of nothing, first create!*
> *O! heavy lightness! serious vanity!*
> *Misshapen chaos of well-seeming forms!*
>
> "That's it," replied Booth. "If it were not for this girl I could feel easy. Think of it, John, that at my time of life—just starting as it were—I should be in love!"[8]

Although Matthews knew who the girl was, he refrained from disclosing it, but it can be surmised that it was Bessie Hale, the senator's daughter.

Although Booth's flowing cape with collar of curly lamb's wool became his trade mark of pleasure seeking in Washington, his plotting, conspiracies, and mysterious connections with many underground groups also took up much of his time. He seemed to disregard all offers for theatrical engagements, yet he had indicated to Matthews that his career was just beginning. After the tremendous success of his five-week engagement in Boston and the sell-out in New York, one can be sure that Booth could have written his own terms of any engagement. His drawing power was evident in many letters such as this one from manager J.H. McVicker, Chicago, dated December 25, 1864:

> What do you say to filling three weeks with me, May 29th? I have not yet filled your time in January, and see no chance of doing so with an attraction equal to yourself. There are plenty of little fish but I don't want them if I can help it. So, if you can come then, come at the above date....[9]

Booth, however, continued to ignore all offers. Also there were many requests from actor friends asking him to play for their benefit performances, knowing full well that the Booth name in itself guaranteed a large box office return.

His business manager, Joseph Simonds, unable to understand him, wrote this to him in February 1865:

I hardly know what to make of you this winter — so different from your usual self. Have you lost all your ambition or what is the matter? Don't get offended with me John, but I cannot but think you are wasting your time spending the entire season in Washington doing nothing where it must be expensive to live and all for no other purpose beyond pleasure....[10]

His mother, whom many have described as psychic, sensed that something was wrong. From New York, March 26, 1865, she wrote Wilkes: "...I have never doubted your love and devotion to me — in fact I always gave you praise for being the fondest of all my boys, but since you leave me in grief I must doubt it. I am no Roman mother. I love my dear ones before country or anything else. Heaven guard you, is my constant prayer...."[11]

Booth's answer to this letter is obviously the April, 1865, five-page letter to his mother recently located by researcher James O. Hall of Virginia.[12] Booth states in part: "Dearest beloved Mother — Heaven knows how dearly I love you, and may our kind Father in Heaven ... watch over, comfort and protect you in my absence. May He soften the blow of my departure, granting you peace and happiness for many, many years to come.... I have always endeavored to be a good and dutiful son, and even now would wish to die sooner than give you pain. But dearest Mother, though I owe you all, there is another duty, a noble duty for the sake of liberty and humanity due to my country.... I may, by the grace of God, live through this war, dear Mother, if so, the rest of my life shall be more devoted to you than has been my former.... And should the last bolt strike your son, dear Mother, bear it patiently and think at the best life is short, and not at all times happy...."

Spending his time in Washington with few theatrical engagements, Booth gave the impression of lounging and inactivity. But letters indicate that he was planning strategy for his cause, covering up as a "dram-drinker" of brandy smashes as well as a fashion plate. He frequently remarked that he never got drunk in his legs, that he never staggered. Instead of patronizing saloons where his fellow actors went, he preferred to go to less pretentious places. One such place he preferred was run by a Mrs. Volkner, a German widow, on 10th Street above E Street. Stagehands seemed to suit his introspective moodiness better than his fellow actors. Reporter "Gath" Townsend verified this further by his comment: "He seldom tolerated his equals from the stage, but would take mere vagrants up and use them for his willful rides and strolls."[13]

According to Joseph Hazelton, program boy at Ford's Theatre, Booth held actors in disdain. He classified them as "Mummers of the quality of skinned milk. There are not half a dozen really good players in America, and in all Europe less than a score. Actors they call themselves, forsooth. Pouf! They know little, think less, and understand next to nothing."[14]

As with the elder Booth, Wilkes had a disgust with the claptrap of the stage, and readily expressed his impatience with an audience that could not appreciate good playing. A story is told of the elder Booth which draws an interesting comparison between the elder and the younger Booths. Wilkes might have done the same thing had he been in the same situation. After having been extremely successful in London, where his professional life commenced, the elder Booth made an engagement with a Manchester manager. Manchester, then as now a manufacturing town, was devoted largely to the production of buttons. The elder Booth appeared before his new audience determined to make a hit, so he threw his heart and soul into his work. But, alas, the house remained cold. His choicest efforts were thrown away, and his heart began to sink within him and self-distrust to steal over him. Then there came a part in the play where a fight scene was to occur. The elder Booth went into it with such a hearty zest that cheers and shouts, thus far repressed, broke out in a storm. Booth caught the secret, and so fought his fellow actor so hard that he literally yelled in pain. The applause was unbounded. Booth then knew what would please them. He sat down in his chair, stretched his neck toward the audience, and "with a face on which depicted the most bitter contempt and disgust, exclaimed in a way all his own: 'What do you think of *that*, you damned button-makers?'"[15] And it was said that he was obliged to leave the stage as well as the city with a mob of the button-makers on his track.

On the other hand, the son Wilkes in all his stage appearances was more dignified, though he reserved similar opinions of such matters to be spoken off stage. Wilkes too, realized what would move an audience: if not art, then violence. Harden and faster with the swords in *Richard*!

The comparison between father and son continued even off stage; it was said of the elder Booth, "his perfect bondage to his cups was the cause of all his troubles...."

John Deery, Wilkes Booth's close friend, the keeper of a billiard saloon in Washington where Booth spent much time, remembered him thus:

> He was, like many another brilliant man who had been over-fond of his glass, one of the most charming of men. I think he was the most fascinating personality I ever met in my long life. He was as handsome as a young God, with his clear, pale, olive complexion, classical regular features, and hair and mustache literally black as night; but his appearance was not more seductive than his manners. In common intercourse he was utterly devoid of that artificiality and staginess so common to men of his profession. In his ways with his intimates he was as simple and affectionate as a child. John Wilkes Booth cast a spell over most men with whom he came in contact, and I believe all women without exception. In liquor, of which he could absorb an astonishing quantity and still retain the bearings of a gentleman, he would sometimes flash out an angry word, but it was a hard matter to provoke him to a quarrel. For a period of about ten days before the assassination, he visited my place every day, sometimes in the afternoon, sometimes in the evenings.... During that week at Washington he sometimes drank at my bar as much as a quart of brandy in the space of less than two hours.... It was more than a spree, I could see that, and yet Booth was not given to sprees.... Few men have known John Wilkes Booth better than I have known him, and despite his terrible crime and deplorable ending, no man have I known who possessed a more winning personality....[16]

Wilkes' personality allowed him to speak freely his political opinions without getting into serious trouble. Of all the Booths, Wilkes was the most politically active. He had definite ideas and never hesitated to express them, much to the concern of his theater managers. The slightest snide remark could set off his demon temper, where his power of fascination seemed to subdue his opponents. He was once provoked by a remark made against

Jefferson Davis by his brother-in-law, John Sleeper Clarke, whom Booth almost strangled. "Never, if you value your life," he said tensely, "never speak in that way to me of a man and a cause I hold sacred."[17]

There are many tales of his near fights over arguments, but the following one illustrates his intense hatred of Secretary of War Edwin M. Stanton. It is ironic, as future disclosures have indicated that Stanton and Lincoln were at odds on various issues. Stanton, for example, was dead on actors and theaters and tried to get Lincoln not to attend these "places of the devil." If Booth had but known how much support he had as an actor from Lincoln, Booth might have directed his fire against the reactionary Stanton instead of Lincoln. An example of this was recorded by a member of Booth's New York company during the 1862 engagement:

> Not a word of politics was ever heard from Booth during the first week of his engagement, although he was an attentive listener to the angry discussions pro and con, till one morning somebody read from a newspaper on the arrest of Marshal George P. Kane in Baltimore, and his incarceration in Fort McHenry by order of Stanton.

There was an argument among the cast—some approved, while others said that Stanton should be shot. At the suggestion of getting rid of Stanton in this manner, a voice tremulous with emotion rang out from back stage:

> "Yes, sir, you are right!" It was Booth's. "I know George P. Kane well; he is my friend, and the man who could drag him from the bosom of his family for no crime whatever, but a mere suspicion that he *may* commit one some time, deserves a dog's death!" It was not the matter of what he said; it was the manner and general appearance of the speaker, that awed us. It would remind you of Lucifer's defiance at the council. He stood there the embodiment of evil. But it was for a moment only, for in the next breath with a sharp, ringing voice, he exclaimed, "Go on with the rehearsal!" ... I could never forget the scene; the statuesque figure of the young man uttering those few words in the centre of the old stage of Wallack's can never be forgotten....[18]

As the days of war continued Booth became more and more obsessed with its tragedy. It was time for a drastic decision to be made. "I know how foolish I shall be deemed for undertaking such a step as this," he wrote in one of his rationales, "...I have many friends and everything to make me happy, where my profession alone has gained me an income of more than $20,000 a year, and where my great personal ambition in my profession has been a great field for labor.... To give up all this ... my mother and sisters whom I love so dearly ... seems insane; but God is my judge.... Many, I know—the vulgar herd will blame me for what I am about to do, but posterity, I am sure, will justify me....[19] The names of those unhappy men, who have fallen in the defense of their country on the battle fields, and who now repose uncoffined and unshrouded, put into the earth like dogs, will be appeased, and their pale shadows will no longer wander unavenged...."[20] The original of Booth's letter, published in the April 19, 1865, edition of the *Philadelphia Inquirer*, lost for 112 years, was recently found.[21]

CHAPTER 26: Drifting–Plotting– Deterioration: The Final Stage Is Set

As the war progressed in its mounting horror, Booth's emotions heightened into a turmoil of dark machinations. As one historian has put it, "There was something violent, relentless, vindictive, in this partnership — especially in his peculiar manner of clothing it with the habiliments natural to his profession."[1]

Or, the old family "weakness" as some have described it, that was present in the famous father. Some said of the two most famous brothers: Wilkes inherited his father's weakness, Edwin, his father's strength. As for the other two brothers, Junius Brutus, Jr., a capable actor, but never inspired with the divine Booth spark, occupies a middle position, that of categorical mediocrity. Joseph, the youngest son, exhibited even more mediocrity upon the stage. He was hissed off the stage by his brother Edwin's fury at his poor performance: "Get off the stage!" Edwin swore under his breath. Joseph later became a doctor.

But Wilkes' strangeness seemed to be in command of his talent. Perhaps in different times his talent might have proved to be as great as that of his father, but the brooding, plotting and obsessive dwelling on the horrors on the war had taken a toll on him. Wilkes

> had measured the virtue of the world by the stage, and considered himself of a theatrical and political aristocracy.... He could no longer study even the plays with conscientious devotion. Too early success in acting, and admiration, flattery, and worldly lusts, had made one of the most self-contained idiots in Washington. There stood the powerful fiber of an athlete, the exterior of a gentleman, and the apparent descent of genius, without discipline, humility, or much reality, deceiving himself and everybody. The fabric was false in everything but headstrong pride....[2]

Increasingly, he seemed to be living in a melodrama in the world of his plays. His mind was completely engrossed in conspiracy plans. The unreality of the stage had become the real; he was living the great drama in which he found himself the star. Gradually people who had welcomed him with open arms were being crushed. Most of the Southern theaters where he had played were shut down. His former patrons were treading the stage of the battlefield where fighting, carnage and the death struggle were only too vivid.

Continuing the melodrama as Booth saw it, it is interesting to examine the "oath scene" as it is said to have occurred in Mrs. Surratt's boarding house among the conspirators. Mrs. Surratt was commanded to bring out a sculptured representation of the Savior. Booth lit three candles he had brought with him and turned out the gaslights. Booth began the oath but was stopped by Mrs. Surratt, saying she would not permit it in her house. At this Booth sternly told her: "The oath shall be taken! Is this child's play, or have we come here merely to have a little sport? ... Disobey me at your peril." Two of the conspirators stood over her with loaded pistols as Booth prepared to take the oath. His "aside" to Mrs. Surratt was "Utter a word or make a movement and you shall die." Booth pronounced the following words:

> I do solemnly swear, by the passion of our Lord Jesus Christ, by his agony in the garden, by the sorrow which pierced his soul when Peter denied him, and by the spotless purity of his Holy Mother, that I will aid and abet, by all the means in my power, the plot which has just been planned; and I further swear by all that man holds sacred, both in this world and the next, that should any one attempt to reveal the plot or any part of it, that I will pursue him with the utmost vengeance, no matter how closely connected with me.

He then kissed the crucifix. Each in turn advanced and took the oath, not excepting Mrs. Surratt, who was livid with terror. Booth observed to her, "Madam, should you see fit to inform the authorities of this night's transactions, your life shall pay the forfeit...." After Booth left the boarding house, he stepped into the nearest hotel and wrote the following brief note to an unidentified recipient. Could this person have been the master of whom Booth has been called the "tool"? "The plot is all arranged," wrote Booth, "expect great developments. The blow will be inflicted in twenty-four hours or less time. The die is cast, and I cannot, if I would, retrace my steps."[3]

Just how much of this is fiction, no one can tell, but the scene is so much like a performance, especially like one of Booth's little "intimate" hotel characterizations. Mrs. Surratt became the first woman to be hanged in America, most probably on insufficient evidence for complicity in the assassination of Lincoln. It is generally conceded today she was innocent.

Anyone who has read or seen enacted the plays *The Apostate* or *Richard III* or *The Chamber of Death* or *The Corsican Brothers* or *Lucretia Borgia*, to name a few of Booth's villainous roles, will recognize a similarity between the above scene and these stage melodramas. Apparently, Booth was taking the oath purely for its dramatic effect, as well as to impress and frighten the others, most of whom were devout Catholics. Booth himself was not a religious man, and subscribed to no creed, yet he was clever enough to know the impression such an oath would have on the more religious members of the group.

Robert Brigham, postmaster at Franklin, Pennsylvania, who had become acquainted with Booth while in the oil fields, said in 1866:

> In religion Booth was what is called a "free thinker." He tied himself down to no one dogma or creed. He believed in an all powerful head and master of all the universe, but reserved for himself the right to think out and live according to the teaching of the Bible and of nature, as he himself understood it.[4]

It has been said that Booth was a Mason, a Catholic, a Jew, a Methodist, an atheist, a subscriber to other groups, but like his father, he was acquainted with and understood many diverse creeds, exacting from these whatever beliefs suited his own way of thinking.

Toward the end of his career, Booth became increasingly confused, distracted and preoccupied, and his theater engagements became fewer. At this time in his life we note the concern of friends and family which were reflected in letters. We find the following letter to his older brother Junius, which suggests the ill feeling which had begun to mar the brotherly closeness of Wilkes and Edwin:

Washington
Jan. 17 [1865]

Dear Brother

I have just received yours from Philadelphia in which you complain of my not writing. I wrote you some days ago to Philadelphia and I know my letter must have been waiting for you, yet by yours, you have not received it directed to Chestnut Street Theater. I therein stated why I had not written before. You ask me what I am doing. Well, a thousand things, yet no more, hardly than what I could attend to if I was home. But dear brother, you must not think me childish when I say that the old feeling roused by our loving brother has not yet died out. I am sure he thinks I live upon him. And its only for dear Mother that I have gone there at all when in New York, and as I cannot live in that city without him at home, and as this season I would be home all the time, I thought it best not to be in the city at all, and as I like this place next, and my business calls me here I thought I would here make my stand. I hope you received my last, it was a little better than this, as this is in haste. Give my love to all. When does John come here. If I was him I would put it off till March as all's dull now. I don't know how the Philadelphia papers will use you, but if they are as kind to you as to me, why God help you, say I.

Your loving brother,
John.

I received Joe's [his younger brother's] letter.

At the top of the letter is written in a valuable verification of a performance: "P.S. I play Romeo for Avonia Jones' Ben. [benefit] Friday."[5]

As indicated in the postscript, Wilkes did offer his services for a benefit performance for Avonia Jones, on Friday, January 20, 1865. They appeared in *Romeo and Juliet* at Grover's Theatre in Washington. Earlier during the previous year, Miss Jones had appeared with Edwin in the same play at the Winter Garden on behalf of the Shakespeare statue fund, so now Wilkes was returning the favor by benefitting her.

Because of the loss of Wilkes' ill-fated wardrobe trunk, he had to play Romeo in borrowed costumes. It will be remembered that in October 1864, Booth had his trunk shipped to Montreal in anticipation of an engagement with the Theatre Royal. When he left Canada, his idea was to have his trunk ready for him in Richmond, Virginia, safely in Southern territory where he himself would flee after his plans for conspiracy against the government were complete.

But such plans were not to materialize. The trunk was put aboard the blockade-running *Marie Victoria* on her way to Nassau, but the ship was wrecked, and although the trunk was salvaged, its contents were damaged by the salt water. The trunk was seized, and it was not until the contents were sold at public auction in July 1865 by decree of the vice-admiralty court that it was known what happened to the trunk. John Wilkes Booth never learned what happened to his celebrated wardrobe. Valued at $25,000, the auction brought only about $500. Most of the items and the trunk itself were purchased by George Rankin, brother of actor McKee Rankin. Eight years later Edwin Booth managed to get hold of the trunk and the remaining contents, and proceeded to burn the whole thing in a midnight ceremony.

Thus the few remaining performances in John Wilkes Booth's career were played in borrowed costumes. Even though he was not playing very much in the theaters at this time, he was as usual entertaining friends with his talent wherever he happened to be. We get an account of these last days in Washington from a journal kept by a Miss Porterfield, then visiting the capital city. She had become acquainted with Booth through mutual friends at the National Hotel. There she had enjoyed Booth's recitations in the parlor of the hotel, where they attracted and impressed large groups of guests. She relates that she and her friends were all eager to listen to his rendition of poems, as "The Beautiful Snow" and Poe's "The Raven," as well as scenes from plays.

John Wilkes Booth was probably the first to initiate the "intimate theater" or theater-in-the-round as we know it today. His recitations in the private rooms of the National Hotel were popular social functions, where the fashionable eagerly sought an invitation to see "his almost glittering face and trim, powerful figure, in classical or melodramatic characters.... He was the poetical character of that crowded house."[6]

Miss Porterfield recorded these impressions of Wilkes in her journal:

> He soon fascinated me and my girl friend.... He often talked to me and my companion, and knowing that we were schoolgirls, tried to impress us with the need of speaking clearly and understandingly; and on occasion asked us to read a few lines from Shakespeare's *Henry VIII*, carefully criticizing our expression and accent as we read. Although we were misses, he treated us with the utmost deference and respect, and we finally became so well acquainted with him that he gave each of us his photograph, signed by himself.[7]

Booth, always seeming to be the perfect gentleman, was the star attraction at hotel gatherings where he was "looked upon adversely by prudent mothers; he was the exciting principle in many a daughter's heart, who could not separate artificial from real heroism. Maidens with fathers at the front of war, and foolish or unprincipled wives whose husbands were in ships on blockading or cruising service, or upon the military staff, felt the dark wizardry of his eyes, his confidential, low tone, and the touch of a hand daring in its mingled respect and familiarity."[8] Indeed, we are told that Booth had "an almost aphrodisiac effect upon women."[9]

Wilkes' last stage appearance was for another benefit for a friend, John McCullough, who had appeared with him on countless stages throughout the country. On March 18, 1865, Ford's rich drop curtain decorated with a landscape and bust of Shakespeare, rose for the last time on John Wilkes Booth. Washington on that Saturday night was alive with tourists, and as usual were directed by a yelling boy stationed at the corner of 10th and E Streets: "This way to Ford's! Tonight John Wilkes Booth!" he cried, as he distributed the yard-long playbills and announcements.

This same program boy who yelled theater announcements from street corners and delivered playbills to the arriving audiences was Joseph Hazelton, then a small, towheaded, wide-eyed lad, befriended by Booth and Lincoln alike, and encouraged by both of them to make the stage his profession. Years later, Hazelton in writing of his youth remembered Booth as

an interesting and intense personality. Handsome beyond the ordinary, a poseur undoubtedly, a wastrel by instinct, a visionary without doubt, and—I am satisfied beyond question—more than a little abnormal in his mental processes. But whatever he was, there clung about him a romantic aura, and he thoroughly fascinated the boy of 12. With all his faults he was a good actor, indeed, with a trifle more balance, he would have developed into a great actor. At this late date it surely can do no harm for me to say that, looking back through the years. I believe him to have been the best actor in the Booth family. There was a quirk in him, however, that set him apart from his kind. He did not care to associate much with the acting fraternity, but either ran by himself, or consorted with those who were his social and professional inferiors.... Stage mechanics

Playbill of Booth in The Apostate, *his last stage appearance. Ford's Theatre, Washington, D.C., March 18, 1865. From the Harvard College Library Theatre Collection. Previously unpublished.*

FORD'S THEATRE
TENTH STREET, ABOVE E.

SEASON II........ WEEK XXVIII........NIGHT 174
WHOLE NUMBER OF NIGHTS, 483.

JOHN T. FORD...PROPRIETOR AND MANAGER
(Also of Holliday St. Theatre, Baltimore, and Academy of Music, Phil'a.)
Stage Manager..J. B. WRIGHT
Treasurer..H. CLAY FORD

Saturday Evening, March 18, 1865

BENEFIT
OF

JOHN M'CULLOUGH

ON WHICH OCCASION
THE EMINENT YOUNG AMERICAN TRAGEDIAN,
MR. J. WILKES

BOOTH

Having kindly Volunteered his services, will render his Great Character of

PESCARA!

W. H. Hamblin.......................as.......................Malec
(By permission of Messrs. E. L. Davenport and J. W. Wallack, Jr.)
Miss Alice Gray......................as.......................Florinda
John McCullough.....................as.......................Hemeya
C. B. Bishop.........................as.......................Caleb Scrimmidge

First time this season of Richard Taylor's Great Tragedy of THE

APOSTATE!

Pescara...........by............J. WILKES BOOTH
Hemeya............by............JOHN McCULLOUGH
Malec.............by............W. H. HAMP'T
Hamet...J. MATTHEWS
Haly..D. E. REILLY
Alvarez...CHARLES WARWICK
Gomez...J. H. EVANS
James...W. J. FERGUSON
The Cadi..C. V. HESS
Gonzague..L. CARLAND
1st Moor..J. PARKHURST
2d Moor...J. L. DeBONAY
3d Moor...C. BYRNES
4th Moor..
Florinda..Miss Alice Gray

The Great Domestic Drama, founded upon fact, called

JONATHAN BRADFORD!
OR, THE MURDER AT THE ROADSIDE INN.

Caleb Scrimmidge.................................C. B. BISHOP
Jonathan Bradford................................D. E. REILLY
Dan Macaboy.....................................J. F. WHEELOCK
Jack..J. H. EVANS
Mr. Hayes.......................................W. J. FERGUSON
Dozer...L. CARLAND
Rodpole...C. V. HESS
Sergeant Sam....................................J. PARKHURST
Corporal..J. L. De BONAY
Jailor..Miss J. GOURLAY
Annie Bradford...................................Mrs J. R. SCOTT
Sally...
The Children....................................Misses NICHOLS and WATSON

A GRAND SACRED CONCERT
SUNDAY EVENING, MARCH 19, 1865,

BENEFIT OF JAS. R. O'BRYON,
OF FORD'S THEATRE.

The most eminent Artists of this City, have volunteered their services for this special occasion.

MONDAY EVENING, THE DISTINGUISHED TRAGEDIAN,

MR. JOSEPH PROCTOR
Will render his Great Character, the

JIBBENAINOSAY, IN NICK OF THE WOODS!

John McCullough......................as.......................Roaring Ralph
Miss Alice Gray......................as.......................Tillie Dee

Business Manager. J. R. FORD

fitted his introspective moodiness better than his fellow actors. My most vivid impression is that he was a solitary. I do not recall that he was either popular or unpopular with the players at Ford's. He and they were of the same mold, but his intimacies were reserved for the stage crew, a few truckmen, and a mechanic or two from other walks of life. In his leisure he liked to stand in the front of the theatre, twirling his mustache and frankly exhibiting himself. He was not without his vanities, his artificialities, and his petty foibles, but he was intensely human, and I came to be good friends with him. I do not know why he was kindly toward me, but ... he was....[10]

For what was destined to be Wilkes' Booth's last stage appearance he chose his father's role of Pescara in *The Apostate*. McCullough appeared as Hemeya, and Alice Grey as Florinda. Notice of the performance in the following day's paper stated that the audience was unusually demonstrative and manifested its appreciation of his efforts by stamping on the floor and cheering loudly when Booth appeared.

Miss Porterfield's journal confirms the enthusiasm of the audience at this last performance. She related:

A few days after our arrival in Washington, my mother and I were members of a party that attended Ford's Theatre and witnessed a benefit performance for John McCullough. Booth played the part of Pescara, and it seemed to me he was applauded more than any one else in the play. The audience was unusually demonstrative, stamping the floor, cheering, and otherwise manifesting its appreciation of his acting. McCullough came before the curtain, but notwithstanding the marked demonstration in his behalf, Booth refused to respond.[11]

How unlike John Wilkes Booth this was, refusing to acknowledge the overwhelming praise of the audience! Perhaps this is another symptom of his psychotic behavior, or possibly he wished to give the whole show to his friend John McCullough who was being benefitted.

There is one story which indicates that Lincoln was present at this final Booth performance. An account by Mary B. Clay, daughter of Cassius M. Clay (a major general in the Union Army and ambassador to Russia under Lincoln) states that the presidential party attended a Booth performance in the winter of 1865, and occupied the same box Lincoln was to use on the fatal night of April 14th. Said she:

I do not recall the play, but Wilkes Booth played the part of villain. The box was right on the stage, with a railing around it. Mr. Lincoln sat next to the rail, I next to Mrs. Lincoln, Miss Sally Clay and the other gentlemen [the secretaries Nicolay and Hay] further around. Twice Booth in uttering threats to the play came very near and put his finger close to Mr. Lincoln's face; when he came a third time I was impressed by it, and said, "Mr. Lincoln, he looks as if he meant it for you." "Well," he said, "he does look pretty sharp at me, doesn't he?"[12]

This could not have been the same box "where Wilkes slew Lincoln" if it were "right on the stage" as Mary B. Clay states. This must have been the lower box which was at a stage level, with floor below stage level. Evidently, the customary presidential box was not used for this party of six who came in two carriages followed by eight mounted guards.

We are told by Noah Brooks, Lincoln's favorite newspaperman, and later a replacement secretary, that at times the box was not readily available. Brooks relates that he and Lincoln sat in the lower box directly under the presidential box.[13] The upper box from which Booth jumped after the murder was 11 feet 6 inches from the stage floor.[14] So this must have been *The Apostate* to which Mary B. Clay refers. Wilkes played only one other engagement in 1865, *Romeo and Juliet,* and this was at Grover's Theatre.

So the last of John Wilkes Booth's professional engagements was brought to a close. Others had been planned, and this was by no means intended as the last, since promises had been made for future productions.

William E. Sinn, associate manager with Leonard Grover, of the National Theatre in Washington, remembered seeing Wilkes three or four days before the tragedy. It was at the stage door of the Chestnut Street Theatre in Philadelphia one night just before Booth was to catch a train for Washington: Walking down Chestnut Street, Wilkes was taking the "lovely dancer" Kate Pennoyer to lunch. They had been friends since appearing on the same engagements in Richmond. In passing Sinn, Booth said he was to go that night to Washington after seeing the play at the Chestnut Street Theatre. Booth said to Sinn: "You will hear from me in Washington. I am going to make a hit." Replied Sinn, "Good luck to you. You're a pretty good sort of an actor; I guess you will."[15]

The play scheduled for Washington at that time was another benefit performance, this time for another favorite leading lady, Susan Denin. However, none of these plans were to materialize.

There are at least two sides to every character; Booth had many facets to his; some have spoken of Booth's darker side—his manic depressive moods, the "strangeness," which interfered with his acting. W.J. Ferguson, who was callboy and bit player at Ford's Theater said:

> Pictures of him disclose him as saturnine, showing little of the quick excitability, nothing of his love of fun, no trace of his joyousness. For these qualities, which completely concealed from us of Ford's Theatre the dark side of his character, in common with all the members of our company I held him in admiration and high esteem. With me the extent of my regard and respect for Booth fell nothing short of hero worship.... If he was insane or bordering on insanity, John Wilkes Booth gave me no such idea at the time I had passed but three years into my teens. To me he was a marvelously clever and amusing demigod. Practical jokes of his invention appealed to me as the quintessence of humor. His verve and fire as an actor made him stand high in the scale of my ideals.[16]

Popular reporter "Gath" Townsend agreed that none of the pictures he had ever seen did justice to Booth. He spoke of Booth's "vital beauty ... the thoughtfully stern sweep of two direct, dark eyes, meaning to women a snare, and to men a search warrant.... He seemed throatfull of introspections, ambitious self-examinings, eye-strides into the future, as if it withheld him something to which he had a right." Townsend felt that Booth's personality was magnetic, that it was not what he said, but how he said it. "I seemed, when he had spoken, to lean toward this man. His attitude spoke to me; with as easy familiarity as I ever observed.... When I left him it was with the feeling that a most agreeable fellow had pased by...."[17]

Full-length portrait of Booth, one hand on chair, the other holding a cane, taken April 10, 1865. According to E.C. Miller it was the last photograph. It is one of a series of different poses with similar background, made at the same time. From the collection of Lloyd Ostendorf, Dayton, Ohio. This is possibly the last photograph extant of Booth.

William Winter, considered to be the foremost dramatic critical authority in America for 35 years, was convinced that Edwin Booth was the greatest of all actors, and certainly no other Booth could approach him. In regards to Wilkes, Winter said: "As an actor, John, whose acting I saw and carefully observed, was raw and crude, and much given to boisterous declamation and violent demeanor, but he was talented, and if he had lived longer and carefully studied his art he might have attained to a high position. He was handsome and dashing; he gained some measure of public admiration, and with members of the dramatic profession he was a favorite ... a fact which speaks for his good qualities..."[18]

Wilkes' closest actor friends at this time were John McCullough, John Matthews, and E.A. Emerson all of whom were players at Ford's Theater. Emerson remembered Booth with kindly feelings. He wrote:

> I knew John Wilkes Booth well, having played with him in dozens of cities throughout the East and Middle West. He was a kind-hearted, genial person, and no cleverer gentleman ever lived. Everybody loved him on the stage, though he was a little excitable and eccentric. The day before President Lincoln was shot, I was standing in front of Ford's Theater, when John walked up, evidently in an agitated state of mind. He grabbed the cane from my hands and said: "Ned, did you hear what that old scoundrel did the other day?" I asked him who he was talking about, and he answered, "Why, that old scoundrel, Lincoln. He went into Jeff Davis' house in Richmond, sat down and threw his long legs over the arm of a chair and squirted tobacco juice all over the place. Somebody ought to kill him." I said, "For God's sake, John, stop where you are! I am going to quit you." With that he pulled my cane down over his shoulders with such force that it broke in four places. I still have that cane.[19]

Then the "illumination" came to Washington City. The following events lashed out in rapid succession: on April 3, 1865, Richmond fell, on April 9th Lee surrendered at Appomattox, on April 11th Mobile was evacuated and on April 12th Montgomery, last capital of the Confederacy, was captured. Washington was ablaze with lights, displays, and riotous celebration. Illuminations were ordered for all governmental departments. Over 3,500 candles were lighted in the Post Office windows, and nearly 6,000 were required for the Patent Office. Everyone was expected to supply his home with plentiful candlelight. The candlestickmakers could not turn out their products fast enough. The supply of flags was exhausted. Lincoln himself ordered all musicians to play *Dixie*, which he declared had become the lawful property of the Union. There was something ominous in the wild enthusiasm. Revelry continued with more and more displays, music, shouting and drinking, combining with the thousands of burning candles all night, turning the city into a nightmarish carnival. On the morning of April 13th, Wilkes Booth exclaimed to a friend who was on the way to purchase more candles: "What do you want with more candles? The windows are full of them now, and when they are lighted I wish they would burn every house to the ground. I would rejoice at the sight. I guess I'm a little desperate this morning, and, do you know, I feel like mounting my horse and tearing up and down the streets, waving a Rebel flag in each hand, till I have driven the poor animal to death."[20]

At 2:00, the morning of the tragic April 15th, John Wilkes Booth wrote this message to his mother:

> Washington
> April 14th, 1865
> 2 A.M.
>
> Dearest Mother
>
> I know you expect a letter from me, and am sure you will hardly forgive me. But indeed I have had nothing to write about. Everything is dull; that is, has been until last night. Everything was bright and splendid. More so in my eyes if it had been a display in a nobler cause. But so goes the world. Might makes right. I only drop you these few lines to let you know I am well, and to say I have not heard from you. Excuse brevity; am in haste. Had one from Rose [i.e., a letter from his sister Rosalie]. With best love to you all,
>
> I am your affectionate son ever,
>
> John.[21]

All during the past few months, Booth had been in and out of the National Hotel in a restless, secretive manner. Friends and family kept asking why he seemingly wasted his time. The old Booth manic depression was upon him. It was during this time that a pathetic incident occurred, indicating the clash of the two Booths within him; a mind more full of horrors than any part he had played on stage. On Sunday evening, March 25, 1865, when he was sharing room no. 231 with his friend John McCullough, a significant scene was played. McCullough, suddenly awakened by tears dropping on his face from someone leaning over him, looked up to see Booth at the side of his bed. "Why, what is the matter?" asked McCullough. "My God, my God, how peacefully you were sleeping! I cannot sleep," replied Booth.[22]

The next day John McCullough left for Canada. The actor with the remarkable memory would see his friend no more; he would not remember anything more.

Chapter Notes[*]

CHAPTER 1

1. Wilson, *John Wilkes Booth*, p.19.
2. Some encyclopedias note that he quit the stage in failure in 1863, though his last appearance was on March 18, 1865, less than a month before the assassination,. Some of his longest and most successful runs were in 1864.
3. Stories relating to the assassination have reached the porportion of folklore. It has been retold and reenacted in every possible medium from the Robinson's Show attraction *Sig Vanodi, the Greatest Living Worker in Wax Presents the Assassination,* which toured in late 1865, to the supposed mummy of Booth that toured carnivals, to the present day television 90-minute extravaganzas.
4. Letter from Booth to Dr. Richard H. Stewart, Virginia, April 4, 1865. Original in National Archives, Washington, D.C. Published in Oldroyd, *Assassination*, p.285.
5. Hanchett, "Booth's Diary."
6. Skinner, *Footlights and Spotlights*, pp.179–184.
7. Lockridge, *Darling of Misfortune*, p.172.
8. Morris, *Stage Confidences*, p.14.
9. Miller, *John Wilkes Booth — Oil Man*, p.48.
10. *Ibid.*
11. *Great Conspiracy*, p.22.
12. *National Republican*, May 3, 1865.
13. Kunhardt and Kunhardt, *Twenty Days*, p.107.
14. Moody, *Edwin Forrest*, p.351.
15. Herndon, *Herndon's Life of Lincoln*, p.402.
16. Hershell, "A Former Actress."
17. *Ibid.*
18. Towse, *Sixty Years*, p.150.
19. Morris, "Some Recollections."
20. *Ibid.*
21. Forrester, *This One Mad Act*, p.237.
22. Edwin Booth, *Recollections...*, p.227.
23. Wilson, *John Wilkes Booth*, p.19.
24. Barringer, *Lincoln's Rise to Power*, p.312.
25. Miller, *John Wilkes Booth — Oil Man*, p.57.
26. Perhaps the largest collections of these assembled items are those in the Harvard Library Theatre Collection, the Yale Library Theatre Collection, the New York Public Library Theatre Collection, the Library of the Players' Club, New York, the William Seymour Theatre Collection at Princeton University, and the Folger Shakespeare Library, Washington, D.C. Also there are various items held by state historical societies and in private collections.
27. Daly, *Life of Augustin Daly*, pp.19-20.

[*]*See Bibliography, beginning on page 191, for complete citations.*

28. A check of *American Book Prices Current* reveals the rise in prices paid for Booth letters and autographed scraps. One of his letters was sold at auction for $160 in 1944, again for $230 one year later, then again in 1955 for $500, and in 1977 for $2,500. A page ripped from a Baltimore hotel register bearing his signature brought $50 in 1955; a similar one from a Washington hotel register brought $360 in 1962. A check made payable to himself for $75 sold for $1,300 in 1977. The paper cover of his playscript *The Spectre Bridegroom*, autographed, dated 1858, Arch St. Theatre, by him, was sold for $400. Playbills for the evening of April 14, 1865, in which Booth was not in the cast, will bring from $175 upward, depending upon condition and edition. There was a hastily revised playbill issued when it was learned that Lincoln would attend.

29. Southern author and newspaper editor famous for his Uncle Remus folktales, and a contemporary of Booth.

30. Harris, *On the Wings of Occasions*, p.74.

31. Weissman, "Why Booth Killed Lincoln."

32. Feldman, "Abe Lincoln."

33. Greeley, *American Conflict*, Vol. 2, p.749.

34. Morse, *Abraham Lincoln*, Vol. 2, pp.346–349.

35. Sandburg, *Abraham Lincoln*, Vol. 4, p.501.

36. Stebbins, *Charlotte Cushman*, pp.11–12.

37. Skinner, *Last Tragedian*, p.63.

38. Roscoe, *Web of Conspiracy*, p.321.

39. *Detroit Free Press*, April 21, 1865.

CHAPTER 2

1. Stout, "Recolations."

2. *New York Sun*, Jan. 16, 1889.

3. Mahoney, *Sketches of Tudor Hall*, p.18.

4. Shettel, "J. Wilkes Booth at School."

5. Kimmel, *Mad Booths*, p.352.

6. Clarke, *Unlocked Book*, pp.53–56.

7. Sheldon, *Mask for Treason*, p.245.

8. Clarke, *Unlocked Book*, p.66.

9. Statement attributed to Rufus Chote, prominent U.S. Senator and lawyer. Quoted in Ruggles, *Prince of Players*, p.62.

10. Today we call them "walk-ons," the nearest term to describe the "walking gentleman" of the 1850s. Actually the term meant more then. It was a training period with distinctions of first, second, or third walking gentleman or lady. They had small roles, but were required to have ready many larger roles they could take over quickly. The supernumeraries, or "supers," of today are not the same. A great deal more was required of walking gentlemen.

CHAPTER 3

1. This theater was better known at the time as Laura Keane's Theatre, although it had changed names many times since. It was originally known as the Howard Athenaeum in 1848. There were at least three changes of name between then and 1853, when in December the theater was leased by Laura Keene, who called it the Charles Street Theatre, but it was remembered from then on as Laura Keene's Theatre.

2. May, "History of the Holliday Street Theater."

3. Clarke, *Unlocked Book*, p.106.

4. Kimmel, *Mad Booths*, p.352.

5. Clarke, *Unlocked Book*, p.72–73.
6. Kimmel, *Mad Booths*, p.67.
7. Clarke, *Unlocked Book*, p.66.
8. *Ibid.*, p.81.
9. Ruggles, *Prince of Players*, p.80.
10. Clarke, *Unlocked Book*, p.59.

CHAPTER 4

1. Kimmel, *Mad Booths*, p.150.
2. Townsend, *Life, Crime and Capture*, p.21.
3. Kimmel, *Mad Booths*, p.150.
4. Clarke, *Unlocked Book*, p.109.

CHAPTER 5

1. Admission prices: Dress Circle & Parquette 50¢ (no charge for secured seats), Second Tier or Family Circle 25¢, Eastern Gallery, for boys only, 12½¢, Western Gallery 25¢, Centre Gallery 50¢.
2. U.S., Works Progress Administration, *San Francisco Theatre*, Vol. 4: The Booth Family, p.112.
3. H.A. Langdon was leading man with the company. The Richmond *Dispatch* called him a fair actor, uneven in his playing, presenting a fine person, with perfect self-possession.
4. Letter to Edwin Booth. Original in the collection of The Players' Club, New York City. First published in Bryan, *Great American Myth*, p.85.
5. Richmond *Dispatch*, Oct. 1, 1858. Roles played by prominent performers were often repeated on the bill for added emphasis.
6. Wilson, *John Wilkes Booth*, p.17.
7. Kimmel, *Mad Booths*, p.152.
8. Ruggles, *Prince of Players*, p.95.
9. It should be noted that Valentine meant afternoon when he said "evening." This is a Southern expression, still in use. Unpublished material in the Valentine Museum, Richmond, Va.
10. Daly, *Life of Augustin Daly*, pp.64–65.
11. A correspondent's account of the two plays is recorded in the *Petersburg* (Va.) *Daily Express*, Dec. 20, 1858.
12. Grover, "Lincoln's Interest."

CHAPTER 6

1. Edwin Booth, *Recollections*, pp.189–90.
2. Barron, "With Wilkes Booth."
3. Wise, *End of an Era*, pp.93–94.
4. Letter to E.V. Valentine from George Crutchfield, Richmond, Va., July 5, 1909. Original in the Valentine Museum, Richmond.
5. Richmond *Enquirer*, Nov. 28, 1859.
6. Grover," "Lincoln's Interest."
7. Clarke, *Unlocked Book*, p.113.
8. Holland, "A Visit to Lincoln Country."
9. Richmond *Dispatch*, May 31, 1860.
10. Richard III was also known as the "Crook'd Back Tyrant."

11. Letter to E.V. Valentine [note 4].
12. Barron, "With Wilkes Booth."
13. Kimmel, *Mad Booths*, p.157.
14. Letter of Edward M. Alfriend. Quoted in Forrester, *This One Mad Act*, p.166.

CHAPTER 7

1. Kimmel, *Mad Booths*, p.156.
2. Mearns, *Largely Lincoln*, pp.9–10. The biographical sketch of Booth was found on Canning's person when he was arrested in Philadelphia, April 15, 1865. The date, 1859, he gives, is incorrect, as it was 1860 when Booth joined Canning's Company.
3. *Ibid.* Mrs. Canning is quoted in a letter to the Provost Marshal General in an attempt to get Canning released and to help identify Booth.
4. Lewis, *Myths After Lincoln*, p.149.

CHAPTER 8

1. Ellsler, *Stage Memories*, pp.77–78.
2. Ruggles, *Prince of Players*, p.97.
3. *Great Conspiracy*, p.38.
4. Shettel, "J. Wilkes Booth at School."
5. Wilson, *John Wilkes Booth*, p.13.
6. Barbee, "A Letter to William Rose Benet."

CHAPTER 9

1. Phelps, *Players of a Century*, pp.324–327.
2. *Post Scrapbook*, Vol. 2, pp.102–104. Maine Historical Society, Portland, Me.
3. From an unpublished letter; private collection.

CHAPTER 10

1. Letter from Booth to Joseph Simmonds. St. Louis, Mo., January 10, 1862. Original in the de Coppet Collection, Princeton University, N.J. Previously unpublished.
2. Dedmon, *Fabulous Chicago*, p.88.
3. Chicago *Post*, April 16, 1865.

CHAPTER 11

1. Ruggles, *Prince of Players*, p.93.
2. Hay, *Lincoln and the Civil War*, p.118.

CHAPTER 12

1. Jennings, *Theatrical and Circus Life*, pp.484–491.

2. *Ibid.*
3. *Great Conspiracy*, p.22.
4. Winslow [Reignolds], *Yesterdays with Actors*, pp.140–142. Probably, the inorganic constituents of sodium, potassium, calcium, bromine, phosphorous and sulphur found in oysters was believed to have medicinal effects in the relief of cuts and bruises.
5. Stoddart, *Recollections of a Player*, pp.116–117.
6. Brown, *History of the American Stage*. Biographical sketches in encyclopedic form. Tilton, who was reported to be an excellent swordsman and quite capable of defending himself against Booth, was also a powerful man over six feet in height, considerably taller and bigger than Booth (Booth was five feet eight). On the night of the accident, the curtain rang down as Tilton climbed out of the orchestra pit while the audience stomped and yelled. The final scene could not be played.
7. Morris, "Some Recollections."
8. Whitman, *Walt Whitman and the Civil War*, "City Photographs: The Bowery: VI The Old Theatre." As originally published in the N.Y. *Ledger*, March 15–May 17, 1862.
9. Leman, *Memoirs of an Old Actor*, pp.53–54.
10. Crawford, *Romance of the American Theatre*, p.170.
11. Ellsler, *Stage Memories*, p.124.
12. Letter from Booth to Joseph Simonds. St. Nicholas Hotel, N.Y., March 23, 1862. Original in the de Coppet Collection, Princeton University Library. Previously unpublished.

CHAPTER 13

1. Miller, "John Wilkes Booth in the Pennsylvania Oil Region."
2. Traubel, *With Walt Whitman in Camden*, Vol. 1, pp.355, 456.
3. *Ibid.*, Vol. 4, p.485.
4. Morris, "Some Recollections."
5. Kimmel, *Mad Booths*, p.153.
6. Mosby, "The Night That Lincoln Was Shot."
7. *Ibid.*
8. Clarke, *Unlocked Book*, p.68.
9. Bishop, *The Day Lincoln Was Shot*, p.204.
10. Winslow, *Yesterday with Actors*.
11. Traubel, *With Walt Whitman in Camden*, Vol. 4, p.485.

CHAPTER 14

1. Sherman, *Drama Cyclopedia*, p.217. Sherman gives Walter Grisdale as being the first to play this work — in New York in 1866; however, Weisert, *A Large and Fashionable Audience*, p.119, states that Booth played it on July 1, 1862.
2. Letter from Booth to T.V. Butsch. Philadelphia, August 3, 1862. Original in Henry E. Huntington Library & Art Gallery, San Marino, Calif. Previously unpublished.
3. Letter from Booth to Joseph Simonds. Tremont House, Chicago, December 6, 1862. Original in de Coppet Collection, Princeton University Library. Previously unpublished.
4. Letter from Booth to E.F. Keach, Chicago, December 8, 1862. Original in Gratz Collection, Historical Society of Pennsylvania. Complete letter previously unpublished.
5. Skinner, *Last Tragedian*, p.63.

CHAPTER 15

1. Kimmel, *Mad Booths*, p.170.
2. Townsend, *Life, Crime and Capture*, p.23.
3. Letter from Booth to Joseph Simonds. Philadelphia, Feb. 28, 1863. Original in de Coppet Collection, Princeton University Library. Previously unpublished.
4. Letter from Booth to Joseph Simonds. Philadelphia, March 1, 1863. Original in de Coppet Collection Princeton University Library. Previously unpublished.
5. Kimmel, *Mad Booths*, p.197.
6. Bryan, *Great American Myth*, p.85.
7. Bates, "Booth, John Wilkes," *Dictionary...*
8. Strang, *Famous Actors of the Day*, p.303.
9. MacCulloch, "This Man Saw Lincoln Shot." An interview with Joseph Hazelton, who was program boy at Ford's Theatre.
10. Letter from Booth to Joseph Simonds. Philadelphia, April 3, 1863. Original in de Coppet Collection, Princeton University Library. Previously unpublished.

CHAPTER 16

1. Hunter, *New National Theatre*. Lincoln's attendance at this performance is further discussed in Atkinson, *A Great Curtain Falls*, p.49.
2. Brooks, "Personal Reminiscences of Lincoln."
3. May, "Mark of the Scalpel."
4. Royle, *Edwin Booth as I Knew Him*, p.9.
5. Miller, "John Wilkes Booth in the Pennsylvania Oil Region," p.31.
6. Crawford, *Romance of the American Theatre*, p.169.
7. Letter from Booth to Joseph Simonds. Washington, D.C., April 19, 1863. Original in the de Coppet Collection, Princeton University Library. Previously unpublished.
8. *Great Conspiracy*, p.38.
9. Townsend, *Katy of Catoctin*, p.461.
10. "John Wilkes Booth: An Interview with the Press with Sir Charles Wyndham," New York *Herald*.

CHAPTER 17

1. Morris, "Some Recollections."
2. Hartnoll, *Oxford Companion*, p.399.
3. *Ibid.*, p.312.
4. Got, *Journal de Edmond Got.*
5. Bullard, "When — If Ever"; "A Plausible Solution of the Mystery."
6. Barbee, "The Bixby Letter Not There."
7. Letter from Booth to Ben De Bar. September 22, 1863. Original in the National Archives, Washington, D.C. Published in Kimmel, *Mad Booths*, p.374.
8. U.S., Works Progress Administration, *San Francisco Theatre*, p.125–26.

CHAPTER 18

1. Leech, *Reveille in Washington*, p.277.
2. Mearns, *Largely Lincoln*, p.147.
3. Brooks, "Personal Reminiscences."

4. Grover, "Lincoln's Interest," p.944.
5. Mearns, *Largely Lincoln*, p.147.
6. New York *World*, April 19, 1865.
7. Ellsler, *Stage Memories*, p.129.
8. George, "The Night John Wilkes Booth Played Before Abraham Lincoln."
9. Hay, *Lincoln and the Civil War*, p.118. Booth obviously was not up to his usual standard on this performance, for his rendition of the dual role was known to be one of his most spellbinding achievements on the stage. It is believed that reports of a Union victory at Rappahannock Station, where Meade had surprised Lee and captured many prisoners, together with the presence of Lincoln, had brought on one of Booth's despondent, moody spells under which he labored frequently. See also Kimmel, "Lincoln Had Deep Appreciation."
10. Nicolay and Hay, *Abraham Lincoln*, Vol. 10, pp.289–312.
11. Mearns, *Largely Lincoln*, p.116.
12. Brooks, *Washington in Lincoln's Time*, p.72.
13. Mearns, *Largely Lincoln*, p.122.
14. Taylor, "A New Story of the Assassination of Lincoln."
15. Grover, "Lincoln's Interest," p.948.
16. Ferguson, *I Saw Booth Shoot Lincoln*, p.15.
17. Ford, "Behind the Curtains."
18. Poore, *Perley's Reminiscences*, Vol. 2, pp.174–75.

CHAPTER 19

1. Townsend, *Life, Crime and Capture*, p.24.
2. Morris, "Some Recollections."
3. *Ibid.*
4. Ruggles, *Prince of Players*, p.197.
5. Lockridge, *Darling of Misfortune*, p.111.
6. Townsend, *Katy of Catoctin*, p.343.
7. For a series of articles on Booth's girl friends see *New York Daily Tribune*, April 17, 27, May 9, 1865.
8. Lockridge, *Darling of Misfortune*, p.25.
9. Weissman, *Creativity in the Theater*, p.8.
10. Carroll, *The Matinee Idols*, pp.31–35.

CHAPTER 20

1. Rose, *Cleveland*, p.323.
2. Bates, "Booth, John Wilkes." *Dictionary...*
3. Morris, *Life on the Stage*, pp.97–98.
4. Townsend, *Katy of Catoctin*, pp.461–62.
5. *Annals of Cleveland, 1818–1935.* A Digest and Index of the Newspaper Record of Events and Opinions Abstracted from the Files of the *Cleveland Leader.* WPA Project. Cleveland, Ohio, 1937. Vols. 46–47 (1863–64).

CHAPTER 21

1. Herbstruth, *Benedict De Bar.*
2. Letter from Booth to Mr. Kimbal. St. Joseph, Mo., Jan. 2, 1864. Original in the Charles C. Hart Collection, Library of Congress. Previously unpublished.
3. Letter from Booth to John Ellsler. Cleveland, Jan. 23, 1864. Original in Western Reserve Historical Society. Published in Ellsler, *Stage Memories*, p.126.

4. Statement of Col. H.D. McConnell, who administered the oath of allegiance to John Wilkes Booth after he had been arrested for using a disloyal expression. Records of the Judg Advocate's Office, April 24, 1865. National Archives, Washington, D.C.

5. Weisert, *A Large and Fashionable Audience.*

6. Rankin, "The News of Lincoln's Death."

7. *Ibid.*

8. Letter from Booth to E.F. Keach. Wood's Theatre, Louisville, Ky., Jan. 30, 1864. Private collection.

9. Gilbert, *Stage Reminiscences,* pp.57–61.

10. Letter from Booth to "Monty" (R.M. Field). Wood's Theatre, Cincinnati, Feb. 22, 1864. Original in the manuscript collection, Princeton University; copy in Library of Congress. Previously unpublished.

CHAPTER 22

1. Gilbert, *Stage Reminiscences,* pp.63–68.

2. Letter from Booth: "To whom it may concern." Left with John Sleeper Clarke during Nov. 1864. First published in Philadelphia *Press,* April 19, 1865, and in Boykin, *Living Letters from American History,* pp.340–44.

3. Townsend, *Katy of Catoctin,* p.368–69.

4. Kendall, *Golden Age,* pp.498–500.

5. Benjamin Franklin Butler was a Union general and commander in the capture of New Orleans and military governor of that city. He was highly unpopular with Southerners.

6. Kendall, *Golden Age,* pp.498–500.

7. Daly, *Life of Augustin Daly,* p.58.

8. Adam Badeau was a Union officer on General Grant's staff. He had recuperated in Edwin Booth's home from a battle wound. He had been saved from the New York riots by Wilkes Booth, when he was bodily carried by Wilkes to Edwin's house. Wilkes Booth cared for him and nursed him back to health.

9. Ruggles, *Prince of Players,* p.93.

10. Letter from Edwin Booth to Henry E. Abbey, his manager and impresario, Hotel Brunswick, undated. Unpublished letter from a private collection.

11. Clarke, *Unlocked Book,* pp.56–57.

CHAPTER 23

1. Gray, *Conspiracy in Canada,* p.51.

2. George, "F. Lauriston Bullard."

3. Norcross, "A Child's Memory."

4. Bates, *Diary, 1859–66;* American Historical Assoc., *Annual Report, 1930.* Vol. 4, p.371.

5. It is interesting to note that although Mrs. Howe and Booth held distinct opposite views, she wrote a poem to him after the assassination called "Pardon."

6. Norcross, "A Child's Memory."

7. Ryan, *Old Boston Museum Days.*

CHAPTER 24

1. Substitute for tobacco containing ingredients such as dried sumac leaves and the inner bark of dogwood or willow.

2. Ellsler, *Stage Memories*, p.127–28.
3. Kennelly, *The Spur*, p.91.
4. Miller, "John Wilkes Booth in the Pennsylvania Oil Region."
5. *Ibid.*
6. *Ibid.*
7. *Ibid.*
8. "Booth Came to Meadville," *Tribune-Republican*, Meadville, Pa.; Mason, "Four Lincoln Conspiracies"; Scott, "Our Omnibus-Box."
9. *Lincoln Lore.* "Within the last few hours this city has been the scene of the most terrible tragedies." Letters from Albert Daggett and Others. April 1961, no. 1478. Daggett was a clerk in the Dept. of State from Troy, N.Y. He stated that "John Wilkes Booth [was] an actor who has appeared on the stage in Troy on several occasions." A search has failed to uncover any advertised performances in Troy, so these must have been solo impromptu readings.
10. This story is detailed in Miller, *John Wilkes Booth — Oil Man.*
11. Probably this is I.B. Phillips, actor-manager known to his coworkers as "Old Phil."
12. Miller, "John Wilkes Booth in the Pennsylvania Oil Region."

CHAPTER 25

1. Clarke, *Unlocked Book*, p.116.
2. Clarke, *The Elder and the Younger Booth*, p.159.
3. Kimmel, *Mad Booths*, pp.382–383.
4. "En Passant: Further Particulars as to the Statements of John Wilkes Booth."
5. *Great Conspiracy*, pp.171–72.
6. Forrester, *This One Mad Act*, p.38.
7. *Great Conspiracy*, p.38.
8. Matthews, Ford, *et al.*, "Lincoln's Last Night."
9. Bryan, *Great American Myth*, p.103.
10. Miller, *John Wilkes Booth — Oil Man*, p.57.
11. Kimmel, *Mad Booths*, p.352.
12. *Lincoln Lore.* "Important Letters by Lincoln's Assassin."
13. Townsend, *Katy of Catoctin*, p.343.
14. MacCulloch, "This Man Saw Lincoln Shot."
15. "The Great Booth Is Dead."
16. Deery, "The Last of Wilkes Booth."
17. Bryan, *Great American Myth*, p.142.
18. Jennings, *Theatrical and Circus Life*, pp.448–491.
19. Letter from Booth, "To My Countrymen," Washington, D.C., April 14, 1865. Given to John Matthews to be delivered to the editor, *National Intelligencer*. Matthews committed it to memory and then burned it. Published in Forrester, *This One Mad Act*, p.230.
20. Letter from Booth "To the Proprietors of the *National Intelligencer*." Published in *Great Conspiracy*, p.172.
21. *Lincoln Lore.* "Important Letters by Lincoln's Assassin."

CHAPTER 26

1. U.S., Works Progress Administration, *San Francisco Theatre*, p.127.
2. Townsend, *Katy of Catoctin*, p.434.
3. *Great Conspiracy*, p.22.

4. Miller, *John Wilkes Booth — Oil Man*, p.26–47.

5. Letter from Booth to Junius Brutus Booth, Jr. Washington, D.C., Jan. 17, 1865. Original in the manuscript collection, Princeton University Library. Published in Kimmel, *Mad Booths*, p.197.

6. Townsend, *Katy of Catoctin*, p.433.

7. Weik, "A New Story of Lincoln's Assassination."

8. Townsend, *Katy of Catoctin*, p.433.

9. Shelton, *Mask for Treason*, p.242.

10. MacCulloch, "This Man Saw Lincoln Shot."

11. Weik, "A New Story of Lincoln's Assassination."

12. Helm, *Mary, Wife of Lincoln*, pp.241–43.

13. Brooks, "Personal Reminiscences of Lincoln."

14. Olszewski, *Restoration of Ford's Theatre*, p.51.

15. Sinn, "A Theatrical Manager's Reminiscences," p.171.

16. Ferguson, *I Saw Booth Shoot Lincoln*, pp.13–15.

17. Townsend, *Life, Crime, and Capture*, p.26.

18. Winter, *Vagrant Memories*, p.169–70.

19. Emerson, "How John Wilkes Booth's Friend Described His Crime."

20. Weik, "A New Story of Lincoln's Assassination."

21. Letter from Booth to his mother, Mary Ann Holmes Booth, Washington, D.C., April 14 [i.e., 15], 1865. Original in National Archives, Washington, D.C. Printed in three New York newspapers April 30–May 1, 1865. Published in Bryan, *Great American Myth*, p.148.

22. Alger, *Life of Edwin Forrest*, Vol. 2, p.146.

Bibliography

Alger, William. *Life of Edwin Forrest, the American Tragedian*, vol. 2. Philadelphia: Lippincott, 1877.

Annals of Cleveland, 1818-1935. A Digest and Index of the Newspaper Record of Events and Opinions Abstracted from the Files of the *Cleveland Leader*, vols. 46–47. WPA Project. Cleveland, Ohio, 1937.

Atkinson, George. *A Great Curtain Falls; The Story of the National Theatre, Washington, D.C.* New York: Strand Press, 1951.

Badeau, Adam. "Edwin Booth On and Off the Stage; Personal Recollections." *McClure's*, vol. 1, Aug. 1893.

Barbee, David Rankin. "The Bixby Letter Not There." *Tyler's Quarterly Historical*, vol. 28, 1947.

_____. "A Letter to William Rose Benet Concerning the Criticism of John Wilkes Booth's Acting." *Saturday Review of Literature*, vol. 29, Feb. 16, 1946.

Barringer, William. *Lincoln's Rise to Power*. Boston: Little, Brown, 1937.

Barron, John M. "With John Wilkes Booth in His Days as an Actor." *Baltimore Sun*, March 17, 1907.

Bates, Edward. *Diary, 1859-1866*, ed. by Howard K. Beale. American Historical Association *Annual Report*, vol. 4, 1930. Washington, D.C.: Gov. Print. Off., 1930.

Bates, Ernest Sutherland. "Booth, John Wilkes." *Dictionary of American Biography*, vol. 2. New York: Scribner's, 1928-1936.

Bishop, James A. *The Day Lincoln Was Shot*. New York: Harper, 1955.

Booth, Edwin. *Edwin Booth: Recollections by His Daughter Edwina Booth Grossmann, and Letters to Her and to His Friends*. New York: Century, 1894.

"Booth Came to Meadville — Actor Spent Night Here in Year 1864." Meadville, Pa., *Tribune-Republican*. Sesqui-Centennial Ed., Section G. (From clipping file in Reis Library, Allegheny College, Meadville, Pa.)

"Booth's Girl Friends — A Series of Articles." New York *Daily Tribune*, April 17, 27, May 9, 1865.

Brooks, Noah. "Personal Reminiscences of Lincoln." *Scribner's Monthly*, vol. 15, March 1878.

_____. *Washington in Lincoln's Time*. New York: Century, 1895. New edition ed. by Herbert Mitgang. New York: Rinehart, 1958.

Brown, Thomas Allston. *History of the American Stage*. New York: Dick & Fitzgerald, 1870.

Bryan, George S. *Great American Myth*. New York: Carrick & Evans, 1940.

Bullard, F. Lauriston. "A Plausible Solution of the Mystery of John Wilkes Booth's Alleged Visit to Paris." *Lincoln Herald*, vol. 52., Oct. 1950.

_____. "When — If Ever — Was John Wilkes Booth in Paris?" *Lincoln Herald*, vol. 50, June 1948.

Carroll, David. *The Matinee Idols*. New York: Arbor House, 1972.

Clarke, Asia Booth. *The Unlocked Book: A Memoir of John Wilkes Booth by His Sister*. New York: Putnam, 1938.

Crawford, Mary Caroline. *Romance of the American Theatre*. Boston: Little, Brown, 1913.

Daly, Joseph Francis. *Life of Augustin Daly*. New York: Macmillan, 1917.

Dedmon, Emmett. *Fabulous Chicago*. New York: Random House, 1953.

Deery, John. "The Last of Wilkes Booth." New York *Sunday Telegram*, May 23, 1909.

Ellsler, John A. *The Stage Memories of John A. Ellsler*. Cleveland: Rofant Club, 1950.

Emerson, E.A. "How John Wilkes Booth's Friend Described His Crime." *Literary Digest*, vol. 88, March 6, 1926.

"En Passant: Further Particulars as to the Statements of John Wilkes Booth." *Theatre* (London), vol. 1 (n.s.), Oct. 1, 1878.

Ferguson, William J. *I Saw Booth Shoot Lincoln*. Boston: Houghton, Mifflin, 1930.

Ford, George D. *These Were Actors*. Epilogue: The Booths. New York: Library Publishers, 1955.

Ford, John T. "Behind the Curtains of a Conspiracy." *North American Review*, vol. 148, April 1889.

Forrester, Izola Louise. *This One Mad Act: The Unknown Story of John Wilkes Booth and His Family by His Granddaughter*. Boston: Hale, Cushman & Flint, 1937.

"The Four Booths: A Human, Intimate Story of the Great American Actor Family." *Green Book Magazine*, vol. 14, July 1915.

George, Joseph, Jr. "F. Lauriston Bullard as a Lincoln Scholar." *Lincoln Herald*, vol. 62, Winter 1960.

————. "The Night John Wilkes Booth Played Before Abraham Lincoln." *Lincoln Herald*, vol. 59, Summer 1957.

Gilbert, Anne Hartley. *The Stage Reminiscences of Mrs. Gilbert*. New York: Scribner's, 1901.

Got, Edmond. *Journal de Edmond Got*. Paris: Sociétaire de la Comédie Française, Plon-Nourrit et Cie, 1910.

Gray, Glayton. *Conspiracy in Canada*. Montreal: L'Atelier Press, 1957.

"The Great Booth Is Dead." *Springfield [Ohio] Republican*, Dec. 6, 1852.

The Great Conspiracy. Philadelphia: Barclay & Co., 1866.

Greeley, Horace. *The American Conflict, a History of the Great Rebellion in the United States of America*, vol. 2, 1860–65. Hartford, Conn.: O.D. Case & Co., 1866.

Grover, Leonard. "Lincoln's Interest in the Theatre." *Century Magazine*, vol. 77, April 1909.

Hanchett, William. "Booth's Diary." *Journal of the Illinois State Historical Society*, vol. 72, no. 1, Feb. 1979.

Harris, Joel Chandler. *On the Wings of Occasions*. New York: Doubleday, Page, 1900.

Hartnoll, Phyllis, ed. *Oxford Companion to the Theatre*, 3d ed. London: Oxford University Press, 1967.

Hay, John. *Lincoln and the Civil War in the Diaries and Letters of John Hay*. New York: Dodd, Mead, 1939.

Helm, Katherine. *Mary, Wife of Lincoln*. New York: Harper, 1928.

Herbstruth, Grant M. *Benedict De Bar and the Grand Opera House in St. Louis, 1855–79*. Thesis, State University of Iowa, 1955.

Herndon, William Henry. *Herndon's Life of Lincoln*. New ed., with introd. & notes by Paul Angle. Greenwich, Conn.: Fawcett, 1961.

Hershell, Norman. "A Former Actress in *Our American Cousin* Tells the Story of the Assassination; An Interview with Jennie Gourlay." *Minneapolis Journal*, April 27, 1914.

Holland, G.S.P. "A Visit to Lincoln Country." *Tyler's Quarterly Historical and Genealogical Magazine*, vol. 10, July 1928.

Hunter, Alexander. *New National Theatre, Washington, D.C., Grover's: A Record of Fifty Years*. Washington, D.C.: R.O. Polkinhorn & Son, Printers, 1885.

Jennings, John Joseph. *Theatrical and Circus Life; or, Secrets of the Stage, Green-Room and Sawdust Arena*. St. Louis: Sun Pub. Co., 1882.

Jones, J.B. *A Rebel War Clerk's Diary*. New York: Old Hickory Bookshop, 1935.
Kendall, John S. *The Golden Age of the New Orleans Theatre*. Baton Rouge: Louisiana State University Press, 1952.
Kennelly, Ardyth. *The Spur*. New York: Messner, 1951.
Keill, Norman, ed. *Psychological Studies of Famous Americans: The Civil War Era*. "Why Booth Killed Lincoln," by Philip Weissman; "Abe Lincoln: The Psychology of a Cult," by A. Bronson Feldman. New York: Twayne, 1964.
Kimmel, Stanley. "Lincoln Had Deep Appreciation of Acting of John Wilkes Booth." Washington *Sunday Star*, April 15, 1941.
————. *The Mad Booths of Maryland*. Indianapolis: Bobbs-Merrill, 1940. Rev. & enl. ed., New York: Dover, 1969.
Kunhardt, Dorothy Merserve, & Kunhardt, Philip B., Jr. *Twenty Days*. New York: Harper & Row, 1965.
Leech, Margaret. *Reveille in Washington, 1860–1865*. New York: Harper, 1941.
Leman, Walter M. *Memoirs of an Old Actor*. San Francisco: A. Roman, 1886.
Lewis, Lloyd. *Myths After Lincoln*. New York: Press of the Readers Club, 1941.
Lincoln Lore. "Important Letters by Lincoln's Assassin Found!" vol. 2, May–June, 1977.
Lincoln Lore. "Within the last few hours this city has been the scene of the most terrible tragedies." Leters of Albert Daggett and others. No. 1478, April, 1961.
Lockridge, Richard. *Darling of Misfortune, Edwin Booth: 1833–1893*. New York: Century, 1932.
MacCulloch, Campbell. "This Man Saw Lincoln Shot. An Interview with Joseph Hazelton, Who Was Program Boy at Ford's Theatre." *Good Housekeeping*, vol. 84, Feb. 1927.
Mahoney, Ella V. *Sketches of Tudor Hall and the Booth Family*. Baltimore: Franklin Printing Co., 1925.
Mason, Victor Lewis. "Four Lincoln Conspiracies." *Century Magazine*, vol. 51, April 1896.
Matthews, John. "Lincoln's Last Night," by John Matthews, John Ford and others. Philadelphia *Press*, Dec. 3–4, 1881.
May, Alonzo. *The History of the Holliday Street Theatre in Baltimore*. Unpublished manuscript in Maryland Historical Society.
May, John Frederick. "Mark of the Scalpel." *Columbia Historical Society Records*, vol. 13, 1910.
Means, David C. *Largely Lincoln*. New York: St. Martin's Press, 1961.
Miller, Ernest Conrad. "John Wilkes Booth in the Pennsylvania Oil Region." *Western Pennsylvania Historical Magazine*, vol. 31, March–June 1948.
————. *John Wilkes Booth – Oil Man*. New York: Exposition Press, 1947.
Moody, Richard. *Edwin Forrest*. New York: Knopf, 1960.
Morris, Clara. *Life on the Stage: My Personal Experiences and Recollections*. New York: McClure, Phillips, 1901.
————. "Some Recollections of John Wilkes Booth." *McClurg's Magazine*, vol. 16, 1901.
————. *Stage Confidences*. Boston: Lathrop, 1902.
Morse, John T., Jr. *Abraham Lincoln*, vol. 2. Boston: Houghton, Mifflin, 1893.
Mosby, John S., Jr. "The Night That Lincoln Was Shot." *The Theatre*, vol. 17, June 1913.
Nicolay, John G. and Hay, John. *Abraham Lincoln; A History*, vol. 10. New York: Century, 1890.
Norcross, A.F. "A Child's Memory of the Boston Theatre." *Theatre Magazine*, vol. 25, May 1926.
Oldroyd, Osborn H. *The Assassination of Abraham Lincoln*. Washington, D.C.: privately printed, 1901.
Olszewski, George J. *Restoration of Ford's Theatre*. Washington, D.C.: National Park Service, U.S. Dept. of the Interior, 1963.

Phelps, Henry Pitt. *Players of a Century; A Record of the Albany Stage.* New York: McDonough, 1860.

Poore, Ben Perley. *Perley's Reminiscences of 60 Years in the National Metropolis.* Philadelphia: Hubbard Brothers, 1886.

Post Scrapbook, vol. 2 (n.d.). Portland, Maine, Historical Society.

Rankin, Mrs. McKee (Kitty Blanchard). "The News of Lincoln's Death, Including Storiers of John Wilkes Booth." *American Magazine,* vol. 67, Jan. 1909.

Roscoe, Theodore. *Web of Conspiracy: The Complete Story of the Men Who Murdered Abraham Lincoln.* Englewood Cliffs, N.J.: Prentice-Hall, 1959.

Rose, William G. *Cleveland; The Making of a City.* Cleveland: World, 1950.

Royle, Edwin M. *Edwin Booth as I Knew Him.* New York: Players Club, 1933.

Ruggles, Eleanor. *Prince of Players: Edwin Booth.* New York: Norton, 1953.

Ryan, Kate. *Old Boston Museum Days.* Boston: Little, Brown, 1915.

Sandburg, Carl. *Abraham Lincoln: The Prairie Years and the War Years.* New York: Harcourt, Brace, 1954.

Scott, Clement. "Our Omnibus-Box." *The Theatre* (London), v. 1 (n.s.), March 1, 1880.

Sheldon, Vaughn. *Mask for Treason: The Lincoln Murder Trial.* Harrisburg, Pa.: Stackpole, 1965.

Sherman, Robert L. *Drama Cyclopedia.* Chicago: the author, 1944.

Shettel, James W. "J. Wilkes Booth at School." *The New York Dramatic Mirror,* Feb. 26, 1916.

Sinn, William E. *Abraham Lincoln, Tributes from His Associates: A Theatrical Manager's Reminiscences.* New York: Crowell, 1895.

Skinner, Otis. *Footlights and Spotlights.* Indianapolis: Bobbs-Merrill, 1924.

————. *The Last Tragedian.* New York: Dodd, Mead, 1939.

Stebbins, Emma. *Charlotte Cushman: Her Letters and Memories of Her Life.* Boston: Houghton, Osgood, 1878.

Stoddart, James E. *Recollections of a Player.* New York: Century, 1902.

Stout, George L. "Recolations." Baltimore *American,* July 27, 1902.

Strang, Lewis C. *Famous Actors of the Day.* Boston: Page, 1899.

Taylor, W.H. "A New Story of the Assassination of Lincoln." *Leslie's Weekly,* vol. 106, March 26, 1908.

Townsend, George Alfred. *Katy of Catoctin: The Chain-Breakers, a National Romance.* New York: Dick & Fitzgerald, 1886. New edition ed. by Harold R. Manakee. Cambridge, Md.: Tidewater Publishers, 1959.

————. *The Life, Crime and Capture of John Wilkes Booth, with a Full Sketch of the Conspiracy of Which He Was the Leader, and the Pursuit, Trial and Execution of His Accomplices.* New York: Dick & Fitzgerald, 1865.

Towse, John Rankin. *Sixty Years of the Theater.* New York: Funk & Wagnalls, 1916.

Traubel, Horace. *With Walt Whitman in Camden.* New York: Mitchell Kennerley, 1905.

U.S. Works Progress Administration. *San Francisco Theatre Research.* 1st ser., vol. 4: The Booth Family. San Francisco: WPA, 1938.

Weik, Jesse W. "A New Story of Lincoln's Assassination." *Century Magazine,* vol. 85, Feb. 1913.

Weisert, John J. *A Large and Fashionable Audience: A Checklist of Performances at the Louisville Theater, 1846–1866.* Ph.D. dissertation, University of Louisville, Ky., 1955.

Weissman, Philip. *Creativity in the Theater; a Psychoanalytic Study.* New York: Basic Books, 1965.

Whitman, Walt. *Walt Whitman and the Civil War.* "City Photographs: The Bowery, VI The Old Theatre." Philadelphia: University of Pennsylvania Press, 1933. Orig. pub. in *New York Ledger,* March 15–May 17, 1862.

Wilson, Francis. *John Wilkes Booth: Fact and Fiction of Lincoln's Assassination.* Boston: Houghton, Mifflin, 1929.

Winslow, Mrs. Catherine Mary (Reignolds). *Yesterday with Actors*, by Kate Reignolds. Boston: Cupples & Ward, 1887.

Winter, William. *Vagrant Memories*. New York: Doran, 1915.

Wise, John Sergeant. *The End of an Era*. Boston: Houghton, Mifflin, 1899.

Wyndham, Sir Charles. "John Wilkes Booth: An Interview with the Press." New York *Herald*, Magazine Section, June 27, 1909.

A Chronology
of the Theatrical Performances
# of John Wilkes Booth

1855
Wheatley's Arch Street Theatre, Philadelphia

Tuesday, August 14: as Richmond in *Richard III*

1857
Wheatley's Arch Street Theatre, Philadelphia

Saturday, August 15: as Second Mask in *The Belle's Stratagem* / *State Secrets*
Monday, August 17: as The Courier in *The Wife; or, A Tale of Mantua* / *State Secrets*
Tuesday, August 18: *Charity's Love; or, The Trials of the Heart* / *No; or, The Glorious Minority*
Wednesday, August 19: *Charity's Love; or, The Trials of the Heart* / *My Precious Betsy*
Thursday, August 20: *Charity's Love; or, The Trials of the Heart* / *My Precious Betsy*
Friday, August 21: *Charity's Love; or, The Trials of the Heart* / *The Dramatist*
Saturday, August 22: *Richard III* / *The Toodles*
Monday, August 24: *The Lady of Lyons* / *P.P.; or, The Man and the Tiger*
Tuesday, August 25: *Love's Sacrifice* / *My Precious Betsy*
Wednesday, August 26: *Richard III* / *The Toodles*
Thursday, August 27: *St. Marc* / *My Precious Betsy*
Friday, August 28: *St. Marc* / *The Married Bachelor*
Saturday, August 29: *St. Marc* / *Paul Pry*
Monday, August 31: *The Stranger* / *Honey Moon*
Tuesday, September 1: *The Hunchback* / *The Handsome Husband*
Wednesday, September 2: *Fazio; or, The Italian Wife* / *The Handsome Husband*
Thursday, September 3: *The Hunchback* / *The Married Bachelor*
Friday, September 4: *Jane Shore* / *The Toodles*
Saturday, September 5: *Romeo and Juliet* / *The Golden Farmer*
Monday, September 7: *Much Ado About Nothing* / *The Handsome Husband*
Tuesday, September 8: *The Merchant of Venice* / *The Toodles*
Wednesday, September 9: *Charity's Love; or, The Trials of the Heart* / *A Serious Family*
Thursday, September 10: *A Serious Family* / *The Toodles*
Friday, September 11: *The Merchant of Venice* / *A Serious Family*
Saturday, September 12: *The Apostate* / *Cape May*
Monday, September 14: *A New Way to Pay Old Debts* / *Cape May*
Tuesday, September 15: *St. Marc* / *Cape May*

(1857, continued)

Wednesday, September 16: *Hamlet* / *Cape May*
Thursday, September 17: *Richard III* / *Cape May*
Friday, September 18: *Hamlet* / *Swiss Swains*
Saturday, September 19: *A New Way to Pay Old Debts* / *The Robber's Wife*
Monday, September 21: *Hamlet* / *Sketches in India*
Tuesday, September 22: *Camille* / *Swiss Swains*
Wednesday, September 23: *The Brigand* / *Willow Copse*
Thursday, September 24: *The Belle's Stratagem* / *The Brigand*
Friday, September 25: *Camille* / *The Brigand*
Saturday, September 26: *Hamlet* / *A Conjugal Lesson*
Monday, September 28: *Othello* / *A Conjugal Lesson*
Tuesday, September 29: *The Victims* / *The Brigand*
Wednesday, September 30: *The Victims* / *The Dramatist*
Thursday, October 1: *The Victims* / *Wild Oats*
Friday, October 2: *The Victims* / *The Brigand*
Saturday, October 3: *The Robbers* / *Sudden Thoughts*
Monday, October 5: *The Victims* / *The Brigand*
Tuesday, October 6: *Eustache* / *That Blessed Baby*
Wednesday, October 7: *The Robbers* / *The Victims*
Thursday, October 8: *Extremes* / *Beware of Garroters*
Friday, October 9: *The Robbers* / *Paul Pry*
Saturday, October 10: *Jack Cade* / *Love in Livery*
Monday, October 12: *Jane Shore* / *The Brigand*
Tuesday, October 13: *Much Ado About Nothing* / *The Dramatist*
Wednesday, October 14: *Jack Cade* / *My Neighbor's Wife*
Thursday, October 15: *Jack Cade* / *Love in Livery*
Friday, October 16: *Jack Cade* / *The Bridegroom*
Saturday, October 17: *Jack Cade* / *My Neighbor's Wife*
Monday, October 19: *Hamlet* / *Perfection*
Tuesday, October 20: *Jack Cade* / *Sudden Thoughts*
Wednesday, October 21: *Jack Cade* / *A Handsome Husband*
Thursday, October 22: *Macbeth* / *Rough Diamond*
Friday, October 23: *Jack Cade* / *Katharine and Petruchio*
Saturday, October 24: *Civilization* / *Paul Pry*
Monday, October 26: *Macbeth* / *My Neighbor's Wife*
Tuesday, October 27: *Civilization* / *The Robber's Wife*
Wednesday, October 28: *Julius Caesar* / *The Toodles*
Thursday, October 29: *Civilization* / *Guy Mannering*
Friday, October 30: *The Model of a Wife* / *The Stage Struck Barber* / *A Glance at New York*
Saturday, October 31: *Julius Caesar* / *Catherine and Petruchio*
Monday, November 2: *The Queen of Spades* / *Black Eyed Susan*
Tuesday, November 3: *The Queen of Spades* / *Black Eyed Susan*
Wednesday, November 4: *The Queen of Spades* / *Black Eyed Susan*
Thursday, November 5: *The Queen of Spades* / *Black Eyed Susan*
Friday, November 6: *The Queen of Spades* / *Black Eyed Susan*
Saturday, November 7: *Ingomar* / *Black Eyed Susan*
Monday, November 9: *The Jealous Wife* / *Black Eyed Susan*
Tuesday, November 10: *The King's Rival* / *Swiss Swains*
Wednesday, November 11: *Jack Cade* / *Honey Moon*
Thursday, November 12: *Camille* / *The Robber's Wife*
Friday, November 13: *The King's Rival* / *The Golden Farmer*
Saturday, November 14: *Richard III* / *P.P.; or, The Man and the Tiger*

(1857, continued)

Monday, November 16: *Hamlet* / *The Married Bachelor*
Tuesday, November 17: *Rob Roy* / *Laugh When You Can*
Wednesday, November 18: *The Merchant of Venice* / *Guy Mannering*
Thursday, November 19: *Charity's Love; or, The Trials of the Heart* / *Rob Roy*
Friday, November 20: *Richelieu* / *Time Tries All*
Saturday, November 21: *Sea of Ice* / *Love in Livery*
Monday, November 23: *Richelieu* / *Time Tries All*
Tuesday, November 24: *Sea of Ice* / *My Precious Betsy*
Wednesday, November 25: *Fazio; or The Italian Wife* / *The Hypocrite*
Thursday, November 26 (afternoon): *P.P.; or, The Man and the Tiger* / *Scandal Mag; or, The Village Gossip* / *Out for Thanksgiving*
Thursday, November 26 (evening): *Sea of Ice* / *The Midnight Watch*
Friday, November 27: *Leap Year* / *Retribution*
Saturday, November 28: *The Hypocrite* / *Retribution*
Monday, November 30: *Jack Cade* / *A Day Well Spent*
Tuesday, December 1: *London Assurance* / *Madelaine*
Wednesday, December 2: *Leap Year* / *Madelaine*
Thursday, December 3: *London Assurance* / *The Midnight Watch*
Friday, December 4: *Still Waters Run Deep* / *The Second Love*
Saturday, December 5: *Othello* / *The Toodles*
Monday, December 7: *London Assurance* / *Paul Pry*
Tuesday, December 8: *The Day After the Wedding* / *Annette, the Forsaken* / *The Bride of Lammermoor*
Wednesday, December 9: *Still Waters Run Deep* / *Laugh When You Can*
Thursday, December 10: *The Jealous Wife* / *The Bride of Lammermoor*
Friday, December 11: *The Lady of Lyons* / *A Serious Family*
Saturday, December 12: *Richard III* / *Sudden Thoughts*
Monday, December 14: *The Merchant of Venice* / *Annette, the Forsaken*
Tuesday, December 15: *Speed the Plough* / *The Carpenter of Rouen*
Wednesday, December 16: *Beatrice; or, The False and the True* / *The Spectre Bridegroom*
Thursday, December 17: *Beatrice; or, The False and the True* / *Love in Livery*
Friday, December 18: *Beatrice; or, The False and the True* / *Swiss Swains*
Saturday, December 19: *Beatrice; or, The False and the True* / *The Carpenter of Rouen*
Monday, December 21: *Beatrice; or, The False and the True* / *Sarah's Young Man*
Tuesday, December 22: *Beatrice; or, The False and the True* / *Sarah's Young Man*
Wednesday, December 23: *Beatrice; or, The False and the True* / *My Precious Betsy*
Thursday, December 24: *Beatrice; or, The False and the True* / *Christmas Adventures; or, Major Jones' Courtship*
Friday, December 25: *The Last Days of Pompeii* / *Sarah's Young Man*
Saturday, December 26: *The Last Days of Pompeii* / *Sarah's Young Man*
Monday, December 28: *The Last Days of Pompeii* / *Rival Pages*
Tuesday, December 29: *The Last Days of Pompeii* / *Rival Pages*
Wednesday, December 30: *The Last Days of Pompeii* / *Still Waters Run Deep*
Thursday, December 31: *The Last Days of Pompeii* / *A Serious Family*

1858

Friday, January 1: *The Last Days of Pompeii* / *Clara, Maid of Milan*
Saturday, January 2: *The Last Days of Pompeii* / *The Scalp Hunters*
Monday, January 4: *The Last Days of Pompeii* / *The Scalp Hunters*

(1858, continued)

Tuesday, January 5: *The Last Days of Pompeii* / *The Scalp Hunters*

Wednesday, January 6: *The Last Days of Pompeii* / *The Scalp Hunters*

Thursday, January 7: *The Last Days of Pompeii* / *The Scalp Hunters*

Friday, January 8: *The Last Days of Pompeii* / *The Scalp Hunters*

Saturday, January 9: *The Last Days of Pompeii* / *The Scalp Hunters*

Monday, January 11: *The Last Days of Pompeii* / *Don Caesar De Bazan*

Tuesday, January 12: *The Last Days of Pompeii* / *The Rent Day*

Wednesday, January 13: *The Last Days of Pompeii* / *The Merchant of Venice*

Thursday, January 14: *The Last Days of Pompeii* / *The Scalp Hunters*

Friday, January 15: *The Lady of Lyons* / *The Hypocrite*

Saturday, January 16: *Fraud and Its Victims; or, The Poor of Philadelphia* / *Sarah's Young Man*

Monday, January 18: *Fraud and Victims; or, The Poor of Philadelphia* / *Rival Pages*

Tuesday, January 19: *Fraud and Its Victims; or, The Poor of Philadelphia* / *Sarah's Young Man*

Wednesday, January 20: *Fraud and Its Victims; or, The Poor of Philadelphia*

Thursday, January 21: *Fraud and Its Victims; or, The Poor of Philadelphia* / *To Parents and Guardians*

Friday, January 22: *Fraud and Its Victims; or, The Poor of Philadelphia* / *Rival Pages*

Saturday, January 23: *Fraud and Its Victims; or, The Poor of Philadelphia* / *A Happy Family*

Monday, January 25: *Fraud and Its Victims; or, The Poor of Philadelphia* / *A Happy Family*

Tuesday, January 26: *Fraud and Its Victims; or, The Poor of Philadelphia* / *To Parents and Guardians*

Wednesday, January 27: *Fraud and Its Victims; or, The Poor of Philadelphia* / *The Hypocrite*

Thursday, January 28: *Fraud and Its Victims; or, The Poor of Philadelphia* / *Sweethearts and Wives*

Friday, January 29: *Fraud and Its Victims* / *Laugh When You Can*

Saturday, January 30: *Wallace, Hero of Scotland* / *A Cure for the Heartache*

Monday, February 1: *Damon and Pythias* / *Paul Pry*

Tuesday, February 2: *She Stoops to Conquer* / *Wallace, Hero of Scotland*

Wednesday, February 3: *Wives as They Were and Maids as They Are* / *Wallace, Hero of Scotland*

Thursday, February 4: *Brian Boroihme* / *Sweethearts and Wives*

Friday, February 5: *Money* / *Brian Boroihme*

Saturday, February 6: *The Plough* / *Brian Boriohme*

Monday, February 8: *Virginius* / *The Happy Family*

Tuesday, February 9: *Wives as They Were and Maids as They Are* / *The Carpenter of Rouen*

Wednesday, February 10: *Ambition; or, The Tomb, the Throne, and the Scaffold* / *The Spectre Bridegroom*

Thursday, February 11: *Ambition; or, The Tomb, the Throne, and the Scaffold* / *The Happy Family*

Friday, February 12: *Ambition; or, The Tomb, the Throne, and the Scaffold* / *Sarah's Young Man*

Saturday, February 13: *Ambition; or, The Tomb, the Throne, and the Scaffold* / *My Neighbor's Wife*

Monday, February 15: *Ambition; or, The Tomb, the Throne, and the Scaffold* / *Nothing to Nurse*

Tuesday, February 16: *Ambition; or, The Tomb, the Throne, and the Scaffold* / *Nothing to Nurse*

(1858, continued)

Wednesday, February 17: *Ambition; or, The Tomb, the Throne, and the Scaffold / The Buzzards*

Thursday, February 18: *Ambition; or, The Tom, the Throne, and the Scaffold / Nothing to Nurse*

Friday, February 19: as Richmond in *Richard III / Iron Chest / Poor Gentleman*

Saturday, February 20 (engagement of Mrs. Farren and Mr. Vezin): *The Stranger / The Honeymoon*

Monday, February 22: *The Tragedy of Bertram / The Wonder*

Tuesday, February 23: as Petruchio Pandolfe in *Lucretia Borgia / A Bold Stroke for a Husband*

Wednesday, February 24: As Dawson in *The Gamester / Simpson & Co.*

Thursday, February 25: *Ingomar / Lucretia Borgia*

Friday, February 26: *Mary Tutor / A Bold Stroke for a Husband / Nothing to Nurse*

Saturday, February 27 (engagement of Mme Ponisi, J.S. Clarke, Susan Denin): *Romeo and Juliet / The Toodles*

Monday, March 1: *Jane Shore / To Parents and Guardians*

Tuesday, March 2: *Money / Sudden Thoughts*

Wednesday, March 3: *Douglas / Poor Gentleman*

Thursday, March 4: *Romeo and Juliet / The Happy Family*

Friday, March 5: *Rule a Wife and Have a Wife / Roland for an Oliver*

Saturday, March 6: *Douglas / Willow Copse*

Monday–Friday, March 8–19: *The Declaration of Independence; or, Philadelphia in the Olden Time*

Saturday, March 20: *Douglas / Willow Copse*

Monday, March 22: *Asmondus; or, The Little D—L's Share / The Drunkard*

Tuesday, March 23: *A Husband for an Hour / Robert Macaire*

Wednesday, March 24: *The Country Squire; or, Two Days at the Hall / A Husband for an Hour*

Thursday, March 25: *The Rivals / A Kiss in the Dark*

Friday, March 26: *The Country Squire; or, Two Days at the Hall / A Husband for an Hour*

Saturday, March 27: *Venice Preserved / Robert Macaire*

Monday, March 29: *The Country Squire; or, Two Days at the Hall / Ugolino*

Tuesday, March 30: *Heir at Law / Rose of Ettrick Vale*

Wednesday, March 31: *School for Scandal / Nature and Philosophy*

Thursday, April 1: *A Husband for an Hour / Ugolino*

Friday, April 2: *Gambler's Fate / A Cure for the Heartache*

Saturday, April 3: *School for Scandal / Gambler's Fate*

Monday, April 5: *Brutus; or, The Fall of Tarquin / A Hard Struggle*

Tuesday, April 6: *Richard III / A Hard Struggle*

Wednesday, April 7: *Fashion / William Tell*

Thursday, April 8: *Fashion / Love and Charity*

Friday, April 9: *The Egyptian / Black Eyed Susan*

Saturday, April 10: *Damon and Pythias / The Carpenter of Rouen*

Monday, April 12: *Paul Pry in America / Jonathan Bradford; or, Murder at the Roadside Inn / The Toodles* (Act 2)

Tuesday, April 13: *Wild Oats / Robert Macaire*

Wednesday, April 14: *Paul Pry in America / Jonathan Bradford; or, Murder at the Roadside Inn / The Toodles* (Act 2)

Thursday, April 15: *The Way to Get Married / Turning the Tables*

Friday, April 16: *Town and Country / Love in Livery*

Saturday, April 17: *The Way to Get Married / Jonathan Bradford; or, Murder at the Roadside Inn*

(1858, continued)

Monday, April 19: *Jonathan Bradford; or, Murder at the Roadside Inn* / *Virginia Mummy*

Tuesday, April 20: *King Henry IV* / *House Dog*

Wednesday, April 21: *The Merry Wives of Windsor* / *Turning the Tables*

Thursday, April 22: *King Henry IV* / *House Dog*

Friday, April 23: *King Henry IV* / *Catharine and Petruchio*

Saturday, April 24: *Mons Mallet* / *Colonel Wildfire, The Kentuckian of 1815*

Monday, April 26 (engagement of Agnes Robertson and Dion Bourcicault): *Jessie Brown* / *The Irish Tutor*

Tuesday, April 27: *Jessie Brown* / *The Irish Tutor*

Wednesday, April 28: *Jessie Brown* / *Omnibus*

Thursday, April 29: *Jessie Brown* / *Omnibus*

Friday, April 30: *Jessie Brown* / *The Limrick Boy*

Saturday, May 1: *Jessie Brown* / *The Limrick Boy*

Monday, May 3: *Jessie Brown* / *Tableau: The Arrival of General Havelock* / *The Limrick Boy*

Tuesday, May 4: *Jessie Brown* / *Tableau: The Arrival of General Havelock* / *The Irish Broom Maker*

Wednesday–Saturday, May 5–22: *Jessie Brown* / (and a favorite farce)

Monday, May 24: (engagement of Charlotte Cushman): *The Stranger* / *Turning the Tables*

Tuesday, May 25: as First Apparition in *Macbeth* / *A Thumping Legacy*

Wednesday, May 26: As Capucius in *Henry VIII* / *A Kiss in the Dark*

Thursday, May 27: *Guy Mannering* / (and a favorite farce)

Friday, May 28: as Silvius in *As You Like It* / *Simpson & Co.*

Saturday, May 29 (afternoon only): *Guy Mannering* / *Retribution* / *William Tell*

Monday, May 31 (engagement of Mr. Couldock): *The Willow Copse* / *Nothing to Nurse*

Tuesday, June 1: *School of Scandal* / *Turning the Tables*

Wednesday, June 2: *Louis XI* / *P.P.; or, The Man and the Tiger*

Thursday, June 3: *Louis XI* / *The Spectre Bridegroom*

Friday, June 4: *Louis XI* / *The School of Reform*

Saturday, June 5: *King Lear*

Monday, June 7 (engagement of John Brougham): *Dombey & Son* / *Sketches in India*

Tuesday, June 8: *David Copperfield* / *Robert Macaire*

Wednesday, June 9: *Po-ca-hon-tas; or, Ye Gentleman Savage* / *The Nervous Man*

Thursday, June 10: *Po-ca-hon-tas; or, Ye Gentleman Savage* / *The Stage Struck Irishman* / *My Neighbor's Wife*

Friday, June 11: *The Musard Ball* / *The Limrick Boy* / *Po-ca-hon-tas; or, Ye Gentleman Savage*

Saturday, June 12: *The Musard Ball* / *The Limrick Boy* / *Po-ca-hon-tas; or, Ye Gentleman Savage*

Monday, June 14: *Columbus el Filibustero* / *Paddy Miles*

Tuesday, June 15: *Columbus el Filibustero* / *Paddy Miles*

Wednesday, June 16: *Columbus el Filibustero* / *Brian O'Lynn* / *Lend Me Five Shillings*

Thursday, June 17: *Columbus el Filibustero* / *The Pleasant Neighbor* / *Two Gregories*

Friday, June 18: *Columbus el Filibustero* / *Po-ca-hon-tas; or, Ye Gentleman Savage* / *Dr. O'Toole*

Saturday, June 19: *The Happy Man* / *Columbus el Filibustero* / *Brian O'Lynn* (last night of the season)

(1858, continued)
Holliday Street Theatre, Baltimore

Friday, August 27 (engagement of Edwin Booth): as Richmond in *Richard III*

Richmond Theatre, Richmond

Saturday, September 4: *Town and Country; or, Which Is Best?* / *1000 Milliners Wanted for the Frazer River Gold Diggins*
Monday, September 6: *School for Scandal*
Tuesday, September 7: *Extremes* / *Jenny Lind*
Wednesday, September 8: as Count Florio in *The Wife; or, My Father's Grave* / *Swiss Swains*
Thursday, September 9: as Cool in *London Assurance*
Friday, September 10: *Old Heads and Young Hearts*
Saturday, September 11: *La Tour de Nesle; or, The Chamber of Death* / *The Lottery Ticket*
Monday, September 13 (engagement of Maggie Mitchell): *The Young Prince* / *The Four Sisters*
Tuesday, September 14: *Margot, The Poultry Dealer* / *The Young Prince*
Wednesday, September 15: *Milly, The Maid with the Milking Pail* / *Katy O'Sheil* / *The Lottery Ticket*
Thursday, September 16: *Wept of Wish-Ton-Wish* / *Margot, The Poultry Dealer*
Friday, September 17: *Pet of the Petticoats* / *Katy O'Sheil* / *Lady of Lyons*
Saturday, September 18: *The French Spy; or, The Fall of Algiers* / *La Tour de Nesle; or, The Chamber of Death*
Monday, September 20: *The Wild Irish Girl* / *Countess of Zytomie*
Tuesday, September 21: *Wept of Wish-Ton-Wish* / *The Wild Irish Girl*
Wednesday, September 22: *The French Spy; or, The Fall of Algiers* / *Husband at Night*
Thursday, September 23: *Satan in Paris* / *Wanderin Boys*
Friday, September 24: *Jessie Brown* / *Captain Charlotte*
Saturday, September 25: *Green Bushes* / *Jessie Brown*
Monday, September 27 (engagement of Edwin Booth): *The Apostate* / *Family Jars*
Tuesday, September 28: *Richilieu; or, The Conspiracy* / *Nature and Philosophy; or, The Youth That Never Saw a Woman*
Wednesday, September 29: *A New Way to Pay Old Debts*
Thursday, September 30: *The Iron Chest* / *Katharine and Petruchio*
Friday, October 1: as Richmond in *Richard III* / *The Secret; or, The Hole in the Wall*
Saturday, October 2: *Macbeth* / *Nature and Philosophy; or, The Youth that Never Saw a Woman*
Monday, October 4: *Romeo and Juliet*
Tuesday, October 5: *Hamlet*
Wednesday, October 6: *Macbeth*
Thursday, October 7: *Othello* / *All the World's a Stage*
Friday, October 8: *The Merchant of Venice* / *Taming of the Shrew*
Saturday, October 9: as Richmond in *Richard III*
Monday, October 11: *Henry V* / *Poor Pillicody*
Tuesday, October 12: *Henry V* / *The Lottery Ticket*
Wednesday, October 13: *King Lear*
Thursday, October 14: *Brutus* / *All the World's a Stage*
Friday, October 15: *Much Ado about Nothing* / *In and Out of Place*
Saturday, October 16: *La Tour de Nesle; or, The Chamber of Death* / *Factory Girl*
Monday, October 18: *Sea of Ice* / *Alpine Maid*

(1858, continued)

Tuesday, October 19: *Sea of Ice* / *Jenny Lind*
Wednesday, October 20: *Sea of Ice* / *Factory Girl*
Thursday, October 21: *Shoemaker of Toulouse; or, The Avenger of Humble Life* / *Family Jars*
Friday, October 22: *Shoemaker of Toulouse; or, The Avenger of Humble Life* / *Family Jars*
Saturday, October 23: *People's Lawyer* / *Jessie Brown*
Monday, October 25: as Traddles in *David Copperfield* / *Family Jars*
Tuesday, October 26: *All that Glitters Is Not Gold* / *Jessie Brown*
Wednesday, October 27: *The Dutch Governor* / *Poor Pillicoddy* / *In and Out of Place*
Thursday, October 28: *Sea of Ice* / *The Lottery Ticket*
Friday, October 29: *Triple Murder; or, The Chamber of Death* / *Yankee Teamster*
Saturday, October 30: *Dombey and Son* / *The Mysterious Panel*

Dudley Hall, Lynchburg, Va.

Monday, November 1: as Count Florio in *The Wife; or, My Father's Grave* / *Poor Pillicoddy*
Tuesday, November 2: as Paris in *Romeo and Juliet* / *The Lottery Ticket*
Wednesday, November 3: as Traddles in *David Copperfield* / *Family Jars*
Thursday, November 4: *Othello* / *Swiss Swains*
Friday, November 5: as Paris in *Romeo and Juliet* / *The Lottery Ticket*
Saturday, November 6: *Factory Girl* / *La Tour de Nesle; or, The Chamber of Death*
Monday, November 8: *School for Scandal* / *In and Out of Place*
Tuesday, November 9: *Macbeth* / *The Secret; or, The Hole in the Wall*
Wednesday–Friday, November 10–12: *Sea of Ice*
Saturday, November 13: as Buckingham in *Richard III* / *Sea of Ice* (Act 2)

Richmond Theatre, Richmond

Monday, November 15 (engagement of Avonia Jones): *Evadne; or, The Statue* / *Poor Pillicoddy*
Tuesday, November 16: *Ingomar* / *The Lottery Ticket*
Wednesday, November 17: *The Bride of Lammermoor* / *Sudden Thoughts*
Thursday, November 18: *Armand* / *Prince and Peasant*
Friday, November 19: as Paisson in *Adrienne the Actress* / as "Her Cheroot" in *Jenny Lind*
Saturday, November 20: *Lucretia Borgia* / *Paul Pry; or, I Hope I Don't Intrude*
Monday, November 22: *Sybil* / *Sudden Thoughts*
Tuesday, November 23: *Sybil* / *Our Gal*
Wednesday, November 24: *La Tiobe; or, The Spt. of St. Marce* / *Boots at the Swan*
Thursday, November 25: as Paisson in *Adrienne the Actress* / *Our Gal*
Friday, November 26: *Katharine and Petruchio* / *Sybil*
Saturday, November 27: *Sybil* / *Lucretia Borgia* / *Wizard of the Moon*
Monday, November 29 (engagement of J.W. Wallack): *The Iron Mask*
Tuesday, November 30: *The Iron Mask*
Wednesday, December 1: *King of the Commons* / *Boots at the Swan*
Thursday, December 2: *Virginius* / *Dead Shot*
Friday, December 3: *Tragedy of Werner* / *My Aunt*
Saturday, December 4: *Life and Death of Richard III*
Monday, December 6: *Civilization* / *Boots at the Swan*
Tuesday, December 7: *The Iron Mask*

(1858, continued)

Wednesday, December 8: *Civilization / Dead Shot*
Thursday, December 9: *King of Commons / Sudden Thoughts*
Friday, December 10: *Macbeth / A Day in Paris*
Saturday, December 11: *William Tell / Black Eyed Susan / Robbers of the Heath*
Monday, December 13 (engagement of Mrs. Julia Dean): *The Hunchback / The Lottery Ticket*
Tuesday, December 14: *Evadne; or, The Statue / Love in All Corners*
Wednesday, December 15: *Love / A Dead Shot*
Thursday, December 16: *Old Heads and Young Hearts / Our Gal*

Powhatan Hotel, Richmond

Saturday, December 18: *Fazio; or, The Italian Wife / The Love Chase*

Petersburg Theatre, Petersburg, Va.

Monday, December 20: *Fazio; or, The Italian Wife / The Love Chase*
Tuesday–Saturday, December 21–25 (Variety of short plays previously given)

1859

Monday–Saturday, December 28–January 1 (engagement of Maggie Mitchell): as Uncas in *Wept of Wish-Ton-Wish* / and daily small parts in Miss Mitchell's pieces

Richmond Theatre, Richmond, Va.

Friday, January 7 (engagement of Signor Felix Carlo, acrobat): *David Copperfield*
Saturday, January 8: *Rake's Progress*
Monday, January 10: *Ernest Maltravers; or, A Father's Curse / Faint Heart Never Won Fair Lady*
Monday, January 17 (engagement of J.A. Neafie): *The Corsican Brothers*
Tuesday, January 18: *Hamlet / Married Rake*
Wednesday, January 19: *Richilieu / Rather Excited*
Thursday, January 20: *Pizarro / A Dead Shot*
Friday, January 21: *Harolde, The Merchant of Calais / Faint Heart Never Won Fair Lady*
Saturday, January 22: *The Corsican Brothers / Black Eyed Susan*
Monday–Saturday, January 24–29, as Danglars in *Monte Christo*
Tuesday–Wednesday, February 1–2: *Cricket on the Hearth / The Printer's Apprentice / the Carnival Scene from Monte Christo*
Thursday, February 3: *Oak of Croisary; or, Theresa's Vow / The Printer's Apprentice*
Friday, February 4: *The Spirit of 76; or, The Time that Tried Men's Souls / The Sergeant's Wedding*
Saturday, February 5: *La Tour de Nesle; or, The Chamber of Death / The Spirit of '76*
Monday, February 7 (engagement of Maggie Mitchell): *Margot, The Poultry Dealer / Katy O'Shiel*
Tuesday, February 8: *The French Spy / Milly, The Maid with the Milking Pail*
Wednesday, February 9: as Uncas in *Wept of Wish-Won-Wish / The Four Sisters*
Thursday, February 10: *The Young Prince / The Queen of the Abruzzel*
Friday, February 11: *The Wild Hunters of Mississippi / The Lady's Stratagem*
Saturday, February 12: *The French Spy / Katy O'Shiel*
Friday, February 25: as Paris in *Romeo and Juliet / The Widow's Victim*

(1858, continued)

Saturday, February 26: *The French Spy* / *Katy O'Shiel*

Monday, February 28 (engagement of William Wheatley and J.S. Clarke): *Our American Cousin* / *The Widow's Victim*

Tuesday, March 1: *Our American Cousin* / *Rather Excited*

Wednesday, March 2: *Our American Cousin* / *A Quiet Family*

Thursday, March 3: *Our American Cousin* / *The Sergeant's Wedding*

Friday, March 4: *Our American Cousin* / *The Toodles* / *The Hypocrite*

Saturday, March 5: *Our American Cousin* / *Man and His Tiger* / *The Spectre Bridegroom; or, A Ghost in Spite of Himself*

Monday, March 7: *Our American Cousin* / *The Dramatist*

Tuesday, March 8: *Our American Cousin* / *Willow Copse*

Wednesday, March 9: *Our American Cousin* / *Laugh When You Can*

Thursday, March 10: *Our American Cousin* / *Wild Oats* / *Turning the Tables*

Friday, March 11: *Inconstant; or, Wine Works Wonders* / *Midnight Watch* / *Sudden Thoughts*

Saturday, March 12: *William Tell* / *Our American Cousin* / *The Toodles* (Act 2)

Monday, March 14 (engagement of James E. Murdock): *Inconstant; or, Wine Works Wonders* / *A Quiet Family*

Tuesday, March 15: *Hamlet* / *Married Rake*

Wednesday, March 16: as Dawson in *The Gamester* / *Swiss Swains*

Thursday, March 17: *Macbeth* / *Married Rake*

Friday, March 18: *The Stranger* / *My Aunt; or, Love and Champagne*

Saturday, March 19: *The Robbers* / *Our Gal*

Monday–Wednesday, March 21–23: *De Soto, Hero of the Mississippi*

Thursday, March 24: *Victims* / *Old Guard*

Friday, March 25: *Marble Heart*

Saturday, March 26 (engagement of Mr. & Mrs. W.J. Florence): *The Irish Immigrant* / *Mischevious Annie*

Monday, March 28: *Pardeen O'Rafferty* / *A Lesson for Husbands* / *Happy Man*

Tuesday, March 29: *Knight of Arva* / *The Young Actress* / *Paddy Miles' Boy*

Wednesday, March 30: *Irish Hussar; or, The King and the Deserter* / *Mischevious Annie*

Thursday, March 31: *Irish Assurance and Yankee Modesty* / *Working the Oracle*

Friday, April 1: *How to Get Out of It* / *Yankee Housekeeper* / *Irish Lion*

Saturday, April 2: *Ireland as It Is* / *The Young Actress* / *Florence Worried by Johnston*

Monday, April 4: *White Horse of the Peppers* / *Lola Montez* / *The Good for Nothing*

Tuesday, April 5: *The Irish Mormon* / *Thrice Married*

Wednesday, April 6: *Mat of the Iron Hand; or, Tom Cringle's Log Book* / *The Sergeant's Wedding*

Thursday–Saturday, April 7–9: *The Naiad Queen*

Tuesday, April 12 (engagement of Barry Sullivan): *Richilieu* / *Organic Affection*

Wednesday, April 13: as Dawson in *The Gamester* / *The Sergeant's Wedding*

Thursday, April 14: *Hamlet*

Friday, April 15: *The Merchant of Venice* / *The Taming of the Shrew*

Saturday, April 16: as Buckingham in *Richard III*

Monday, April 18 (engagement of Edwin Booth): *The Apostate*

Tuesday, April 19: *The Iron Chest*

Wednesday, April 20: *King Lear*

Thursday, April 21: *Macbeth*

Friday, April 22: as Richmond in *Richard III*

Saturday, April 23: *Brutus* / *P.P.; or, The Man and His Tiger*

Monday, April 25: *King Lear*

(1859, continued)

Tuesday, April 26: *A New Way to Pay Old Debts*
Wednesday, April 27: as Horatio in *Hamlet* (theatre closed April 27–30)
Monday, May 2 (end of Edwin Booth's engagement): Othello in *Othello* (benefit)
Tuesday, May 3 (engagement of Mrs. W.C. Gladstane and John W. Adams): *Lucretia Borgia*
Wednesday, May 4: as Cool in *London Assurance*
Thursday, May 5: *Louise de Lignerolles*
Friday, May 6: as Lord Tinsel in *The Hunchback* / *Rough Diamond*
Saturday, May 7: *The Robber's Wife; or, The Coiner's Grave* / *Our Eastern Shore Cousin in Richmond*
Monday, May 9: *Masks and Faces* / the Screen Scene from *School for Scandal* / Our Eastern Shore Cousin in Richmond
Tuesday, May 10: *Masks and Faces* / the Screen Scene from *School for Scandal* / Our *Eastern Shore Cousin in Richmond* / *Louise de Lignerolles*
Wednesday, May 11: *Masks and Faces* / *Our Eastern Shore Cousin in Richmond* / *Agnes de Vere; or, A Wife's Revenge*
Thursday, May 12: *Masks and Faces* / *Our Eastern Shore Cousin in Richmond* / *A Serious Family*
Friday, May 13: *Ladies Battle* / Readings from Longfellow: *Hiawatha* / Scenes from *Masks and Faces*
Saturday, May 14: *The Female Gambler* / *The Lottery Ticket*
Monday, May 16 (last night of the season): *Masks and Faces* / a Washington Allegorical Tableau

Richmond Theatre, Richmond

Saturday, September 3: as Henry Moreland in *Heir at Law* / *Out to Nurse*
Monday, September 5: *Marble Heart* / *A Kiss in the Dark*
Tuesday, September 6: *Everybody's Friend* / *Your Life's in Danger*
Wednesday, September 7: *The Rivals* / *Paddy Miles' Boy*
Thursday, September 8: *Everybody's Friend* / *Our Country Cousin*
Friday, September 9: *Nine Points of the Law* / *The Stage Struck Barber*
Saturday, September 10: as Buckingham in *Richard III* / *Your Life's in Danger*
Monday, September 12 (engagement of Mr. & Mrs. Waller): *The Duchess of Malfi*
Tuesday, September 13: *The Duchess of Malfi* / *Why Don't She Marry?*
Wednesday, September 14: *Macbeth*
Thursday, September 15: *Othello*
Friday, September 16: *Guy Mannering* / *Therese*
Saturday, September 17: *The Tragedy of Bertram* / *Horse-Shoe Robinson*
Monday, September 19: *Pauline; or, The Assassins of the Chateau* / *Buried Alive*
Tuesday, September 20: *The Stranger* / *The Lady of Lyons*
Wednesday, September 21: *Pauline; or, The Assassins of the Chateau* / *Deeds of Dreadful Note; or, Crimson Crimes*
Thursday, September 22: *Midas* / *Apollo*
Friday, September 23: as Lord Tinsel in *The Hunchback* / *Guy Mannering*
Saturday, September 24: *The Mas'd Riders* / *Apollo*
Monday, September 26 (engagement of Jane Coombs): *Love's Sacrifice*
Tuesday, September 27: *School for Scandal*
Wednesday, September 28: as Paris in *Romeo and Juliet* / *A Kiss in the Dark*
Thursday, September 29: as Alastor in *Ingomar; or, The Power of Love* / *Ireland as It Is*
Friday, September 30: as Glavis in *The Lady of Lyons* / as Trueworth in *The Love Chase*

(1859, continued)

Saturday, October 1: as Alaster in *Ingomar, The Barbarian* / *Tom and Jerry; or, Life in London*

Monday, October 3: *The Wife's Revenge* / *His Last Legs*

Tuesday, October 4: as Cool in *London Assurance*

Wednesday, October 5: *Actress of Padua* / *My Friend in the Straps*

Thursday, October 6: *The Stranger* / *Ireland as It Is*

Friday, October 7: as Paris in *Romeo and Juliet* / as Lord Tinsel in *The Hunchback* / *School for Scandal* / *His Last Legs*

Saturday, October 8: *Black Rangers; or, The Battle of Germantown* / *Tom and Jerry; or, Life in London*

Monday, October 10 (engagement of Maggie Mitchell): *The Young Prince* / *Katy O'Shiel* / *The Black Rangers*

Tuesday, October 11: *Margot, The Poultry Dealer* / *Pet of the Petticoats*

Wednesday, October 12: as Uncas in *Wept of Wish-Ton-Wish* / *The Little Savage*

Thursday, October 13: *The French Spy* / *The Four Sisters*

Friday, October 14: *Wild Huntress of the Mississippi* / *A Lady's Stratagem*

Saturday, October 15: *Beauty and the Beast*

Dudley Hall, Lynchburg, Va.

Monday, October 17: as Glavis in *Lady of Lyons* / *Our Country Cousin*

Tuesday, October 18: *The Stage Struck Barber* / *The Loan of a Lover* / *The Wandering Minstrel*

Wednesday, October 19: *The College Boy* / *Jumbo Jim; or, The Honest Shoe Black* / *The Farmer's Story; or, The Trials of Toodles*

Thursday, October 20: *My Aunt* / *The Rough Diamond* / *Paddy Miles' Boy*

Friday, October 21: *The Stranger* / *The Loan of a Lover*

Saturday, October 22: *Dumb Belle* / as Buckingham in *Richard III* / *A Kiss in the Dark*

Richmond Theatre, Richmond

Monday, October 17 (engagement of Maggie Mitchell): *Beauty and the Beast*

Tuesday, October 18: *Beauty and the Beast* / *My Grandfather's Will; or, The Man in the Straw*

Wednesday, October 19: *The Wandering Boys* / *The Milk Maid* / *Beauty and the Beast*

Thursday, October 20: *Olympia, The Brigand Queen* / *Beauty and the Beast*

Friday, October 21: *Beauty and the Beast*

Saturday, October 22 (afternoon only): *Beauty and the Beast* / *The Little Treasure*

Monday, October 24: *Everybody's Friend* / *Horse-Shoe Robinson*

Tuesday, October 25: as Henry Moreland in *Heir at Law*

Howard Athenaeum, Boston

Wednesday, October 26 (second week of Edwin Booth): as Blount in *Richard III*

Thursday, October 27: *Richelieu*

Friday, October 28: *The Stranger* / *Don Caesar de Bazan*

Richmond Theatre, Richmond

Monday, October 31 (engagement of Barry Sullivan): as Horatio in *Hamlet*

Tuesday, November 1: *Richelieu*

(1859, continued)

Wednesday, November 2: as Dawson in *The Gamester*
Thursday, November 3: *Money*
Friday, November 4: *The Merchant of Venice* / *The Taming of the Shrew*
Saturday, November 5: as Buckingham in *Richard III*
Monday, November 7: *A New Way to Pay Old Debts* / *More Blunders Than One*
Tuesday, November 8: *King Lear*
Wednesday, November 9: *King Henry IV*
Thursday, November 10: cast as Don Pedro but did not appear in *Much Ado About Nothing*; left company until the 14th
Monday, November 14 (engagement of Mrs. Hughes and W.E. Burton): *The Toodles* / *A Breach of Promise*
Tuesday, November 15: *A Serious Family* / *Guy Goodluck*
Wednesday, November 16: *A 1000 Young Milliners Wanted*
Thursday, November 17: *Dombey and Son* / *Wandering Minstrel*
Friday, November 18: *Paul Pry* / *Blue Devils*
Saturday, November 19: *The Original Jacobs of New York* / *Timothy Toodles*
Monday, November 21: *Eustache* / *Beauty and the Beast*
Tuesday, November 22: *She Stoops to Conquer; or, The Mistakes of a Night* / *Deeds of Dreadful Note*
Wednesday, November 23: *The Lost Ship* / *His Last Legs*
Thursday, November 24: *Eustache*
Friday, November 25: left to join Richmond Grays in guarding and hanging of John Brown; returned week of Dec. 5th
Saturday–Wednesday, December 3–7 (continued engagement of Mrs. Charles Howard and H. Watkins): *The Hidden Hand* / *The Ledger Story*
Thursday–Friday, December 8–9: *Smiles and Tears* / *A Mother's Prayer* / *Aline, the Rose*
Saturday, December 10: *The Ledger Romance* / *Pioneer Patriot*
Monday, December 12 (engagement of the Marsh juvenile comedians): *Brigand* / *The Toodles*
Tuesday, December 13: *The Bottle Imp* / *Brian O'Lynn*
Wednesday, December 14: *The Forty Thieves* / *My Neighbor's Wife*
Thursday, December 15: *The Naiad Queen* / *Good for Nothing*
Friday, December 16: *Ingomar, the Barbarian* / *The Wandering Minstrel*
Saturday, December 17: *Our American Cousin* / *A Trip to Coney Island* / *The Naiad Queen* (matinee)
Monday, December 19: *Sea of Ice* / *A Mother's Prayer*
Tuesday, December 20: *Fortunio; or, The Seven Servants* / pantomime of M. Dechalumeaux (matinee and evening same)
Wednesday, December 21: *Cinderella* / *The Spectre Bridegroom* (matinee and evening same)
Thursday, December 22: *Jenny Twitcher in England* / *The Bottle Imp*
Friday, December 23: *Kim-ka, the Aeronaut* / *The Miser and the Three Thieves* (matinee and evening same)
Saturday, December 24: *Cinderella* / *The Six Degrees of Crime*
Monday, December 26: *The Hidden Hand* / *Poor Smike* (matinee)
Tuesday, December 27: as Lord Arthur Brandon in *Dreams of Delusion* / as Lamp in *Wild Oats*
Wednesday, December 28: *The Ledger Romance*
Thursday, December 29: *A Game of Chess* / *Jenny Lind* / a Medical Lecture by Dr. Graham Dumps "Quack Martyrs"
Friday, December 30: *A Sheep in Wolf's Clothing* / *Everybody's Friend* / *Siamese Twins*
Saturday, December 31: *Pioneer Patriot*

1860

Monday, January 2 (engagement of Caroline Richings and Peter Richings): *Daughter of the Regiment* / *The Little Savage*

Tuesday, January 3: *Louise Muller* / *The Bonnie Fish Wife*

Wednesday, January 4: variety musical program / *Washington Allegory*

Thursday, January 5: *The Spirit of the Rhine* / *The Chaplain of the Regiment* / *Washington Allegory*

Friday, January 6: *Fashion* / *Washington Allegory*

Saturday, January 7: *Napoleon's Old Guard* / *The Spirit of the Rhine* / *Washington Allegory*

Monday, January 9: *Fashion* / *Washington Allegory*

Tuesday, January 10: *The Chaplain of the Regiment* / *The Spirit of the Rhine*

Wednesday–Tuesday, January 11–24: *The Enchantress*

Wednesday, January 25: *The Chaplain of the Regiment* / *The Bonnie Fish Wife* / *The Spirit of the Rhine*

Thursday, January 26: *The Daughter of the Regiment* / *The Little Savage*

Friday, January 27: *Extremes* / with gymnastic exercises and songs

Saturday, January 28: Musical program (mat.) / *Clari, Private and Confidential* (eve.)

Monday, January 30 (engagement of James E. Murdock): *Wild Oats* / *Your Life's in Danger*

Tuesday, January 31: *Money*

Wednesday, February 1: *Hamlet*

Thursday, February 2: as Dawson in *The Gamester* / as Mr. Glimmer in *The Buzzards*

Friday, February 3: *The Inconstant* / *My Aunt; or, Love and Champagne*

Saturday, February 4: *The Robbers* / as Mr. Glimmer in *The Buzzards*

Monday, February 6: *Doom of Deville; or, The Maiden's Vow* / *Dreams of Delusion*

Tuesday, February 7: *Marble Heart* / *Crimson Crimes*

Wednesday, February 8: *Sheep in Wolf's Clothing* / *A Glance at New York*

Thursday, February 9: *Horse-Shoe Robinson* / *A Glance at New York*

Friday, February 10: *Sheep in Wolf's Clothing* / *Ireland as It Is* / *The Buzzards*

Saturday, February 11: *Bacon's Rebellion* / *A Husband to Order*

Monday, February 13: *A Husband to Order* / *The Drunkard*

Tuesday, February 14: *Bacon's Rebellion* / *A Husband to Order*

Wednesday, February 15: *Don Caesar de Bazan* / *A Husband to Order*

Thursday, February 16: *The Idiot Witness; or, A Tale of Blood* / *Doom of Deville*

Friday, February 17: *The Broken Sword* / *Village Lawyer* / *Jumbo Jim*

Saturday, February 18: *Wolfgang; or, The Wrecker's Beacon* / *The Broken Sword*

Monday, February 20 (engagement of J.B. Roberts): as Buckingham in *Richard III* / *The Omnibus; or, Ten Miles Out of Town*

Tuesday, February 21: *A New Way to Pay Old Debts*

Wednesday, February 22: *Louis XI* / *The Omnibus; or, Ten Miles Out of Town*

Thursday, February 23: *Louis XI* / *The Omnibus*

Friday, February 24: *Louis XI* / *Ruy Gomez*

Saturday, February 25: *The Apostate; or, The Moors of Spain* / as Romeo Jaffier Jenkins in *Too Much for Good Nature*

Monday, February 27 (engagement of Mrs. Julia Dean): *The Lady of Lyons* / as Romeo Jaffier Jenkins in *Too Much for Good Nature*

Tuesday, February 28: *Ingomar, the Barbarian* / *Too Much for Good Nature*

Wednesday, February 29: as Lord Tinsel in *The Hunchback* / as Romeo Jaffier Jenkins in *Too Much for Good Nature*

Thursday, March 1: as Cool in *London Assurance* / *The Rifle; or, How to Use It*

Friday, March 2: *Evadne* / *Rough Diamond*

Saturday, March 3: *Lucretia Borgia* / *Aunt Charlotte's Maid*

(1860, continued)

Monday, March 5 (engagement of Louise Wells and her equestrian troupe): *Buck Bison* / *Americans Abroad*

Tuesday, March 6: *Eagle Eye; or, The Maiden of Delaware* / *Americans Abroad*

Wednesday, March 7: *Eagle Eye* / *Paddy Miles' Boy*

Thursday, March 8: *Margaret Catchpole; or, The Female Horse Thief* / *Break of Day Boys*

Friday, March 9: *Sybil, of Rookwood* / *Zoloe* (from the operatic spectacle *La Bayadare*)

Saturday, March 10: *Jack Shepard, The Horsebreaker* / *Jonathan Wilde, The Thief-Taker*

Monday–Tuesday, March 12–13: *Mazeppa; or, The Wilde Horse of Tartary*

Wednesday, March 14: *Sybil of Rockwood; or, The Life and Death of Dick Turpin*

Thursday, March 15: *Putnam* / *Irish Assurance and Yankee Modesty*

Friday, March 16: as Uncas in *Wept of Wish-Ton-Wish* / *Jack Sheppard, The Horse-breaker*

Saturday, March 17: *The French Spy; or, Richard III on Horseback* / *Paddy, The Piper*

Monday, March 19 (engagement of J.S. Clarke): *Leap Year* / *The Toodles*

Tuesday, March 20 (engagement of J.S. Clarke): *Jonathan Bradford; or, Murder at the Roadside Inn* / *Leap Year*

Wednesday, March 21: *School of Reform; or, How to Rule a Husband* / *The Spectre Bridegroom; or, A Ghost in Spite of Himself*

Thursday, March 22: *Paul Pry* / *The Toodles* / *The Hypocrite* / a Lecture on the Times

Friday, March 23: *Our American Cousin* / *Jack, The Exciseman* / *Old Times in Virginia*

Saturday, March 24: *Our American Cousin* / *Jack Sheppard; or, The Old Offender*

Monday, March 26: *Sheep in Wolf's Clothing* / *Everybody's Friend* / *Aunt Charlotte's Maid*

Tuesday, March 27: *Dreams of Delusion* / *Don Caesar de Bazan*

Wednesday, March 28: *All That Glitters Is Not Gold; or, The Poor Factory Girl* / *Black Eyed Susan*

Thursday, March 29: *The Stranger* / *Whitebait at Greenwich*

Friday, March 30: *Willow Copse* / *Aunt Charlotte's Maid*

Saturday, March 31: *Rake's Progress* / *The Solitary of the Heath*

Monday, April 2 (engagement of Lucille and Helen Western): *Flowers of the Forest* / *The Swedish Nightingale*

Tuesday, April 3: *The Ladies' Stratagem* / *The French Spy* / *The Wandering Boys*

Wednesday, April 4: *Our Female American Cousin* / *The Belle of Ireland* / *The Young Student*

Thursday, April 5: *Wept of Wish-Ton-Wish* / *The House Breaker*

Friday, April 6: *Satan in Paris* / *Our Female American Cousin*

Saturday, April 7: *The Hot Corn Girl* / *The French Spy*

Monday, April 9: *Three Fast Men; or, The Female Robinson Crusoes*

Tuesday, April 10: *Our Female American Cousin* / *Nature and Philosophy*

Wednesday, April 11: *Flowers of the Forest* / *Loan of a Lover*

Thursday, April 12: *Wild Hunters of the Mississippi* / *The Ladies' Stratagem*

Friday, April 13: *The Hidden Hand* / *Lover's Disguise*

Saturday, April 14: *The French Spy* / *Yankee Cousin*

Monday–Saturday, April 16–21: *Three Fast Men* / *Female Minstrels*

Monday, April 23 (engagement of Mrs. John C. Heenan): *The French Spy* / *A Day in Paris*

Tuesday, April 24: *The Soldier's Daughter*

(1860, continued)

Wednesday, April 25: *An Unprotected Female* / *The Irish Heiress* / *The Stage-Struck Barber*

Thursday, April 26: *An Unprotected Female* / *Benicia Boy of England*

Friday, April 27: *Orphan of Geneva* / *Dreams of Delusion* / *Benicia Boy in England*

Saturday, April 28: *Wreckers of Norway; or, A Vision of the Dead* / *Golden Farmer*

Monday, April 30 (engagement of F.S. Chanfau): *The Toodles* / *The Widow's Victim* / imitations of Booth, Forrest, Kean, et al.

Tuesday, May 1: *A Yankee Teamster* / *A French Actor* / *A Drunk Corporal*

Wednesday, May 2: *A Yankee Sailor* / *An Old Frenchman* / *A Raw Irishman* / *The First Night, A Peep Behind the Curtain*

Thursday, May 3: Last Scene from *Therese* / *Model of a Wife* / *The Toodles*

Friday, May 4: *A Glance at New York* / *The Ocean Child* / *Mose*

Saturday, May 5: *The Spat* / *A Glance at New York*

Monday–Saturday, May 7–12: theatre closed

Monday–Tuesday, May 14–15: as Aramis in *Three Guardsmen*

Wednesday–Thursday, May 16–17: *The Flying Dutchman; or, The Phantom Ship*

Friday, May 18: as M. de Bevannes, a Man of the World, in *Romance of a Poor Young Man* / *The Queen's Own*

Saturday, May 19: *The Flying Dutchman* / *Horse-Shoe Robinson*

Monday–Thursday, May 21–24: *The Wood Demon*

Friday, May 25: *Romance of a Poor Young Man* / *The Widow's Victim*

Saturday, May 26: *Poor Smike* / *The Lost Ship*

Tuesday, May 28 (close of the season): *A Husband to Order* / *Everybody's Friend*

Thursday, May 31 (extra night; benefit): as Victim in *The Son of Malta* / as Sayers in *My Fellow Clerk* / as Richard in *Richard III* (Act 5)

Petersburg Theatre, Petersburg, Va.

Saturday, June 3: as Victim in *The Son of Malta* / as Sayers in *My Fellow Clerk* / as Richard in *Richard III*

Columbus Theatre, Columbus, Ga.

Monday, October 1: as Romeo in *Romeo and Juliet*

Tuesday, October 2: as The Stranger in *The Stranger*

Wednesday, October 3: as Ludovico in *Evadne; or, The Statue*

Thursday, October 4: as Julian St. Pierre in *The Wife*

Friday, October 5: as Richard in *Richard III*

Saturday, October 6: as Pescara in *The Apostate*

Monday, October 8: as Phidias and Raphael in *The Marble Heart*

Tuesday, October 9: as Claude Melnotte in *The Lady of Lyons*

Wednesday, October 10: as Julian St. Pierre in *The Wife*

Thursday, October 11: as Icebrook in *Everybody's Friend*

Friday, October 12 (benefit): scheduled for *Hamlet*; did not appear because of shooting accident

Saturday, October 13: as Charles De Moor in *The Robbers*

Monday–Friday, October 15–19: (benefit) did not appear

Saturday, October 20: as Mark Antony in *Julius Caesar* in Forum Scene / *The Drunkard* / *The Hidden Hand*

Montgomery Theatre, Montgomery

Tuesday–Saturday, October 23–27: announced; did not appear

(1860, continued)

Monday, October 29: as Pescara in *The Apostate*
Tuesday, October 30: as Julian St. Pierre in *The Wife*
Wednesday, October 31: as Hamlet in *Hamlet*
Thursday, November 1: as Richard in *Richard III*
Friday, November 2 (benefit): as Romeo in *Romeo and Juliet*
Saturday, November 3 (last performance of engagement): as Charles De Moor in *The Robbers*
Friday, November 16 (engagement of Kate Bateman): as Romeo in *Romeo and Juliet*
Saturday, December 1 (engagement of Maggie Mitchell; Booth benefit): as Count Rafaelle in *Rafaelle* / as Richard in *Richard III* (Act 5) / Katy O'Shiel

1861

Metropolitan Theatre, Rochester, N.Y.

Monday, January 21: as Romeo in *Romeo and Juliet*
Tuesday, January 22: as Claude Melnotte in *The Lady of Lyons*
Wednesday, January 23: as Othello in *Othello*
Thursday, January 24: as Julian St. Pierre in *The Wife*
Friday, January 25 (benefit): as Richard in *Richard III*
Saturday, January 26: as Raffael in *Raffael, The Reprobate*
Monday, January 28: as Phidias and Raphael in *The Marble Heart*
Tuesday, January 29: as Ludovico in *Evadne; or, The Statue*
Wednesday, January 30: as Don Caesar in *Don Caesar de Bazan*
Thursday, January 31: as Richard in *Richard III*
Friday, February 1 (benefit): as Fabien and Louis in *The Corsican Brothers*
Saturday, February 2: as Fabien and Louis in *The Corsican Brothers*

Green Street Gayety Theatre, Albany, N.Y.

Monday, February 11: as Romeo in *Romeo and Juliet*
Tuesday, February 12: as Pescara in *The Apostate*
Wednesday–Saturday, February 13–16: did not appear because of accident on the 12th
Monday, February 18: as Pescara in *The Apostate*
Tuesday, February 19: as Julian St. Pierre in *The Wife*
Wednesday, February 20: as Othello in *Othello*
Thursday, February 21: as The Stranger in *The Stranger*
Friday, February 22 (benefit): as Richard in *Richard III*
Saturday, February 23: as Charles De Moor in *The Robbers*

(Same theatre, after a break)
Monday, March 4: as Richard in *Richard III*
Tuesday, March 5: as Richard in *Richard III*
Wednesday, March 6: as Hamlet in *Hamlet*
Thursday, March 7: as Claude Melnotte in *The Lady of Lyons*
Friday, March 8: as Macbeth in *Macbeth*
Saturday, March 9: as Macbeth in *Macbeth*
Monday, March 11: as Shylock in *The Merchant of Venice*
Tuesday, March 12: as Shylock in *The Merchant of Venice*
Wednesday, March 13: as Phidias and Raphael in *The Marble Heart*
Thursday, March 14: as Fabien and Louis in *The Corsican Brothers*
Friday, March 15: as Fabien and Louis in *The Corsican Brothers*

(1861, continued)

Portland Theatre, Portland, Me.

Monday, March 18: as Richard in *Richard III*
Tuesday, March 19: as Othello in *Othello*
Wednesday, March 20: as Hamlet in *Hamlet*
Thursday, March 21: as Richard in *Richard III*
Friday, March 22 (benefit): as Macbeth in *Macbeth*
Saturday, March 23 (afternoon only): as Claude Melnotte in *The Lady of Lyons*
Monday, March 25: as Romeo in *Romeo and Juliet*
Tuesday, March 26: as Shylock in *The Merchant of Venice*
Wednesday, March 27: as Pescara in *The Apostate*
Thursday, March 28: as Phidias and Raphael in *The Marble Heart*
Friday, March 29 (farewell benefit): as Rafaelle in *Rafaelle, The Reprobate* / as Fabien
    and Louis in *The Corsican Brothers*
Saturday, March 30 (afternoon only): as Fabien and Louis in *The Corsican Brothers*

Green Street Gayety Theatre, Albany, N.Y.

Monday, April 22: as Richard in Richard III
Tuesday, April 23: as Charles De Moor in *The Robbers*
Wednesday–Saturday, April 24–27: as Ludovico in *Evadne; or, The Statue* (stabbed
    by leading lady Henrietta Irving)

Metropolitan Theatre, Buffalo, N.Y.

Monday, October 28: as Pescara in *The Apostate*
Tuesday, October 29: as Hamlet in *Hamlet*
Wednesday, October 30: as Othello in *Othello*
Thursday, October 31: as Julian St. Pierre in *The Wife*
Friday, November 1 (benefit): as Richard in *Richard III*
Saturday, November 2: as Charles De Moor in *The Robbers*
Monday, November 4: as Romeo in *Romeo and Juliet*
Tuesday, November 5: as Claude Melnotte in *The Lady of Lyons*
Wednesday, November 6: as Macbeth in *Macbeth*
Thursday, November 7: as Richard in *Richard III*
Friday, November 8 (benefit): as Phidias and Raphael in *The Marble Heart*
Saturday, November 9: as Fabien and Louis in *The Corsican Brothers*

Mrs. H.A. Perry's Metropolitan Theatre, Detroit

Monday, November 11: as Julian St. Pierre in *The Wife*
Tuesday, November 12: as Macbeth in *Macbeth*
Wednesday, November 13: as Othello in *Othello*
Thursday, November 14: as Othello in *Othello*
Friday, November 15 (benefit): as Richard in *Richard III* / as Romeo Jaffier Jenkins in
    Too Much For Good Nature
Saturday, November 16: as Hamlet in *Hamlet*
Monday, November 18: as Richard in *Richard III*

Wood's Theatre, Cincinnati (Sycamore St. Theatre)

Monday, November 25: as Richard in *Richard III*
Tuesday, November 26: as Othello in *Othello*

(1861, continued)

Wednesday, November 27: as Claude Melnotte in *The Lady of Lyons*
Thursday, November 28: as Charles De Moor in *The Robbers*
Friday, November 29 (benefit): as Macbeth in *Macbeth*
Saturday, November 30: as Richard in *Richard III*
Monday, December 2: as Phidias and Raphael in *The Marble Heart*
Tuesday, December 3: as Phidias and Raphael in *The Marble Heart*
Wednesday, December 4: as Hamlet in *Hamlet*
Thursday, December 5 (Cincinnati newspapers disagreed; possibly the bill was
    changed between the morning and evening editions): as Julian St. Pierre in *The
    Wife* and as Macbeth in *Macbeth* (Act 5) according to the *Daily Commercial*; as
    Mark Antony in *Julius Caesar* according to the *Daily Gazette*
Friday, December 6 (benefit): as Shylock in *The Merchant of Venice* / as Romeo
    Jaffier Jenkins in *Too Much for Good Nature*
Saturday, December 7: as Charles De Moor in *The Robbers*

Louisville Theatre, Louisville

Monday, December 9: as Richard in *Richard III*
Tuesday, December 10: as Claude Melnotte in *The Lady of Lyons*
Wednesday, December 11: as Macbeth in *Macbeth*
Thursday, December 12: as Richard in *Richard III*
Friday, December 13 (benefit): as Hamlet in *Hamlet*
Saturday, December 14: as Charles De Moor in *The Robbers*
Monday, December 16: as Pescara in *The Apostate*
Tuesday, December 17: as Charles de Moor in *The Robbers*
Wednesday, December 18: as Shylock in *The Merchant of Venice* / as Macbeth in
    Macbeth (act 5)
Thursday, December 19: as The Stranger in *The Stranger*
Friday, December 20 (benefit): as Phidias and Raphael in *The Marble Heart* / as
    Romeo Jaffier Jenkins in *Too Much for Good Nature*
Saturday, December 21: as Richard in *Richard III*
Monday, December 23: as Phidias and Raphael in *The Marble Heart*
Tuesday, December 24: as the Demon in *The Fairy and the Demon*
Wednesday, December 25: as the Demon in *The Fairy and the Demon*
Thursday, December 26: as the Demon in *The Fairy and the Demon*
Friday, December 27: as the Demon in *The Fairy and the Demon*
Saturday, December 28: as the Demon in *The Fairy and the Demon*
Monday, December 30: as the Demon in *The Fairy and the Demon*
Tuesday, December 31: as the Demon in *The Fairy and the Demon*

1862

Wednesday, January 1: as the Demon in *The Fairy and the Demon*
Thursday, January 2: as the Demon in *The Fairy and the Demon*
Friday, January 3: as the Demon in *The Fairy and the Demon*
Saturday, January 4: as the Demon in *The Fairy and the Demon*

Ben Debar's St. Louis Theatre, St. Louis

Monday, January 6: as Richard in *Richard III*
Tuesday, January 7: as Hamlet in *Hamlet*
Wednesday, January 8: as Macbeth in *Macbeth*

(1862, continued)

Thursday, January 9: as Othello in *Othello*
Friday, January 10 (benefit): as Pescara in *The Apostate*
Saturday, January 11: as Richard in *Richard III*
Monday, January 13: as Charles De Moor in *The Robbers*
Tuesday, January 14: as Julian St. Pierre in *The Wife*
Wednesday, January 15: as Phidias and Raphael in *The Marble Heart*
Thursday, January 16: as Richard in *Richard III*
Friday, January 17 (benefit): as Claude Melnotte in *The Lady of Lyons* / as Romeo Jaffier Jenkins in *Too Much for Good Nature*
Saturday, January 18: as Phidias and Raphael in *The Marble Heart* / as Romeo Jaffier Jenkins in *Too Much for Good Nature*

McVicker's Theatre, Chicago

Monday, January 20: as Richard in *Richard III*
Tuesday, January 21: as Claude Melnotte in *The Lady of Lyons*
Wednesday, January 22: as Pescara in *The Apostate*
Thursday, January 23: as Romeo in *Romeo and Juliet*
Friday, January 24 (benefit): as Richard in *Richard III*
Saturday, January 25: as Charles De Moor in *The Robbers*
Monday, January 27: as Hamlet in *Hamlet*
Tuesday, January 28: as Hamlet in *Hamlet*
Wednesday, January 29: as Othello in *Othello*
Thursday, January 30: as Pescara in *The Apostate*
Friday, January 31 (benefit): as Macbeth in *Macbeth*
Saturday, February 1: as Richard in *Richard III*

Holliday Street Theatre, Baltimore

Monday, February 17: as Richard in *Richard III*
Tuesday, February 18: as Richard in *Richard III*
Wednesday, February 19: as Romeo in *Romeo and Juliet*
Thursday, February 20: as Fabien and Louis in *The Corsican Brothers*
Friday, February 21 (benefit): as Pescara in *The Apostate*
Saturday, February 22: as Richard in *Richard III*
Monday, February 24: as Hamlet in *Hamlet*
Tuesday, February 25: as The Stranger in *The Stranger*
Wednesday, February 26: as Richard in *Richard III*
Thursday, February 27: as Macbeth in *Macbeth*
Friday, February 28 (benefit): as Hamlet in *Hamlet*
Saturday, March 1: as Pescara in *The Apostate*
Monday, March 3: as Phidias and Raphael in *The Marble Heart*
Tuesday, March 4: as Charles De Moor in *The Robbers*
Wednesday, March 5: as Phidias and Raphael in *The Marble Heart*
Thursday, March 6: as Romeo in *Romeo and Juliet*
Friday, March 7 (benefit): as Charles De Moor in *The Robbers* / as Shylock in Scenes from *The Merchant of Venice*
Saturday, March 8: as Richard in *Richard III*

Mary Provost's Theatre, New York

Monday, March 17: as Richard in *Richard III*
Tuesday, March 18: as Richard in *Richard III*

(1862, continued)

Wednesday, March 19: as Charles De Moor in *The Robbers*
Thursday–Saturday, March 20–22: as Richard in *Richard III*
Monday, March 24: as Hamlet in *Hamlet*
Tuesday–Wednesday, March 25–26: as Pescara in *The Apostate*
Thursday, March 27: as Richard in *Richard III*
Friday, March 28 (benefit): as Macbeth in *Macbeth*
Saturday, March 29: as Richard in *Richard III*
Monday–Tuesday, March 31–April 1: as Richard in *Richard III*
Wednesday, April 2: as Shylock in *The Merchant of Venice*
Thursday, April 3: as Richard in *Richard III*
Friday, April 4: as Charles De Moor in *The Robbers*
Saturday, April 5: as Richard in *Richard III*

Ben Debar's St. Louis Theatre, St. Louis

Monday, April 21: as Charles De Moor in *The Robbers*
Tuesday, April 22: as Hamlet in *Hamlet*
Wednesday, April 23: as Macbeth in *Macbeth*
Thursday, April 24: as Pescara in *The Apostate*
Friday–Saturday, April 25–26: as Richard in *Richard III* (benefit the 25th)
Monday–Tuesday, April 28–29: as Phidias and Raphael in *The Marble Heart*
Wednesday, April 30: as Shylock in *The Merchant of Venice*
Thursday, May 1: as Richard in *Richard III*
Friday, May 2 (benefit): as Romeo in *Romeo and Juliet*
Saturday, May 3: as Phidias and Raphael in *The Marble Heart*

Boston Museum, Boston

Monday, May 12: as Richard in *Richard III*
Tuesday, May 13: as Romeo in *Romeo and Juliet*
Wednesday, May 14: as Charles De Moor in *The Robbers*
Thursday, May 15: as Richard in *Richard III*
Friday, May 16: as Hamlet in *Hamlet*
Saturday, May 17: as Romeo in *Romeo and Juliet*
Monday, May 19: as Pescara in *The Apostate*
Tuesday, May 20: as The Stranger in *The Stranger*
Wednesday, May 21: as Charles De Moor in *The Robbers* / as Romeo Jaffier Jenkins
    in *Too Much for Good Nature*
Thursday, May 22: as Claude Melnotte in *The Lady of Lyons*
Friday, May 23: as Richard in *Richard III*

McVicker's Theatre, Chicago

Monday, June 2: as Richard in *Richard III*
Tuesday, June 3: as Pescara in *The Apostate*
Wednesday, June 4 (afternoon): as Shylock in *Shylock the Jew* / as Richard in *Richard
    III*
Wednesday, June 4 (evening): as Charles De Moor in *The Robbers*
Thursday, June 5: as Claude Melnotte in *The Lady of Lyons*
Friday, June 6: as Pescara in *The Apostate*
Saturday, June 7: as Richard in *Richard III*
Monday–Tuesday, June 9–10: as Hamlet in *Hamlet*
Wednesday, June 11: as Romeo in *Romeo and Juliet*

(1862, continued)

Thursday, June 12: as Pescara in *The Apostate*
Friday, June 13: as Phidias and Raphael in *The Marble Heart*
Saturday, June 14: as Richard in *Richard III*
Monday, June 16: as Macbeth in *Macbeth*
Tuesday, June 17: as Othello in *Othello*
Wednesday, June 18: as Phidias and Raphael in *The Marble Heart*
Thursday, June 19: as Richard in *Richard III*
Friday, June 20: as Charles De Moor in *The Robbers*
Saturday, June 21: as Claude Melnotte in *The Lady of Lyons*

Louisville Theatre, Louisville

Wednesday, June 25: as Richard in *Richard III*
Thursday, June 26: as Hamlet in *Hamlet*
Friday, June 27 (benefit): as Charles De Moor in *The Robbers*
Saturday, June 28: as Richard in *Richard III*
Monday, June 30: as Shylock in *The Merchant of Venice*
Tuesday, July 1: as Ruric Nelville in *The Gunmaker of Moscow*

The Opera House, Lexington, Ky.

Thursday, October 23: as Richard in *Richard III*
Friday, October 24: as Charles De Moor in *The Robbers*

Louisville Theatre, Louisville

Monday, October 27: as Claude Melnotte in *The Lady of Lyons*
Tuesday, October 28: as Richard in *Richard III*
Wednesday, October 29: as Pescara in *The Apostate*
Thursday, October 30: as Macbeth in *Macbeth*
Friday, October 31 (benefit): as Phidias and Raphael in *The Marble Heart*
Saturday, November 1: as Richard in *Richard III*
Monday, November 3: as Charles De Moor in *The Robbers*
Tuesday, November 4: as Macbeth in *Macbeth*
Wednesday, November 5: as Richard in *Richard III*
Thursday, November 6: as Shylock in *The Merchant of Venice*
Friday, November 7 (benefit): as Alfred Evelyn in *Money*
Saturday, November 8: as Fabien and Louis in *The Corsican Brothers*

National Theatre, Cincinnati

Monday, November 10: as Richard in *Richard III*
Tuesday, November 11: as Claude Melnotte in *Lady of Lyons*
Wednesday, November 12: as Macbeth in *Macbeth*
Thursday, November 13: as Fabien and Louis in *The Corsican Brothers*
Friday, November 14: as Richard in *Richard III*
Saturday, November 15: as Charles De Moor in *The Robbers*
Monday, November 17: as Hamlet in *Hamlet*
Tuesday, November 18: as Othello in *Othello*
Wednesday, November 19: as Pescara in *The Apostate*
Thursday, November 20: as Charles De Moor in *The Robbers*
Friday, November 21: as Alfred Evelyn in *Money*
Saturday, November 22: as Pescara in *The Apostate*

(1862, continued)

McVicker's Theatre, Chicago

Monday, December 1: as Claude Melnotte in *The Lady of Lyons*
Tuesday, December 2: as Richard in *Richard III*
Wednesday, December 3: as Shylock in *The Merchant of Venice*
Thursday, December 4: as Othello in *Othello*
Friday, December 5: as Hamlet in *Hamlet*
Saturday, December 6: as Pescara in *The Apostate*
Monday, December 8: as Phidias and Raphael in *The Marble Heart*
Tuesday, December 9: as Phidias and Raphael in *The Marble Heart*
Wednesday, December 10: as Macbeth in *Macbeth*
Thursday, December 11: as The Stranger in *The Stranger*
Friday, December 12: as Richard in *Richard III*
Saturday, December 13: as Charles De Moor in *The Robbers*
Monday, December 15: as Alfred Evelyn in *Money*
Tuesday, December 16: as Pescara in *The Apostate*
Wednesday, December 17: as Romeo in *Romeo and Juliet*
Thursday, December 18: as Macbeth in *Macbeth*
Friday, December 19: as Shylock in *The Merchant of Venice*
Saturday, December 20: as Richard in *Richard III*

Ben Debar's St. Louis Theatre, St. Louis

Monday, December 22: as Richard in *Richard III*
Tuesday, December 23: as Hamlet in *Hamlet*
Wednesday, December 24: as Pescara in *The Apostate*
Thursday, December 25: as Macbeth in *Macbeth*
Friday, December 26: title not announced
Saturday, December 27 (benefit): as Richard in *Richard III*
Monday, December 29: as Phidias and Raphael in *The Marble Heart*
Tuesday, December 30: as Hamlet in *Hamlet*
Wednesday, December 31: as Phidias and Raphael in *The Marble Heart*

1863

Thursday, January 1: as Fabien and Louis in *The Corsican Brothers*
Friday, January 2: as Alfred Evelyn in *Money*
Saturday, January 3 (benefit): as Shylock in *The Merchant of Venice* / as Petruchio in
    Katharine and Petruchio

Boston Museum, Boston

Monday, January 19: as Richard in *Richard III*
Tuesday, January 20: as Claude Melnotte in *The Lady of Lyons*
Wednesday, January 21: as Pescara in *The Apostate*
Thursday, January 22: as Alfred Evelyn in *Money*
Friday, January 23: as Richard in *Richard III*
Saturday, January 24: as Claude Melnotte in *The Lady of Lyons*
Monday, January 26: as Macbeth in *Macbeth*
Tuesday, January 27: as Alfred Evelyn in *Money*
Wednesday, January 28: as Othello in *Othello*
Thursday, January 29: as Charles De Moor in *The Robbers*

(1863, continued)

Friday, January 30: as Romeo in *Romeo and Juliet*
Saturday, January 31: as Phidias and Raphael in *The Marble Heart*
Monday, February 2: as Phidias and Raphael in *The Marble Heart*
Tuesday, February 3: as Phidias and Raphael in *The Marble Heart*
Wednesday, February 4 (afternoon): as Phidias and Raphael in *The Marble Heart*
Wednesday, February 4 (evening): as Phidias and Raphael in *The Marble Heart*
Thursday, February 5: as Pescara in *The Apostate*
Friday, February 6: as Richard in *Richard III*
Saturday, February 7: as Phidias and Raphael in *The Marble Heart*
Monday, February 9: as Fabien and Louis in *The Corsican Brothers*
Tuesday, February 10: as Fabien and Louis in *The Corsican Brothers*
Wednesday, February 11: as Fabien and Louis in *The Corsican Brothers*
Thursday, February 12 (afternoon): as Fabien and Louis in *The Corsican Brothers*
Thursday, February 12 (evening): as Richard in *Richard III*
Friday, February 13 (farewell benefit): as Shylock in *The Merchant of Venice* / as Petruchio in *Katharine and Petruchio*

Mrs. Drew's Arch Street Theatre, Philadelphia

Monday, March 2: as Richard in *Richard III*
Tuesday, March 3: as Phidias and Raphael in *The Marble Heart*
Wednesday, March 4: as Richard in *Richard III*
Thursday, March 5: as Pescara in *The Apostate*
Friday, March 6 (benefit): as Shylock in *The Merchant of Venice* / as Petruchio in *Katharine and Petruchio*
Saturday, March 7: as Charles De Moor in *The Robbers*
Monday, March 9: as Hamlet in *Hamlet*
Tuesday, March 10: as Alfred Evelyn in *Money*
Wednesday, March 11: as Phidias and Raphael in *The Marble Heart*
Thursday, March 12: as Charles De Moor in *The Robbers*
Friday, March 13: as Macbeth in *Macbeth*
Saturday, March 14: as Pescara in *The Apostate*

Grover's Theatre, Washington

Saturday, April 11: as Richard in *Richard III*
Monday, April 13: as Phidias and Raphael in *The Marble Heart*
Tuesday, April 14: as Hamlet in *Hamlet*
Wednesday, April 15: as Claude Melnotte in *The Lady of Lyons*
Thursday, April 16: as Alfred Evelyn in *Money*
Friday, April 17 (benefit): as Shylock in *The Merchant of Venice* / as Petruchio in *Katharine and Petruchio*
Saturday, April 18: as Phidias and Raphael in *The Marble Heart*

Washington Theatre, Washington

Monday, April 27: as Richard in *Richard III*
Tuesday, April 28: as Pescara in *The Apostate*
Wednesday, April 29: as Phidias and Raphael in *The Marble Heart*
Thursday, April 30: as Romeo in *Romeo and Juliet*
Friday, May 1 (benefit): as The Stranger in *The Stranger* / as Petruchio in *Katharine and Petruchio*
Saturday, May 2: as Charles De Moor in *The Robbers*

(1863, continued)

Monday, May 4: as Fabien and Louis in *The Corsican Brothers*
Tuesday, May 5: as Othello in *Othello*
Wednesday–Thursday, May 6–7: time relinquished to J. Grau's Italian opera troupe
Friday, May 8 (benefit): as Macbeth in *Macbeth*
Saturday, May 9: as Charles De Moor in *The Robbers*

Ben Debar's St. Louis Theatre, St. Louis

Monday, June 15: as Richard in *Richard III*
Tuesday, June 16: as Hamlet in *Hamlet*
Wednesday, June 17: as Pescara in *The Apostate*
Thursday, June 18: as The Stranger in *The Stranger*
Friday–Saturday, June 19–20: Fabien and Louis in *The Corsican Brothers* (benefit 19th)
Monday, June 22: as Phidias and Raphael in *The Marble Heart*
Tuesday, June 23: as Charles De Moor in *The Robbers*
Wednesday, June 24: as Shylock in *The Merchant of Venice* / as Petruchio in *Katharine and Petruchio*
Thursday, June 25: as Richard in *Richard III*
Friday, June 26 (farewell benefit): as Alfred Evelyn in *Money*

Academy of Music, Cleveland

Tuesday, June 30: as Richard in *Richard III*
Wednesday, July 1: as Hamlet in *Hamlet*
Thursday, July 2: as Alfred Evelyn in *Money*
Friday, July 3 (benefit): as Charles De Moor in *The Robbers*

Willard's Howard Athenaeum, Boston

Monday, September 28: as Claude Melnotte in *The Lady of Lyons*
Tuesday, September 29: as Richard in *Richard III*
Wednesday, September 30: as Hamlet in *Hamlet*
Thursday, October 1: as Richard in *Richard III*
Friday, October 2: as Pescara in *The Apostate*
Saturday, October 3: as Charles De Moor in *The Robbers*
Monday, October 5: as Othello in *Othello*
Tuesday, October 6: as Phidias and Raphael in *The Marble Heart*
Wednesday, October 7: as Macbeth in *Macbeth*
Thursday, October 8: as Pescara in *The Apostate*
Friday, October 9: as Shylock in *The Merchant of Venice* / as Petruchio in *Katharine and Petruchio*
Saturday, October 10 (afternoon): as Phidias and Raphael in *The Marble Heart*
Saturday, October 10 (evening): as Richard in *Richard III*

Academy of Music, Providence

Saturday, October 17: as Claude Melnotte in *The Lady of Lyons*

Allyn Hall, Hartford

Tuesday, October 20: as Richard in *Richard III*
Wednesday, October 21: as Claude Melnotte in *The Lady of Lyons*
Thursday, October 22: as Hamlet in *Hamlet*

(1863, continued)

Academy of Music, Brooklyn

Saturday, October 24: as Richard in *Richard III*
Monday, October 26: as Phidias and Raphael in *The Marble Heart*

Music Hall, New Haven

Tuesday, October 27: as Phidias and Raphael in *The Marble Heart*
Wednesday, October 28: as Richard in *Richard III*

Ford's Theatre, Washington

Monday, November 2: as Richard in *Richard III*
Tuesday, November 3: as Pescara in *The Apostate*
Wednesday, November 4: as Charles De Moor in *The Robbers*
Thursday, November 5: as Claude Melnotte in *The Lady of Lyons*
Friday, November 6: as Shylock in *The Merchant of Venice* / as Petruchio in *Taming of the Shrew*
Saturday, November 7: as Richard in *Richard III*
Monday, November 9: as Phidias and Raphael in *The Marble Heart*
Tuesday, November 10: as Hamlet in *Hamlet*
Wednesday, November 11: as Romeo in *Romeo and Juliet*
Thursday, November 12: as Alfred Evelyn in *Money*
Friday, November 13: as Richard in *Richard III*
Saturday, November 14: as Charles De Moor in *The Robbers*

Academy of Music, Cleveland

Thursday, November 26: as Claude Melnotte in *The Lady of Lyons*
Saturday, November 28: as Richard in *Richard III*
Monday, November 30: as Phidias and Raphael in *The Marble Heart*
Saturday, December 5: as Charles De Moor in *The Robbers*

1864

Ben Debar's St. Louis Theatre, St. Louis

Monday–Monday, January 4–11: announced but did not appear
Tuesday, January 12: as Richard in *Richard III*
Wednesday, January 13: as Hamlet in *Hamlet*
Thursday, January 14: as Charles De Moor in *The Robbers*
Friday, January 15 (benefit): as Alfred Evelyn in *Money* / as Petruchio in *Katharine and Petruchio*
Saturday, January 16: as Richard in *Richard III*

Wood's Theatre, Louisville

Monday, January 18: as Richard in *Richard III*
Tuesday, January 19: as Othello in *Othello*
Wednesday, January 20: as Charles De Moor in *The Robbers*
Thursday, January 21: as Pescara in *The Apostate*
Friday, January 22 (benefit): as Alfred Evelyn in *Money*
Saturday, January 23: as Pescara in *The Apostate*

(1864, continued)

Monday, January 25: as Richelieu in *Richelieu*
Tuesday, January 26: as Richard in *Richard III*
Wednesday–Thursday, January 27–28: as Fabien and Louis in *The Corsican Brothers*
Friday, January 29: as Damon in *Damon and Pythias*
Saturday, January 30 (benefit): as Macbeth in *Macbeth*

Wood's Theatre, Nashville

Monday, February 1: as Richard in *Richard III*
Tuesday, February 2: as Pescara in *The Apostate*
Wednesday, February 3: as Richelieu in *Richelieu*
Thursday, February 4: as Hamlet in *Hamlet*
Friday, February 5: as Alfred Evelyn in *Money*
Saturday, February 6: as Charles De Moor in *The Robbers*
Monday, February 8: as Othello in *Othello*
Tuesday, February 9: as Richard in *Richard III*
Wednesday, February 10: as Fabien and Louis in *The Corsican Brothers*
Thursday, February 11: as Damon in *Damon and Pythias*
Friday, February 12: as Shylock in *The Merchant of Venice*
Saturday, February 13: as Fabien and Louis in *The Corsican Brothers*

Wood's Theatre, Cincinnati

Monday, February 15: as Iago in *Othello* (scheduled to play *Richard III*, but played
     lighter role because of indisposition)
Tuesday, February 16: as Pescara in *The Apostate*
Wednesday, February 17: as Charles De Moor in *The Robbers* (because of indis-
     position, part was played by Mr. Meeker)
Thursday, February 18: as Richilieu in *Richilieu*
Friday, February 19: as Alfred Evelyn in *Money*
Saturday, February 20: as Richard in *Richard III*
Monday, February 22: as Hamlet in *Hamlet*
Tuesday, February 23: as Fabian and Louis in *The Corsican Brothers*
Wednesday, February 24: as Claude Melnotte in *The Lady of Lyons*
Thursday, February 25: as Macbeth in *Macbeth*
Friday, February 26 (final performance and benefit): as Shylock in *The Merchant of
     Venice* / as Petruchio in *Katharine and Petruchio*

St. Charles Theatre, New Orleans

Monday, March 14: as Richard in *Richard III*
Tuesday, March 15: as Hamlet in *Hamlet*
Wednesday, March 16: as Pescara in *The Apostate*
Thursday, March 17: as Richelieu in *Richelieu*
Friday, March 18 (benefit): as Alfred Evelyn in *Money; or, Duplicity Exposed*
Saturday, March 19: as Charles De Moor in *The Robbers; or, The Forrest of Bohemia*
Sunday, March 20: as Richard in *Richard III*
Monday, March 21: as Othello in *Othello*
Tuesday, March 22: as Claude Melnotte in *The Lady of Lyons; or, Love and Pride*
Wednesday, March 23: as Macbeth in *Macbeth*
Thursday, March 24: as Romeo in *Romeo and Juliet*
Friday, March 25 (benefit): as Shylock in *The Merchant of Venice* / as Petruchio in
     Katharine and Petruchio

(1864, continued)

Saturday–Sunday, March 26–27: performances cancelled because of illness
Monday, March 28: performance cancelled because of illness
Tuesday, March 29 (benefit): as Phidias and Raphael in *The Marble Heart; or, The Sculptor's Dream*
Wednesday, March 30: as Fabian and Louis in *The Corsican Brothers* / *Loan of a Lover*
Thursday, March 31: as Phidias and Raphael in *The Marble Heart*
Friday, April 1: as Claude Melnotte in *The Lady of Lyons* / as Petruchio in *Katharine and Petruchio*
Saturday, April 2: as Fabian and Louis in *The Corsican Brothers* / *Ireland as It Is*
Sunday, April 3: as Richard in *Richard III*

Boston Museum, Boston

Monday, April 25: as Richard in *Richard III*
Tuesday, April 26: as Alfred Evelyn in *Money*
Wednesday, April 27 (evening): as Pescara in *The Apostate*
Thursday, April 28: as Claude Melnotte in *The Lady of Lyons*
Friday, April 29: as Richard in *Richard III*
Saturday, April 30 (afternoon): as Alfred Evelyn in *Money*
Monday, May 2: as Othello in *Othello*
Tuesday, May 3: as Romeo in *Romeo and Juliet*
Wednesday, May 4 (evening): as Damon in *Damon and Pythias*
Thursday, May 5: as Pescara in *The Apostate*
Friday, May 6: as Hamlet in *Hamlet*
Saturday, May 7 (afternoon): as Romeo in *Romeo and Juliet*
Monday, May 9: as Richelieu in *Richelieu*
Tuesday, May 10: as Iago in *Othello*
Wednesday, May 11 (evening): as Charles De Moor in *The Robbers*
Thursday, May 12: as Richard in *Richard III*
Friday, May 13: as Petruchio in *Katharine and Petruchio* / as Shylock in *The Merchant of Venice*
Saturday, May 14 (afternoon): as Claude Melnotte in *The Lady of Lyons*
Monday–Tuesday, May 16–17: as Phidias and Raphael in *The Marble Heart*
Wednesday, May 18 (evening): as Damon in *Damon and Pythias*
Thursday, May 19: as Julian St. Pierre in *The Wife*
Friday, May 20: as Macbeth in *Macbeth*
Saturday, May 21 (afternoon): as Phidias and Raphael in *The Marble Heart*
Monday, May 23: as Fabian and Louis in *The Corsican Brothers*
Tuesday, May 24: as Phidias and Raphael in *The Marble Heart*
Wednesday, May 25 (afternoon): as Phidias and Raphael in *The Marble Heart*
Wednesday, May 25 (evening): as Fabian and Louis in *The Corsican Brothers*
Thursday, May 26: as Phidias and Raphael in *The Marble Heart*
Friday, May 27: as Count Ugolino in *Ugolino*

Corby's Hall, Montreal

Saturday, October 24: solo dramatic readings—as Shylock and Portia in *The Merchant of Venice* (trial scene) / as Mark Antony in *Julius Caesar* (forum scene) / "The Charge of the Light Brigade" / "Remorse of the Fallen One; or, Beautiful Snow" / *Hamlet* (selections)

Winter Garden, New York

Friday, November 25: as Mark Antony in *Julius Caesar*

1865

Grover's Theatre, Washington

Friday, January 29: as Romeo in *Romeo and Juliet*

Ford's Theatre, Washington

Saturday, March 18: as Pescara in *The Apostate*

Newspapers Consulted for the Chronology
(Theatres, Amusements, Local Matters, 1855–1865)

Atlas and Argus, Albany, N.Y.
Baltimore American & Commercial Advertiser
Baltimore Sun
Boston Transcript
Buffalo Sentinel
Chicago Tribune
Cincinnati *Daily Commercial*
Cincinnati *Daily Gazette*
Cincinnati *Enquirer*
Cleveland Leader
Cleveland Plain Dealer
Columbus [Ga.] *Daily Enquirer*
Columbus [Ga.] *Times*
Columbus [Ga.] *Sun*
Daily Advertiser, Boston
Daily Missouri Democrat, St. Louis
Daily Picayune, New Orleans
Daily True Delta, New Orleans
Detroit *Daily Advertiser*
Detroit Free Press

Hartford *Courant*
Lexington Observer & Reporter
Louisville *Daily Courier*
Louisville *Daily Democrat*
Louisville *Daily Journal*
Lynchburg *Daily Virginian*
Montgomery *Daily Mail*
Montgomery *Daily Post*
Nashville Dispatch
New York *Herald*
National Intelligencer, Washington
Petersburg, Va., *Daily Express*
Philadelphia *North American*
Philadelphia *Press*
Philadelphia *Public Ledger*
Providence Daily Journal
Richmond Dispatch
Spirit of the Times, New York
Union & Advertiser, Rochester, N.Y.
Washington Evening Star
Washington *Sunday Morning Chronicle*

Representative Casts

Wheatley's Arch Street Theatre, Philadelphia (August 15, 1857)*

Sole Lessee Wm. Wheatley, *Acting & Stage Manager* W.S. Fredericks. The Lessee most respectfully announces to the public that this popular establishment will open for the regular fall and winter season To-morrow (Saturday) Evening, August 15th, 1857.

During the late recess, the entire premises have been (regardless of expense) remodeled and improved, repainted, papered, carpeted, &c. The Orchestra stalls have been greatly enlarged and enhanced in comfort; the Dress Circle entirely reconstructed; and the extensive alterations in the Second Tier or Family Circle have, while adding to its capacity, established a most thorough ventilation. In short, all that could add to the comfort and convenience of visitors has been secured, and no effort spared to render the Auditorium fully equal to any similar establishment in the world.

The Celebrated Star Company has been greatly augmented and improved, forming a combination of Artistic Talent equal to the perfect production of the highest order of Dramatic Literature, on a scale of surpassing excellence, and will consist of the following distinguished names: MR. E.L. DAVENPORT The celebrated American Tragedian (1st appearance at this theatre), MR. WM. WHEATLEY, MR. JOHN DOLMAN, MR. J.S. CLARKE, MR. E.N. THAYER, MR. F. TANNERHILL from the Boston Theatres (His first appearance in Philadelphia), ▶ MR. J.B. WILKS from the N. York Theatres (His first appearance in Philadelphia), MR. WALLIS, MR. FISHER, MR. STEARNES, MR. RIELLY, MR. MCCULLOUGH (His first appearance here), MR. BROOKS, MR. ANDERSON (His first appearance here), MR. LOWE (His first appearance here), MR. AIKEN (His first appearance here), MR. WM. S. FREDERICKS, MRS. E.L. DAVENPORT (Late Miss Fanny Vining, from the Theatre Royale, London. Her first appearance at this theatre), MRS. ELMORE from the Theatre Royale, Haymarket, London (Her first appearance at this theatre), MISS ELLEN MORANT from the New Orleans Theatres, MISS ANNA CRUISE, MISS E.N. THAYER, MISS TANNERHILL, MISS DEWALD, MISS GRAHAM, MISS GREER, MISS ROBERTS, MISS CLIFTON, MISS REED.

The Orchestra greatly improved in numbers and efficiency will be under the popular leader and composer CHARLES R. DODWORTH. The Scenic Department will continue under the direction of the celebrated artist MR. JOHN WISER; Stage Director, MR. FREDERICK CHURCH; Master of the Wardrobe, MR. F. JOHNSON; Machinists, MR. JOSEPH STRAHAN and Assistants; Appointments by MR. BARRETT and Assistants.

The alterations in the Auditorium have been completed under the supervision of the distinguished architect MR. CHARLES RUBICAM; The carpeting by MR. CHARLES WATSON; The oil paintings by MESSRS. KILLINGSWORTH and REYNOLDS; The paper hanging by MESSRS. BURTON and LANNING; The upholdstering by MR. EDWARD BURKE and; The gas fixtures by MR. G. LEWIS.

Scale of Prices: Orchestra Stalls 50¢, Dress Circle (no charge for secured seats) 50¢, Family Circle & Amphitheatre 25¢, Seats in Private Boxes 75¢, Whole Private Box $6, Gallery 15¢, Gallery for Colored Persons 25¢, Private Box in Gallery for Colored Persons $3. Box Book Now Open. *Treasurer* J.M.B. WHITTON.

*Transcribed from the complete handbill.

Wheatley's Arch Street Theatre, Philadelphia
(May 25, 1858) — *Macbeth*

Macbeth MR. DOLMAN, Macduff MR. J.E. M'DONOUGH, Banguo, first appearance here in 3 yrs, MR. GILE, Duncan MR. BRADLEY, Malcolm MR. WM. H. MYERS, Donalbain MISS ROBERTS, Rosse MR. MCCULLOUGH, Lennox MR. TANNEHILL, Seyton MR. REILLY, Fleance MISS A. FISHER, Seyward MR. LITTLE, Physician MR. FISHER, First Witch MR. THAYER, Second Witch MR. WALLIS, Third Witch MR. JOHNSON, First Officer MR. STREET, Bleeding Captain MR. JONES, Second Officer MR. LEWIS, Gentlewoman MRS. TANNEHILL, First Singing Witch MISS FAAS, Second Singing Witch MISS E. TAYLOR, Third Singing Witch MISS JONES ► First Apparition MR. WILKS, Second Apparition MR. HESS, Third Apparition MISS C. REED, Lady Macbeth MISS C. CUSHMAN.

Wheatley's Arch Street Theatre, Philadelphia
(May 26, 1858) — *Henry VIII*

King Henry VIII MR. DOLMAN, Cardinal Wolsey MR. J.E. M'DONOUGH, Cardinal Campeius MR. FISHER, Cromwell MR. WM. H. MYERS, Duke of Buckingham MR. GILE, Duke of Norfolk MR. STREET, Lord Sands MR. THAYER, Lord Chamberlain MR. TANNEHILL, Bishop of Winchester MR. BENN, Sir Thomas Lovell MR. LITTLE, Earl of Surry MR. WALLIS, Sir Henry Guilford MR. LEWIS, Surveyor of Buckingham MR. MCCULLOUGH, Brandon MR. REILLY, ► Capucius MR. WILKS, Clerk of the Court MR. ANDERSON, Lady Denny MRS. THAYER, Anne Boleyn MISS E. TAYLOR, Marchioness of Dorset MISS SNYDER, Patience MISS JONES, Agatha MISS ROBERTS, Ciecily MISS C. REED, Queen Katharine MISS C. CUSHMAN, Lords, Guests, Bishops, Soldiers.

Wheatley's Arch Street Theatre, Philadelphia
(May 28, 1858) — *As You Like It*

Banished Duke MR. GILE, Duke Frederick MR. BRADLEY, Jacques MR. DOLMAN, Amiens MR. JAS. DUNN, Orlando MR. WM. WHEATLEY, Oliver MR. WM. H. MYERS, Jaques Dubois MR. REILLY, Adam MR. THAYER, Touchstone MR. J.S. CLARKE, Corin MR. MCCULLOUGH, Le Beau MR. WALLIS, ► Silvius MR. WILKS, William MR. TANNEHILL, Charles, the Wrestler MR. F. JOHNSON, Celia MISS E. TAYLOR, Phoebe MRS. TANNEHILL, Audrey MRS. THAYER, Rosalind MISS C. CUSHMAN, Courtiers, Shepherds, Hunters, &c., &c.

Richmond Theatre (Oct. 25, 1858) — *David Copperfield*

Uriah Heep (His original character) MR. T.B. JOHNSON, David Copperfield MR. B. RINGGOLD, James Steerforth MR. D.M. HARKINS, Watkins Micawber MR. W.H. BAILEY, ► Traddles MR. J.B. WILKES, Rose Dartle MISS JULIA IRVING, Betsy Trotwood MRS. J.H. REID, Mrs. Micawber MISS KATE FISHER, Emily MISS TAYLOR, Agnes MISS KATE PENNOYER

Dudley Hall, Lynchburg, Va. (Nov. 1, 1858) —
The Wife; or, My Father's Grave

Julian St. Pierre MR. H.A. LANGDON, Leonard Gonzago MR. D.H. HARKINS, Ferrado Gonzago MR. S.K. CHESTER, Antonio (a curate) MR. W.H. BAILEY, Lorenzo MR. B.T.

RINGGOLD, ▶ Count Florio MR. J.B. WILKES, Bartolo MR. T.B. JOHNSTON, Bernardo MR. W.T. JOHNSON, Carlo MR. I.B. PHILLIPS, Cosmo MR. W. MORTIMER, Mariana, the Wife MRS. I.B. PHILLIPS, Floribel MISS KATE PENNOYER, Courier MISS TAYLOR.

Richmond Theatre, (Nov. 19, 1858) —
Adrienne, the Actress

Adrienne Lecouvrer MISS AVONIA JONES, Count Maurice de Saxe H.A. LANGDON, L'Abbe D.H. HARKINS, Michouet W.H. BAILEY, Duke D'Aumont B.T. RINGGOLD, Quinault (an actor) S.K. CHESTER, ▶ Paisson J.B. WILKES, Valet W. MORTIMER, Princess D'Bouillon MRS. I.B. PHILLIPS, M'lle Angelique MISS JULIA IRVING, M'lle Jouvenot MISS FISHER, M'lle Dangerville MISS KATE PENNOYER, Marchioness MISS TAYLOR, Actors, Actresses, Gents., &c. Grand Spanish Dance MISS KATE PENNOYER.

[Same night] — Jenny Lind

Baron Swigitoof B. RINGGOLD, Mr. Leatherlungs W.H. BAILEY, Granby Gag T.B. JOHNSTON ▶ Her Cheroot J.B. WILKES, Herr Kanaster W. MORTIMER, Her Spittoon C.H. FRENCH, Her Koff R. MEER, Jenny Leatherlungs (with songs) MISS KATE FISHER.

Richmond Theatre (Jan. 24, 1859) — Monte Christo

Edmond Dante MR. H.A. LANGDON, The Captain MR. H.A. LANGDON, Abbe Buoni, MR. H.A. LANGDON, Sinbad the Sailor MR. H.A. LANGDON, Count of Monte Christo MR. H.A. LANGDON, Caderouse MR. W.H. BAILEY, Ferdinand (a Young Frenchman in love with Mercedes) MR. D.H. HARKINS, Max Morrell MR. S.K. CHESTER, ▶ Danglars (a Supercargo) MR. J.B. WILKES, Albert De Mortef MR. B.T. RINGGOLD, Old Dantes MR. R. MEER, Emanuel MR. CLARKE, Villefort MR. W. MORTIMER, Jacopo (smuggler) MR. I.B. PHILLIPS, Gantaus (Smuggler) MR. C. BROOKE, Ali (the faithful dumb slave) MR. T. RAWLINGS, Mercedes (a Catalan peasant girl) MRS. I.B. PHILLIPS, La Caronte MRS. J.H. REID, Julia MISS TAYLOR, Citizens, Grand'Arms, Sailors, Smugglers, Markers, Catalans, Peasants, etc.

Richmond Theatre (Feb. 25, 1859) — Romeo and Juliet

Benefit of Thomas L. Moxley. Romeo MISS MAGGIE MITCHELL, Juliet MRS. I.B. PHILLIPS, Nurse MRS. J.H. REID, Lady Capulet MRS. ADIE PROCTOR, Friar Lawrence MR. H.A. LANGDON, Mercutio MR. D.H. HARKINS, Capulet MR. W.H. BAILEY, Peter MR. T.B. JOHNSTON, Tybalt MR. S.K. CHESTER, Benvolio MR. B.T. RINGGOLD, ▶ Paris MR. J.B. WILKES, Apothecary MR. W.T. JOHNSON, Balthazar MR. H. HANCKER, Gregory MR. C.H. FRENCH, Page MRS. W.T. JOHNSON.

Richmond Theatre (May 6, 1859) — Hunchback

Benefit of Mrs. W.C. Gladstane. Julia MRS. W.C. GLADSTANE, Helen MRS. I.B. PHILLIPS, Master Walter MR. F. HARDENBERG, Sir Thos. Clifford MR. D.H. HARKINS, Fathom MR. T.B. JOHNSTON, Modus MR. B.T. RINGGOLD, Rockdale MR. S.K. CHESTER, ▶ Lord Tinsel MR. J.B. WILKES, Master Heartwell MR. W. JOHNSON, Gaylove MR. H. HANCKER, Stephen MR. R. MEER, Thomas MR. C.H. FRENCH.

Richmond Theatre (Sept. 3, 1859) — *Heir at Law*

Dr. Pangloss (his first appearance here) MR. B.G. ROGERS, Dick Dowlas MR. EDWIN ADAMS, Lord Duberly MR. W.H. BAILEY, ▶ Henry Moreland MR. J.B. WILKES, Steadfast MR. S.K. CHESTER, Zekiel Homespun MR. W. JOHNSON, Kenrick MR. R. MEER, John MR. O.B. MASON, Waiter at the Blue Boar MR. F. DURAND, Lady Duberly (first appearance) MRS. C. DE BAR, Cicily Homespun MRS. I.B. PHILLIPS, Caroline Dormer (first appearance) MISS ELLA WREN (in which she will sing a beautiful ballad).

Richmond Theatre (Sept. 10, 1859) — *Richard III; or, The Battle of Bosworth Field*

Richard, Duke of Gloster (first time) MR. EDWIN ADAMS, Richmond MR. J.W. COLLIER, ▶ Buckingham MR. J.B. WILKES, King Henry MR. W.H. BAILEY, Lord Mayor MR. B.G. ROGERS, Terrel MR. S.K. CHESTER, Lord Stanley MR. W. JOHNSON, Queen Elizabeth MRS. I.B. PHILLIPS, Duchess of York MRS. C. DE BAR, Lady Anne MISS ELLA M. WREN, Prince of Wales MISS MARY WHITE, Duke of York LA PETITE FANNIE.

Richmond Theatre (Sept. 23, 1859) — *Hunchback*

Julia MRS. WALLER, Master Walter MR. WALLER, Helen MRS. J.B. PHILLIPS, Modas MR. EDWIN ADAMS, Fathom MR. J.W. COLLIER, ▶ Lord Tinsel MR. J.B. WILKES, Rochdale MR. S.K. CHESTER, Heartwell MR. W. JOHNSON, Thomas MR. G.W. WREN, Stephan MR. J.B. PHILLIPS, Gaylove MR. E. DILLON, pas seul MISS SALOME.

Richmond Theatre (Sept. 28, 1859) — *Romeo and Juliet*

Juliet MISS JANE COOMBS, Romeo (first time) MR. EDWIN ADAMS, Mercutio MR. J.W. COLLIER, Friar Lawrence MR. W.H. BAILEY, Peter MR. B.G. ROGERS, ▶ Paris MR. J.B. WILKES, Benvolio MR. E. DILLON, Tybolt MR. S.K. CHESTER, Capulet MR. W. JOHNSON, Apothecary MR. R. MEER, Balthazzar MR. O.B. MASON, Nurse MRS. C. BE BAR, Lady Capulet MRS. E. MONELL.

Richmond Theatre (Sept. 29, 1859) — *Ingomar; or, The Power of Love*

Greek Maiden MISS JANE COOMBS, Ingomar ADAMS, Myron BAILEY, ▶ Alaster WILKES, Polidor CHESTER, Timaich DILLON, Ambivar JOHNSON.

Richmond Theatre (Sept. 30, 1859) — *Lady of Lyons* and *Love Chase*

Pauline MISS JANE COOMBS, Constance MISS JANE COOMBS, Lydia MRS. J.B. PHILLIPS, Widow Green and Madame Donchappins MRS. C. DE BAR, Widow Melnotte MRS. C. MONELL, Claude Melnotte and Sir Wm. Fendlove MR. EDWIN ADAMS, ▶ Glavis and Trueworth MR. J.B. WILKES, Beaumont and Waller MR. S.K. CHESTER, Monsieur Donchappins MR. WM. JOHNSON, Gasper and Neville MR. E. DILLON, Humphreys MR. R. MEER.

Richmond Theatre (Oct. 4, 1859) — *London Assurance*

Lady Gay Spanker MISS JANE COOMBS, Grace Harkaway MISS ELLA M. WREN, Pert MRS. EDWIN ADAMS, Dazzle MR. J.W. COLLIER, Charles Courtly MR. EDWIN ADAMS, Sir Harcourt Courtly MR. W.H. BAILEY, Max Harkaway MR. B.G. ROGERS, Dolly Spanker MR. W. JOHNSON, ▶ Cool MR. J.B. WILKES, Martin MR. R. MEER, James MR. O.B. MASON, Solomon MR. F. DURAND.

Richmond Theatre (Oct. 31, 1859) — *Hamlet*

Hamlet MR. BARRY SULLIVAN, Ophelia MRS. I.B. PHILLIPS, Queen Gertrude MISS ELLA M. WREN, Osrick MRS. EDWIN ADAMS, The Ghost MR. EDWIN ADAMS, Laertes MR. J.W. COLLIER, King Claudius MR. S.K. CHESTER, Polonius MR. W.H. BAILEY, ▶ Horatio MR. J.B. WILKES, Rosencrantz MR. J.M. BARRON, Marcellus MR. W. JOHNSON, Geldernstern MR. R. MEER, The Grave Digger MR. I.B. PHILLIPS.

Howard Athenaeum, Boston (Oct. 28, 1859) — *Richard III*

Duke of Gloster, afterwards Richard III MR. EDWIN BOOTH, King Henry MR. HANCHETT, Richmond MR. HARDENBURG, Duke of Buckingham MR. RAND, Lord Stanley MR. W.H. CURTIS, Tressel MR. REYNOLDS, Catesby MR. SELWYN, Ratcliffe MR. BROWNE, Duke of Norfolk MR. PRICE, Lieut. of Tower MR. VERNEY, Lord Mayor MR. LENNOX, Tyrell MR. OTIS, ▶ Blount MR. WILKES, Oxford MR. SNOWDEN, Officer MR. HILLS, Prince of Wales MISS F. PRICE, Duke of York MISS JONES, Queen Elizabeth MISS MESTAYER, Lady Anne MISS SYLVIA, Duchess of York MRS. HANCHETT.

Richmond Theatre (Oct. 25, 1859) — *Heir at Law* and *Illustrious Stranger*

Cicily Homespun MRS. J.B. PHILLIPS, Caroline Dormer MISS ELLA M. WREN, Priscilla Irza MRS. EDWIN ADAMS, Fatima MISS ELIZA WREN, Dick Dowlas MR. EDWIN ADAMS, Dr. Pangloss and Billy Bowbell MR. B.G. ROGERS, Lord Duberly MR. WM. H. BAILEY, ▶ Henry Moreland MR. J.B. WILKES, Zekiel Homespun MR. W. JOHNSON, Steadfast MR. S.K. CHESTER, Kenrick MR. R. MEER, Abonlifar MR. G.W. WREN.

Richmond Theatre (Nov. 2, 1859) — *The Gamester*

Beverly BARRY SULLIVAN, Mrs. Beverly MRS. I.B. PHILLIPS, Charlotte MISS ELLA M. WREN, Stukely MR. EDWIN ADAMS, Leuson MR. J.W. COLLIER, Jarvis MR. W.H. BAILEY, Bates MR. S.K. CHESTER, ▶ Dawson MR. J.B. WILKES.

Richmond Theatre (Feb. 2, 1860) — *The Gamester*

Mr. Beverly MR. JAMES E. MURDOCK, Charlotte MISS ELLA M. WREN, Stukely MR. EDWIN ADAMS, Jarvis MR. W.H. BAILEY, Lewson MR. J.W. COLLIER, Bates MR. S.K. CHESTER, ▶ Dawson MR. J.B. WILKES.

[Same night] — *The Buzzards*

John Small MR. B.G. ROGERS, Mr. Benjamin Buzzard MR. W.H. BAILEY, ▶ Mr.

Glimmer MR. J.B. WILKES, Miss Lucretia Buzzard MRS. C. DE BAR, Sally MRS. EDWIN
ADAMS.

Richmond Theatre (Feb. 29, 1860) — *Hunchback*

Julia MRS. JULIA DEAN HAYNE, Helen MRS. I.B. PHILLIPS, Sir Thos. Clifford MR. ED-
WIN ADAMS, Fathom MR. B.G. ROGERS, Modus MR. J.W. COLLIER, Master Walter
MR. S.K. CHESTER, ► Lord Tinsel MR. J.B. WILKES, Earl of Rochdale MR. E. DILLON,
Stephen MR. R. MEER, Gaylove MR. G.W. WREN, Thomas MR. O.B. MASON.

[Same night] — *Too Much for Good Nature*

Mr. Adolphus (a good natured man) MR. B.G. ROGERS, ► Romeo Jaffier Jenkins (love-
sick swain) MR. J.B. WILKES, Mr. Septimus Spalding (a scientific mesmerizer) MR. R.
MEER, Mrs. Adolphus (overflowing with affection) MRS. ELLA M. WREN, Matilda Jane
Jenkins (fond of Jenkins) MISS ELIZA WREN, Mrs. Chummy (an irascible lady, violen-
lently opposed to Jenkins) MRS. C. DE BAR, Miss Precise (an eventempered lady) MRS.
MORRELL, Mrs. Jones (opposed to the science of mesmerism) MRS. JOHNSON, Miss
Jones (a martyr of the same) MISS MORRELL, Mrs. Spalding (a strong-minded woman)
MADAME MERINO.

Richmond Theatre (May 14, 1860 — *Three Guardsmen; or, The Siege of Rochelle*

D'Artagan MR. EDWIN ADAMS, The Three Guardsmen: Athos MR. J.W. COLLIER, Por-
tos MR. S.K. CHESTER, ► Aramis MR. J.B. WILKES; Richelieu MR. W.H. BAILEY, Pian-
chet MR. B.G. ROGERS, Musquetoon MR. W. JOHNSON, Bonaucieux MR. R. MEER,
Buckingham MR. E. DILLON, Louis MR. I.B. PHILLIPS, Grimand MR. O.B. MASON,
Lady Winter MRS. I.B. PHILLIPS, Anne of Austria MISS ELLA M. WREN, Constance
MRS. E. ADAMS. In the Carnival Scene, a grand dance by 24 ladies and gentlemen.

Richmond Theatre (May 18, 1860) — *Romance of a Poor Young Man*

Annual benefit of Mrs. I.B. Phillips. Manuel (Marquis de Champcey) MR. E. ADAMS,
Doctor Desmarets (formerly of the French Army) MR. W.H. BAILEY, ► M. de Bevan-
nes (a man of the world) MR. J.B. WILKES, Gasper Laroque (an aged man, formerly
Captain of the Privateer) MR. S.K. CHESTER, Alain (a confidential domestic) MR. W.
JOHNSON, M. Nouret (a notary) MR. O.B. MASON, Yvonnet (a Breton shepherd) MR.
R. MEER, Henry MR. F. DURAND, Louis MR. JACKSON, Madame Laroque (daughter-in-
law to Gasper) MRS. MONELL, Marguerite (her daughter) MRS. I.B. PHILLIPS,
Madame Aubery (a relative of the Laroque family) MRS. DE BAR, Louise Vauberger
(formerly nurse to Manuel, now keeper of a lodging house) MRS. JOHNSON, Christine
(a Breton peasant girl) LITTLE MARIE, Guests, Servants, Peasantry, &c, &c.

Mrs. H.A. Perry's Metropolitan Theatre, Detroit (November 15, 1861) — *Richard III*

► Richard III MR. J. WILKES BOOTH, Richmond MR. J.W. ALBAUGH, King Henry MR.
T.E. WOLFE, Buckingham MR. E.F. MARDEN, Lord Stanley MR. C.P. DEGROAT,

Catesby MR. G.W. CAMPBELL, Lieut. of the Tower MR. M.L. GRAYSON, Lord Norfolk MR. JNO. POWERS, Ratcliffe MR. WM. JONES, Tressel MR. J.B. RURNER, Terrel MR. W. SPELLANE, Lord Mayor of London MR. C. WILLIAMSON, Blunt MR. CHAS. BUTLER, Oxford MR. JOHN SPAUDLING, Prince of Wales MISS UTIE CLIFFORD, Duke of York MISS GATLAND, Lady Anne MRS. H.A. PERRY, Queen MISS NASH, Duchess MRS. BURROUGHS.

[Same night] — *Too Much for Good Nature*

▶ Mr. Romeo Jaffier Jenkins (a Romantic Youth) MR. J. WILKES BOOTH, Mr. Adolphus (a very good-natured gentleman) MR. T.E. WOLFE, Louisa (Mr. Adolphus' wife) MRS. H.A. PERRY, Mr. Spaulding (a scientific, mesmeric experimenter) MR. C.P. DEGROAT, Miss Precise (her aunt) MISS NASH, Mrs. Chumney (an irascible woman) MISS MAYNARD, Miss Matilda Jane Chumney (the beloved of Jenkins) MISS CLIFFORD, Betty (a chambermaid of no little experience) MRS. BURROUGHS, Mrs. Jones (a stupid woman, adverse to science) MISS WILFORD, Mrs. Spaulding (a lady quite independent of "Female Protectionary Laws") MISS JONES.

Holliday Street Theatre, Baltimore (February 24, 1862) — *Hamlet*

▶ Hamlet MR. JOHN WILKES BOOTH, Queen Gertrude MRS. FARREN, Ophelia MISS ANNE GRAHAM, The Ghost MR. E.L. TILTON, Laertes MR. KNIGHT, King Claudius MR. S.K. CHESTER, Polonius MR. HALL, Horatio MR. HERNE, First Grave Digger MR. BISHOP, Second Grave Digger MR. PARKER.

Mary Provost's Theatre, New York (March 28, 1862) — *Macbeth*

▶ Macbeth (King of Scotland) J. WILKES BOOTH, Lady Macbeth MRS. FARREN, Macduff MR. E.L. TILTON, King Duncan MR. GEORGE RYER, Banquo MR. CARTER, Rosse MR. J.W. COLLIER, Malcolm MR. RAND, Donalbain MISS SMITH, Fleance MISS MARY BULLOCK, Hecate MR. SPACKMAN, 1st Witch MR. LEWIS BAKER, 2nd Witch MR. MCCLOSKEY, 3d Witch MRS. RAND, Bleeding Captain MR. PEMBERTON, Chamberlain MR. THOMPSON, Singing Witch MRS. CHANFRAU, Gentelwoman MRS. FLOYD, Physician MR. CROUTA, Apparitions: MRS. FLOYD, MRS. RAND, MISS BULLOCK; 1st Officer MR. WARD, 2nd Officer MR. WALSH. Singing Witches MESSRS. REA, OLIVER, WALDRON, MORTIMER. Witches, Soldiers, Nobles, Retainers, &c. by Auxiliary Corps.

Mary Provost's Theatre, New York (March 29, 1862) — *Richard III*

▶ Richard J. WILKES BOOTH, Queen Elizabeth MRS. FARREN, Lady Anne MRS. CHANRAU, Duchess of York MRS. RAND, Prince of Wales MRS. FLOYD, Duke of York LITTLE MARY BULLOCK, Earl of Richmond MR. E.L. TILTON, Tressell MR. LEWIS BAKER, King Henry VI MR. GEORGE RYER, Duke of Buckingham MR. CARTER, Lord Stanly MR. SPACKMAN, Catesby MR. COLLIER, Duke of Norfolk MR. WALSH, Ratcliffe MR. T.J. WARD, Lord Mayor MR. CROUTS, Lieut. of Tower MR. MCCLOSKEY, Blunt MR. DAVENPORT, Tirrell MR. WALTER BIRCH, Officers, Soldiers, Lords, Ladies, Pages, &c. by Auxiliary Corps.

Boston Museum (May 20, 1862) — *The Stranger*

▶ The Stranger MR. J. WILKES BOOTH, Baron Steinfort MR. F. HARDENBURGH, Count Wintersen MR. J. WHITING, Francis MR. J. WILSON, Solomon MR. R.F. MCCLANNIN, Peter MR. W. WARREN, Tobias MR. SOL SMITH, JR., Karl MR. DELANO, Wilhelm MR. BARTLETT, George MR. BENNETT, Countess Wintersen MISS L. ANDERSON, Charlotte MISS JOSEPHINE ORTON, Annette, with Ballad, "I have a silent sorrow here" MISS ORIANA MARSHALL, Claudine MISS L. BAKER, Mrs. Haller MISS KATE REIGNOLDS, La Manola MISS ROSE WOOD.

Boston Museum (January 27, 1863) — *Money*

▶ Alfred Evelyn J. WILKES BOOTH, Graves MR. W. WARREN, Sir John Vesey R.F. MCCLANNIN, Sir Frederick Blount J.A. SMITH, Lord Glossmore J. WHEELOCK, Stout F. HARDENBURGH, Captain Dudley Smooth J. WILSON, Old Member J.H. RING, Sharp G.F. KETCHUM, Flat W.J. HILL, Greene H. PEAKES, Sir John's Servant HUNTER, Toke DELANO, Waiter at the Club PITMAN, Clara Douglas KATE REIGNOLDS, Lady Franklin MISS EMILY MESTAYER, Georgina MISS ANNIE CLARKE.

Boston Museum (Feb. 9–11, 1863) — *The Corsican Brothers*

▶ Fabian Dei Franchi and Louis Dei Franchi (twin brothers) MR. J. WILKES BOOTH, Chateau Renaud MR. WM. WHALLEY, Alfred Maynard MR. L. MESTAYER, Baron Martelli MR. J. WILSON, Baron de Montgiron MR. J.A. SMITH, M. Beauchamp MR. J. PEAKES, M. Verner MR. PITMAN, Judge MR. W. BENN, Orlando MR. G.F. KETCHUM, Colonna SOL. SMITH, JR., Griffot MR. HUNTER, Boisec MR. J.H. RING, Tomaso MR. DELANO, Francois MR. BARTIETT. Citizens, Masqueraders, &c.: Emilie dei Lesparre KATE REIGNOLDS, Madame dei Franchi EMILY MESTAYER, Marie MRS. J. WHEELOCK, Coralie MISS L. BAKER, Estelle MISS ANNIE CLARKE, Celestine MISS M. ANDREWS.

Mrs. John Drew's Arch Street Theatre, Philadelphia (March 6, 1863) — *The Merchant of Venice*

▶ Shylock MR. JOHN WILKES BOOTH, Portia MRS. JOHN DREW, Merissa MRS. CHAS. HENRI, Jessica MISS E. PRICE, Bassinio MR. BARION HILL, Gratiano MR. FRANK DREW, Antonio MR. ALBAUGH, Lorenzo MR. RINGGOLD, Launcelot Gobbo MR. SEYMOUR, Old Gobbo MR. FISHER, Salarino MR. CRAIG, Salanio MR. LITTLE, Tubal MR. CHAS. HENRI, Balthazar MR. ROGERS, Stephano MR. WILSON. Magnificos, Officers of Justice, &c. The Orchestra, led by Mr. Chas. R. Dodworth, will perform a variety Popular Musical Selections.

[Same night] — *Catharine and Petruchio*

▶ Petruchio MR. JOHN WILKES BOOTH, Baptista MR. WALLIS, Grumio MR. FRANK DREW, Biondello MR. RINGGOLD, Hortensio MR. CRAIG, Music Master MR. CHAS. HENRI, Tailor MR. SEYMOUR, Cook MR. FISHER, Gregory MR. ROGERS, Ralph MR. WILSON, Walter MR. WORTH, Pedro MR. LITTLE, Catharine MRS. JOHN DREW, Bianca MISS GARDINIER, Curtis MRS. JONES.

Grover's Theatre, Washington (April 11, 1863) — *Richard III*

▶ Richard, Duke of Gloster J. WILKES BOOTH, Queen Elizabeth SUSAN DENIN,

Henry, Earl of Richmond J.M. WARD, Duke of Buckingham J.E. WHITING, Lord
Tressel J.V. DAILEY, King Henry VI BEN ROGERS, Lord Stanley W.H. BOKEE, Sir
Robert Brackenbury E.B. WILLIAMS, Edward, Prince of Wales ADA MONK, Richard,
Duke of York SUSIE PARKER, Duke of Norfolk WM. BARRON, Sir William Catesby E.S.
TARR, Sir Richard Ratcliff M.A. KENNEDY, Sir James Tyrrell E.P. HAWLEY, Earl of Ox-
ford H. MCDOUALL, Lord Mayor of London HARRY CLIFFORD, Sir Thomas Vaughn N.
COLLIER, Duchess of York MRS. G.C. GERMON, Lady Anne SOPHIE GIMBER.

Grover's Theatre, Washington (April 14, 1863) — *Hamlet*

► Hamlet, Nephew to King Claudius J. WILKES BOOTH, Queen Gertrude SUSAN
DENIN, Ophelia, daughter of Polonius EFFIE GERMON, Ghost of Hamlet's father W.H.
BOKEE, Polonius, Lord Chamberlain BEN G. ROGERS, Laertes, son to Polonius J.M.
WARD, Horatio, friend to Hamlet J.E. WHITING, Rosencrantz J.V. DAILEY, Guilden-
stern WM. BARRON, Marcellus E.S. TARR, Bernardo M.A. KENNEDY, Francisco, a
soldier N. COLLIER, First actor HARRY CLIFFORD, Second actor F.A. MONTAGUE, First
gravedigger HARRY CLIFFORD, Second gravedigger EBEN AYLMER, Osrick CHAS.
WYNDHAM, Priest J.B. EVANS, Player Queen FANNY RYAN.

Willard's Howard Athenaeum, Boston
(October 10, 1863) — *Marble Heart*

► Phidias, the sculptor and Raphael Duchalet MR. J. WILKES BOOTH, Diogenes, the
cynic philosopher MR. JAS. DUFF,Gorgias, a rich Athenian MR. D.N. JONES, Alcibiades, the general MR. J.C. BOYD, Starbon, a slave MR. J.H. CONNER, Aspasia MRS.
JULIA BENNETT BARROW, Lais MRS. L. ANDERSON, Phyrne MISS MOLLIE NEWTON,
Thea, a slave MISS LIZZIE ANDERSON. Soldiers, Citizens, Slaves, &c.

St. Charles Theatre, New Orleans
(March 25, 1864) — *The Merchant of Venice*

► Shylock J. WILKES BOOTH, Duke J. WELKINS, Antonio E.L. MORTIMER, Bassanio
G.D. CHAPLIN, Gratiano E.M. MARBLE, Lorenzo, with song MISS L. MADDERN,
Salanio C.L. FREEMAN, Salarino E. MACKWAY, Old Gobbo A.H. CAMPBELL, Laun-
celot J.A. GRAVER, Tubal H. MELMER, Balthazar H. MELLEN, Portia MRS. C.P.
WALTERS, Jessica MISS E. CASSEL, Nerissa MRS. CHIPPENDALE.

[Same night] — *Katharine and Petruchio; or, Taming the Shrew*

► Petruchio J. WILKES BOOTH, Baptista G.G. TURNER, Hortensio C.L. FREEMAN,
Biondello MR. LEONARD, Grumio J.A. GRAVER, Music Master A.H. CAMPBELL, Pedro
E. MACKWAY, Tailor T. DAVEY, Cook H. MELNER, Servant H. MELLEN, Katharine
MRS. C.F. WALTERS, Curtis MRS. J.W. THORPE, Hortensia MISS E. CASSEL.

Boston Museum (May 2, 1864) — *Othello*

► Othello J. WILKES BOOTH, Iago MR. L.R. SHEWELL, Cassio MR. J. WILSON, Duke of
Venice MR. J. WHEELOCK, Roderigo MR. J.A. SMITH, Brabantio MR. F. HARDEN-
BURGH, Ludovico MR. G.F. KETCHUM, Gratiano MR. T.M. HUNTER, Montano MR.
WALTER BENN, Julio MR. J.E. ADAMS, Marco MR. J. PEAKES, Messinger MR. J.
DELANO. Senators, Gentlemen, etc. Desdemona MISS KATE REIGNOLDS, Emelia MISS
EMILY MESTAYER, Dance (Ariel!) MISS ROSE & THERESE WOOD.

Boston Museum (May 3, 1864) — *Romeo and Juliet*

▶ Romeo J. WILKES BOOTH, Mercutio MR. L.R. SHEWELL, Benvolio MR. J. WILSON, Tybalt MR. J. WHEELOCK, Capulet MR. R.F. MCCLANNIN, Friar Lawrence MR. F. HARDENBURGH, Paris MR. WALTER BENN, Peter MR. J.H. RING, Apothecary MR. SOL. SMITH, JR., Balthazar MR. T.M. HUNTER, Gregory MR. J. DELANO, Page MRS. T.M. HUNTER, Juliet MISS KATE REIGNOLDS, Nurse MRS. J.R. VINCENT, Lady Capulet MISS M. PARKER, Dance (Ariel) MISS ROSE AND THERESE WOOD, Orchestra selections MR. EICHBERG'S ORCHESTRA.

Winter Garden, New York (November 25, 1864) — *Julius Caesar*

Cassius JUNIUS BRUTUS BOOTH, Brutus EDWIN BOOTH, ▶ Marc Antony JOHN WILKES BOOTH, Julius Caesar MR. E. VARREY, Casca MR. C. KEMBLE MASON, Octavius Caesar MR. C. WALCOT, JR., Trebonius MR. S.K. CHESTER, Decius MR. J.W. BURGESS, Metellus MR. T.C. CLINE, Titinnius MR. C.S. THOMAS, Cinna MR. J. DUELL, Varro MR. D. JOHNSTONE, Pindarus MR. E. POST, Soothsayer MR. P. EVANS, Popillius Lenas MR. N. DECKER, Servius MR. W.F. BURROUGHS, Flavius MR. B.F. WILLIAMS, Lucius MISS FANNY PRESTIGE, 1st Plebian E.A. EBERLE, 2nd Plebian O.S. FAWCET, 3rd Plebian A.E. ANDERSON, 4th Plebian S.F. OLIVER, Porcia MRS. F.S. CHANFRAU, Calphurnia MRS. C. WALCOT, JR. Guards, Lictors, Matrons, Virgins & Plebeians.

Ford's Theatre, Washington (March 18, 1865) — *The Apostate*

▶ Pescara J. WILKES BOOTH, Hemeya JOHN MCCULLOUGH, Malec W.H. HAMBLIN, Hamet J. MATTHEWS, Haly D.E. REILLY, Alvarez CHARLES WARWICK, Gamez J.H. EVANS, The Cadi W.J. FERGUSON, Gonzague C.V. HESS, 1st Moor L. CARLAND, 2nd Moor J. PARKHURST, 3rd Moor J.L. DEBONAY, 4th Moor C. BYRNES, Florinda MISS ALICE GRAY.

Index

Adams, Edwin, leading man in Richmond Co., 35-36; on Booth's tale of being snowbound, 135

Albaugh, John, in Booth's first play, 16; on Booth, 138; substitutes for Booth, 138; supports Booth at Arch St. Theatre, 98-99

The Apostate, 49, 59, 73-74, 83-84, 97, 122, 128, 146, 176

Arch St. Theatre, Phila., 19-23, 98-99, 101, 225

Badeau, Adam, wounded Union officer nursed by Booth, 147, 188

Barron, John M., on Booth in Richmond Co., 36, 43

Booth, Asia, *see* Clarke, Asia Booth

Booth, Edwin, acting compared to brother John Wilkes, 89, 106, 116; acts with John Wilkes, 24, 27-28, 34, 38; on acting, 54, 110; on bowdlerized verions of Shakespeare, 35; on John Wilkes Booth, 4, 11, 89, 97, 165; on tour with father, Junius Brutus, 81; suffered same hoarseness as brother Wilkes, 147

Booth, John Wilkes, acting appraised, 1, 4-5, 8, 20, 24, 37, 43-45, 49, 58, 60, 63, 65-66, 76-84, 88-90, 97, 102, 107, 113, 116, 123, 143, 146-147, 162-165, 171; admitted to governmental functions by senator's daughters, 167; appeal to women, 21, 44, 61, 113, 117-119, 129-131, 167, 174; arrested for disloyal expressions against Lincoln's administration, 138; attitude toward women, 130-131; blackens faces of actors on stage, 108; called cynic of the most pronounced type, 158; compared to Edgar Allan Poe, 121; comparison with brother Edwin, 89-90, 106, 113, 116; comparison with father, Junius Brutus, 49, 55, 59, 63, 65, 72, 76, 80-84, 88, 106, 116, 147, 157, 168-169; diamond-scratched windowpane message of Lincoln's death, 158;

diary, 3; earnings, 2, 25, 52, 61, 92, 95, 99, 104, 119, 128, 155, 170; education, 12, 14, 54; effects of his father's image, 90; erratic behavior, 36, 44, 107-108, 117-118, 139, 157-158, 171-173; falls asleep on stage, 139; fan mail, 92, 129, 131; fierce realism on stage bruises leading lady, 90-91; fistfight and fined in police court, 55; forms Dramatic Oil Co., 155-156; fortuneteller predicts future, 148; identifying scars, 133; illness, 113, 140-141, 146; incorporates Civil War songs into *Richard III*, 124; influence of other actors, 55; influence over the conspirators, 112, 171-172; innovative staging, 56, 61, 76-77, 82-84, 88, 95, 97, 103, 105, 108-109, 113, 116, 128; interpretation of roles, 54-55, 69, 76-77, 87-88, 102-103, 113, 127-128, 144-145; intense hatred of Secretary of War Stanton, 170; joins Richmond Grays, 40; kindness toward children, 104; knocks player (Ward) into president's box, 105; knocks player (Tilton) into orchestra pit, 132-133, 185; letter to Dr. Richard Stewart, 3; letter to Ted (Edwin Booth), 26; letters to Joseph H. Simonds, 61, 67-68, 93, 99, 104, 110; letter to T.V. Butsch, 92; letter to E.F. Keach, 94-95; letter to Ben De Bar, 119; letter to "Kim" Kimbal, 134; letter to John A. Ellsler, 135; letter to Monty (R.M. Field), 141; letter to Ella Turner Star, 166; letters to his mother, 168, 180; letter to Junius Brutus Booth, Jr., 173; letter "To whom it may concern," 142, 165, 170; melodramatic "oath scene," 171-172; military pass issued by Gen. Grant, 142, 162; nurses wounded Union officer fiend, 147, 188; on actors, 168; on his aid to the Confederacy, 162, 168; on tales about his father, 90; on the horrors of war, 142, 170; on the town in New Orleans, 145; one-man show in a portrait gallery, 160; performs